THE
LION
★★★★ AND THE ★★★★
LAMB

The Holocaust story of a powerful Nazi leader and a Dutch resistance worker

CHARLES CAUSEY

Edited by Vicki Zimmer

WESTBOW
PRESS®
A DIVISION OF THOMAS NELSON
& ZONDERVAN

WestBow Press books may be ordered through booksellers or by contacting:

WestBow Press
A Division of Thomas Nelson & Zondervan
1663 Liberty Drive
Bloomington, IN 47403
www.westbowpress.com
1 (866) 928-1240

Cover art:
On Wings and a Prayer, ©William S. Phillips.
Licensed by The Greenwich Workshop, Inc.

ISBN: 978-1-5127-6109-2 (sc)
ISBN: 978-1-5127-6110-8 (hc)
ISBN: 978-1-5127-6108-5 (e)

Library of Congress Control Number: 2016917770

Print information available on the last page.

WestBow Press rev. date: 4/19/2017

Dedicated with gratitude

to

The Fearless 1980's CU Boulder CRU Staff

Director John & Nancy Lamb
Doug
Rabs
Connie
JJ
Bridget
Johnny O
Shelly
Kelly
Paul
Martha

May the torches you lit shine like the stars
and illumine the four corners

"THE HAND OF THE AGGRESSOR IS STAYED BY
STRENGTH AND STRENGTH ALONE."

Dwight D. Eisenhower

CONTENTS

FOREWORD

Albert Speer was born in 1905 into a wealthy family. His father was an architect and ensured that his children received a good education. Albert wanted to become a mathematician, but he chose to study architecture instead, to please his father. Early in his career he came into contact with Hitler and the Nazi party, the NSDAP, and joined it in 1931. Speer quickly gained a good reputation within the NSDAP. When Hitler and the NSDAP seized power in 1933, Speer came into contact with the new leader.

Hitler loved art. When he was younger, he actually wanted to become an architect. It is therefore not so strange that Hitler took an interest in Speer. Hitler and Speer became friends and worked on many projects together. In 1942 Hitler appointed Speer as Minister of Armaments and War Production. Speer was now responsible for arming the ever more demanding Nazi war machine. To increase production and feed the hunger of the Nazi army, Speer used almost two million prisoners of war in his factories. Thanks to Speer's efforts, the war may have lasted a year longer than otherwise would have been the case. It is sad to note, that in the last year of the war, as many people died as in the previous four years combined.

Corrie ten Boom grew up in a harmonious Christian family in Holland. Corrie's father, Caspar ten Boom, was a well-known watchmaker who raised his children to have respect and compassion for their fellow man and to love the Jewish people. Corrie followed in her father's footsteps and became a watchmaker as well. Early on, the Ten Booms noticed the dangers of the rising anti-Semitism movement led by the Nazi party in Germany. When Nazi Germany conquered the Netherlands in May 1940 and started to hunt down and murder Jews, Corrie became the leader of a non-violent resistance group, consisting of more than 80 persons. Together with her father and sister Betsie, Corrie took in and sheltered Jews.

In a very special way, Charles Causey has interwoven the stories of Albert Speer and Corrie ten Boom, allowing the reader a glimpse into the choices Speer and Corrie made during their lives. In terms of ideology, both protagonists are diametrically opposed. Speer chose to destroy the lives of millions of people in order to please Hitler. He enjoyed the powers given to him; human lives mean rather little to him. Corrie, on the other hand, showed love and attention for every human being. She was even willing to put her life on the line to save a single person from death. In this book, we are confronted with some stark choices people can make in their lives: either to cause death and destruction, or to serve your fellowman and point towards a heavenly and divine future.

By describing the histories of Speer and Corrie, Charles Causey has provided us with hours of stimulating reading. What is more, he has also succeeded in making an important contribution to the answer of this crucial question: "What will I do, if a regime comes to power that aims to destroy its opponents or entire peoples, like the Jews?"

Corrie did not stand aloof, but, empowered by God, she rose up to protect His people. Here am I!

Frits Nieuwstraten
Director of the Corrie ten Boom House Foundation
The Netherlands

Albert Speer werd in 1905 geboren in een welgesteld gezin. Zijn vader was architect en zorgde dat zijn kinderen een goede opleiding konden krijgen. Hoewel Albert wiskundige wilde worden, koos hij toch voor de studie architectuur om zijn vader een plezier te doen. Tijdens zijn werk kwam hij in kontakt met de nazipartij en werd hij in 1931 lid. Al snel groeide zijn reputatie in de nazipartij en toen de nazipartij in 1933 de macht grepen kwam hij in kontakt met Hitler.

Hitler hield van kunst en wilde eigenlijk in zijn jonge jaren ook architect worden. Hitler en Albert Speer werden vrienden en werkten samen aan veel projecten. In 1942 werd Speer aangesteld als de minister van Bewapening en oorlogsproductie. Speer werd verantwoordelijk voor de wapenproductie en om deze tot hoge productie te kunnen opvoeren gebruikte hij bijna 2 miljoen krijgsgevangenen. Door deze inzet van Speer heeft de oorlog misschien wel een jaar langer geduurd dan anders het geval zou zijn geweest. Het is triest te bedenken dat in dat laatste jaar net zoveel doden vielen als in de gezamenlijke vier jaren daarvoor.

Corrie ten Boom groeide op in een harmonieus christelijk gezin. Haar vader was een bekende horlogemaker en voedde zijn kinderen op met respect en mededogen voor de medemens en liefde voor het Joodse Volk. Corrie werd net als haar vader een horlogemaakster. Zij zette zich, samen met de andere familieleden Ten Boom, in voor de zwakkeren in de samenleving. Al in een vroegtijdig stadium zagen de Ten Booms de gevaren van het opkomende antisemitisme, aangevoerd door de nazipartij in Duitsland. Toen nazi-Duitsland ook Nederland veroverde en de joden ging vervolgen en uitmoorden, werd Corrie leidster van een geweldloze verzetsgroep die door meer dan 80 personen werd gevormd. Samen met haar vader en zuster Betsie, die net als zij ongehuwd was gebleven, namen zij Joodse mensen in huis.

Op bijzondere wijze heeft Charles Causey deze beide personen naast elkaar geportretteerd waardoor we een inkijkje hebben in de keuzes die ze maakten in hun leven. De beide hoofdpersonen staan qua ideologie lijnrecht tegenover elkaar. Speer kiest gewetenloos voor vernietiging van miljoenen mensen. Een mensen leven is niet in tel bij hem. Hij geniet van de macht die hij krijgt. Corrie heeft aandacht en liefde voor ieder menselijk wezen. Is zelfs bereid om haar leven in de waagschaal te leggen om een enkele persoon te redden van de dood. We worden in dit boek geconfronteerd met de keuzes die mensen maken in hun leven: dood en verderf zaaien of je inzetten voor de medemens en uitzicht op een hemels goddelijk leven.

Door beschrijving van deze onderdelen van de geschiedenis van meer dan 70 jaar geleden bezorgd Charles ons boeiende lees-uren en geeft hij een belangrijke bijdrage aan de beantwoording van de vraag: "wat doe ik als een regiem aan de macht komt die uit is op vernietiging van tegenstanders of hele bevolkingsgroepen, zoals de Joden."

Corrie bleef niet aan de kant staan, maar in Gods kracht stond zij op om Zijn volk te beschermen. Here am I!

Frits Nieuwstraten
Director Corrie ten Boom House Foundation
The Netherlands

TO THE READER

You are about to read a true story filled with betrayals, conspiracies, treachery and hope. It is the story of the last half of World War II told from the viewpoints of Albert Speer and Corrie ten Boom, two pivotal characters who, in their own unique way, not only survived the most horrific days of the twentieth century, but countermanded the evil of Adolf Hitler. It is an entirely true story, yet a novel by definition because there are thoughts added not recorded in history. Instead of reading their wartime accounts as cold historical data, my intent was to let the reader experience the feelings of *being* there: how it felt to hide Jews, to live in a concentration camp, or to have worked alongside Hermann Göring and to answer for Hitler's atrocities at the Nuremberg trials.

The Lion and the Lamb was written for the reader to glimpse how the central characters experienced life in real time and as part of their own unique community. The voices you hear are theirs and will ring true with the historical record. Their actions are described as accurately as I can portray them without being an eye witness. I have not consciously changed any fact, but I have condensed some of the events for clarity. Every person in *The Lion and the Lamb* exists in history. They are where they are supposed to be, when they are supposed to be there, and doing what they actually did.

The irony in combining these two lives will be felt from the very beginning. Corrie, a devout Christian seeking to help Jews, is contrasted with Herr Speer, a powerful Third Reich leader who became as close a friend to Germany's Führer as anyone ever came. Both stories, I feel, need to be told simultaneously so that the reader can gaze into the two lenses of cause and effect in war, and grasp how seemingly trivial personal choices result in weighty moral consequences. I also wanted the reader to face the intense dread suffered by both the victims *and* their captors as World War II concluded.

These characterizations are my own.

Charles Causey

THE PEOPLE

Martin Bormann—The Führer's private secretary. Though other cabinet members competed for power, Bormann always retained a permanent position in Hitler's inner circle and rarely left the Führer's side. He controlled all information coming in and out of the Chancellor's office and he was the leading proponent for persecution against the Christian church, the Jews, and the Russians. Considered a weasel and despised by the other Reich leaders, Bormann maintained Hitler's favor.

Joseph Goebbels—Leader of the Propaganda Ministry. Goebbels used speeches and flyers to solidify the Nazi Party during its early days. He controlled Germany's news media, entertainment and performing arts programs, and he extensively used the radio to promote Nazi hatred for Jews. Goebbels was ill as a child and suffered with a club foot deformity. He wore a metal brace and walked with a limp throughout his life. Despite this physical setback, he held a PhD and was known as quite a lady's man. He advanced as a politician alongside Hitler for being a fierce promulgater of Nazi policies.

Hermann Göring—Leading Nazi Party official. Hitler gave Göring the honorary military rank of Reichsmarschall which made Göring the number two man in Germany. Flamboyant Göring used the war to his advantage, siphoning spoils from the persecuted Jews to furnish his estates with priceless treasures while most Germans lived on rations. He earned imperishable honor as a flying ace in World War I, flying missions alongside Manfred Von Richthofen, the Red Baron. In the early days, Hitler leveraged his alliance with the popular war hero, Göring, to solidify his political status.

Rudolf Hess—Deputy Führer since 1934. On May 10, 1941, Rudolf Hess left Adolf Hitler without sanction on an impossible secret mission of peace. He climbed into a Messerschmitt 110 fighter, loaded it with extra fuel tanks, and embarked on a daring five-hour, 900-mile flight over the North Sea to Scotland. Hess hoped to speak to the British and negotiate peace, but they knew this rogue defector did not speak for Hitler so Winston Churchill locked him in prison until the end of the war.

Heinrich Himmler—Leader of the SS and the architect of the Final Solution. Known as the Reichsführer, Himmler was in charge of all the Gestapo, the concentration camps, and all secret operations within the state. Constantly plotting and possessing unusual shrewdness, most on Hitler's cabinet were frightened of Himmler and speculated that he kept a secret dossier on each of them.

Adolf Hitler—Executive head of Germany as the Führer (leader and sole source of power) since 1934. Hitler, as Germany's Chancellor, started WWII in September 1939 when he invaded Poland. He conquered Czechoslovakia, Denmark, Holland, Belgium and France in the next twelve months. Believing he was on the verge of world domination, it was Germany's faltering near Stalingrad in 1942 when Hitler's emperor status was no longer a foregone conclusion.

Albert Speer—Armaments Chief and former German architect. Speer joined the Nazi Party in 1931 after listening to an impassioned speech by Adolf Hitler. Nazi Party functionaries hired Speer to oversee building projects and, through a seemingly stroke of good luck, he was asked to design the 1933 Nuremburg Rally, placing him in direct contact with Adolf Hitler. Speer soon became Hitler's chief architect whereby he designed the Reich Chancellery in Berlin and the Party Palace in Nuremberg. Hitler secretly commissioned Speer to redesign the entire city of Berlin, which — upon completion — would be renamed Germania for the future 1,000-year rule of the Reich.

Corrie ten Boom—Dutch Resistance worker and former watchmaker. Corrie was the youngest daughter of Casper ten Boom, a skilled watchmaker who sold clocks and watches in the storefront of their family home in Haarlem, Holland. As a young woman Corrie led Christian girls' clubs, taught mentally disabled children, and worked with the YWCA until the Germans invaded Holland. Corrie had boundless energy, she loved to laugh, listen to Bach, and play the piano. One of Corrie's favorite pre-war activities was to stroll through Haarlem's streets alongside her father after every midday meal before the shop reopened at two.

The SS—Nickname used for the *Schutzstaffel*, the protection squad of the Nazi Party. Before the war, the SS was primarily used as a bodyguard for Adolf Hitler. Members were selected by proving Aryan ancestry and a devotion to the Nazi Party and Germany. The SS boasted over a million members divided into three components: The Waffen-SS (military units that fought as separate, mobile infantry regiments alongside the regular Wehrmacht units); the Allgemeine-SS (known as the Gestapo, the police force who patrolled city streets and acted as the vanguards of National Socialism and racial purity); and the SS-Totenkopfverbände (SS guards who ran the concentration camps and extermination centers). The SS motto was "My honor is loyalty."

The Gauleiters—Regional leaders of the Nazi Party. These party elites possessed a paramilitary rank and were given direct appointments from Adolf Hitler to govern geographical areas in the Third Reich. They had unquestioned authority in their region and advised the local governments they oversaw on how to conduct affairs in a German occupied country. The Gauleiters coordinated regional Nazi Party events, hosted visits from the Führer, and were the supreme civil administrators in their assigned territory.

The Sonderkommandos—Jewish men living in death camps assigned to work in special detachments that assisted the SS in exterminating significant numbers of their victims. The word itself meant 'special units' and was used because these Jewish prisoners were exposed to the top-secret operations of the Final Solution.

"Nazi Expansion in 1942"

PROLOGUE

In Germany

Albert Speer sat on the floor of his living room surrounded by recently discarded Christmas wrapping paper. Speer's children, intent on playing with their presents, sprawled beside him, and his oldest daughter, Hilde, sat on his lap with a white bow in her hair. Margarete, Speer's wife, lounged on the sofa, thankful all the gifts were appreciated and the children were happy.

The phone rang, and Speer answered using his official voice.

"Speer, this is Todt," came the throaty voice on the other end. "Merry Christmas."

"Merry Christmas," Speer replied with a lingering question in his mind, wondering what the holiday call could be about. Fritz Todt was his boss, and Speer noticed an urgency in his greeting.

"Sorry to bother your time with your family, it's only..." Todt hesitated. "It's only that the Führer has finally approved our plan for more construction workers in the East."

"That is good," Speer replied as he glanced apologetically toward his wife.

This is Christmas! Margarete's eyes cattily conveyed.

"Yes, that is good," responded Todt. "An order will be coming forthwith. However, as you know, I've just returned, and what I've seen is not good. The war is going against us, Speer. These new workers may not change the status quo. Our soldiers do not have the hardiness of the Russians."

Speer did not respond. For months it had seemed a foregone conclusion that the Soviets would be wiped from the map. Now, with reports like these coming from those who had visited Russia, it did not seem so sure that the Nazis would win.

"I need you to go there, and oversee the deployment of the workers personally," said Todt.

Speer looked around the room, at his gleeful children, his weary wife. "What did you have in mind?"

"It will take thirty days to mobilize the workers. Plan to depart for Dnepropetrovsk in one month. And Speer — be careful."

Speer replaced the receiver in its cradle and stepped back into the warm, glowing room. He would go, and abandon his family for the war effort once again. But for today, he decided to cherish the time with those he loved the most.

In Holland

"Soldiers are coming!" the boys exclaimed as they ran into the kitchen. "They are two doors down and coming quick."

"Get into the cellar!" Corrie said anxiously.

The two boys moved the table and the rug, opened the trapdoor, and slipped down onto the cold, dark earth. Corrie and Betsie dropped the door shut, replaced the rug, and slid the kitchen table over the hiding place. Corrie threw a table cloth over the table and began putting dishes on it with Nollie's daughter Cocky.

Crash!

A Nazi soldier burst open the front door with the butt of his rifle. Two uniformed Germans ran into the kitchen, rifles leveled.

"Stay where you are, and don't move."

The disturbance sparked Cocky to drop a china teacup onto the wooden floor.

More soldiers entered the home and maneuvered through the other rooms on the main floor and up the stairs. It was a Nazi tactic called *the razzia:* a lightning-fast search and seizure method the SS used throughout Holland's communities that year. Without warning they surrounded a block of buildings with large trucks and swept through an entire neighborhood door-to-door looking for Dutchmen between the ages of sixteen and thirty to work in German munitions factories.

"Where are your men?" one of the soldiers asked bright-eyed Cocky.

"This is my grandfather," Cocky said, pointing to Casper ten Boom. "My father is at work, and my brother is at college."

"How many brothers do you have?" the Nazi officer asked in thickly-accented Dutch.

Cocky had been taught not to lie under any circumstances. She lowered her head and stared at the floor.

"I asked how many brothers you have!"

"Three," Cocky said softly.

"Where are the other two?"

Cocky again looked down and did not answer.

The officer walked over to her and jerked her upright.

"Where are they?" he asked coarsely.

Cocky looked up and smiled, "Why, they're under the table."

Corrie nearly gasped out loud at Cocky's honesty. Nollie and her husband Flip had made the addition to their kitchen a few weeks ago because they were worried about their sons, Peter and Bob, being taken by the Nazis; *yet Cocky just directed the captors right to them!*

Motioning all of the Ten Booms away from the table, one SS man aimed his rifle a foot below the table top. The German officer in charge walked over and yanked the cloth off of it, hurling plates of china into the air.

Cocky suddenly burst out into spasms of hysterical, nervous laughter.

The soldiers all glared at her.

"Do you take us as fools?" the officer exploded in German.

The intruders quickly dispersed out of the home, pocketing the Ten Boom's cookies and tea, but leaving the more precious, hidden cargo.

———◆◆◆———

Fourteen-year-old Martin Adolf Bormann was home from his Bavarian boarding school for the Christmas holiday. He and his kid sister, Eike, loved spending time on the Obersalzberg, sledding and playing games in the snow with their friends. Martin often ran errands for his father, or for his godfather, Adolf Hitler. Martin was quick and helpful; he dashed around the mountain to different meetings near Hitler's headquarters with films, maps, and war photographs.

Martin and Eike were invited one day to visit the house of a neighbor, Hedwig Potthast, for tea. They did not know her well but she seemed nice, plus she served chocolate cake that was lip-smacking. Martin wondered about this interesting woman. He knew Fräulein Potthast was in a secret relationship with the SS leader, Heinrich Himmler, who worked alongside his father to help Adolf Hitler win the war. He did not know what she did during the day or why she lived alone.

The visit was going well, but after the trio finished their treats, Fräulein Potthast stood and told the children she had something she wanted to show them in the attic if they were interested: a special trove of secret treasures.

Martin and his younger sister looked at each other, silently consulting, then nodded excitedly. The children stood and followed their hostess up the back stairs to the attic.

"Now, children," said Fräulein Potthast sternly, "you must promise me you will never tell anyone about the things you are about to see. I am showing you because I think you will find them as fascinating as I do. It is a rare assortment of treasures that my friend, Herr Himmler, collected and stores here."

"We promise," Martin and Eike said together.

"Okay, I trust you. Look over here." Fräulein Potthast pointed to a table and chairs and explained them in a scientific manner. The children looked at the furniture with curiosity.

"The furniture up here is made entirely out of human body parts. You see this chair, it is made of human bones. See the arms? They are human arms. See the legs? Those are actual legs on human feet. Look at the seat; it is made of a human pelvis bone. You can sit on it if you like, it's sturdy."

"I don't want to," shrieked Eike, visibly upset.

Martin grabbed his sister's hand, "Don't worry, Eike. You don't have to." He himself was also full of fear, and desired to leave the attic.

Fräulein Potthast was not disheartened, "Take a look at this." She picked up a book from a pile and handed it to Martin.

Martin reached for the book, recognizing it as Adolf Hitler's treatise *Mein Kampf*. Martin had seen it many times before. This one had a cover that felt leathery.

"This cover is made from a very unique material," said Fräulein Potthast smiling while Martin held it. "The prisoners at Dachau made these books with covers out of human skin. They used the skin from the center of the back. Isn't that interesting?"

"Martin, I want to go now," yowled Eike.

So did Martin. He swiftly handed the book back to Fräulein Potthast, and hastily said goodbye without looking at her. He grabbed Eike's hand and maneuvered toward the back stairway.

"Don't you want to see the other things?" asked Fräulein Potthast with disappointment.

The children did not acknowledge the question as they were already halfway down the stairs. They could not leave fast enough. Eike pushed her brother down the narrow stairs as Martin's feet tried to find each step to avoid tripping. They left the house and raced all the way home into the arms of their mother.

Though they never returned to the house of Fräulein Potthast, the memory haunted them. As much as they tried to forget about it, they were stained with the images they witnessed in the attic.

Part I

THE SCOURING
OF EUROPE

CHAPTER 1

The Russians Are Coming

"*Mach Schnell!* Let's go," Albert Speer bellowed out to the train conductor. "We need to leave now!"

It was February 6, 1942. Snow was falling heavily and drifts covered the tracks in front of them. On this frigid, overcast day, Speer learned from a German scout that a Russian tank battalion was closing in on the city of Dnepropetrovsk. He wanted to depart immediately.

Speer had just finished a six-day stint working to open up the railroads in the south-central region of Ukraine. He was there solely to inspect the efforts of his construction workers and had no desire to become a prisoner of war. With the Russians only twelve miles away, it was simply a matter of time before they stormed the city.

Without a verbal response, the train conductor immediately stroked the levers, making the train lurch forward and away from the danger. The rest of the construction workers left behind looked around for rifles and sharp tools to delay the advance of the enemy, with hand-to-hand combat if necessary. Like their leader Speer, they were not trained fighters and not at all eager to confront the Russians, but they had orders from the Führer to protect Dnepropetrovsk at all costs.

After the German invasion of the Soviet Union in 1941, the Red Army had withdrawn from Dnepropetrovsk and destroyed everything that might aid their adversaries. The railroad lines were smashed, the locomotive sheds burned, and the water storage facilities left exposed to freeze. Even the snow-clearing equipment was damaged and rendered useless for the Germans.

And now Albert Speer, who served as Adolf Hitler's personal architect, was in charge of overseeing the progress made by the construction teams. Born in 1905, Speer was one of the youngest men to join team Hitler. In 1934, at just twenty-nine years of age, Hitler appointed Speer chief of construction for the Third Reich.

Once the war began in 1939, Speer worked as an assistant to Dr. Fritz Todt, the Reich Minister for Armaments and Ammunition. Under Todt's leadership, Speer led thousands of men on construction teams throughout the Third Reich Empire, many of which were assigned to the Eastern Front where they restored bridges, tunnels, airstrips and mangled railroad tracks.

These tasks in mind, Speer, with his sad eyes and smooth-shaven face, kissed his wife, Margarete, goodbye that winter and traveled to Dnepropetrovsk. The Christmas holidays were over, his oldest two children were back in grammar school, and Speer was anxious to discover if his construction workers had made progress opening up the eastern railroads.

Speer arrived in the city during a terrible blizzard. What he found was that the German soldiers on the front lines desperately needed supplies. As he inspected the area, he made a grisly discovery. A nearby train headed for Berlin had stalled just miles from Dnepropetrovsk and the wounded soldiers and the medical staff attending them had all frozen to death. Everything, it seemed, was snowed under and the

2

Germans could not maintain their stronghold. As a result, the Russians started to creep back and reclaim territory.

This was not good news to Albert Speer. He pondered this realization as he now sat on the westward train, chugging forward at seven miles an hour. Nonetheless, Speer was relieved to be returning to Berlin and safety. The wind howled against the railcars as the day faded into evening, and occasionally some of the workmen had to climb out in the dark, frigid night to clear the rail lines of the dense snow. Speer eventually fell fast asleep in a makeshift bunk toward the rear of the train.

Albert Speer awoke at dawn and found the train had pulled into a station that looked somewhat familiar. He rubbed his fist on the fogged window and peered out to see burnt buildings, high drifts of snow and civilian workers clearing off a runway.

"Where are we?" Speer shouted when one of the train operators poked his head into his cabin.

"Back in Dnepropetrovsk," the man replied. "We had to turn around last night because of the snow drifts. They were ten feet tall."

"Dnepropetrovsk!" Speer's heart raced. *Will I have to fight?* He was not mentally prepared for this setback so a near panic attack set in.

He placed his right hand on his left breast a moment as if to steady his pounding heart, and then quickly gathered his things and left the train. The workers who had celebrated his departure the night before seemed discouraged to see him back at the station. Speer asked about the Russians' progress but thankfully found they had not advanced on the city during the night. *Perhaps the weather stalled them as well,* Speer hoped.

Speer reluctantly grasped that with the temperature at a chilly zero degrees and the snow piling up, he was trapped there indefinitely. Just when he had resolved himself to stay and help the men fight the enemy, he was approached by a pilot who was also hoping to evacuate from the area before the Russians came.

"I'm not going to Berlin but I can fly you to the Wolf's Lair," said the pilot, who was returning to Hitler's Eastern Headquarters. "I depart in one hour."

"Yes, I'll accept," said Speer as he smiled, thankful to finally be leaving the place. "Do you think there is enough of a runway to get out of here?"

"It doesn't matter. We're going to make it work."

"What about the wind?"

"Leave that problem to me."

Speer appreciated the pilot's optimism.

An entire crew of men feverishly shoveled a wide path on the runway, and within an hour, their plane took off.

Speer glanced at the wasteland below him. The roads and rails were covered with snow, and the few buildings on the outskirts of town were destroyed. In the next moment, as the plane ascended and headed west, all Speer could see for miles was a vast, white territory. The muddy marshes from a few months ago had transformed into ice-covered drifts of snow.

This did not bode well for the ongoing German invasion into the East.

The Wolf's Lair was Adolf Hitler's military headquarters for the Eastern Front. The German war with the Soviet Union created the need for a top-secret facility near the front lines. The meeting rooms and sleeping quarters were bunkers with concrete walls that were six feet thick and reinforced with steel. Though located near the city of Rastenburg, Poland, the Wolf's Lair sat on many acres of a heavily wooded rural area with several layers of security protecting it. In addition to three zones of barbed wire fence and land mines throughout, there were hundreds of Nazi soldiers guarding the gates and roving the grounds with dogs around the clock. The Wolf's Lair was an impenetrable fortress.

Albert Speer arrived safely at the narrow airport surrounded by tall pines. He called on the hangar phone to let them know he was there, and within a few minutes, a soldier driving a car from the Führer's motor pool came to pick him up. When they entered the clandestine facility and passed all of the checkpoints, Speer had the driver deliver him to the mess hall since he had not eaten for two days.

He was informed that his boss, Dr. Todt, was also at the Wolf's Lair. Todt, a decorated veteran of World War I, had been a member of the Nazi Party since its inception in the early 1920s. His stoicism bothered Adolf Hitler but not Albert Speer. Speer thought Todt's realism was desperately needed now that the invasion of the Soviet Union had stalled.

At that very moment, Todt was briefing Hitler with reports on the Eastern Front and the logistical mess there. Speer waited patiently for Todt so he could provide an update on his trip. He also inquired about the next plane leaving for Berlin.

When Fritz Todt came out of his meeting with the Führer, Speer thought he looked weary. The two men drank a glass of wine and discussed the current mood of the Reich Chancellor.

"How did your meeting go?" asked Speer.

"He is not willing to listen, Speer," said Todt. "The blitzkrieg did not work in the east; we need a new strategy. He does not understand and keeps reliving his earlier successes."

They spoke openly to each other, knowing what they said would stay between the two of them. Speer was naturally shy and quiet, and though he might think of disagreeing with Hitler, he would never speak it openly like Todt.

"You seem saddened by this," said Speer, raising his dark eyebrows to receive the expected answer.

A slight nod from Todt. "A country cannot be governed by one man. There is no way to have a dissenting voice on strategy. Hitler's voice always wins. If he would listen to the generals, or to me…"

Speer accepted this kind of shattered mood from his supervisor. Hitler called it defeatism, but Speer knew Todt could be optimistic if he thought there was a chance.

The two men discussed some of the problems Speer encountered on his trip and then finally entered their favorite topic: their mutual dislike of Martin Bormann, Hitler's personal secretary. Todt felt the man was a usurper and not a helpful administrator of Third Reich business.

Dr. Todt eventually rose from the table and offered Speer a ride back to Berlin on his plane early the next morning. Speer happily accepted.

"I will see you in the morning," Speer said as his boss walked away.

A few minutes after Todt left for his quarters, an aide summoned Speer to meet with Adolf Hitler. Though it was already 1 a.m. and Speer was exhausted, he knew he could not refuse to see the Führer.

———◆◆◆———

"I know you like the snow, Speer, but I cannot imagine why," Adolf Hitler mused after Speer joined him in the Reich Chancellor's meeting room.

"Margarete and I love to ski…," started Speer.

"So does Eva," Hitler interrupted. "But I don't know why. You can break your leg on those sticks. Just look at what the snow and ice have done to my campaign in Russia. Yet you three play in it like little elves."

Speer noticed a slight tone of mourning in his voice that night.

Hitler, with his smudge of a mustache, wide face and left-sided forelock, smiled with excitement in his eyes and said, "I like fire. I like the hot sun. Remember the summer nights at my Berghof? That's what I love. Give me a warm sunny day to this miserable cold any time."

Albert Speer was used to the rants of Hitler and his irritation with the cold and snow. The man loved fire and was never more thrilled than watching bombs fall on London, and flames burning in Warsaw. Hitler was obsessed with his campaign movies showing the destruction his military brought on the enemy.

In the evenings at Hitler's home in the mountains he would show his companions films given to him by army generals. When a target was hit resulting in a large explosion, Hitler would shout triumphantly and look to others to be as excited as he was. Speer knew that Hitler's dream was to see the cities of Moscow and New York engulfed in flames. In fact, the obsession to bomb New York City led Hitler to command Fritz Todt to manufacture bombers with a longer range.

"Tell me what you have seen out there, in the East. I have heard from Todt and listened to his dreary perspective. Now I want to hear about it from you."

"I left Dnepropetrovsk today," said Speer. "The Russians are approaching but had not arrived before I left, and I did not see them from the plane."

"No, they have not reached the city and they will not. I sent word to hold Dnepropetrovsk at all costs."

"Yes, I understand. However, there are not many of our men there…"

"There are enough! They just need to be bold and stand their ground and fight. It is no different than when we stood our ground with the British and eventually pushed them back until they fled."

Speer knew it was no use arguing so he did not discuss the lack of soldiers and insufficient arms for the construction workers. Hitler would never allow someone to countermand his decisions on military strategy. Speer had seen generals of the Wehrmacht who had served for over thirty years belittled when they introduced a variation on a strategy Hitler had proposed. Speer decided to speak to Hitler on other things unrelated to strategy: the construction workers, the railroad lines, and the lack of medical equipment at the hospital outpost.

Hitler was curious to hear some of the positive aspects of what Speer had witnessed. He wanted to know about the morale of the men, and what they were doing to help win the war. Speer told him about the work of the engineers during the day, the blizzards, and about the sad songs the soldiers would sing at night.

Hitler inquired about the words of the songs, and when told they were of a melancholy nature, he was irritated the workers were singing such defeatist songs, as if they knew the war was already lost. Speer accepted that it simply made the men feel better and he attempted to promote their loyalty, but Hitler remained suspicious and distrusted their motives.

After a long discussion lasting until 3 a.m., their meeting finally concluded and Albert Speer left the Führer to find a cot on which to sleep for the rest of the night. Before he settled down, he spoke to an aide to alert Dr. Todt that he could not join him for his early flight. The exhausted Speer would find another way back to Berlin after he had slept at least six hours.

<hr />

When Speer awoke he could hear people moving around in the hallway and whispering in an urgent manner. Something had happened and Speer was certain it was the town of Dnepropetrovsk falling back to the Russians. He quickly dressed, but before he left the room he was told he had an urgent call from his friend, Dr. Karl Brandt.

"Todt is dead," Brandt said to Speer on the phone. "His Heinkel 111 crashed this morning and there were no survivors."

"What?"

"Albert, Dr. Todt has been killed."

Speer looked down the hallway at those moving to and fro and speaking with hushed voices. He knew they were discussing the plane crash.

"How did it happen?" Speer asked.

"We don't know. He was due back in Munich this morning after a brief stop in Berlin, so the plane departed just after daybreak but it was cloudy. They had barely left the runway when the plane exploded killing everyone onboard."

"Sabotage?"

"It is being investigated."

This news rattled Speer. For the second time in twenty-four hours Speer's heart began pounding out of control. He was supposed to have been on that flight but at the last minute changed his mind.

A few moments later, Hitler called Speer into his office. Without any greeting or mourning, the Führer appointed Speer to take Todt's old position.

Still in shock, Speer attempted to argue. "But I don't know anything about the armaments. And..."

"It doesn't matter; I have confidence in you," Hitler interrupted. "You will have my complete backing," he assured Speer.

The job was enormous. Dr. Fritz Todt had fundamentally consolidated several ministries into one. He had been in charge of all the roads, the navigable waterways, the power plants, the construction industry, the defensive bunkers, the U-boat shelters, and the roads in all of the new territory Germany held in Western Europe and Russia. He was also the minister who worked directly with the Industrialists who built and supplied the Reich with tanks, planes, submarines and weaponry.

Albert Speer, overwhelmed with the magnitude of the task, was nonetheless energized by the responsibility the Führer entrusted to him. Though he could not explain it, Speer loved and appreciated being the one counted on by Hitler, not only as a friend, but as a professional. In this appointment, the German Chancellor was entrusting Speer with a tremendous amount of responsibility.

Speer was dismissed and turned to leave when the door opened and an aide said to Hitler, "The Reichsmarschall is here and urgently wishes to speak to you."

Hitler sighed. "Send him in," he said, then instructed Speer to stay.

Through the doorway came the hefty frame of Hermann Göring, who bustled in with a flourish. "Greetings, mein Führer, I am so sorry for your loss of Dr. Todt," he said.

Speer was astonished at his entrance. Göring had come from his special hunting lodge in Rominten on a train. He was not dressed in uniform but in hunter's garb with a long knife at his side.

"Best if I take over Dr. Todt's assignments, mein Führer," said Göring assuredly. "I am certain it has already come to your mind?"

Hitler looked into Göring's eyes and with a fierceness declared, "I have already appointed his successor. Reich Minister Speer has assumed all of Dr. Todt's offices as of this moment."

Göring, utterly deflated, did not have a rejoinder. As the number two man in the Reich, he had assumed that Todt's responsibilities would now fall under his jurisdiction, giving him undeniable power. Göring stood there a moment as if to respond, but was so taken aback by Hitler's unequivocal decision and tone, he did not dare challenge it.

Instead, Göring's confident expression on his round face disintegrated, as did his erect posture. With an obvious attempt to change the subject, he pronounced, "I hope you will understand, mein Führer, if I do not attend Dr. Todt's funeral. You know the battles I had with him."

"I hope *you* will understand," Hitler responded, "that the man next in line as Reich Chancellor must be present at Todt's funeral or people will talk."

Göring froze. All visible warmth evaporated from his plump face. He gathered himself enough to acknowledge, "Of course, mein Führer." Then he exited without bidding farewell.

Unimaginably, Albert Speer had won out over Hermann Göring. As Speer headed back to Berlin, he replayed every conversation he had in the last twenty-four hours. There was so much to think about and he realized how few people in history were ever afforded a task of such magnitude.

He did not discover until later that, as Todt's successor, he was looked upon with suspicion when the news of Todt's demise blanketed Germany. This was especially true since Speer had changed his mind about the flight just hours before its scheduled departure. He would also find out that the officer in Dnepropetrovsk who led the sad songs was court-martialed on orders from the Führer.

CHAPTER 2

Resistance

T he Ten Boom's criminal activity began so incidentally and their hospitality to Jewish neighbors so innocent, it did not seem as if they were engaging in risky business. Like a fresh afternoon breeze that harkens a deadly storm, their initial experience resisting the Nazis was invigorating, but it signaled a time that would endanger them and change their idyllic lives forever.

———⊷◆⊷———

"How many ration cards do you require?" the older man tentatively asked the Dutch woman across the counter from him.

Corrie ten Boom opened her mouth to say five, but the number that popped out was "One hundred."

"That's too many! I can't do that for you."

"Please, sir. I wouldn't ask if the need wasn't great."

"But this is criminal activity."

Corrie nodded soberly.

Fred Koornstra looked at the younger woman with sympathy. She was the same age as his daughter. He knew her family well — the Ten Booms — and how they always cared for people in need. Fred used to be the meter man who would stop by their house each month. Corrie's father, Casper, was the most respected man in Haarlem and arguably one of the best clockmakers in all Holland.

Fred knew the brave woman in front of him was taking a tremendous risk to help strangers who were in need. Her entire family — including her aged father — could be arrested and sent to Germany if the Gestapo discovered Corrie was harboring Jews. Nevertheless, she stood there with her large, shining eyes pleading with Fred to help her.

"You know, Miss Ten Boom, one hundred ration cards will not come easily. I am a trusted government worker." Then, as if contemplating the consequences, he added, "I could stage a robbery here, and have a friend beat me up to smuggle them for you, but if found out I would not only lose my position, but be sent to prison in Amsterdam or to a work camp."

"I know, sir, I know," Corrie replied, empathizing with his fear. "I realize the risk you are taking. It is just that the family we have now is quite needy, and with child. They look to us for sympathy and guidance."

"Jews?" Fred asked with a knowing tone.

"Yes. All we have helped so far have been Jews."

"You can't possibly save them all."

"I know, sir, but God wants me to save this family, and the ones coming tomorrow night, and the next night. I realize now that this is a work God has given to me. We need the ration cards or these people will not be allowed to move into the country for safer accommodations. The cards are their passage."

On May 10, 1940, the German Army had stealthily invaded Holland without a declaration of war. The royal family fled to Britain and the Dutch Army surrendered on the fifth day. Since then, the Nazi military and the Gestapo had infiltrated virtually every community in Holland, disrupting commerce and transporting many "undesirables" from their homes. Now, in May 1942, it was an act of treason to aid Jews.

Fred worked for the Food Office, a government enterprise that disbursed ration cards to each family so they could buy food for the month. When the Nazis arrived, they forbade Jews from having ration cards, thus limiting their ability to live in Holland because the ration cards were necessary to obtain bread, meat, cheese and milk. Each month, new ration cards were issued when one turned in the stub from last month's card. They were meticulously counted and given out only in places monitored closely by the Gestapo.

Fred knew the cost, but he could not resist the dauntless woman who taught his mentally disabled daughter to read the Bible. He peered at her, with a twinge of respect at the edge of his lips and eyes.

They were both startled when they heard marching in the streets and orders shouted in German.

"I'll see," he said abruptly, hoping she would leave before the next customer stopped in.

"That's all I ask," Corrie said with a delightful smile, making sure she locked eyes with the older man, and then hurried out of the shop.

More knocks at the door.

More Jews to hide.

More danger of being detected.

Corrie's house was filling up with people to hide. She now worked full-time to find places in the country where her refugees could go. She needed the ration cards but thought Fred had let her down, until the day he walked into their clock shop.

"Oh, my goodness, Mr. Koornstra, look at you!" Corrie exclaimed, knowing she had caused his injuries.

Fred Koornstra had two black eyes, and from the look of it, a broken nose. His lower lip was sliced and swollen. Before Corrie could run to him, Fred opened his face into a large smile.

"My friend took the hold-up a little too seriously," the bruised man said. "He wanted it to look as real as possible."

"I would say he did a very realistic job," said Betsie, Corrie's sister, who entered the room.

"Yes, but look what I have for you," Fred pulled a package out of his pocket and opened the top to reveal a mass of ration cards.

"Oh, Mr. Koonstra, you dear man," said Corrie joyfully.

"I can give you the same amount each month," he said proudly. "See, I have torn off the continuing coupon from each one."

9

The trio worked out a plan to have Fred stop by the back of the house, or the Beje, as it was affectionately called by its inhabitants because of the street they lived on in Haarlem, the Barteljorisstraat. Fred would wear an old uniform and act as if he was checking the meter, but he would deliver the ration cards by lifting the first step off the back staircase and placing them in a hollow space underneath. With this method, Corrie could avoid visiting the Food Office, and Fred could pretend to have a legitimate reason to regularly stop by the Beje.

———◆———

A mother and three babies came.

Then a couple without children.

Then an older, single Jew who had lost his wife.

Corrie not only needed more space, she needed it insulated somehow. *What if the babies are heard out in the street when the Gestapo marches by?* Corrie wondered.

It was no longer adequate to hide the Beje stowaways on the third floor and tell them to keep quiet. Corrie needed a special room that could not be detected if the house were inspected, and it must be soundproof. This project is what drew Corrie into the underground.

Many Dutch people objected to the occupation by the Third Reich and senseless acts against the Hebrew people. These Jews were friends and neighbors who were disappearing, all because they believed in the God of Abraham and Isaac. Hollanders resisted Hitler and his Nazi regime in various ways. Some of them decided to offer armed resistance; others utilized the press with illegal newspapers and Radio Orange; still others decided to help by hiding people such as the Landelijke Organisatie voor Hulp aan Onderduikers (National Organization for Help to Persons in Hiding), or the LO. Corrie's relative, Kik, was involved with the LO.

One night, Kik stopped by the Beje to invite Corrie to a clandestine meeting to connect with people who could help her.

"Get your bicycle," Kik said brusquely.

"Now? After curfew?" asked Corrie, feeling a little bossed.

"And bring a sweater, it's cold!" Kik ordered.

Corrie obliged.

After a long bike ride through the darkened Haarlem streets, then into the country on gravel roads, they slipped under a bridge and alongside a canal. Corrie could smell the sea air and realized they were traveling toward the coast. Coming to a halt, Kik picked up the bicycles, and led Corrie by foot down a long, winding lane surrounded by tall trees. He led her up the front steps of a dark brick house and turned to face her.

"This is it, Corrie," Kik said, somewhat out of breath from carrying the bicycles. "This meeting will expose you to the underground and all that is happening across Holland. There are some of the most fascinating men and women you will ever meet in this house. They are in liaison with the English and the Free Dutch forces operating in Western Europe. They control the underground railroad, not only for Jews escaping Germany, but also for Allied fighter pilots who are shot down and making their way back to England."

"Why did you bring me here, Kik?" Corrie asked, feeling out of her league. She simply helped a few strangers who came to her house each night, giving them some warm food and a bed.

"These people have heard about you and want to help. I told them you were leading a resistance group in Haarlem."

"You did what?" Corrie's eyes widened.

"They are going to help you build a secret room, and they can help you with false identity papers, transportation, medicine, and even weapons and explosives — though I know you would never use them. This meeting will probably change your life but it will be worth it. Are you ready?"

Corrie was a little winded, but thoroughly excited, wondering what she would find once she entered the strange home they had come so far to visit.

"The Lord wants me to do this, so I know He will give me the strength and courage to endure the future, whatever it may hold. It is my Christian duty to help the hurting. So, lead on."

"Well, I'm glad you feel that way."

Grasping her hand, Kik opened the back door and gently pulled Corrie over the threshold.

CHAPTER 3

Assassination

The Architect was grieving. The man who was to be his successor, Reinhard Heydrich, was no more. Reinhard was his best friend, and a mastermind on how to destroy Jews, the number one enemy of the state. But now, at 38, Reinhard had gone to the abyss, destroyed by assassins.

The tragedy happened on May 27, 1942, near Prague. Two Czech agents — obviously connected to the British underground — attacked Heydrich's convertible when his driver slowed for a sharp curve in the road. One man stepped out of the bushes with a machine gun, which immediately jammed.

The other agent threw a bomb toward the car, but he missed his target. However, the shrapnel from the explosion eventually performed its duty on the victim and within eight days, a crucial leader of the SS, Reinhard Heydrich, was dead from severe infection.

———◆◆◆———

They will pay! The Architect vowed to himself. *It is now my life's mission to destroy our true enemy. I will call my plan* Operation Reinhard.

CHAPTER 4

Carinhall

On Hermann Göring's right hand was an exquisite ring set with six diamonds. His left hand sported an immense square emerald ring, at least an inch in diameter. Göring walked just ahead of Albert Speer and spoke to his guest quietly, as if others were trying to eavesdrop on them.

"You know, Speer, the Führer appears to be getting more and more tired; it is the work schedule he keeps. Bormann isn't helping him at all. If only *I* had been summoned to lead the staff and watch over him, we would not have suffered the recent setbacks with the Soviets."

Speer did not respond. He knew that while they walked he should not jump to the crux of the issue he wanted to discuss. Besides, to agree too hastily when one showed discontentment with the war effort was risky; it could be a trap. He followed Göring on his tour, noticing the erect carriage of his shoulders and massive girth.

Speer, with his new cabinet position as Minister of Armaments and Munitions, still grieved the loss of his predecessor, Dr. Fritz Todt. The investigation into the airplane accident was inconclusive, and Speer intentionally disregarded the frequent chatter of espionage and treason surrounding the event. He was not to blame, and his new responsibilities as Minister occupied every waking moment. Even his young family took a back seat while Speer dove head first into his work.

Speer, having once been Hitler's chief architect, designed the Reich Chancellery in Berlin and the Party Palace in Nuremberg. What most people did not know was that Hitler had secretly commissioned Speer to redesign the entire city of Berlin for the future 1,000-year rule of the Reich. But presently, his role was to deliver airplanes, tanks and machine guns to the German Army.

Reichsmarschall Hermann Göring, Speer's host that afternoon, kept finding himself on the outs with Adolf Hitler even though Göring was Hitler's second-in-command. Göring knew he had lost the Führer's confidence the past year, yet Albert Speer managed to uphold Hitler's full admiration. Speer was a personal friend of the Führer and others envied their close relationship.

Göring invited Speer to Carinhall that day. What he did not know was that Speer had held a prior meeting with Joseph Goebbels whereby they plotted together on how to reinstate the Reichsmarschall as the leader over Hitler's day to day affairs. Speer was happy for the timely invitation and Carinhall was the perfect place for such a meeting.

Carinhall was Göring's country residence, a mansion located on his sylvan estate northeast of Berlin. Carinhall was as opulent and excessive as the jewelry Göring wore and the clothes he constantly changed to impress his guests. Built in 1933 by the same architect who designed the Olympic stadium in Berlin, Carinhall was a grand hunting lodge with high, arched ceilings and massive, crisscrossing wooden beams. Named after Hermann's first wife, Carin, Carinhall was easily the finest estate in all of Germany.

The Carinhall reception room was filled with hundreds of paintings four tiers high. The broad corridors held statues and exquisite furniture, many with a history Göring loved to explain. Göring led Speer through his cellar and many galleries filled with priceless, classical pieces from the Naples Museum and museums in southern France. He showed Speer the Sterzing Altar presented to him by Mussolini two years prior. Each of the four highly prized panels depicted scenes from "The Life of the Virgin" and were considered the most important pieces of art in Sterzing, Italy. Göring beamed with pride as he revealed to Speer the historical significance of the precious alterpiece.

There were cupboards of French soaps and perfumes, trays of diamonds and other precious stones, fur coats, and medals given Göring from foreign diplomats all over the world. He stopped to explain each gift that he received from foreign governments, and each painting along with the master painter who put color to canvas. Speer wondered how much of it was acquired from the Jews without payment, but he held his tongue.

Hermann Göring was a large man, much larger than he had been when he earned imperishable honor as a flying ace in World War I. Flying missions alongside Manfred Von Richthofen, the Red Baron, Göring was one of the great heroes of Germany with twenty-two air victories. He often wore his spectacular medals when sporting his dress uniforms. Yet, in between wars, Göring's girth became larger and larger, his clothing more ostentatious, and the curious reddening of his face and mood swings were indicative of someone with a drug addiction.

Göring was quite unreliable with his emotions, Speer knew; at one moment gracious and warm, and the next moment brash and insulting. You dealt with Hermann Göring by keeping your cards close to your chest, especially when he warmed up to you. The Reichsmarschall was one of the most dangerous men in Germany, capable of excessive brutality and intrigues.

When considering Hitler's inner cabinet, Speer held the belief that they were not the best politicians. One could not help but sense an extreme sense of entitlement and overcompensation with the men, rather than being true statesmen. Reichsmarschall Hermann Göring; propaganda minister Joseph Goebbels; and SS chief Heinrich Himmler all had special access to the Führer because of their unique relationship with him when Nazism was founded. Thus, it was entirely irrelevant what kind of credentials they held; Hitler was loyal to those who had been loyal to him.

What these men all had in common was their devotion to the Führer and his agenda of National Socialism. They constantly maneuvered against each other to remain in the good graces of their leader as his number one confidant, but that position was usurped by the man they all hated, Martin Bormann, Hitler's personal secretary.

"Have a seat, Speer, while I go change," Göring said curtly as he strode toward the massive staircase. "We will have our discussion when I return."

While waiting, Speer looked around the lodge at the heads of slain beasts from Africa, Asia and Europe. The stone, timber and metal used throughout the fortress was simply breathtaking. Speer studied the thick beams and columns of oak and marble, so intricately designed and put together in a way that any king would be impressed with the details. The one-hundred-thousand acres of woods surrounding

Carinhall possessed its own beauty apart from the great structure. The deer, fox, bear and swans made this estate wonderful and private, a Garden of Eden excluded from the darkness of war.

The fact that Göring inhabited Carinhall, however, seemed out of place. The man was not a king, merely someone who had taken advantage of war and the spoils that came with it. As Adolf Hitler promoted the Reichsmarschall and gave him increasing authority over government and commerce, Hermann's estates flourished and grew almost out of control. While most Germans were tasked to ration and cut back, Göring built edifices throughout Germany and exported vintage paintings and other relics to his fortress in the woods. It was obsessive, it was vulgar, and if the German laborers knew about it he would certainly hang. But Speer recognized there was no accountability because everyone was distracted with the war effort.

Speer thought on Hermann Göring's rise to power in the last decade, and how he often bullied people to get what he wanted. A good example was when Germany's Foreign Minister, Joachim von Ribbentrop, was given the highest civilian award in Italy called the Order of Annunziata. Göring believed he had earned the honor and was more entitled to the award than Ribbentrop. He made his indignation known to Benito Mussolini, the fascist dictator of Italy, and soon, the honor of the Order of Annunziata was also bestowed on the Reichsmarschall.

Looking at Carinhall, Speer thought it would be an interesting study in economics to learn how Göring had accumulated his great wealth. It was during the early months of the war that were probably the most thrilling for Göring. The luxury goods he was able to confiscate would be fascinating to index and to learn their history.

Speer heard from his friend, Erhard Milch, that in Paris alone over 38,000 Jewish homes were seized, then sealed so their contents could be confiscated. The tapestries, paintings, statues and furniture were nothing less than exquisite. Over a span of two years, an average of 30 railroad cars per day poured from France into Germany for Göring to personally decide the destination of the priceless items — reside at Carinhall, or be shipped on to the Führer as gifts. One time, the Führer noted that a specific painting should have come to him instead of Göring so it was immediately shipped to Berlin, but most of the treasures ended up at Carinhall.

Drifting back into the room, Göring warmly said, "Ah, yes, Herr Speer, you've chosen my chaise made with leather from southern Italy. Mussolini himself sat in that chair and enjoyed its comfort."

Speer looked up to see the flamboyant outfit Göring sported, decorated with an oversized ruby brooch on his green velvet dressing gown. Göring could have been in a fashion magazine representing the baroque era. Speer had to keep himself from laughing aloud and turned his mind back to the conversation at hand.

Göring began, "I don't like Martin Bormann and the influence he has on our Führer. Every time I speak, Bormann's putting in a word or two edgewise, like a serpent slithering around the Führer night and day. This has to stop, don't you agree, Herr Speer?"

Speer took little time to respond, knowing the meeting was already off to a great start, "Yes, of course, a little snake. I agree with you."

"Bormann is aiming at nothing less than the succession of Adolf Hitler," said Göring. "If he doesn't overthrow our Führer, he wants to be there when Hitler breathes his last so he can reign as Germany's chancellor in his place."

"I agree with you, and I can also tell you that Martin Bormann speaks about you cynically every chance he gets," said Speer. "Bormann belittles you to the Führer and this is partially why you have lost Hitler's respect."

"I knew it!" cried Göring. "That snake wants all the glory for himself. I have decreased this year as Bormann has increased."

"He is definitely the man with the hedge-clippers," said Speer.

"What do you mean?"

"He seems to use his cunning to keep all the men around Hitler at a certain level. He doesn't let anyone get too much power or influence with the Führer."

"You are right, Speer. I have noticed that myself. I wish Bormann were more like you. You have a tactful way with the Führer. I can tell he likes you very much, with your handsome looks and intelligent eyes. He likes that you are a descendent from the bourgeois class and that you've come through for him on more than one occassion."

With this comment Speer was reminded of Göring's own tactics and the time Hitler commissioned Göring to help the Desert Fox, General Erwin Rommel. Hitler told Göring, "I want you to work with General Rommel and his 7th Panzer Division to ensure he has everything he needs to beat back the Americans. Spare not the bombers, armor, ammunition and fuel needed to accomplish his mission and hold on to Tripoli. We must not lose Africa."

"You can pile everything on my shoulders, mein Führer," responded Göring confidently. "I will see to this myself."

Göring took General Rommel and his wife, Lucia, on a ride in his personal train down to Rome to help the North African campaign. However, Göring stayed in the Excelsior Hotel and toured museums instead of visiting the front lines. The Rommels eventually parted company with the Reichsmarschall when they realized he was with them only in an attempt to earn him favor with the Führer, not help with the African war effort.

Speer could remember many times Göring had let Germany down, but Speer was bound to promote him to Hitler once more. Göring was a much better organizer than Bormann, and the war needed a military strategist at the helm. In fact, in Speer's mind, nearly anyone would be an improvement over the spineless Bormann.

"So what can we do?" asked Göring.

"Well, I have spoken to Goebbels and he has a plan. It is to put you back in your rightful place as second in power, thus limiting Bormann, and eventually showing the Führer that Bormann is a traitor."

"I already like the plan," said Göring, looking off with a smile sweeping his face.

Speer knew that promoting Göring to the Führer would gain the Reichsmarschall's interest in the plan. Now he just had to convince him that it would work.

"I think it is time to meet with the Führer without Bormann present and allow Goebbels and me the chance to convince him that you are his rightful successor. As Reichsmarschall you should have more say in matters of the state. You should be leading this war."

"I love it, I love it. Please tell me more, tell me more." Göring rubbed his hands together, giddy with enthusiasm. He reminded Speer of a little boy when told he could visit the beach.

"It begins with a meeting at Berchtesgaden."

CHAPTER 5

Courage

Corrie dashed out of the Beje screaming, "Betsie, hurry! The Weils are under attack!"

Corrie ran down the road toward the commotion. There was a small crowd beginning to grow on the street outside of Weil's Furrier Shop. One German soldier with a combat helmet and rifle stood outside as guard but it was obvious many more soldiers were inside the shop breaking glass and destroying furniture. Poor Mr. Weil stood alone, near the guard and a few of his neighbors.

The windows opened above them and clothes and books rained down on the street. Loud German shouting echoed from the inside of the house. It appeared they were looking for something they could not find.

Betsie grabbed Corrie's arm, letting her know she was now by her side. They both stared at Mr. Weil. They could see his eyes welling up with tears.

"Where is Mrs. Weil?" Corrie asked their neighbor.

No response. Mr. Weil looked straight ahead as if in shock.

"We need to get him away from here," said Betsie as pajamas and socks floated down to the street from the third story window.

The guard had stepped inside the house and Corrie saw her opportunity.

"Quick, Mr. Weil, come with me to safety."

Corrie grabbed the older gentleman's arm and started to propel him in the direction of the Beje. Betsie grabbed his other arm making resistance futile for the dazed Jew. Thankfully, the crowd was large enough that most did not notice that the owner was disappearing with the Ten Boom sisters.

Once they were safely inside the Beje, Corrie glanced back down the street and saw two German soldiers walk out of the house with arms full of furs. They were distracted, and this was good. The Ten Booms learned that Mrs. Weil was out of town, and this was also advantageous. Thankfully, no one was hurt that day but it marked the end of an era: Jews could no longer hide quietly in their homes in Holland.

One of Corrie's new sources told her that a Mr. Smit would visit regarding their special room within three days of her meeting with the underground. Like clockwork, three days later, there was a knock at the door and a Mr. Smit entered their watch shop to inspect the Beje for a possible hiding place.

"Good afternoon, Mr. Ten Boom, Miss Ten Boom," said their visitor. "I have come with a special purpose. Since you use this house as a headquarters of operations for your underground work in Haarlem, we must try to make it as safe as possible for your visitors. I will look to see if there is a place in your home to build a secret room, where your guests can hide in case of a search."

Eighty-three-year-old Casper ten Boom, who loved to make connections with people he might know, scratched his beard and asked, "Are you related to the Smits on the Prinsengracht?"

Corrie frowned, "No, Father, he isn't. It's an alias."

Mr. Smit smiled at Casper then began climbing the staircase. When he reached the top where Corrie's room was located, he whistled in delight at their luck.

"This is wonderful!" he exclaimed.

"Why?" asked Corrie.

"The way the ceiling is designed I can put up a fake wall here in this bedroom and make it look like it is part of the original structure," Mr. Smit replied. "No one will ever suspect there is a secret room behind it."

During the next few days, several different "Mr. Smits" appeared at the door, all hiding something in their clothes or in newspapers — trowels, paintbrushes, bricks and plaster. One by one, they came to assist, but the original Mr. Smit was there most often. They decided to use brick so the wall would not sound hollow. They also had to redo all the molding and make the paint look aged to match the original.

When they finished, even the Ten Booms struggled to identify how the wall might look out of place, since it matched the rest of the room so perfectly. A water stain on the new wall somehow looked decades old. These men were obviously master carpenters.

The original Mr. Smit came alone the final day and gave them some special instructions to diligently follow.

"There is an air vent to the outside in the hiding place. Keep a fresh jug of water in here at all times, as well as vitamins and hard tack biscuits. When you have visitors, they must keep their personal belongings in the room at all times. Being on the top floor will help your stowaways hide while the search begins downstairs, but they cannot have the added burden of luggage while they flee to the room; it would be far too risky. Do you have any questions?"

Casper asked, "Are you related to any Smit families in Amsterdam?"

As Jews disappeared from the city, there were more knocks on the Beje door, with additional people to feed and find safe places for in the country. Thankfully, the resources and number of workers had grown along with the need. Corrie and Betsie now worked with more than eighty associates in the Dutch underground, many who dined with them and stopped by the shop throughout the day. The

Beje had eighteen messengers who would run or bike throughout Haarlem and the surrounding countryside.

As the leader, Corrie developed strategic contacts throughout Haarlem and Amsterdam to help her. She knew who to call for medicine or when a Jew needed surgery; which guard to speak with when a loved one was in prison or needed a favor; what to do when they needed extra money to pay off someone in the underground who must perform an extraordinary risk; how to dispose of a Jewish body if a child died during the night.

Through the final months of 1942 and into 1943, Corrie's operation drew so many people in and out of the watch shop that they began to feel uneasy about being discovered. *Why would a clock repair shop have so many visitors each day?*

One day a neighbor stopped by and asked Corrie and Betsie if they could keep their Jews from singing so loudly. Eventually the day came when Corrie received a message from the Chief of Police, beckoning her to the station to speak with him.

Corrie bravely walked to the police station alone. She followed a guard down a corridor to a door marked "CHIEF." She knocked three times, then patted down her brown, windblown hair before the door was opened by a heavy, balding man. He smiled when he saw her and asked her to sit down. He reached for his radio and turned it up. He then confided to Corrie that he knew all about her operation and applauded her for her bravery.

"Yes, our clock repair work takes much courage these days, we…"

"That is not what I was talking about!" said the Chief abruptly. "I meant your other work. Your more important work."

Corrie started to speak, then pressed her lips together and stared into the Chief's dark eyes.

"Yes, I know what you and Betsie do. You are an inspiration to our entire nation. That is why I need your help. I am fearful for your lives."

"Go on, sir."

"I have a dirty job to do, and I need someone to help me with it," the Chief said.

"What is this dirty job?" asked Corrie, hesitantly.

The police chief reached over and turned up the radio even louder.

"There is a Dutch man on our force who turns in his own people to the Gestapo," said the Chief. "He collaborates with the Nazis and has been selling out our countrymen, even friends and family. He has no heart. We must rid ourselves of this man. Do you understand me? So I ask you, Miss Ten Boom, do you know someone who could do away with him for me? This might save your own life and the lives of those you help."

"To kill him?" asked Corrie. "You want to know if I know someone who would kill another human being?"

"Yes, I thought with all your contacts there might be someone who…"

"No sir! This I cannot and will not help you with. My family is in this business to save lives — precious lives — and *this* is the work God has for us. I could never help you murder someone."

The police chief stared back at Corrie, expressionless.

"Sir, I understand your dilemma," said Corrie more calmly. "Let us pray together for God to help this situation. Would you like to pray with me for God to help this man and change his heart?"

"Yes."

The two bowed their heads in the Haarlem police station while Corrie prayed fervently to God to change the man's heart, to understand his own worth and the worth of every other human being. When she finished, the two briefly hugged and Corrie left the station, but not before seeing the police chief emotionally moved with damp eyes. More than anything, this encounter reminded Corrie that she had taken many risks.

So many people know. The operation must soon be found out, Corrie thought. *We cannot expect God's continued protection in the face of so many obstacles and dangers. Or can we?*

———◆———

Mr. Smit came again early one morning. He stepped into the Beje and removed his wristwatch as if he wanted Casper to look at it. Several other underground workers were in the shop but since he did not know them, he acted like a customer needing a watch repair.

"Greetings, Mr. Smit!" Casper ten Boom's face lit up when he saw the man who had helped them with the secret room.

Corrie saw that Mr. Smit looked nervous and tried to reassure him, "It's okay, Mr. Smit. We can talk openly with them. They are here to bring supplies and take messages out into the city for us. You have been so kind to us; what can we help you with today?"

"Hello, Miss Ten Boom. I came today because I want to make your home safer. This house needs an alarm system to warn people if someone comes into the clock shop who wants to harm you. A buzzer near the front door can be pushed to alert people in every room in the house to go to the hiding place. Do you understand? In our other houses like this, we have sent an electrician to wire the entire house with an alarm system. Do you have any objections to this? It could save many lives."

"No, sir," answered Corrie. "We have no objections. Please send the electrician, and do tell those wonderful people helping us hello for me."

"I will. One other thing. You need a warning not just for those inside, but for those outside the shop. What happens if your home is raided and Gestapo agents are inside just waiting for people in the underground to come by the watch shop? Please put a sign in the window so they know when it is safe to come by. Perhaps one could quickly remove the sign from the window if the house is raided."

"That is a good idea. We will attend to that at once."

"I will send a man tomorrow; his name is Leenderd Kip. In exchange for his services, perhaps he could reside here for a while? He is a Jew."

"Absolutely," answered Corrie.

And with that, Mr. Smit left the clock shop and never returned. Leenderd came the following day. Though not an electrician by trade, he provided excellent service and wired several buttons on the first floor that sounded an alarm upstairs in the bedrooms. He then asked if he could stay at the Beje.

"Of course," exclaimed Corrie with outstretched arms. Leenderd bowed, and Corrie led him to his room.

In addition to this development, Corrie found she had a contact at the central telephone exchange who worked new lines for people. With a slight reworking of some of his new numbers, he was able to reconnect the Ten Boom's phone, which had been out of service for two years since the war started. It was illegal to have this luxury, but Corrie knew they needed it to alert people in other towns regarding raids and tips they received from the police force.

The Ten Booms were encouraged to know that an orange-haired Dutch police officer named Rolf was sympathetic to their secret activities. He stopped by regularly to chat with the elder Ten Boom and let them know which neighborhood was on the docket to be raided the next day. This information saved many lives. The secret reconnected telephone allowed for urgent warnings when their messengers could not make it in time.

One day, a pastor stopped by to greet the Ten Booms. Corrie was not sure, but thought this might be a sign from God that he could help them with their work. The pastor lived off the road in the woods and his secluded home would be ideal to house a family for a short while.

"*Goede morgen*, pastor," said Corrie warmly. "What brings you to town today?"

"Well, my clock is no longer working and I believe Casper is the only one who can fix it," the pastor replied. "I have tried, but I don't have the gift that your father has with these machines." The pastor set his clock on the counter near the workshop.

"We would love to repair your clock for you, but we also have something we need to ask you as well," said Corrie a little more seriously.

The pastor smiled, "Anything for you and your family."

Corrie stepped closer and said quietly, "We have a Jewish woman and her baby here who need a place to stay for a while. Could you please take them in for us? Your house is secluded and no one will hear the baby cry in the country."

All the warmth and friendliness drained from the pastor's face.

"How dare you ask me such a thing!" he said as he stepped back from Corrie. "Is this some kind of sick trick you are playing on me to get me in trouble? As a pastor, I cannot partake in criminal activity! I hope your family is not involved in this business. You could all go to prison."

Corrie had an idea.

"Wait here," she said. Corrie ran upstairs, leaving the pastor with her father.

Corrie went into Betsie's room where their special guests resided. A young mother was resting on the bed while Betsie held her baby on her lap.

"Give her to me for a moment, Betsie," said Corrie. "I may have a home for her."

Betsie handed her younger sister the baby and Corrie flew back down the stairs. She approached the pastor who was now standing near the door.

"Please, pastor," Corrie said. "Please look at this little one. Have you ever seen such cute cheeks?"

The pastor reluctantly looked down into her arms at the delicate infant and stroked her face with the side of his hand. Corrie lit up inside, thinking she had found a home for this fractured family.

Suddenly the man removed his hand and with a serious tone said, "No, ma'am, I cannot do this. God does not want us to be foolhardy with the ministry He has provided us. My wife and I could lose our lives for this Jewish child."

As Corrie came to grips with this news, Casper ten Boom walked silently behind her.

"Hand the baby to me, Corrie," said the old watchmaker.

Casper ten Boom cradled the baby in his arms, and allowed the infant to peer up into his eyes and smile. "You say we could lose our lives for this child? I would consider that the greatest honor that could come to my family."

The pastor turned abruptly and walked out of the shop. Though a little disheartened, Corrie felt empowered in her work, knowing her father grasped the danger she brought on them all.

The Jewish mother and baby ended up at a truck farm just outside of town. The Gestapo had recently raided the buildings so Corrie thought it would be safe for a few nights. If the baby screamed, she would not be heard.

Several days later, the farm was raided again and both the mother and her infant screamed out in fear. They were discovered and taken away by the Gestapo, never seen again by the Ten Booms. Corrie hoped the mother did not reveal that they previously stayed at a clock shop in Haarlem.

CHAPTER 6

Zyklon B

The Architect's retribution against Reinhard Heydrich's assassins was swift and severe. First, the Bohemian village of Lidice was surrounded by the Gestapo, and all 172 male inhabitants over the age of twelve were taken to a nearby orchard and shot in groups of ten against a barn wall. The 200 female residents of Lidice were immediately shipped to Ravensbrück Concentration Camp. The four pregnant women were taken to a maternity clinic in Prague where their babies were delivered, then killed. All of the 90 Lidice children except for seven were gassed at Chelmno in Poland.

After emptying Lidice of its residents, the city was systematically set on fire. The homes and businesses not burned completely to the ground were blown up with explosives or bulldozed. Then the entire city was scraped and leveled by dozers, with salt sown in the charred soil.

The cemetery beside Lidice was dug up and the rotting corpses removed. The town was swept clean of any sign of its prior inhabitants living or dead. To the

Architect, it was of no significance that Lidice was eventually found not to be the village that housed the assassins of his murdered friend. *German reprisal for such an incident must be severe!* Lidice was reduced to a vacant field, and its inhabitants a memory.

———•••———

The Architect looked over a column of large figures indicating the number of people present in each territory on the map in front of him. *How to deal with the peasantry?*

The Architect studied a new report on the poisonous gas Zyklon-B. It might be the miracle for which he was looking to help him with Operation Reinhard.

I. G. Farben owned the pesticide patent and the hydrogen cyanide crystals could be purchased in bulk from two German chemical firms in Hamburg. Its normal function was to fumigate buildings. But if the extremely poisonous gas was inhaled, it would kill in a few breaths by inhibiting oxidative metabolism.

Zyklon-B bound hemoglobin in the blood, blocking the process by which oxygen is transferred to the cells. It was tested on dogs and in three minutes the canines were killed with just 300 parts per million by creating a form of internal asphyxiation.

The Architect read that as little as 70 milligrams of hydrogen cyanide could kill a person in two minutes. He quickly scribbled some figures on a piece of paper, deducted the evaporation rate, and found that in a large chamber — where perhaps several hundred people could stand — a couple hundred grams of gas could occupy the entire area in two to three minutes. A can of Zyklon-B contained 200 grams of hydrogen cyanide and could effectively poison 550 cubic meters of air in a few minutes. *So what if we used five cans per chamber?*

This would be an extremely fast way for a large group to die. The slowest part of this process would be to get rid of the bodies, the cremation. An entire team of people would be needed to clear out the chamber and load all the bodies into the furnace. Each camp would need more than guards to do this job; they would need volunteer Jews because the SS would not want to be in charge of the night and day furnace operations.

The Architect recalled that before Reinhard Heydrich's assassination, Hermann Göring had ordered Heydrich to come up with a final solution to the Jewish problem. Heydrich outlined during the Wannsee Conference a pogrom where Germany would not wait until after the war to exterminate the Jews. Heydrich explained that the final solution could be completed during the war in concentration camps in Poland.

The problem was that Heydrich did not live long enough to realize the plan. He had not developed a workable method. He was still killing Jews with diesel fumes in the back of large vans at Belzec and Treblinka, but killing Jews by the vanload would never accommodate the millions who needed to be destroyed. *Zyklon-B could be the grand solution!* Thousands of Jews could be killed every day in large warehouses with just a little bit of the gas. The Architect read that another positive aspect of Zyklon-B was that it could be lethal even in freezing temperatures, whereas sometimes the diesel engines would not start in the cold, winter months.

———◆◆◆———

The Architect authorized his specialists to experiment with Zyklon-B to kill Soviet prisoners of war and see if it was effective. The first batch poisoned 850 Russian soldiers and it worked remarkably well. The second test killed an additional 900 Russian soldiers. Zyklon-B was the ideal gas to do the job quickly. The Architect did not feel the need to be governed by the Hague or Geneva Conventions of War for POWs. Russia did not adhere to these pacts, so Germany was not obliged to treat the Soviets accordingly.

Oh, how he would be praised by the Führer for this solution! *Despite a few moments of fear, dizziness and vomiting, these prisoners will feel no pain*, the Architect thought. It was an exceedingly humane way to die while others are bombed or starved. He was quite pleased with himself, the humanitarian.

The Architect wrote a note that ordered several men to be trained as Zyklon-B specialists. They would join the 96 men he already recruited from his T4 euthanasia project in Berlin who had been sent to Poland to build and operate the four Operation Reinhard extermination centers. He would have Dr. Joachim Mugrowski, head of the SS health department, procure the gas, and then have it distributed discreetly to the camps. Other former T4 men would oversee initial operations to ensure the job would continue satisfactorily. *It will take a mini-army to complete the mission of* Operation Reinhard!

The Architect was sad that his friend was not around to be a witness. According to Heydrich's vision, Chelmno, Belzec, Sobibor and Treblinka — all located within 200 miles of Warsaw — were operational to eliminate the Jews. The men who were sent to construct these camps had delivered in the nick of time because the Jewish ghettos in Warsaw were overflowing.

After mulling over the situation, the Architect decided to write another note ordering Rudolf Höss, the SS kommandant at Auschwitz, to immediately refit his camp as a large-scale gassing location. He specified that the two farmhouses adjacent to the Auschwitz-Birkenau Camp were to be converted to gas chambers of at least 200 square meters each. He knew that after meeting with the Führer and explaining the potential of Zyklon-B, even more gas chambers and crematoria would be needed.

The Architect also knew the Nazis could not just continue to gas those Jews who were unfit for work. For Germany to have room to grow and colonize to the East, virtually all the Jews rounded up throughout Europe would have to perish immediately, whether they could work or not. His friend Heydrich had been right; this could not wait until after the war. *With the effectiveness of Zyklon-B, the final solution could be accomplished in a few months!*

CHAPTER 7

An Attempt to Save Germany

"What is the Führer's mood, Herr Speer?" Joseph Goebbels asked upon his arrival at Berchtesgaden, the mountain town near Adolf Hitler's alpine home.

"Well, the Führer is not feeling very fond of Göring at the moment," replied Albert Speer. "It would probably be better not to press the matter right now unless his mood changes."

The two men greeted each other at the Hof Hotel, then drove together toward the Berghof, the German retreat headquarters where the Führer received his guests and would sometimes invite them to take afternoon walks with him to his teehaus. The Berghof was Hitler's home away from Berlin and it possessed a massive study, library, and a great hall where the Reich Chancellor met with Nazis and foreign dignitaries.

Adolf Hitler would hike to the teehaus with people he especially liked. Together they would recline on sofas for long discussions and naps before making the one kilometer trek back to the Berghof. This walk featured breathtaking views of the Alps and the Berchtesgaden Valley. Eva Braun, Hitler's longtime companion, was usually part of the teehaus group, and sometimes Speer — but always Bormann.

When Goebbels and Speer arrived at the Berghof, it was Martin Bormann who received them at the entrance and escorted them up to the great hall. Speer had already had his fill of Bormann after sitting through meetings with him and the other staff for the last twenty-four hours. Goebbels was warm to Bormann and extended his hand in a personal greeting. No *Heil Hitlers* were used at the Berghof by those on the national staff, only visitors.

Martin Bormann was the personal secretary of Adolf Hitler and oversaw all correspondence coming to the Führer. This gave him immense power as gatekeeper to the supreme leader of Germany. Bormann was a large man — though not as large as Göring — and he possessed a bulldog face with dark eyes. He was known as a conniver, and Speer knew better than to enter into his confidences.

In previous meetings, Goebbels, Speer and Göring acknowledged Germany had entered a "leader crisis." Hitler was receiving most of his advisement from one man, Bormann, and not relying on his other advisors. Göring and Goebbels had been with Hitler from the beginning; they were long-time allies of the Führer, but Bormann limited their influence. Even Heinrich Himmler, head of the SS, no longer had the access he once enjoyed. *But perhaps this visit to the Berghof would change the status quo.*

"Will we be allowed to meet with the Führer soon?" asked Goebbels.

"Yes, very soon," replied Bormann. "He is meeting with Count Ciano presently, but I know he is looking forward to your meeting."

Speer knew how Bormann operated. He was slick and appeasing to one's face; but as soon as one was out of sight Bormann would turn on him. He would kill the individual's character with kindness by giving faint praise to Hitler, only to let the

Führer disagree with him and explain why the individual should not be praised. Bormann always managed to achieve his desired result.

Bormann took the men to the outside veranda decorated with different colored canvas awnings which gave the log and stone home a contemporary feel. They all sat and waited for the Führer to finish his conference with the Italian diplomat. Soon, there was some movement inside so Bormann left them for a moment, then returned to receive them into the Führer's study.

Their meeting was cordial. Speer gave the Führer updated reports about armaments production throughout Germany he had received by cable within the last few hours. Plane and tank production was up from the previous month. There was nothing shocking in his reports.

Goebbels spoke to the Führer about what was going on politically in Berlin and updated him on some of the trials and court-martials taking place. Hitler was always interested in which actress was performing in the opera or theater and Goebbels obliged him with gossip.

Adolf Hitler seemed in a relatively good mood and Martin Bormann had stepped out of the meeting to address some issues with the staff. *Now is the time to strike*, thought Speer.

Hitler gave the men a warm smile, "Shall we walk to the teehaus together?"

"That would be wonderful," answered Goebbels.

"Let me get Blondi," said Hitler of his female Alsatian.

Speer felt confident the three men would now be able to have an open discussion about Hitler's internal decision-making process. Hopefully, broadening the people who had access to the Führer would help him in the many decisions he made for Germany. The time had come to end Martin Bormann's undue influence with the Reich leader.

As they were standing up to depart, Bormann came into the room with an alarmed look in his face.

"Mein Führer, there is a heavy air raid over Nuremberg!" he announced.

Goebbels and Speer glanced at each other. Whenever there was air raid information Hitler would go into a tirade about Göring's incompetence as the leader of the Luftwaffe. They both knew their plan to walk to the teehaus had evaporated, and possibly the opportunity to reinstate Göring with the Führer.

———◆◆◆———

Joseph Goebbels, Hermann Göring and Albert Speer met at Göring's palatial country house at Obersalzberg near Hitler's Berghof. Göring immersed his hand in a large crystal bowl filled with beautiful pearls and calmed his nerves by running his fingers through the soft, round gems. Speer knew that Göring needed a distraction to take his mind off the Allied bombing campaign. As a Nazi, Göring's standing had grown in power and position year after year, but lately his shooting star was faltering and heading in the wrong direction. *It is the Führer's stupid war with Russia*, Göring would whisper over and over, mostly to himself.

"We have to somehow break the Führer's inner circle of Bormann, Lammers and

Keitel," said the polished Goebbels. Looking at Speer and pointing to Göring, he said, "If we activate the Reichmarschall now, perhaps we three can become Hitler's inner ring, like an advisory panel. The men around him are not interested in what is best for Germany and the Führer. They are newcomers, and we have been with him from the beginning."

Hans Lammers was the head of Hitler's cabinet and would preside over meetings when Hitler was not present. A Nazi since 1933, he had risen in the ranks quickly and become a trusted adviser to the Führer. Wilhelm Keitel was a German Field Marshal and the head of the general staff. He served on the cabinet as Hitler's war secretary and like Bormann, he was with Hitler every day.

Goebbels spent an hour lambasting Bormann, Keitel, Lammers and others who had surrounded the Führer in an effort to influence him. He and Speer also spoke to Göring on the status of the war and how backward everything seemed to be going with Russia.

"The Führer spends his days with these men brooding and worrying," said Goebbels. "They do not make sure he gets his rest, or gets enough fresh air. You, Hermann, can change all that, and ensure he gets his advice from people who actually know what's going on; people who can speak their mind around him."

"Like you and Speer?" Göring said, smiling.

"Yes, and you will lead us," said Goebbels as he bent to one knee as if pleading. "We need you to wake up, Hermann, and retake control. You are the flying ace. You are the leader of the Luftwaffe. Hitler once trusted you like a brother. His love is still there, just buried."

"I know, I know, but things have changed so much," said Göring. "With Bormann there all the time torpedoing me, I have lost much esteem in the Führer's eyes. Isn't that right, Herr Speer?"

Speer cleared his throat, "Somewhat right, yes, but I think now is the time to act." Speer knew he was slightly out of his league. The two men before him had fought alongside Hitler since the inception of the Nazi movement. Göring was even wounded at Hitler's side during the famous putsch in 1923.

Speer was a relative newcomer, and this feeling never left him. As such, he chose his words cautiously, "If we do not change things at once, the war will surely be lost. The Americans will attack the mainland soon and this will bring troubling times ahead. With Hitler receiving all of his advice from Bormann, we will lose. The man has no military experience. And Joseph and I believe that Bormann is seeking to succeed Hitler. But there is still time to act."

"Having you as the leader, Hermann, would give Hitler the strongest possible alternative to the pseudo cabinet he has now," said Goebbels solemnly. "You should be Hitler's successor, not Bormann."

"Yes, yes, I agree," said Göring, becoming more interested in their plan. "But how will we accomplish this? Think of the bombings, and his ire at me?"

"Well, Speer has a plan, and I think it is a good one," said Goebbels. "Tell him, Albert."

"We all know that Martin Bormann and Fritz Sauckel have an alliance against me," said Speer. "With Sauckel in my own ministry he is able to sabotage my efforts and undermine my standing with the Führer behind my back. But I happen to know from Erhard Milch that Sauckel plays with his numbers. Right now there is a discrepancy of approximately a million workers that Sauckel is reporting as accounted for, but the Industrialists are reporting to me as missing. Milch knows these workers don't exist. I think this would be an opportunity to confront Sauckel and Bormann in this and show that they have been conniving to mislead the Führer for months."

Goebbels continued, "We will hold a meeting at the Berghof with everyone present, and unveil to the Führer the intrigues against him."

"Do you really believe this will work?" asked Göring.

"Yes, I do," answered Goebbels. "But only if we stand beside each other. United, we have the power to convince the Führer."

"Yes," said Speer.

"Yes!" said Göring, laughing with joy.

The three men gave a toast, to Hitler's new advisory team.

On the evening of their planned attack against Bormann, Albert Speer's stomach felt twisted into a knot. He could think of nothing else all day. The driver dropped off Speer and Erhard Milch at Hitler's Berghof headquarters where Bormann received them.

Milch was a field marshal of the Luftwaffe. He worked for both Speer and Göring as the Air Inspector General and was in charge of aircraft production. In terms of chain of command he was essentially Göring's deputy, but the field marshal favored Speer. Speer liked Milch for his pragmatism, so Milch was let in on the plan to reestablish Göring with the Führer that evening.

While waiting for the meeting to begin, Speer found to his astonishment that Goebbels was not there yet; just Göring, Keitel, Sauckel and — of all people — Heinrich Himmler, head of the SS.

"Where is Goebbels?" asked Speer nonchalantly, trying to disguise his panic. He hoped Goebbels was already in the building and meeting with the Chancellor.

Bormann spoke up, "Goebbels sends his regrets, and said he is unable to make it tonight. He phoned earlier, he is having a severe kidney attack."

It was the way Bormann said it. The look in his eyes and the slight smile killed the hope Speer had of their plan working. Speer glanced at Göring and noticed that he was uncharacteristically staring at the floor and not talking. *This doesn't look good. I need to do something,* Speer thought.

Before the meeting with Hitler, Speer pulled Göring aside to remind him of what they were trying to accomplish that night. Speer was rattled that Goebbels was not there and wondered if Göring also suspected a rat.

Göring smiled broadly at him and rubbed his large hands together, "Don't worry. It will all soon be taken care of!"

Speer was a little relieved that Göring seemed confident, and that he actually had a twinkle in his eye. "Remember," Speer said to Göring, "this is to put you in charge of the cabinet so we can save Germany."

"Yes, I can't wait. To save Germany. But be careful of Milch."

"What do you mean?" asked Speer. *This was so typical of Göring to try to subterfuge others behind their back*, thought Speer. But this last minute attempt against their ally before the big meeting was inexcusable.

"He is totally unreliable," answered Göring. "He will seek to take advantage of any opportunity given him and he will drop a friend like a hot iron."

Speer stared into Göring's eyes, but did not have time to address the irrational thought.

"Just keep focused on what we are trying to accomplish," Speer pleaded.

Bormann announced that the Führer was ready to see them and all the men paraded into the chancellery hall.

"Heil, mein Führer!" shouted Göring while raising his stocky outstretched arm and open hand as still as he could.

With a terse, incomprehensible response from Hitler, the men sat at the enormous conference table.

That is when the trouble started.

Hitler promptly asked what the meeting was about and what the issues were. Speer noticed that Göring was not eager to speak up, so Speer went to the main point of argument: he and Erhard Milch attacked Sauckel on the numbers he was reporting to Hitler. Sauckel suggested that two million workers were given to the Industrialists, but the factory owners reported to Speer that they currently only had one million.

Sauckel immediately cried foul and said that he used utmost caution to always give the Führer accurate numbers. Between Sauckel and Bormann, several excuses were given as to why the Industrialists may be wrong with their count. When the accusations quieted down, Hitler turned to Göring to receive his judgment. Speer held his breath with cautious hope.

"My Reichsmarschall, you've been with me from the beginning. Please give me *your* opinion so we can settle this matter," said Hitler.

Speer hoped Göring would now provide the crucial backing they needed to expose Bormann and Sauckel.

"Milch, how dare you question the numbers of our good party comrade, Fritz Sauckel!" Göring thundered. "You should be ashamed of yourself. It is yours and Speer's numbers that are suspect! Our dear Sauckel works hard for the Führer day and night to keep workers in our factories, and you seek to work behind his back to undermine him?"

Speer was speechless. *How could this be? Moments ago Göring was agreeing that this was the plan to shake up Hitler's cabinet, and now he is sabotaging it? Just moments ago he warned me of Milch?*

It seemed that Göring had chosen the wrong phonograph record to play; that his mind was not in the right place at the right time. *Snap out of it!*

Now smiling to the Führer, Göring continued, "I myself have always appreciated Sauckel's work with the Industrialists and our forced labor program."

Just when Speer thought Göring could not make it any worse, Göring concluded his thoughts on Sauckel. "I feel a great debt to him," he said with a martyr-like tone.

Speer noticed Sauckel smile at Göring.

Hitler turned to Bormann and asked him what he thought. Then to Keitel. Then back to Sauckel. Finally, Hitler turned to Himmler who sat quietly through the meeting so far.

"What do you think, Reichsführer?" Hitler asked the leader of the SS.

Himmler looked around the room and then eyed Hitler and stated calmly, "The most likely explanation for the million missing bodies is that they are all dead."

Silence. The remark sent a chill down Speer's spine. People sat awkwardly looking around the room. No one commented on Himmler's idea, but all eyes turned back to the Führer for his leadership of the meeting.

"I think the conversation about missing workers is an internal issue in your ministry, Herr Speer," said Hitler stoically. "Please do not bother me again with discrepancies of numbers like this. It can be taken care of between you and the Reichsmarschall."

Speer glanced at Bormann and saw his delight. Speer then locked eyes with Göring and found him grinning and nodding like they had won a battle. Speer looked at Milch and saw a man totally defeated and ready to cry. *A great Luftwaffe general officer humiliated in front of the Chancellor by his own supervisor.*

Speer found out soon after the meeting that Bormann had bribed Göring with money from the Adolf Hitler Fund. Goebbels was warned by Bormann ahead of time not to come. Therefore, before the meeting even started, the defeat and embarrassment of Albert Speer was secure. Bormann would remain in power and everyone else was diminished.

In a matter of days, Speer heard from two different people. The first was Heinrich Himmler. He told Speer that it was very unwise for him and Goebbels to try to reinstate the Reichsmarschall, and he threatened Speer never to attempt it again. This was irritating to Speer because Himmler was using tools from the old Nazi playbook to insinuate with veiled threats.

The second person was a general closely aligned with Erhard Milch. He approached Speer in Berlin after a meeting one afternoon and said very quietly that all the generals were behind him, and that Speer should keep that in mind.

When Speer told Milch about this meeting the next day, his friend smiled at him.

Milch related, "The generals have heard your name a lot recently. You are looked at as Hitler's successor."

"Interesting," replied Speer. "I thought everyone knew that it is Bormann who will eventually take the throne."

"No, he is incompetent. The generals like you."

Speer then told Milch what Hermann Göring said about him before the meeting with Hitler.

"That's funny," laughed Milch. "Göring told me exactly the same thing about you."

CHAPTER 8

Honesty or Love

Corrie's older sister, Nollie, heard the rumbling of the Nazi trucks on the street in front of her house, then footsteps marching up to the door. Banging. Shouting.

Is this really happening? Nollie feared.

Nollie and Flip van Woerden lived a mile and a half from the Beje, but were very active participants in Corrie's underground work. Oftentimes they would help Corrie smuggle someone out of the city by hiding the person at their house first. However, Nollie held to a different standard than Corrie, and always felt compelled to convey the absolute truth.

Three Gestapo agents entered her home with several Nazi soldiers standing guard outside by the truck.

They must have been tipped off, thought Nollie.

"Where are they hiding?" the leader shouted at Nollie.

On that particular day, Flip was away with the children, and the only two in the house with Nollie were Katrien and Annelies, two Jews with forged identity papers from the Dutch underground. These women worked for Nollie doing housework and helped with the cooking and errands. They never ventured too far from Nollie's home to avoid discovery, but they felt little fear due to their Aryan, non-Jewish looks, and forged documents. Their only problem now was Nollie's honesty.

"We have no Jews in hiding here," Nollie said as seriously as she could. This was technically true because Annelies was standing in the room with her and not in hiding. Katrien was somewhere at the back of the house, out of sight, but not in hiding.

The Gestapo agents searched the house and found nothing suspicious. It seemed they were about to leave when one of them took his rifle and placed the tip of its bore under Annelies' chin.

Annelies tried not to tremble. She was twenty-two-years old with blond hair and blue eyes. She looked to be a very attractive Dutch or German woman and did not have the characteristic appearance of a European Jew.

The guard stared at Annelies and said to Nollie, "Why is she here? Is she your sister?"

"No," Nollie answered. "She is not my sister."

"Then why is she here?"

"Annelies works for me and helps with the chores," Nollie said trying to remain as calm as possible.

Annelies locked eyes with Nollie for a moment as if to communicate something urgent.

"Is she a Jew?" the Gestapo asked.

No response.

"I asked you if she was a Jew?"

Annelies beseeched Nollie with her eyes, *Don't do this thing!*

"Yes, she is a Jew," Nollie said softly.

The words seemed to hover in the air for a brief moment in time. Everyone in the room froze. The guards were stunned at the uncharacteristic honesty from someone housing an illegal citizen. It took them a moment to realize what Nollie just said to them, when suddenly they heard the back door slam shut.

"Who else is here?" the guard asked angrily. "Is that other woman a Jew as well?"

"Yes, she is a Jew as well."

Nollie met Annelies' eyes with sympathy. In that look she pleaded with Annelies to trust in God; that everything would be okay.

Annelies wept as two Gestapo agents led her out of the home and put her on one of the trucks.

The other agent sat down at Nollie's kitchen table and removed his helmet.

"So, since we are being honest today, what other Jews do you house here?"

―――――◆◆◆――――――

Katrien arrived at the Beje out of breath and very distraught. Corrie brought her upstairs where they could speak openly without fear of someone in the watch shop overhearing them.

"She's gone mad!" Katrien cried. "Your sister has gone mad. Her house was invaded by the Gestapo and Nollie told the Gestapo agent that Annelies was Jewish. Nollie didn't have to say that. Why couldn't she have lied for once in her life? She's gone mad!"

"Oh, Nollie, Nollie," said Corrie. "What have you done?"

Corrie felt that Nollie continually tested God to see if He was faithful to His word. She quoted scripture to Corrie and told her younger sister to keep her lips pure.

Corrie did not feel this way, however. Through long talks with her father, Corrie decided to answer in a way which was the most loving. It would be more loving to lie about Jews hiding in your house than to tell the truth and let them be captured by the Nazis; but Nollie felt differently.

Corrie left Katrien at the Beje and rode on her bike the mile and a half to Nollie's house. A block away she stopped and parked beside a large tree on Bos en Hovenstraat. What she saw made her sick to her stomach.

Guards were walking Nollie from her house to their large truck. Nollie looked as if she was about to fall over or pass out on her front walkway, but the guards on each side of her held her upright.

Corrie could not imagine what Nollie might have told them in the spirit of truthfulness. *Would she tell them about the Beje and all of Corrie's underground activities stretching throughout Holland?* Corrie wondered.

The truck started up and, with Nollie in the back still between two guards, it moved down the street in the direction of the police station.

Did the man the police chief wanted to kill tip off the Gestapo about Nollie? Oh, Nollie, why couldn't you lie just this once?

―――――◆◆◆――――――

Corrie's personality had changed since the carefree days before the war. The once somewhat introverted Dutch woman who lived at home with her father and sister had now come alive to become a person upon whom many families depended. Corrie instinctively knew what to do and say at any given moment; it was as if she had been training for this work all of her life. Finding her inner strength from God, Corrie relied on this secret fountain for wisdom and courage. Her quiet times with the Lord had never been so meaningful; her love for country, family and for the visitors she helped had never been stronger. She knew she was not the same person.

Corrie still craved alone time once in a while, but her ability to speak to myriads of Jewish strangers and resistance leaders was so uncharacteristic pre-war Corrie ten Boom. Her actions whispered a profound confidence that she was squarely on God's path for her life, and He was helping her save hundreds of innocent souls in the process. It was thrilling and terrifying at the same time and each day brought a new surprise. Now, people depended on her with their lives to make the right decisions. She did not want to let them down.

And she would not let those in her care be sacrificed to the evil Nazis. *It doesn't matter why Nollie did this, we might all be compromised! All the Jews living at the Beje need to leave for a while. It is for their own safety.*

<hr />

Time and again as some of Corrie's messengers were captured, or when she was warned by her contacts at the police headquarters, the Beje would empty its permanent occupants to safer residences. Usually within a couple of weeks, some of them would come back, but it was always very risky because the Beje was in the middle of a busy Haarlem street.

The Ten Boom house was a regional depot of Jews finding refuge for a night or two, and then leaving the city. Corrie heard reports on hundreds of families she had helped, many of them making their way out of Holland and to freedom. Occasionally one of the farms on the underground railroad was raided, but Corrie's messengers warned her in plenty of time to avoid the catastrophe of sending Jews to a Nazi occupied house.

The Dutch Resistance leaders became concerned about the safety of the Beje and its inhabitants and sent Corrie a secret message. They advised her of the need to conduct drills in her house to ensure that the occupants could make it to the secret hiding place in enough time if the Beje was ever raided. Corrie agreed this was necessary.

<hr />

Corrie was fast asleep one night and dreamed she heard the alarm going off in the house. She awoke to hear someone yelling at her with a flashlight pointed toward her face.

"Where are the nine Jews you are hiding here?"

Corrie rubbed her eyes and said, "We only have seven right now."

Silence.

The light came on in her bedroom and Corrie found she was surrounded by four men, not from the secret police but from the resistance movement. The drill abruptly ended. Corrie knew she had made a mistake.

"Corrie, we know you're tired," one of them said, then paused. "But we really need you to remember to say that you do not have any Jews in hiding here. They will trick you with their questions; they are masters at catching people off guard and discovering their secrets."

"I know, I'm so sorry," Corrie said contritely.

Another man who Corrie had never met added, "Also, your Jews need to learn to flip their mattresses when they take off their covers to carry them to the secret room. I touched their beds just now and could feel the warmth from their bodies. That is one of the Gestapo's favorite tricks. They did well with their clothes this time, but they also need to flip their mattress, so please explain this to your guests."

"Yes, I will tell them," Corrie answered, determined to get everything right the next time.

This was the second drill they had conducted that week. The last drill was a disaster; they found clothes dropped by the Jews on the stairs on their way up to Corrie's bedroom. In their panic to slide through the secret door at the bottom of the bookcase, they left several traces of their presence at the Beje.

The leader gave the all clear and the seven Jews came out of the cramped space, three men and four women.

"Make sure there is enough water in there for at least seventy-two hours," encouraged the man who spoke about the mattresses. "Also, there should be at least one meal for each person, but nothing warm lest the Nazis smell the food through the bookcase. Hopefully within four days someone will be able to let them out of hiding if your home is raided."

"Prison bags," the leader said. "Make sure that each of you who reside here — you, Betsie, and your father — have prison bags ready with essential items."

This caught Corrie by surprise.

"Why do we need prison bags?" she asked.

"Once the raid happens, whether they find any Jews hiding here or not, you will be taken to prison for up to a month, if only to have enough time to interrogate you. You see, when they raid this place it will be because someone has turned on you, a neighbor or a family member being tortured. It won't matter if they find your Jews or not, you will go to prison so you will want to have a few essentials — a change of undergarments, a Bible, a toothbrush and a comb. Not too much or they could take it from you, but enough to get you by for a few days."

Betsie looked terrified over this last piece of news. Corrie's oldest sister was seven years her senior and often ill. She was an indoor person and the thought of leaving the Beje to go to prison was as frightening as anything she could imagine.

Corrie grabbed Betsie's hand.

"It will be okay, sister. God will see us through."

The two exchanged knowing glances. Usually Betsie was the one encouraging her younger sister, but now Corrie was the strong one, the leader. She had the will for this kind of work, enough for all three of the Ten Booms.

―――◆――――

Another home was raided nearby. Another drill. Another Jewish family needing a place to hide. Another visit from Mr. Koonstra. Another day come and gone.

Corrie continued to receive secret messages regarding her sister Nollie. After a few days in the Haarlem jail, Nollie was transferred to the national prison in Amsterdam. Yet messages continued to come. The Dutch Resistance movement was everywhere, with nurses in prison hospitals, factory owners, telephone switchmen and even government officials like the Chief of Police. Nollie's message to her little sister was similar to her last one:

Don't worry about Annelies, Corrie. God will provide for her. He will not make her suffer because I obeyed Him with my lips. She will not be taken to Germany.

Corrie did not enjoy messages like this one. Nollie had no proof, only faith, and Corrie felt that it was blind faith.

Yes, I must worry about Annelies, thought Corrie after reading Nollie's message. *We betrayed her confidence. If she dies, her blood will be on our hands.*

News came that Annelies was transported to Amsterdam, to an old Jewish theater named Hollandse Schouw, located next to a train station. Trains would arrive at that station and transport Jews to Germany nearly every night. The rumor was that these Jews would end up in extermination camps in Germany or Poland. This news of Annelies horrified the Ten Boom family.

Corrie found herself miserable thinking about Nollie and her actions until one day when she realized she had misjudged Nollie. A messenger called on Corrie's secret telephone and told her to meet him across the canal at a specified building. Corrie knew the place well. It was near the house she first went to with Kik in order to learn about the resistance movement.

Corrie rode her bike to a secluded spot and then ran alongside the canal. She turned onto a side street and went to the designated building. Inside the man was waiting for her.

"I have a message for you from the underground," he said. "Do you need a moment to catch your breath?"

"I am okay, go ahead," replied Corrie.

"The old Jewish theater in Amsterdam was raided last night," the messenger said. "The Jews who were waiting there for transportation to Germany were rescued and sent to safe houses throughout Holland. A blond-haired girl was most insistent that Nollie, Corrie ten Boom's sister, knew that Annelies was free. Do you understand this message?"

"Yes, I understand it," answered Corrie. But even as she spoke the words, Corrie did not actually understand it. This was something God did. *Why would He do this to save Nollie from my scorn?* Corrie wondered.

Corrie was filled with relief and joy for Annelies, but inexplicably a little mad at God for removing her fury for her sister. *How could Nollie be so sure?* Corrie pondered this question often. Corrie thought she loved the Jews more than Nollie did, and had a better understanding of God's love as well. But now she wasn't so sure. Corrie's thoughts were temporarily consumed with trying to understand these latest events.

Then, she dove back into her work, caring for those who needed her help, and risking everything in order to save them.

CHAPTER 9

Göring's Birthday Party

Albert Speer was driving the forty-five mile route northeast of Berlin to Carinhall to commemorate Göring's birthday. As the Minister of the Armaments and War Production for the Third Reich, it was expected that he would make an appearance. So Speer kissed Margarete and his children goodbye and reluctantly departed in his white Mercedes. It was January 12, 1944.

With time during the drive to reflect, Speer's mind wandered to the people and events of the war. He considered how poorly the war was going for the Third Reich. Yet it seemed all the other leaders kept their heads buried in the sand. This greatly bothered Speer. Monuments, new buildings, and statues were victoriously planned by the Gauleiters, those Nazi regional party leaders who controlled every district of the new order. Speer continued to protest to Adolf Hitler regarding these men destroying historical castles and churches to make room for victory edifices once the war was won. Göring himself made an official request to the Minister of Finance for a grant of two million marks for the expansion of Carinhall.

This madness must stop, thought Speer. *The war has turned against us!*

It was true. With Rommel's withdrawal from Africa, the German Army suffered 125,000 prisoners of war to Eisenhower's Allied Forces. The invasion of Russia was also not going well. In fact, victory seemed no longer possible. Sensible German men were now thinking of a political end — some type of truce — because the military hope for victory had vanished. The Russian Army broke through the German line north of Stalingrad and virtually surrounded Germany's Sixth Army. When the generals asked Hitler if they could retreat, he flew into a tantrum and declared he would not abandon the Volga!

Hermann Göring did not help at all, thought Speer. Instead of imploring the Führer to abandon Stalingrad and save as many men as possible, Göring asserted to Hitler that they should indeed hold out and that his Luftwaffe would deliver 750 tons of food daily to those encircled at Stalingrad. Speer remembered Göring telling the Führer that he could entrust victory to his Reichsmarschall, *Leave everything to me, mein* Führer!

Hitler had to know those words were meaningless. As Speer could have predicted, Göring barely supplied the promised aid. Due to the blizzard conditions, the insufficient Luftwaffe strength, and a simple lack of urgency, Göring utterly failed the 200,000-person-strong Sixth Army. The German "air bridge" he avowed was never constructed, and only an average of 85 tons of supplies arrived each day, a little over one tenth of what was promised.

The Sixth Army was never rescued. Many German soldiers slowly died of starvation. When the last few German pilots reached their cornered comrades in Stalingrad, they found the soldiers too exhausted from hunger to remove supplies from the planes.

The end came quickly. Though the German 4th Panzer Army arrived within 30 miles of Stalingrad to rescue the Sixth Army and form a pocket of escape, the German commander in the city followed Hitler's orders to the bitter end: not to surrender the city at any cost. The battle concluded with the surrender of 110,000 German soldiers who were transported to Soviet prisoner of war camps where they froze or starved to death. The entire Eastern effort had amassed nearly 800,000 Axis casualties to date.

Albert Speer's own brother, Ernst, was one of the soldiers trapped in Russia. A letter the family received from Ernst indicated he had jaundice and was stricken with fever. He also had swollen legs and severe kidney pains. Ernst relayed there was little food or water left, and that the snowy wind blew directly into the makeshift hospital where men all around him were dying. That was the last they heard from him.

With promptings from his mother, Speer asked Erhard Milch to see if the Luftwaffe could locate and rescue him, but to no avail. He was presumed dead, probably frozen to death in a prisoner of war camp, and Speer felt terrible about it. His parents looked to him for help but he could not deliver.

With these dispiriting thoughts in mind, Speer exited the main road and entered a rural area where he continued to ruminate on the progress of the eastern war and on Hitler and Göring's stubbornness. He recalled one conversation in which he and Milch were trying to convince Göring of the necessity for more fighter planes when they visited him at his castle.

"Welcome to Veldenstein," said the smiling Göring after he had kept them waiting for some time. Wearing aviator attire and a pistol, he snapped his fingers twice for the housekeeper to go make some sandwiches. "What brings you here this evening?"

Milch started, almost frantically, "There's been another massive raid on Hamburg."

"No," uttered a frowning Göring. He had promised the Führer time and time again that the Luftwaffe he commanded would keep Allied bombers out of Germany.

"Yes," said Milch emphatically. "The Chancellor is furious and has called to see you at the Wolf's Lair right away. He has asked for Speer and me to come retrieve you tonight."

"Is this true, Speer?" asked Göring, knowing the very question insulted Milch.

"Yes," said the Armaments Minister, composed and serious. "But that is not all that angers the Führer. He is also upset about our Eastern front. Our aircraft have not been effective over Russia. We are seeing more and more Russian aircraft flying unhindered over our troops, many times dropping bombs and disrupting their movement. We have also seen their new fighters."

"Fighters!" exclaimed Göring. "You cannot win a war with fighters."

"You cannot win a war without fighters," shrieked Milch. "Our cities are being destroyed yet we continue to produce bombers. We must devote thousands of fighters to engage the enemy, something to knock him out of the sky."

"Oh, come now, Milch. You who know so much about how to win this war? I flew with Richthofen. I should know what kind of aircraft the Reich needs."

The discussion was fruitless.

Done with thinking about the past, Speer looked through his windshield and caught a glimpse of Göring's magnificently decorated Carinhall estate.

⁂

It was a beautiful but cold day when Speer's Mercedes tires halted on the crunchy gravel in front of Carinhall. Hermann Göring had invited every important Nazi to a party at Carinhall to celebrate his 51st birthday. Along with invitations, Göring sent out a list of gifts that he expected people to bestow upon him. What Speer found out from Erhard Milch that year was that everyone's government paycheck had an item deduction for the Reichsmarschall's birthday fund, and not just for the month of January, but for every month of the year. *Who authorized this?*

Speer vowed on the trip that this would be the last birthday party for Göring he would ever attend, whether the war was won or not. He could not stand the pomposity and blatant disregard for the suffering of the citizenry. While Germans in Berlin were rationing butter, meat, and cheese, Nazi Party leaders lived like kings, and tonight would be no exception.

In the back of his vehicle, Speer escorted a larger-than-life-size marble bust of Adolf Hitler that Göring had suggested to him to bring as a gift. This seemed some kind of sick joke, knowing that both Speer and Göring had been diminished in the Führer's eyes recently. But Speer decided to go through with the request.

Speer's car was parked for him as he was ushered up the marble walkway to the main entrance. Snow flurries twisted and spun in front of him just above the marble where he walked. Two men behind Speer carried the bust of Hitler he would add to Göring's hoard.

Inside the palatial entrance hall nearly 150 feet wide and awash with expensive paintings, Hermann Göring warmly greeted Speer. It made Speer smile when the Reichsmarschall feigned surprise and humility at the gift he himself requested. It was a show for his guests, realized Speer, and he quickly exited the receiving room to take a look around.

On the gift table in the Carinhall library were the other treasures Göring had requested from his guests: jewels from Tunisia, gold bars from the Balkans, rare books from France, cigars from Holland, statues, paintings, chocolates, soaps, silk clothes and more. To top it off there was a set of building plans as a gift from Göring's architect that would double the size of Carinhall.

Speer removed his eyes from the table where his own gift was about to be placed. He heard music coming from upstairs so he walked up to the attic where Göring had a

37

massive game room complete with a model train. Speer noticed approximately twenty other people avoiding the celebration downstairs of a man turning one year older.

The game room was over eighty feet long and twenty feet wide. A control panel next to a large red armchair operated the model train. One of Göring's assistants dressed in white from head to toe was operating the train that evening to entertain the guests. Speer marveled that one side of the track ran a straight course for sixty feet. He had never seen a model train set so enormous. *My children would love this!* Speer thought.

Next, Speer walked down to the basement where Göring had a gymnasium, a swimming pool, and a second game room. He ran into Erhard Milch, another guest dodging the pomp of the main floor. The two decided to get some fresh air.

They maneuvered out a side entrance of the mansion and walked down the path toward the lake. Göring had constructed an oversized mausoleum for his first wife, Carin, the one for whom the estate was named. It was an impressively decorated tomb with stairs leading down to a chamber where Carin's massive pewter coffin laid at its center. Speer and Milch did not go down the stairs but stood on the opposite side of the structure from the manse, looking out at the frozen lake.

Both men reminisced that Carin Frock Göring was the love of Hermann's life. Though he remarried, it was obvious that by naming his beloved estate after her and designing the mausoleum in her honor, Göring never wanted to let slip from memory their relationship. Carin died from a heart attack after eight years of marriage. She was only forty-two.

It is a nice idea in one sense, but also very odd when you marry another woman, Speer thought.

The fifty-one-year old Milch started the conversation, "It is cold tonight, but I prefer the air out here to the air in there." Milch pointed toward the steep-roofed mansion.

"As do I," Speer agreed, not looking away from the lake.

"Did you hear all the congratulations and flattery being handed out in there?" asked Milch. "It is as if Ol' Fatty has single-handedly won the war for Germany."

"Yes, I heard."

"Did you see his gifts?" asked Milch.

"Remarkable!"

"Did you know that some of his gifts are not displayed?"

"What do you mean?" asked Speer.

Milch thought for a moment before continuing, "My sources tell me that the Göring division sent some packages to Carinhall with famous artwork looted from the museum in Naples that Göring is too sheepish to display."

"That doesn't surprise me," said Speer.

"The paintings are so well known, it would be obvious to anyone they were stolen from Italy. Göring is waiting to display them until after the party, when most of the dignitaries have left. I am sure he will change his attire for the occasion."

Both men laughed, then walked back to the celebration and found the guests gathering around the long, formal table in the dining room. The table was splendidly set with porcelain, crystal, gold, silver and silk. The toastmaster for the evening was Walther Funk, the Reich Minister of Economics and President of the Reichsbank.

"Hail to one of the greatest Germans to have ever lived," proclaimed Funk once he had captured everyone's attention. "The smashing of France, England and Russia is due to the brilliance of Hermann Göring and his Luftwaffe. Hear, hear!"

Soon others stood to toast Göring. It went on for nearly thirty minutes until Göring, already in his third outfit of the evening, finally stood and offered his appreciation for the kind words and all the presents. At one point during his speech, he noted that the jewel on his finger was one of the most valuable in the world.

Göring was indeed lord of the manor, lord of that evening's event, and the lion of the Third Reich's war machine. But there was a larger lion in Europe that evening, secretly devouring more costly possessions.

CHAPTER 10

The Visitor

C orrie was in her bed, not feeling well. This gave her time to think. As the war continued, Corrie noticed more and more Jewish homes and businesses being boarded up.

What did the Germans do with all the stuff they confiscated? Corrie wondered.

Hopefully, the possessions would be saved for these Dutch citizens and returned to them after the war. However, the rumors Corrie heard were that the Jews were not coming back. Corrie did not understand how so much hatred could emanate from Germany, but she feared the rumors of gassing chambers were true.

But what would they do with all the bodies? Corrie didn't like thinking such thoughts. No one seemed to know any of the details; neighbors just heard bits and pieces of news from time to time.

Corrie also thought about the four Jews who were currently occupying the Beje. Two of them had unfavorable characteristics and were not welcomed in other safe houses. Their most interesting visitor was a man nicknamed Eusie. A former cantor in an Amsterdam synagogue, Eusie's real name was Meyer Mossel, and he looked so distinctively like a Jew it hindered his hiding opportunities. He smoked a pipe, sung Scripture passionately, and loved to share humor with Casper. Another visitor was Mary van Itallie, a 76-year-old woman plagued with asthmatic wheezing, who was not welcomed elsewhere because of her constant cough. The Beje took everyone, even when they were considered a high risk.

Corrie's thoughts were interrupted by a knock at the bedroom door; Betsie summoned Corrie downstairs to meet a visitor in the watch shop who was adamant he would only talk to her. Corrie dressed and made her way down the long flight of stairs. At the counter stood a short, sandy-haired man who asked if she was indeed Miss Ten Boom.

"Yes, I am she," Corrie said giving the man as much of a smile as she could while fighting the flu.

"I need your help," the man said. "I have heard you could help people in desperate situations like the one I am in."

"You have a clock that needs a desperate repair?" Corrie asked innocently.

"No, ma'am, not a clock," he replied. "It is my wife. She was taken by the Gestapo for hiding Jews," the man whispered. "There is a man at the police station who can be bribed if I get him enough money. Perhaps I can get her out of jail before they send her to Amsterdam and it is too late."

"I'm sorry, I cannot help you," Corrie said. There was something about the man that really bothered her. It was as if he had rehearsed a script and was trying to get it right. Also, he would not look her in the eye. His eyes seemed fixated between her nose and lips. Corrie could not tell if he was being truthful.

"Please, Miss Ten Boom, it is a matter of life and death. Without six hundred guilders I may never see my wife again. Would you please help me? I heard that you were a compassionate person."

This last comment made Corrie circumspect. She did not feel compassionate that day; she felt like going to bed and letting others deal with their own problems.

Against Corrie's better instincts, she felt compelled to help the visitor. "Come back tomorrow at this time and I will have the money for you."

What if his wife was in jail for helping to rescue Jews? What if the man was simply too insecure to look her in the eyes? But no matter how many times she tried to reassure herself she felt a nagging remorse over the entire encounter. She made her way back upstairs and crawled into bed where she wished she had stayed.

A while later, she was dreaming of the buzzer alarm ringing incessantly, of Gestapo voices downstairs, and of people frantically running past her to hide before they were found.

Part II

EVIL UNLEASHED

CHAPTER 11

Murder by the Numbers

T he Architect was pleased with the reports he was reading from France and Holland. Several underground rings had been exposed, involving the arrest and imprisonment of hundreds of resistance workers and seizure of their assets. He wrote to the local SS that punishment of the French and Dutch workers should take place at German concentration camps and not at their local prisons. However, the resistance workers' demise was only one good report against the backdrop of his mounting unease with his orders from the Führer.

Frustrated by his attempt to solve the Jewish problem by the end of 1942 — which he had promised the Führer — the Architect felt thwarted, in part by leaders in the Nazi Party. Albert Speer continued to persuade the Führer that healthy Jews were needed for his factories. The Architect did not appreciate this kind of interference when trying to accomplish something so special. Speer would have to be dealt with soon. *I will bide my time until an opportune moment.*

Another disturbance rested in the fact that hundreds of thousands of Jews were still alive all over Europe due to protection from their own countries. *This was not for lack of trying*, the Architect consoled himself. By thinking of the gains that had been made over the last eighteen months, his mood began to improve. And they were chillingly significant.

In Helsinki, Finland, over 2,000 Jews were arrested and sent to death camps in Poland; nearly 1,000 Jews from Norway were eliminated; in Ukraine, 16,000 Jews were exterminated in four days in the Pinsk ghetto, with another 50,000 killed over the summer. The Architect looked down the list of other countries and their successes:

> Croatia - 30,000 killed, most by starvation
> Macedonia - 7,000 killed
> Thrace - 3,000 gassed at Treblinka
> Holland - 38,000 gassed at Auschwitz
> Romania - 50,000 killed

The Architect had flown to each major European city to ensure the SS was following his orders with exactitude. Only this kind of personal attention would bring about the completion of his vision. After the initial dirty work in Romania, of the 150,000 Jews spared, 65,000 of them died of hunger or disease a few months afterward. The Architect was assured the remaining Jews were in the process of being shipped to Auschwitz. These were the success stories.

Still, the Architect fretted about Belgium, Greece, and Italy. The governments there were shielding the Jews from him. No matter how many conversations the Architect had with Mussolini, the fascist dictator would not oblige with access to all of Italy's Jews. This stubbornness would have to change … and the Führer would help make it happen.

One encouragement for the Architect was that at least 30,000 Jews who had fled to France for safety were rounded up and sent to Poland. Over 10,000 French citizens who were of Jewish descent were recently handled by the SS, and 2,000 children were sent to Auschwitz. However, there were still tens of thousands more Jews in France who were not being given up by the government. *This weakness of the will must stop!*

Warsaw, Poland was the territory that continually needed to be coaxed into cooperating. Earlier that year, 250,000 Jews were deported to Treblinka, but recently there was an armed rebellion by Jews in the Warsaw ghetto that had to be quashed. As a result, another 80,000 Jews were murdered in the streets. Force called for stronger force, but the Jews had to know their resistance was futile; *it was they who had the death wish*, he thought.

The Architect hoped his subordinates were grateful for his backbone of iron. For instance, when there was a breakout of Jewish prisoners from the Sobibor Camp and resistance shown in Lublin, the Architect ordered all 40,000 Jews in the concentration camps there to be shot in one day — a massacre codenamed Harvest Festival. Thankfully they had the ammunition on hand to complete the task, another accomplishment due to his visionary leadership. *If only his followers could have foresight like this!*

The Architect thought of a speech he gave to the SS and the Wehrmacht generals on the importance of this work:

> *With regards to the extermination of the Jewish people, most of you know what it's like to see 100 corpses lying side by side, or 500 or 1,000 of them piled up. To have coped with this, and to have remained decent, this is what has made us tough, and it is a glorious page in our history. I know that I have sufficiently strong nerves for this, and a sufficiently strong sense of duty to carry these acts out uncompromisingly. As far as the Jewish women and children, in allowing those avengers to grow up in the shape of children who will then murder our fathers and grandchildren; I would have considered that a cowardly thing to do. As a result, this question was solved uncompromisingly, and you all are part of our success. For the survival of our blood we have done this with complete conviction.*

He should have been happy at this point with all of his success in carrying out Operation Reinhard. But the Architect knew there were still thousands of Jews secretly hiding in Europe who were beyond his grasp. He must work harder. His agitation grew due to the fact that time was running out. The Soviets were advancing in the East, and the Americans and British were advancing in Italy. If Europe was to be cleansed of Jewish blood, it would have to be done soon and with more force.

CHAPTER 12

Discovery

"**G**et up this instant!" yelled an angry Sicherheitsdienst (SD) agent in a blue suit. The SD man was part of the Gestapo's intelligence service, sent on special missions like the one today at the Beje.

Corrie sat up in her bed. Her heart was pounding hard. Her mind raced. She had gotten back in bed just in time. *They hadn't noticed!*

A few minutes earlier, the buzzer alarm system woke her up and she saw her illegal visitors move past her with their beddings. One by one, Corrie watched as all six of her guests crawled into the secret door of the bookcase. Eusie, the lighthearted Jewish man, carried his ashtray in his right hand with his pipe rattling around nearly spilling. Corrie then helped the eldest female, Mary, by pushing her through the small opening. One more man fell in behind Mary before Corrie replaced the bottom panel.

There was screaming and battering noises coming from below. Heavy footsteps were heard on the wooden staircase. At the very last moment, Corrie noticed her briefcase with names and records sitting on her bedroom floor. If found it would expose many of their contacts in the underground. Corrie grabbed it, reopened the panel, and threw the case inside the secret room. She then dove for her bed, pulled the covers up and closed her eyes just as her bedroom door burst open.

There were secret police in her bedroom looking at the walls and ceiling, but there was no sign of her special guests.

"What is your name?" the man asked fiercely.

"Cornelia ten Boom," she answered.

"Then you're the ring leader, eh?"

"Sir?"

"Where are the Jews you are hiding?" asked the man dressed in the blue suit.

"There are no Jews here," answered Corrie. She had practiced this script many times when the alarms sounded for their drills.

"Yes, there are, Fräulein, and when I find them you and your family will be in a lot of trouble. We found all of the money and valuables you keep for them in the steps. Where are the ration cards?" he growled.

"I have no ration cards," answered Corrie, again from the rehearsed script in her mind. Immediately, Corrie pictured Nollie's face in her mind but she shook her head a little to stay focused.

"Get dressed, we're going downstairs," the man said. Then he shouted down the stairs, "Willemsen, I have another. This one's the ringleader."

"Good, Kapteyn, bring him down so we can question him," another man shouted from the bottom of the stairs.

Corrie pulled on clothes over her pajamas, still chilled from her illness, then moved toward the door. The one named Kapteyn grabbed her arm and marshaled her in front of him, pushing her down the stairs until they emerged into the tiny kitchen.

Corrie saw her father, Betsie, and three other underground workers all sitting on chairs against the wall. *Oh Papa, such a look on your face*, Corrie thought.

This was the end of the line for them. They all knew this day would come. They had no idea how long the Lord would allow them to continue this dangerous work. As their involvement grew — way beyond their ability to ensure secrecy — a foreboding also grew. Now there were hundreds of ration cards delivered each month from several men, not just Fred Koornstra. Corrie's network included people all over Holland. There must have been close to one hundred affiliates who came and went from the Beje on a weekly basis, bringing supplies, enjoying meals with them, and smuggling Jews to new places. Three of their helpers sat terrified and motionless on the chairs next to her family.

"So the ringleader is a female, huh?" said Willemsen when he saw Corrie enter the kitchen. He had the Jewish valuables spread out on the table in front of him. The secret stash had been accumulating behind the corner cupboard for months. There were diamonds, silver rijksdaalders, jewelry and rolls of bills. "Well, you know what to do with her," he said to the first man in the blue suit, who still gripped Corrie's arm.

The one named Kapteyn took Corrie and pushed her down the five steps into the repair shop. He shoved Corrie against the wall and screamed, "Where are the Jews? Where is the secret room? Where are the ration cards?"

Corrie was so scared. She had never in her life been treated this way. All she could think to say was, "We have no Jews, we have no cards."

The agent flung her around and slapped her face hard.

"You need to answer me! Where are you hiding them?"

Corrie could hear people upstairs prying off boards, splintering wood with an axe and throwing things around in the bedrooms above her. She prayed to God they would not find the secret room where their six special visitors were hiding.

Slap! Another blow. Another question. Another attempt by Corrie to save her special visitors. The agent hit Corrie forcefully with his fist. Her head snapped back hard against the wall. She tasted blood in her mouth.

"Look, we know you have an underground operation here, and you are the ringleader. Tell us where the Jews are and I will stop hitting you."

"I have no Jews," Corrie answered with a bruised cheek and cut eyebrow.

Pow! Another punch to her face.

"Lord Jesus, protect me," Corrie cried aloud. Her head was spinning and she felt like she might pass out.

"Don't!" the man spoke as hatefully as Corrie had ever heard. "Don't you say that name again or I will kill you," Kapteyn hissed through clinched teeth.

Barely conscious, Corrie looked at her attacker expecting another blow to the face. Instead, his hand and arm poised to strike, he hesitated. "You think you can resist? I will get the answers I need."

Kapteyn led Corrie back to the kitchen where Willemsen, the other Ten Booms, and now four underground workers sat. The sign was still in the window indicating it was safe to come inside. More underground messengers and escorts inadvertently arrived and were arrested. Corrie hoped the extra ration cards shipment would not come today.

Kapteyn pushed Corrie into a chair, then yanked Betsie by the arm and led her down the stairs to where Corrie received her beating. Betsie was a little older than Corrie but their bodies were much different. Betsie was thin and weak, and she was always more susceptible to illness. Corrie was strong and rarely sick. Corrie wished she could take this beating for Betsie.

Corrie and Casper could hear the slaps, hear Betsie's screams, but could not move from their chairs. They knew she would not betray the Jews that trusted the Ten Boom family with their lives. Soon Betsie rejoined the family with a bloody lip and disheveled hair. Her face was bruised and puffy.

"Oh, Betsie, they hurt you," Corrie exclaimed.

"Yes. I feel so sorry for them," whispered Betsie. Blood dripped from the corner of her mouth.

"Why?" asked Corrie incredulously. "They just beat you."

"They do not know the love of Jesus, Corrie."

"Silence!" Willemsen shrieked. "Silence. The prisoners will not speak to each other."

Just then the doorbell rang again. Another messenger — a good friend of the Ten Booms — came by with news of another raid, unaware of what was happening at the Beje. Kapteyn opened the door and pretended he was part of the resistance. The messenger, having no reason to believe otherwise, trusted him and gave information to the SD agent.

Please Lord, allow no more visitors to come into this house, Corrie prayed. *Also keep the Jews upstairs hidden from these men.*

"Aha!" cried Willemsen when one of his agents handed him the family radio, found under the stairs. "We knew you people were up to no good. Look, we found your radio. These have been illegal since the occupation. Old man, you call yourself a law-abiding citizen?"

"Yes, I do," answered Casper ten Boom.

Kapteyn scowled at this, "You read your Bible. Do you know what it says about obeying the government?"

"Yes, we are to fear God and honor the king, but in our case it is a queen."

"We are the government now. You are to honor us!" Kapteyn said scornfully. "You are all lawbreakers."

The telephone began to ring.

Oh no, Corrie thought. *Not now.*

"That's a telephone!" exclaimed a surprised Willemsen.

"You people also have a forbidden telephone?" shrieked Kapteyn. "You, ringleader, answer it. And don't give anything away."

Willemsen grabbed Corrie out of her seat and led her down the hall to where the phone was ringing.

"Ten Boom residence and clock shop," answered Corrie as evenly as possible.

"Miss Ten Boom, have you heard?" the voice on the other end was panicked. "You are in terrible danger. Everyone is being arrested today. They found out about the entire operation. You need to take every measure of precaution."

Willemsen grinned. It was the confirmation he had been waiting for. As soon as Corrie put the receiver back down, the telephone rang again. She gave it her uncustomary stiff greeting, hoping the party at the other end would take the hint.

"Miss Ten Boom, Oom Herman has been taken into custody. They are on to all of us, you must be careful today."

Again, a large smile swept across Willemsen's face. When Corrie replaced the receiver, Willemsen pushed her back down the hall into the dining room. There were ten of them there now, including Nollie, who had recently been released from prison. She was helping conduct a Bible study at the Beje that day when the raid began. The study group had been kept captive in an upper bedroom and asked questions. Corrie hoped that Nollie had not told them everything she knew.

Nollie's eyes met Corrie's face with a look of assurance. In that instant, Corrie knew her sister had not betrayed her, or the hidden Jews.

More heavy footsteps marched down the stairs. "Willemsen, there is nothing up there," a uniformed agent said.

"What do you mean?" Willemsen asked. "This is the house, and these are the ringleaders. All the tips point to this place."

"That may be true, but if there is a secret room in this house, then the devil himself built it."

"There is a secret room. Post guards! We are going to starve them out with surveillance. The rest of you, line up in the hallway. We will be leaving soon for the police station. We are taking all of you in for conspiracy."

Kapteyn felt it his duty to yank Corrie from the kitchen first and parade her downstairs to the front of the shop. "Wait here," he barked. "The rest of you, line up behind the ringleader."

Casper ten Boom shuffled over to a large, old, wooden clock. "We mustn't let the clock run down," he said as he pulled the chain to move the weights.

"Get back in line, old man," yelled Kapteyn.

Father, the clock? Now? Corrie stared at her father in disbelief.

When everyone had on their coats and hats and tottered into a line, Willemsen and Kapteyn walked to the front and opened the shop entrance door. The two agents escorted the entire Ten Boom family out into the Haarlem streets and marched them one block away to the police station on Smedestraat.

Through the double doors they all walked, into the same building where Corrie had been summoned by the Chief of Police so many months ago. He was not there now; a German officer was sitting at his desk. The group was led into a waiting area with mats on the floor for them to sit on. Thirty-five people were arrested at the Beje that day, and now they all sat in clumps on the floor next to other prisoners who were also brought to the station. Corrie recognized a few faces but did not see some of her main conspirators in the underground, which she hoped was a good sign.

She worried about those still in hiding at the Beje. She hoped the house would not be occupied by guards for long and that someone would be able to let them out soon. She thought of her cat, left all alone. Perhaps a few of them would be released early because they just happened to be at the shop that day, like Nollie. *Perhaps they would all be released*, but Corrie knew this was more than she could hope for.

Different detectives arrived and asked each of them questions for almost two hours. They took plenty of new data back into the office area, yet they continued to come back with more and more questions. Someone mercifully brought in water and rolls.

Suddenly Rolf, the sympathetic police officer the Ten Booms knew, walked through the door. Corrie thought he looked distressed. She speculated he was upset because he was unable to warn Corrie about the raid. He told them they could use the toilets in the back of the station. He whispered to Corrie's older brother, Willem, that if they shredded their notes carefully they could dispose of incriminating evidence into the toilets. Corrie was happy to see a familiar face. She felt thankful to God for this act of kindness on this darkest of days.

When Corrie returned from the toilets with Betsie, they found a group gathered around their father. He was leading them in evening prayers as he had done at the Beje every day of his life. *Does he not remember where we are?* Corrie wondered. Then she heard his words.

"He who dwells in the shelter of the Most High will abide in the shadow of the Almighty," Casper ten Boom quoted from memory. The eighty-four-year old man with deep blue eyes continued to give encouragement from the Psalms until many drifted off to sleep on the floor. Corrie took comfort in that simple act, a habit they had enjoyed for years.

There was not much rest to be found. With so many people scattered about on the floor, when someone stirred, those around would be knocked against others trying to sleep.

Corrie dozed off and on. She thought of her future. What would God have for her now? She was unmarried and with no children. She did not even have a suitor. *Will we make it out of this alive? Will I ever get married? Will I ever return to the Beje? Will the Jews in hiding escape and find new places to hide?* Corrie wondered and wondered, until at last she opened her eyes to the sun peeking through the large screened windows at the top of the walls, the white paint cracking off their wooden frames.

CHAPTER 13

Herr Speer

"Hello."

"Hello, Speer, it is good to hear your voice," said an enthusiastic Göring after ringing the hospital where Albert Speer was a patient. "Thank you," answered Speer. "It seems I am recovering more and more each day."

After attending Göring's birthday party Speer checked himself into a hospital due to a respiratory condition and a continual feeling of exhaustion. Speer believed it was more than a temporary physical sickness, however, and thought there was something else desperately wrong with him. At only 38, he had no energy or passion for work. He felt as though future years had been sapped from his life. Speer thought that perhaps he had a blood disease, or there was something wrong with his heart.

For twenty days Speer lay flat on his back, unable to walk. Soon, his constant coughing produced blood and he wondered if his condition was life-threatening. Without Speer's consent, and prearranged by Joseph Goebbels and Heinrich Himmler, he was being cared for by a doctor who was Himmler's best friend, Dr. Karl Gebhardt. However, Speer was suspicious and felt Gebhardt was not leveling with him, nor was he including him on the decisions about his medications. It seemed to Speer that the prescriptions he was taking from Dr. Gebhardt were making his condition worse, and he was greatly worried.

Speer wrote an urgent letter to his wife requesting help, and Margarete immediately appealed to Hitler's personal physician, Dr. Karl Brandt, who was Speer's friend. Dr. Brandt ordered a medical professor from Berlin University to take charge of Speer and forbade Gebhardt from issuing any more medical orders in Speer's case. And yet, Speer's condition worsened.

For several days Albert Speer remained in critical condition, with extreme respiratory difficulty, a high fever and a rapid pulse. Speer felt as if he was drifting between life and death; at one moment a sense of euphoria and well-being, at another moment clutching for air and gasping. Speer's new doctor stayed by his side day and night during this period, until Speer turned a corner.

After ten days of intensive care, Speer became fully conscious and was allowed to receive visitors. Erhard Milch visited and whispered to Speer in confidence that Himmler's doctor treated Speer with medicine which would surely have killed him. Milch had received the information directly from Dr. Brandt.

Speer was incensed, but did not know what to do. If he informed Hitler, the Führer could easily side with Himmler on the matter, leaving Milch and Dr. Brandt at great risk.

On the same day, while trying to process the ramifications of being intentionally poisoned, Speer accepted Hermann Göring's phone call. While speaking to the Reichsmarschall, Speer wondered if Göring knew what Gebhardt was doing.

"Well, I'm glad to hear the good news you're feeling better today," said Göring cheerfully.

"Not just today," answered Speer. "I mean I am improving and regaining my strength." Speer pondered which castle Göring was calling from, Carinhall or Veldenstein, and how he might be dressed.

"Oh, come now, Speer. That is not what I hear from Dr. Gebhardt. What you're saying isn't true at all. Dr. Gebhardt told me plainly that you're suffering from a serious heart disease."

"No, that's not true. Dr. Brandt and his associate are looking after me now and I am improving. Dr. Gebhardt is no longer my physician."

"Well, this is just sad. Perhaps I am the first to tell you, but that is okay. I am glad to be a true friend and tell you the truth. You have no hope for improvement! Did you not know that? This is quite awkward telling you on the phone."

"I guess I don't know what to say," Speer said after a wave of nausea passed. He knew that he would not be able to convince the stubborn Reichsmarschall over the phone, but thought he would try one more time.

"My body is doing better and I hope to leave here soon. The x-rays and electrocardiograms are confirming that nothing is wrong with me. Dr. Brandt told me himself."

"Speer, listen to me now as your friend; you have been misinformed. But there is no need to worry. You have done a remarkable job in your career as an architect and as the Minster of Armaments. You will be remembered fondly by all. It is now time to accept the hard truth and get your affairs in order. I'm sorry to say this, but Dr. Gebhardt told me yesterday that you don't have much longer, maybe just days. Himmler agrees with him. Get your affairs in order."

Speer felt sorry for Göring in one sense. He seemed to be attempting some sort of encouragement. But it was obtuse and completely off the mark. The misbegotten jubilation in Göring's voice betrayed his efforts at compassion. It was clear the Reichsmarschall would be perfectly fine if Speer were to die.

A wave of fearful questions suddenly penetrated Speer's mind.

What is being said about me in Berlin?

How is Bormann orchestrating events to minimize my influence with the Führer?

What does Himmler gain by killing me?

After hanging up the phone, Speer lay in bed for hours and contemplated the awkward conversation. A man cannot take news lightly that he is trying to be killed. Either he immediately lashes out and seeks to destroy his destroyer, or he considers his entire life and what might have led him to that dark point. Speer chose the latter. His involvement with the Third Reich and his relationship with Adolf Hitler began so ordinarily that Speer could have had no way of knowing then, at his young age, how he would play such a central role for Germany during a world war.

It was December 1930, and 25-year-old Albert Speer was a new architect, employed to teach students at the Institute of Technology in Berlin. Adolf Hitler was in town to deliver a speech at a beer hall named Hasenheide, and Speer's architecture students urged him to attend with them. Speer reluctantly complied.

The building was dirty, with narrow hallways and decrepit stairways. The upstairs beer hall was packed with students from Berlin University and the Institute of Technology. There were also a few workers, politicians and professors. Many in the crowd adored Adolf Hitler, but others feared or despised him. Everyone wanted to see the controversial man in person and hear him speak.

When Hitler arrived, there was thunderous applause for several minutes. The young Speer was immediately intrigued. The man Speer had seen on posters in full military garb was now wearing a blue business suit. The man who he thought used brute force and angry words to coerce people appeared simple and modest, almost bashful in the presence of his fans as he tried to subdue their applause.

When the time came for him to speak, Speer expected Hitler to be a Nazi fanatic, maniacally shouting lines from his book *Mein Kampf.* But that is not what happened. Slowly and methodically, Adolf Hitler spoke on the history of the German people, on the evils of communism, and of the ideals of Germany. As the speech progressed, his voice rose in volume while using more and more words people wanted to hear such as homeland, economic recovery, German strength, hard-working mothers and fathers and their sacrifices. He had a simple, self-deprecating humor, and Bavarian charm that emerged naturally, not forced. The future chancellor was sure of himself, and this helped to project Adolf Hitler as a natural leader.

Toward the end of the speech, Speer could tell that Hitler had mesmerized the entire room. It seemed Hitler's emotional energy had captured the attention of the students like no other lecture he had ever attended, as student or teacher. Speer sensed no more skepticism or reservations. Everyone in that room was with Hitler until his final word, including himself.

Speer's students wanted to discuss the speech over a glass of beer, but Speer needed to clear his head. He drove his car out of town to a pine forest and took a long walk in the cool December night. Speer liked what he had heard. He was fascinated by this man who spoke as if he could deliver Germany from decades of bad politics, including the disaster of a world war. Hitler seemed to hold the key to relieving people's misery and insecurity.

Was this what Germany needed? Speer wondered. *Could Hitler unify the masses and accomplish something great and historic?* Speer was not moved by the speech as much as by the man himself. The simplicity of the man, and the fundamental message of hope Hitler brought to Germany was alluring. Speer decided that very night in the woods, under the starry skies, that he would investigate the National Socialist German Worker's Party further, and he decided that one day he must meet that remarkable man.

A few weeks later Speer joined the Nazi Party. By 1933, just three years later, Speer was summoned to Hitler's apartment to show him plans for the Nuremburg Party Rally. Upon first meeting Albert Speer, Hitler instantly took a liking to the young man and asked Speer about his origins, his upbringing, and his training as an architect. Speer enjoyed the attention, and remembered the good-natured man in the blue suit who had delivered the inspiring speech at the beer hall. A close bond developed between the two, and soon Speer would not only become the official architect for the Third Reich, he would have intimate access to one of the most powerful men in the entire world.

Adolf Hitler. Confined to his hospital room, the name no longer impressed Speer the way it once had. Perhaps it was Speer's sickness, or perhaps it was the fact that, after so many years, he knew Hitler better than most people. The luster of working closely beside the man was now nearly gone. Speer acknowledged that he was quite idealistic in his younger days with his decision to follow Hitler. He had never read *Mein Kampf,* and had never heard about Hitler's eastern expansion desires. Speer did not realize that the man believed in authoritarian rule and held inside such deep-seated anti-Semitism.

Now Speer possessed a fuller picture, a more complete portrait of the man in the blue suit. Speer could see Hitler's pride, and how he took delight in being the center of attention. Everyone else was simply a Hitler pawn. Every conversation and every meeting revolved around Hitler, his journey through hardships and his *inspired* leadership.

The Führer spent hours comparing himself to Frederick the Great, convincing people they were now living in historic times with a historic leader. Speer could not see the good for Germany as he did in the old days. He now sensed that the entire war and the very fate of Germany was to bring Hitler to his rightful place in the annals of history. This was not a positive power, but a negative, dark power because it was centered on self and not the whole of Germany.

Speer was also tired of competing with Bormann, Himmler, Goebbels and Göring for his standing. He grew increasingly weary of the way Hitler played his top men against each other. It was as if Hitler had a profound contempt for all people, and this contempt manifested itself in the way he manipulated those around him.

Speer heard that while he was sick Hitler allowed Bormann to make decisions impacting Speer's Armaments Ministry work. Therefore Speer contemplated tendering his resignation, and mentioned it to some around him.

Soon after, Speer received a telephone call from Bormann stating that Hitler was traveling to the hospital for a visit.

———◆◆◆———

"Do I hear correctly that you have had thoughts of resigning?" Hitler asked Speer as he sat by his bedside.

Whether it was the hospital lighting or his ongoing recovery from illness, Speer allowed his eyes to look at Adolf Hitler objectively. He noticed the Führer's ashen skin color, large nose, and smudge of a mustache. Speer felt repulsed by Hitler's appearance for the first time in their history together. The man he once loved seemed transparent.

"Is it not true that the Führer is unhappy with my work and seeks to use other men to accomplish the job I am assigned to do?" Speer asked his leader. "If so, then I should resign."

"No, Speer. I do not want you to resign. I have no one else who knows building the way you do. You understand how much my projects mean to me! And you are still my chief architect. I will give you the control you need to perform the construction I need completed. I will let you decide who is to run what project."

Even as Hitler was speaking, and trying to reconcile his relationship with Speer, it was obvious that he was up to his old antics, manipulating situations and people. Speer knew that Hitler's reversal today to reinstate him to his rightful place would infuriate Bormann and Himmler, and perhaps only be temporary.

Speer could now see more fully that this was how Hitler kept balance with his staff. Everyone had to fight for his approval, and this forced all parties to remain loyal to him. When Hitler changed his mind and went back on earlier decisions, it left his staff in a perpetual funk, not knowing what to expect next. This instability and discord kept them more dependent upon the Führer, because they could not predict the future or his likely position. Though frustrating for his subordinates, Speer realized it served the Führer extremely well.

"Dr. Brandt says I am recovering quickly and will be leaving the hospital soon," Speer said.

Speer's words did not appear to register with Hitler, as he listlessly said, "I am also sick, Speer, and my doctors tell me I will be blind one day."

Speer felt no warmth or sympathy from the Führer. The only real emotion Hitler displayed was self-pity at his own ailments. Nonetheless, Speer was reinstated with the promise to be in charge of his entire Ministry, including construction. Soon, Bormann called, and the Führer had to depart.

⊷◆⊷

Predictably, a few weeks later, Hitler went back on his word and appointed a man named Xaver Dorsch — a former deputy of Speer's — to lead Berlin's underground bunker projects. Now Speer's underling had control of what used to be part of Speer's ministerial work for the Reich. The new appointee made promises to Hitler to complete the projects on a timetable that he could never keep. Speer was furious.

Back at work as Germany's Armaments Minister, yet still under the care of his physicians, Speer was able to thoroughly see what was going on inside the Reich and the countries beyond, and it was not encouraging. He took all the actions he felt were necessary to aid the war, even if they countermanded the will of Hitler. He wrote to Hitler and told him how disappointed he was that his Führer had gone back on his original agreement to leave Speer in complete control. With the Russians performing so well in the East, Speer knew that Germany was now in grave danger and feared he might be the only high-ranking government official who could see it. The Wehrmacht generals saw it, but none of Hitler's Cabinet.

Since his sickness, Speer became aware of an alchemy in his loyalties, for he was now more intensely loyal to the German people than he was to their current leader. He now felt compelled to lead by instinct, instead of what he thought might please the Führer. Something new stirred within Speer, and his resulting actions caused immediate damage to his reputation with other Nazi leaders.

When a massive Allied bombing campaign destroyed several large buildings, Speer suspended Dorsch's building of the Berlin bunkers so that those workers could help repair the damage in the city. This was in direct opposition to Hitler's decision that the bunkers were first priority.

Upon hearing this news, Bormann informed Speer sharply that, "The commands of the Führer are to be carried out by every German and cannot be ignored or delayed at will." Also, Hitler declared publicly that, "The Gestapo will instantly arrest any responsible official for acting contrary to an order from the Führer and taken to a concentration camp!"

Speer decided again it was time to resign.

He wrote a letter to Hitler and stated if his actions were unacceptable to the

Führer that he should resign. This action triggered another phone call from Hermann Göring.

"Herr Speer, have I heard correctly that you are threatening resignation again?" asked Göring.

"Yes, that is true," replied Speer.

"You need to listen to me. I have heard from the very highest level that the Führer does not allow resignations among members of his staff. The Führer alone will be the one to dictate when a minister might depart from his service."

"I really don't care what you have heard, my friend. I cannot serve someone who makes sideways threats regarding my decisions. If Hitler likes Dorsch's work so much, then perhaps he should replace me with him."

"You had better watch your actions or harm could unnecessarily come to you and your family."

"I would ask that you leave the mention of my family out of this phone conversation, Hermann." Speer used Göring's first name to show he was serious. "I hope you are not trying to threaten me."

"I am merely trying to be a good friend and warn you, Albert!" cried Göring.

"Okay then, perhaps I will simply slip back into sickness, and after so many months I can quietly disappear from service as a minister until I am no longer missed," suggested Speer.

"Yes, that's the answer!" exclaimed Göring. "That's how we can accomplish your removal. The Führer will surely accept this solution."

Speer could tell that Göring was smiling with enthusiasm like a jolly child.

Is Göring cheering on my removal for his own political advantage?

As a member of Hitler's staff, one could never tell what another official was fully thinking. Hitler had manipulated his staff so fully that everyone acted paranoid. In the back of everyone's mind was a consideration of how they were getting along with the Führer compared to their colleagues.

Speer contemplated the Nazi leaders he worked with. Göring was a dishonest man, yet usually divulged his position by his outward glee or anger; Goebbels was somewhat more calculating and passive-aggressive. He would make snide remarks which could be interpreted in more than one way. But with Himmler's icy exterior, one could never really know what he was up to. Himmler was quiet, ruthless, and inwardly deliberative. When he showed no emotion, Speer knew there was trouble.

※

Speer's resignation by slowly backing away from his ministry did not work. His friend and work associate Erhard Milch brought word to Speer that Hitler demanded a visit by him at his Obersalzberg retreat, and that the Führer wanted to amend their work relationship.

"No, forget about it," Speer declared. "I'm done!"

"You can't be," responded Milch. "The Führer has demanded that you see him. He wants to speak with you in person, and reinstate you once and for all."

"I don't believe it."

"It is true, Albert, and you must go visit him."

"I am done with Hitler. He is a tyrant."

"You really shouldn't say that, even with me."

"It is true, isn't it?"

After hours of arguments and deliberations, with Milch explaining that Hitler wanted Speer back in complete control and would no longer interfere, Speer relented. He would visit Hitler.

Before he could fly, he had to have permission from his physicians. Dr. Brandt, who healed him, gave full permission for Speer to travel. But Dr. Gebhardt said that it was too risky. After a phone call to Heinrich Himmler, however, Gebhardt told Speer he could fly on one condition: Speer must visit with Himmler before he saw Hitler. Speer was tired of all the childish games but accepted the terms.

When Speer arrived at the mountain retreat center, he immediately met with Himmler as promised. The SS leader spoke in a soft voice without looking Speer in the eye.

"I want you to stop causing difficulties," Himmler told Speer. "Göring, Bormann, and I have already held a conference with the Führer and we have decided that a separate agency should be set up for construction, outside of your control."

Speer could have predicted this would happen, yet he was still speechless when Himmler informed him of the new situation.

"Go on," was all Speer could get out.

Himmler finally made eye contact and continued, "So stop writing letters of protest to the Führer and causing difficulties for everyone. Things have changed, Speer, and you had better be on board. The Führer decided to place Xaver Dorsch in charge of construction in the Reich so that the bunker project would not be interrupted because of your other responsibilities. Dorsch's work in Germany will be independent of your Armaments Ministry."

"But Dorsch works for me," Speer protested.

"Not any more. As I said, he is independent now. As far as I see it, this matter is settled. Care for some tea?"

Speer was used to this kind of soft-peddled power from the man before him. Himmler's authority rested solely on the fact that everyone knew that Hitler trusted him with ultra top-secret information. Speer wanted to protest, but realized it was useless to argue with the man standing before him. Himmler had the entire SS at his disposal, while Speer had merely construction and factory workers.

A cold wind blew on the dark Obersalzberg Mountain that evening. Speer arrived at the Berghof and was received by the German Chancellor into his special office. Speer could tell right away that Hitler was happy to have Speer as company, and eager to meet with him about the current events. Hitler gave Speer incredible deference through their initial meetings with Bormann and the other staff present that night. Then Hitler took Speer aside and spoke to him alone.

"Herr Speer, I first want you to know that some of my staff would like to disrupt your operations, but I will never hear of it," started Hitler. "Your work for us over these past months has been crucial and above what I could have asked of any other man. I will not give Xaver Dorsch control of construction within the Reich, you know that."

Hitler paused, as if to give his guest a chance to speak. But Speer was mystified at these statements, and curious how the rest of the conversation would unfold. Speer hesitated, which allowed Hitler to continue his train of thought.

"I have determined it would not be in the best interest of the Reich to separate construction from your armaments work. You are my builder, Speer, you know that. I will approve sight unseen all the measures you think necessary for construction. Now, no more talk of resignation, we have a good arrangement, right?"

Speer felt a little unsettled. This was the direct opposite of what Hitler had just agreed to do during his meeting with Himmler, Göring and Bormann. Speer knew that by agreeing to this plan Hitler was ignoring the advice of all his other ministers. He also knew that Dorsch would be severely put out when news of this decision reached him.

Speer once more thought of Himmler's admonition to stop causing difficulties. However, this decision by the Führer is what was truly needed to insure consistency of work and to utilize laborers only with the most important projects, not for Nazi Party leaders building new homes and offices all over Berlin. Speer could establish quality control and make sure that the war would be fought with all available assets directed toward achieving victory, and not toward personal pleasures. *This is precisely why Himmler, Göring and Bormann dislike my position of authority so much*, Speer thought. *They know they can get away with a lot more of their excesses if one of their lackeys was running construction!*

As happy as Speer was with Hitler's affirmation, he knew that even this decision could change just as quickly as it was made, and this reconciliation between them forgotten. Bormann was always by Hitler's side, whereas Speer saw him only occasionally. With enough time to degrade someone behind their back, Bormann could derail any decision made by the Führer no matter how resolute. Speer had an idea.

"I appreciate the confidence you have in me, and the efforts you are taking on my behalf," Speer answered the Führer. "However, this decision has to be settled on a long-term basis. I would be in an impossible situation if this matter were to ever come up again."

Albert Speer was going out on a limb with Hitler's graciousness that evening, but he had to push the Führer a little to check his resolve. Speer would be compromised if Hitler were to back down and reconsider this decision when Speer was not around.

"My decision is final!" Hitler shouted, visibly annoyed. The Führer jackknifed out of his chair. "I will no longer consider changing it. The issue is closed."

The two men exited the office and reentered the salon where the others were waiting, including Bormann and Eva Braun. Speer was invited to sit with them by the fire and listen to a Richard Wagner aria. Speer was happy to relax for a few minutes before heading back to his nearby house.

Speer felt he had won a personal victory. Yet he knew that soon he would be either despised by the others, or held in higher esteem for having turned the tide against them. Speer undeniably held Hitler's favor once again. He had no idea why it was so important to him to be back in the good graces of the Führer, but in a small way, all seemed right with life again.

The next day, Speer informed both Göring and Himmler of the decision by telephone. Göring responded as expected; in anger initially, then as Speer's best friend stating he had hoped it would be the outcome all along. Himmler made no response, but his eerie silence shouted volumes.

During the afternoon walk to the teehaus, Bormann sidled over to Speer to speak in private. With excessive friendliness Bormann said, "You realize I was never part of the intrigue against you. I just wanted you to know, Speer, so that we can go on as friends. It was Himmler and Göring who were trying to change things and not me."

Speer did not believe him, but he enjoyed the fact that this new arrangement made Bormann so uncomfortable. He recalled a conversation he had with Milch a few months earlier. Milch said that Bormann was telling others that Speer wanted to be Hitler's successor. Of this there was no proof, but Bormann used the accusation to rally support and demean a rival.

Speer smiled at Bormann without affirmation.

He had won!

He would allow Bormann to squirm for a while.

Speer recognized he was now in a new relationship with the Führer. Though he still loved the power of his cabinet position and close relationship with the nation's leader, Speer felt something else burning in his heart even stronger — his love for country. This thought was bundled with the idea that Hitler was not doing what was best for Germany, so the two were now on a collision path.

CHAPTER 14

Casper ten Boom

Corrie awoke in pain and darkness. Her eyesight tried to adjust to the blackness of her chamber, but it was no use. Though she could hear her chamber-mates, she could not make out their forms. There was no window, and absolutely no way for a prisoner to know what side of the cell she might be on except for the faintest glimmer coming from the sides of the thick cell door.

Corrie did not know what time it was.

She did not feel well.

Her body ached from the beating she had received from the SD agent at the Beje.

She coughed up blood.

She had a fever.

Corrie's thoughts raced. *Oh, how is Betsie? Where is father? Are they treating him well?* Corrie also wondered about those in the secret room and if they had escaped. She offered up a simple prayer before her mind returned to her own condition. Another spasm of coughing seized her chest and throat.

Corrie heard a low rumble of an engine outside. She could not tell if it was on the street or in the air, high above. It did not matter. It would not impact her life unless it dropped a bomb on her prison. She was trapped there, for good; *for God's good,* she reminded herself. She wondered who, besides Hitler, was running this war. *Couldn't they see the suffering it was causing?* Corrie turned on her side, where there was not as much pain. She thought of the recent events since they were taken into captivity. She thought about the final moments she had with her family.

⊰•⊱

On the day after the Ten Boom's capture, they were escorted out of the police station where the fresh winter air flushed their faces. Residents of Haarlem stood around the bus where they were being loaded and Corrie heard the people murmuring about Haarlem's Grand Old Man, her father's nickname. Some standing around the bus had tears in their eyes. With Betsie just in front of them, Corrie grabbed her father, helped him into the bus and took a seat next to him near the front. Casper ten Boom smiled at Corrie as they waited for the rest of the Beje prisoners to load onto the bus. They spoke of heaven.

"The best is yet to come," said Casper. It was one of his oft-quoted expressions.

"That's right, father," responded Corrie. "The best is yet to come." She noticed that he was neither restless nor very sad. Corrie knew he did not clearly comprehend what was happening to all of them.

As they drove away, Corrie noticed how beautiful the Grote Markt appeared that winter day. The sun was shining down on the Grote Kerk; the great cathedral seemed impervious not only to that day's events, but to the entire war. The people of Haarlem were proud that Mozart and Handel had both played its magnificent organ.

Casper looked around as well, a proud citizen of Haarlem. There was always a twinkle in his eye when he looked at his city and today was no exception. Casper studied the landscape until they departed Haarlem, then he rested his head on Corrie's arm during the remainder of the trip.

Would they ever see their home again? Corrie wondered. Even while the bus roared away from their beloved Haarlem, Corrie's heart was filled with a strange sense of peace. She knew this day would eventually come. She knew the risks they had been taking. If anything, she was surprised the operation had not been discovered earlier. There were so many people involved, and they worked in the heart of a busy street. Nearly all of the neighbors had to know what was taking place.

Corrie believed that most of the Dutch citizenry despised the Nazis and wanted the war to end. There were just a few citizens who worked with Germany; but these few were all the Gestapo needed. However long the war lasted, hopefully people in Holland would continue to resist the unforgiving rule of their occupiers.

The bus took them along the coast to The Hague, the Dutch city and home to the Bureau of the Gestapo. The Ten Booms were to be interrogated there before taken to their final destination, the nearby national prison in the district of Scheveningen.

In the darkness of Corrie's cell that evening, she mulled over a conversation her father had with one of the Gestapo agents at the Bureau. A couple of the guards wanted to release her father to let him die at home and not put him into prison.

"You, old man," one of the Bureau interrogators said. "Is there really a need for this?"

Corrie's older brother, Willem, led Casper up to the chief interrogator's desk.

"I'd like to send you home, old fellow," the interrogator said. "Just give me your word that you will make no more trouble."

There was a pause in the hearts of all the Ten Booms that perhaps their father might be set free to return to the Beje ... but it did not last long. Corrie remembered seeing the rigid outline of Casper's shoulders as he straightened up to respond to the man.

"If I go home today," her father spoke clearly, "tomorrow I will open my door again to any man in need who knocks."

"Get back in line. *Schnell!* No more delays."

During this episode, Kapteyn, the agent who had been at the Beje, entered the room.

"I could have told you that," Kapteyn said in derision. "All the old man talks about is Jesus, and the queen." He pointed at Corrie and said to the chief interrogator, "She's the ringleader."

Corrie stared at Kapteyn, the man who had beaten her. She was proud to be bruised for strangers in need, and proud of what her father had spoken to these men. It was just the confirmation needed to remind Corrie that the other Ten Booms joined the resistance work willingly and not solely because of the earnestness of their youngest family member. She hoped that Kapteyn would one day discover the truth about Jesus.

An outburst drew everyone's attention down the long hall. A short Jewish man with a yellow star on his jacket was being harassed by several guards about his purse.

"It's mine," the Jew shrieked, clutching the little bag with his bony hands. "You cannot have this, it is mine."

The guards each took turns kicking the man until one boot landed solidly in the middle of the Jew's back sending him to the floor. A guard reached down and ripped the purse from his hand. Other guards kept kicking the Jew in the ribs, legs, and head as he lay helplessly crying.

Corrie felt conflicted in her heart. In one sense she felt pity for the man and for his loss. On the other hand she hated him for being so weak, for allowing the others to treat him so harshly. *Couldn't he see that having money was futile now?* Corrie's feelings of disgust for the man were not rational, she knew, but she wanted the racket to stop and for the Jew to quit crying. Mercifully, a supervisor arrived and pulled the wretched man out of the room.

The guards interrogated the Ten Boom family one by one, verifying their names and family relationships: Betsie, Nollie, Willem, Casper, alongside many Beje resistance workers.

Corrie's family was united in prison, a testament to the Ten Boom family's involvement in the underground. Now none of them would be available for clock repair work; nor would they be available for their most important work, to aid the

Jews. *Who would answer the door at the Beje?* No one. No one would be there to feed the cat or help strangers in need.

Corrie's oldest sibling, Betsie, was interrogated first. Name, age and residence were all asked.

"Married?" the interrogator asked.

"No, unmarried." Betsie responded.

"Number of children?"

"I said I was unmarried."

"I asked number of children!" the man snapped back.

"None."

Soon, Haarlem's Grand Old Man was in front of the chief interrogator again. The questions came quickly. The same questions were repeated over and over again that day.

"Name?" the agent asked.

"Casper ten Boom."

"Age?"

"Eighty-four," answered Casper.

"Married?"

"Yes."

"Wife's name?"

"Cornelia Johanna Arnolda ten Boom."

The interrogator glanced up at the long name, then continued, "Living?"

"No, died in 1921."

"Remarried?"

"No."

"Children?"

"Yes, five."

"Living?"

"Yes, four are living and in this room with me."

"Names of the living?"

"Elisabeth, Willem, Nollie van Woerden and Corrie."

"Occupation?"

"Watchmaker."

"Location?"

"Ten Boom Watch Shop, Barteljorisstraat, Haarlem."

"Religion?"

"Christian."

"Do you know why you're here, old fellow?"

"For helping my queen and my countrymen."

The interrogator rolled his eyes.

"Next!"

When the interrogation was over, the prisoners were taken away by patrol cars to the penitentiary in Scheveningen. When they arrived, they were taken through large iron gates and into an open courtyard. A guard told them to put their noses against the brick wall.

They waited and waited with their noses touching the cold, rough wall. To the right of Corrie was Toos, the Beje bookkeeper, and Nollie; to her left was Willem and Betsie. Corrie could not see her father without moving her nose away from the wall, which would incur the wrath of the guards. Finally, a door opened to the right of the courtyard.

"All women prisoners follow me," the guard shouted.

Corrie turned and began shuffling toward the open door. She scanned along the line of men still facing the wall for her father but could not see him. Finally, Corrie eyed Casper seated on a chair a guard must have brought him.

"Father!" Corrie cried suddenly. "God be with you."

"And with you, my daughters," he said.

Corrie looked at his familiar face, his glasses, and his white hair. This was their goodbye before entering a prison cell. Corrie feared she would not see him again.

The prisoners moved forward, and Corrie left the courtyard where her father remained seated. The door slammed behind them. Betsie grabbed Corrie's hand. They walked to an office where someone behind a desk took all of their personal belongings, their watches, rings and coins.

The women were escorted down a wide corridor. Soon, a guard opened a prison door and called Betsie's name; she was forced inside. They walked a few doors down and Nollie's name was called. The cell door slammed shut behind her. They walked around the corner and down another corridor. Corrie's name was called, a door was opened, and a slight shove thrust her through the doorway of her prison cell. *Slam!* She had arrived.

Goodbye, Papa.

CHAPTER 15

The Max Heiliger Account

The Architect met with Dr. Walther Funk, the president of the Reichsbank. There was a financial situation that needed to be addressed and it had to do with the goods coming from the concentration camps. When prisoners at the concentration camps were gassed, their corpses were picked through and all the gold fillings were taken out of their mouths with pliers. Sometimes the gold would be yanked out before the gassing, but the usual method was to do it after so as not to unnecessarily disturb the prisoners.

This gold, along with many other precious metals found in their discarded luggage, was melted down, molded into bars, and shipped to Berlin. The Architect and Dr. Funk set up a secret SS account under the name of *Max Heiliger*. Deposited into the account were all of the valuables taken from those at concentration camps. It was also where funds were deposited from all of the assets acquired from Jews' homes throughout Europe. Typically, after a forced evacuation of the premises, the Jewish homes were boarded and sealed off until trained SS guards arrived with strict instructions to itemize all the contents and send them to Germany.

The *Max Heiliger* account had grown so large it was to the point of being unmanageable and not above suspicion. Not only were the gold fillings taken, but also gold bracelets, necklaces, rings, watches, earrings and spectacle frames procured from those deported to concentration camps. When the Jews were captured in communities throughout Europe, they were told they were being resettled in new lands to the East, and they were encouraged to carry all of their valuables. Therefore incredible amounts of jewelry, silverware, diamonds, pocket watches, brooches, banknotes and other such items were found in their possession when processing through the camps. There were even gold bars found hidden in some of the suitcases.

Dr. Walther Funk gave a report to the Architect a year ago, telling him that his arrangements were becoming too successful. More deposits kept arriving but all the vaults in the Reichsbank were overflowing beyond their capacity and could handle no more valuables. The idea they developed to solve this problem was brilliant, they thought. The extra goods would go to pawn shops throughout Berlin and then turned into cash to be easily stored in the bank vaults. But now, even the pawn shop owners had reached their limit and told the Reichsbank they could no longer accept valuables from the government. The shops were filled and there was no more space.

So, the Architect and Dr. Funk developed a new plan, one in which even the Allied bombs could not disrupt. They began storing the goods in German mines. There was a salt mine at Merkers in Thuringia, and at Altaussee and Siegen. The men knew that Göring was already using mines as art depositories because mines and caves offer the right humidity and temperature to store paintings properly. *Why not use them to also store gold and other valuables?*

The two men figured out the logistics. The goods would be shipped by trains to the mines and guarded by local SS. There would be nothing written about this, no records kept except for an addendum on the *Max Heiliger* account marked 'mines.' The Architect would also have a detailed map marking precisely where each shipment was stored. *This will be helpful after the war,* he surmised. The pawn shop owners would quit complaining now; there was a new plan in place and shrouded under the utmost secrecy.

CHAPTER 16

Cell 384

C orrie's cell was six paces long and two paces wide. She shared the tiny cement room with four other women. On the first night after she was cast into the crowded room, Corrie could not stop coughing causing one of her cellmates to complain to the guard. The other women were kind and tried to accommodate Corrie by saying she could use the only cot in the chamber. However, Corrie could not control her sickness that was exacerbated by the damp conditions.

"I am so sorry to be in here with you, forcing you to share your space with me," Corrie offered to her hostesses.

"It is not your fault," one of them answered. "We know that."

The prisoners aided Corrie as best they could. One hung up her hat. Another woman shared some bread and water with Corrie for which she was very grateful. She had not eaten all day. They also gave her the cot, moving it over so she could lay down on it; but when Corrie sat on the bed the black dust from the filthy straw mattress sent her into a coughing spasm. Corrie's lungs felt squeezed and she tried to stifle her cough but almost choked in the process.

Eventually her coughing died down and she was able to doze. At the cell door there was a loud knock and then the bolt slid open. It was time for breakfast. Corrie made it through her first night in prison.

The lights turned on and four plates of porridge were passed through an opening in the door.

"We have a new one in here, so we need five portions," one of the prisoners called Frau Mikes said to the guard.

Another plate came through the door.

"If you don't want yours I could help you with it," Frau Mikes offered.

Corrie studied the watery gray porridge and silently handed it to her new acquaintance.

As the hours went on Corrie got to know a little about her cellmates. One had been held prisoner at Scheveningen for the past three years. She could name each of the guards who were passing the cell merely by their voices and the way they shuffled down the hall. Another girl, who was just seventeen years old, had been a baroness. She paced the tiny cell constantly from morning until night; six steps one way, then six steps back, dodging the other occupants with every step. She reminded Corrie of an animal in a cage.

Day after day the hours slowly hammered on. Corrie was beside herself with boredom. Frau Mikes had playing cards she made out of small squares of tissue. She taught Corrie how to play solitaire to help pass the time. It seemed like a harmless activity, and Corrie enjoyed the game until she realized it impacted her disposition too much. If the cards went well it would be a good day, if not it would be a bad day and surely evil was happening to her loved ones.

Corrie ached to hear news about her family. She wondered if her father was doing well in prison, or perhaps even released. She wondered if Betsie had made friends with her cellmates.

Corrie's cough and headaches continued. Every time the thin mattresses and cot were moved to clean the floor, or to lay upon, a billow of dry dust engulfed the prisoners and Corrie would go into another coughing spell.

"Ten Boom, Cornelia," said the prison guard one day when she opened their cell door unexpectedly. "Grab your hat and follow me."

Corrie was escorted out of the prison into the street where a car was waiting for her and two other prisoners. *Where are we going?* Corrie wondered.

Soon they arrived at the hospital in The Hague. While being ushered into the waiting room, a nurse pulled her aside and asked her how she could help.

"Do you have a Bible?" asked Corrie.

"I will try my best," the nurse responded. "Anything else?"

"Yes. A needle and thread, a toothbrush, a bar of soap?" Corrie asked hopefully. She had to leave her prison bag in her room on the day of the raid because it was in front of the secret entrance to the hiding place. The last thing she wanted to do was draw attention to that area, so her bag was left behind.

"I'll see what I can do. So many patients today." Then the nurse left and Corrie's heart was filled with hope. Such kindness, and from a stranger. Love filled her heart at the simple goodness this woman had shown to her.

After a long wait, Corrie had her visit with the doctor. He examined her and then wrote something on a piece of paper. As she was leaving the room he whispered, "I hope I am doing you a favor with this diagnosis."

Corrie had no idea what he meant, but there again was another small show of kindness. As a soldier led her group back down the main corridor toward the door where they would exit the building, the nurse who had spoken to her before walked by Corrie and slipped a small package into her hand.

Corrie was amazed at her subtlety, for the nurse had not altered her pace and continued to look straight ahead the entire time. Corrie could not wait to return to her cell to open the package. She traced with her finger the treasure now in her pocket all the way back to the prison.

When Corrie returned to her cell and the metal door was rebolted behind her, she pulled out the package and opened it with all of her cellmates gathered around her. Even the young girl who paced stopped to see what Corrie received from the nurse.

Inside the package were two bars of prewar soap, a bag of safety pins and the four Gospels. The women were overjoyed at the precious gifts now in Corrie's possession. Frau Mikes covered her mouth to keep from yelping out loud. Corrie divided the goods among her cellmates, but when she offered them the Gospels they all shied away and adamantly refused.

"You get caught with scripture and its *kalte kost* for you, and they might even double your sentence," Frau Mikes announced.

Kalte kost, the punishment given for a day or up to a week, meant only cold food. Usually there was some hot food served but with *kalte kost* there was just the ration of bread and water. It was a threat the guards used to keep prisoners in line, and it worked. If they made too much noise it was *kalte kost*. If they did not move fast enough it was *kalte kost*. If they were caught with forbidden supplies it was *kalte kost*, then maybe more punishment.

Corrie did not care about the threat of *kalte kost*. It would be a small price to pay for being able to read God's Word. Corrie wished her cellmates would also read but she could not force them. Perhaps they would ask her to read them out loud one day. At the very least it would be a way to pass the long, dull hours with nothing to do but sit and wait.

Another day. Another night. Frau Mikes played with her cards, the baroness paced the floor. Corrie read her Gospels. Then, two days after Corrie's visit to the hospital the door opened up and a steel-voiced guard said, "Ten Boom, Cornelia. Grab all of your things and follow me."

"You mean…"

"Silence. No talking. Follow me."

Corrie grabbed her few possessions, said goodbye to her cellmates with her eyes, then left the cell. Her heart filled with hope that she was being released. But instead of returning out the way she had originally entered, they walked the other way, deeper into the maze of prison passageways. Soon the matron stopped and opened a door to an empty cell. Without talking, she motioned for Corrie to enter the new cell.

Corrie wanted to speak to her and ask questions about her siblings and father, and why she was being taken from her cellmates to live alone. She knew it would be *kalte kost*, the guard was so fierce. *Would it be too hard to show some compassion?*

Corrie walked into the new cell — cell 384 — and the door slammed behind her. She walked the six paces to the cot which reeked worse than the last one. She grabbed the blanket to put around her but the last inmate had been sick in it. Corrie could not throw it away fast enough. Her stomach lurched inside of her so she ran to the bucket to relieve its contents.

The memory of the horrific odor from the blanket stayed with her for the next few hours. Her heart sank in desperation. *Will this be the cell I stay in for years like my other cellmate? Will I remain in solitary confinement without any companions or conversation?* While thinking through her new situation, the one light in her cell turned off, engulfing the room in complete darkness.

There was one improvement over her last cell, it had a window with metal bars crisscrossing the opening. But unlike her last cell which was housed within the innards of the prison, her new cell was along the outer walls of Scheveningen, making it a much colder chamber. She could hear the wind beat against the wall. Corrie grabbed her coat tighter around her. She never took it off in her other cell, even when sleeping. Now she would need it more than ever because she could not use the blanket because of the stench. She knew she would have to be strong, brave and mature. She prepared her mind for the silence. But it was hard.

There was knocking on the walls. There were also noises coming from the pipes. "Is this a haunted cell to which I have come?" she asked out loud. "O Savior, take away my anxiety. Take me into Your arms and comfort me."

Corrie had lived at home with family her entire life, and she was never alone. Now she felt so isolated. It was difficult to sleep that night. Memories from the Beje came to her mind, thoughts of her mother and the fun times with her father. Just when Corrie thought she could hear the morning guards beginning their rounds, her eyes closed and she dozed off. The next thing she knew her breakfast was being pushed through the door.

Corrie's sickness worsened. Her fever raged and her head and arm throbbed. She could not get up from her cot to retrieve her food. The room was significantly colder than the last one, and there was no one to talk to. If she only had a sheet, a clean blanket and a pillow life would be so much better, she thought. She had no toothbrush, no extra underwear, and no wash cloth. She missed even the simple luxury of a nail clipper. Corrie tried to believe that God had brought her there for a purpose, but it was very difficult.

Corrie was thankful she had her Scriptures from the brave nurse. Instead of reading just one or two verses, she devoured an entire Gospel at a time. This thrilled her soul to see the full Gospel narrative play out in one reading.

Though doing well spiritually, Corrie suffered physically, and she could no longer stand up to take her food. The man who brought her bread took sympathy for a while and would throw her bread toward her. Sometimes a female prisoner enlisted to push the meal cart would carry the hot gruel to Corrie's cot so she could eat it. Corrie was grateful for their help.

Every so often a male orderly who provided medical services at the prison would come to check Corrie's temperature to verify that she was still sick. Corrie would have to take off her shirt and he would put the thermometer between her arm and her side. One day, Corrie grabbed the man by the arm and asked, "My father is Casper ten Boom, he is 84-years-old and has a full head of white hair and a beard. Have you taken medicine to him?" Corrie was desperate for information. For conversation. For kindness.

"I don't know," the man replied. "Please don't ask me."

Suddenly Corrie's door flew wide open and the intimidating matron stood in the entrance, filling the doorway. "Prisoners are not to talk," she said. "No more questions or it will be *kalte kost* for the duration of your sentence."

Kalte kost. Even the hearing of those two words was a punishment. Corrie was startled at how the matron could say them so cruelly.

One day after the same man took her temperature and left, the matron opened the door and said, "You are no longer sick. So we will no longer wait on you hand and foot. If you don't get out of bed you will starve."

The door clanged shut and the bolt slammed.

Corrie was left alone.

One of the anxieties was not knowing how long she would remain in prison and isolation. Until a hearing or court trial? Until the war was over? She could hear bombers flying high above her at night and she wondered if they were German bombers going to England, or English bombers heading toward Germany. She hoped it was the latter.

Who was running the war? Corrie wondered again. She could not imagine all the logistics it would take to make ships, tanks and airplanes. Corrie's former world was centered on making watches with her father. She knew what tiny parts and special tools were needed to make a clock work right, but who was making the parts and tools for all the war machines being used now?

Corrie shivered and thought about the cross matron who delighted in threatening and mocking her. "Look at the great lady who now just sits in bed," she would say to Corrie. *What does she expect me to do in this tiny cell?*

Corrie wondered what kind of upbringing the matron had. Corrie also wondered if she had a father who loved her as much as Casper ten Boom loved Corrie. She thought of her father, how hard it must be for him to endure such deprivation. *How long could he last in a place like this?* Corrie wondered. *Please Lord, if it be Your will, take him home to live with Jesus. He would be so happy then.*

As the days continued Corrie's strength began to return. Having a window was the only positive to her solitary confinement. When strong enough to use her legs again, Corrie would stand up on her cot and allow her face to absorb the warm rays of the sun which helped nourish her body and spirit. Soon she could walk and the fever had left her.

One day melted into the next, and into the next. More nightly bombers. More threats of *kalte kost*. More isolation. Corrie marked off each day on the wall behind her cot. She did not want to lose track of time. She was arrested on February 28th. On February 29th she was taken to Scheveningen. On March 16th she was brought into solitary confinement. Now it was April 15th and her birthday. Corrie thought she would celebrate by singing a song.

She remembered the wild cherry tree that stood in the Kenaupark of downtown Haarlem. Every spring it produced such large cherry blossoms that the residents called it the "Bride of Haarlem." Its massive branches formed a canopy of what appeared as a white velvet cloud above, then the petals fell and spread into a carpet of white on the brick sidewalk below. There was a children's song written about the tree and Corrie began to sing this joyful song to herself to celebrate her birthday.

"Silence! Solitary prisoners are to be quiet or else."

<hr />

A few days later Corrie was taken out of her cell and brought to the shower room. It was the first time she had bathed since her capture from the Beje. The warm water washed over her matted, stuck hair and down her skin with its festering wounds. Corrie delighted in the event. She chuckled that the simplest thing in life when deprived can bring such pleasure. Even though they could not converse, just to be around other women was a thrill for her. She knew she would never take human relationships for granted again. This closeness with others brought her joy and strength. *How rich is anyone who sees another human face!* Corrie thought.

Corrie returned to her cell with new resolve to live and to thrive. She knew that the next time she went to shower she would bring three of her Gospels to give to the other women. She did not want to horde God's blessings on her life.

Soon after the shower event Corrie received another blessing. A black ant crawled on the floor near where she stepped one morning when returning her bucket to the door. Corrie studied the ant with intensity, marveling at the intricacy and design of the small creature. At suppertime, after the ant had long disappeared, Corrie threw a few bread crumbs at the crack in the floor where she last saw him. Almost immediately the ant appeared and worked feverishly to move the bread crumbs into its hole. Corrie had a new friend, and she thanked God for the small joys in life, even in the face of adversity. Some were joys she had often overlooked before.

One night there was shouting in the hallway. Corrie wondered how the prisoners were talking without being corrected by the guards. She went to her door and listened through the shelf where her food was served. Some people were singing, some were shouting. Some were pleading for people to be quiet so they would not get into trouble.

"What is happening?" Corrie asked. "Why is everyone talking tonight?"

Someone nearby answered, "It is Adolf Hitler's birthday party. All the guards are somewhere celebrating."

Names of inmates were being passed down the hallway. The prisoners were using the opportunity for an information exchange. *Perhaps I can find out about my family*, Corrie thought.

"I am Corrie ten Boom. My father and siblings are here. Casper ten Boom, Betsie ten Boom, Willem ten Boom, Nollie van Woerden. Has anyone seen them?"

Corrie shouted these names over and over again. She also shouted names for others so the information could pass down the hallway. Soon, information on releases and deaths and sicknesses were starting to come back to those in Corrie's hallway. Someone's baby had died, someone's arm was better. Other information about the war and current events also trickled down the hall that night.

"The Allies had invaded Europe."

"The war would soon be over."

Corrie waited patiently to hear information about her family. All of a sudden she heard her sisters' names being relayed down the hall and her heart leapt.

"Betsie ten Boom is in cell 312. She says to tell you that God is good."

That was Betsie! Corrie was so encouraged she laughed out loud. *That was Betsie through and through.*

"Nollie van Woerden was in cell 318 but she was released one month ago."

Nollie! Oh Nollie, you are free! Corrie was so thankful to hear this information about her sisters. She wondered about the men. Information was slower coming from the men's section of the prison. Corrie waited patiently to hear about her father, brother, and nephew.

Soon she heard the news that Toos was released. Corrie's heart soared at this opportunity to receive information about her friends and family who were arrested with her.

"Peter van Woerden. Released."

"Willem ten Boom. Released."

Oh how wonderful, her nephew and brother were released. But there was one more name that Corrie waited for. However, it did not come.

Corrie shouted again, "Casper ten Boom, an 84-year-old watchmaker, white hair and a long beard. Has anyone seen him?"

The name Casper ten Boom traveled down the hallway again and Corrie waited.

No answer came. No one had seen him. No one had heard of him. She took delight in the news she had received but her father's status remained a mystery.

⟤⟡⟢

Another week.

More restless nights.

More boring days.

Corrie took courage with the news that Betsie seemed well and about Nollie being released. Perhaps Betsie and Corrie would be released soon as well.

One day, Corrie's door opened unexpectedly and a prison guard tossed a package wrapped in brown paper on the floor. When the guard left Corrie picked up the package and turned it over and over in her hands. It was from Nollie. What a surprise!

Corrie gently opened the package and could tell that it had been opened and rewrapped at least once, but this did not take away her excitement. She reached in the package and found her light blue embroidered sweater. *Oh, how wonderful to see it again.* Corrie put the sweater around her and reveled in the feeling of luxury. *Thank you Nollie!*

Nollie also included cookies wrapped in red cellophane, vitamins, needle and thread, and a bright red towel. Corrie looked at the colors and how they contrasted with the gray walls and floor of her chamber. Nollie remembered how bleak it was in prison and was intentionally trying to encourage Corrie with color. *Thank you Nollie!*

As Corrie sat looking at all of the contents in the box an idea occurred to her; why not put the cellophane paper around the light bulb in her room to act as a lampshade? She stood on her cot and gently formed a type of lampshade around her bulb. Immediately a soft red glow filled the room.

Corrie looked one more time at the return address and Nollie's handwriting. Her writing was not her normal beautiful script, but seemed to be slanted at an angle and it almost looked like it was pointing toward the postage stamp. *Could it be that Nollie is sending me a message?* Corrie wondered.

When the underground was still in operation at the Beje, sometimes the workers would write on the back of the postage stamp with very small letters to send messages. Corrie chided herself and her imagination, hoping for something more in the package, but thought she would check just to be sure.

Corrie moistened the stamp in the basin water and gently removed it once it was soft enough. Words! There were definitely words underneath the stamp. Corrie could not believe her eyes, but the writing was small and she could not make out the letters without more light.

Corrie stood on her cot again and held the package paper just under the light and read the eight words Nollie had so deliberately written.

All the watches in your closet are safe.

Corrie could not believe her eyes. She reread it just to make sure. Did this mean that the Jews they had been hiding had made it safely out of the Beje? *How wonderful!*

Corrie could not contain her joy. The Jewish friends she protected in the secret room were safe. She put her hand over her mouth to keep from screaming out loud.

Then the tears came and she wept uncontrollably. The four Jews — Eusie, Mary, Meta, and Ronnie — along with two underground workers all made it out of the secret room and past the Gestapo somehow. How did they? *Lord You know, You were there and orchestrated everything.*

Corrie's Jews were safe.

CHAPTER 17

D-Day at the Berghof

Albert Speer had successfully staged a one-man coup. For some reason — which Speer could not explain — the Führer saw through his other advisors and picked Speer to come out on top. Such a victory was unthinkable to Speer because it coincidentally occurred just when he had lost faith in Germany's leader. *Perhaps Hitler could sense that he was losing his young architect?* He could not think on these matters long … the dreaded but inevitable bombings began that spring.

On May 13, 1944, in a daylight attack by the Allies, 749 American Eighth Air Force bombers and 740 fighter planes stormed across Germany and destroyed oil plants in Leipzig and Brux, Czechoslovakia. Soon after the attacks, in a meeting at the Berghof in Obersalzberg, the Führer decided to hear a full report regarding the actual damage and impact it would have on the war effort.

After waiting in the Berghof entrance hall, Hitler's main war strategists entered into the meeting hall with a stiff greeting from the Führer. As usual, Wilhelm Keitel, Hitler's Chief of Defense Minister, and Hermann Göring immediately delivered the typical National Socialist responses stating how everything would be fine, and that very soon the war would change course. Their hubris was nauseating to the others present. The Industrialists, whom Speer invited, gave much more unvarnished responses, even after being warned by Göring ahead of time not to make their reports so doom and gloom.

As soon as Hitler made the comment, "We've been through worse crises," Keitel and Göring were quick to nod and support his line of thinking. Speer often thought they looked like nodding donkeys.

"Oh yes, mein Führer, you are exactly right," said Göring grinning broadly. "We will come back on top. The oil reserves we have now will last at least eighteen months. The Allies cannot attack with this type of deep penetration again for a long while."

It was evident to Speer that Göring was trying to keep the conversation from taking a negative outlook. He did not want the Luftwaffe, or himself, to become a target of criticism for allowing the bombing to happen.

Unfortunately for Göring this became unavoidable. At the end of May, after days of intense repair work to the nation's fuel and chemical plants, another massive Allied bombing attack struck oil refineries in Ploiesti, Romania, which cut the Reich's fuel production in half. The false hope Göring conveyed to Hitler at the Berghof gave Speer the idea that it was an exceptional time to strike, and take revenge on Göring for his treachery months earlier when he humiliated Speer by siding with Sauckel.

On June 4th, Albert Speer spoke to Hitler. "You know, mein Führer, it would be more advantageous to incorporate the production of Air Armaments into my ministry. It would spare the Reichsmarschall the agony of giving an explanation to you every time there is an Allied attack. This would allow Göring to save face and keep focused on his more important duties. I could ensure we have enough bombers and fighters available to prevent some of these horrible attacks."

Speer was not sure what his boss's reaction to this power move would be. Hitler was surely accustomed to this type of maneuvering from Bormann, Goebbels and Göring — but not Speer. Speer prided himself in thinking that he was too preoccupied with real work issues to spend much time at the Berghof coaxing Hitler to backstab one of his fellow cabinet members. Hitler's positive reply surprised him.

"Of course the Air Armaments *must* be incorporated into your ministry, this is not a discussion," Hitler said forcefully. "I will call the Reichsmarschall at once and inform him of my decision, then you two can talk the details of the transfer."

Speer was enthused about the prospect of meeting with Göring to see how the man would handle this setback: in anger, in shame, with calm resolve? Their meeting occurred at the Reichsmarschall's house in the mountains in Obersalzberg.

"It is beyond my imagination how a man can flip flop so much," said Göring, visibly upset. "It was only two weeks ago Hitler was threatening to take away your construction department and give it to me. Now he rips out the heart of everything I am achieving and gives it to you."

"I know," Speer said calmly. "He does change his mind a lot."

"A lot?" Göring barked. "Constantly!"

Speer could barely look at the man before him. Visions of grand horse-and-carriage rides around Göring's massive hunting estates flooded Speer's mind. Göring had taken advantage of the war with the spoils furnishing his mansion, and yet had not held a steady hand with the increasingly important air production. Now, the most technical and prestigious part of his oversight was ripped from him.

After taking a few long breaths, Göring finally spoke. "I will go along with this," he said looking deep into Speer's eyes. "What choice do I have? A few days ago the Führer told me that you had too much on your plate and would take responsibilities away from you, and now this..."

This was news to Speer, and it made him even more irritated with the pompous man before him, this official to the people. But he decided not to humiliate Göring publicly with news of the recent change. Speer suggested that the Reichsmarschall himself issue the decree and let others know, as if it was his own decision for the good of the Reich. Göring liked the idea a lot.

"Yes, that would work nicely," said Göring, rubbing his hands together.

It was in those few days when Speer thought deeply about his country. He felt alone; he could see the road of destruction ahead of Germany because of the war, yet Hitler's other advisors seemed to pay no mind to the frequent setbacks Germany was experiencing.

Speer was distraught at the general acceptance of the Führer's policy of warfare. He could understand how Hitler's Nazi cronies accepted the Reich Chancellor's uncompromising position to continue to fight — those men like Himmler, Goebbels, and Bormann; *but the Wehrmacht generals? Could they not see the futility of the path on which Germany was advancing?* Speer questioned. *And what about Göring? Surely he must acknowledge that the Russians will not only march into Berlin, but take his beloved Carinhall as well.*

It was all only a matter of time. With the loss of Stalingrad, and the capture of hundreds of thousands of German soldiers to the Americans in Africa, Adolf Hitler's dream of the 1,000-year-rule of the Reich would never materialize. *Everyone had to know it, even the Führer himself,* Speer gauged.

As the Minister of Armaments for the Third Reich, Speer was constantly aware of how few supplies Germany had at their disposal compared to the rich resources of Russia. As the Soviets advanced and reacquired the territory Germany had taken from them only months ago, Speer surmised that the battle would now be lost due to a lack of oil fields and metal-producing mines.

There was one great hope everyone had, and it came from Goebbels, the Propaganda Minister. He informed the German citizenry that there was a secret weapon; one special bomb that would bring the Allies to their knees. Speer knew that Hitler himself hoped for one important battlefield victory where the Allies would be compelled to ask for a truce. As the Armaments Minister, however, Speer knew that there was no secret weapon. He would have had to authorize it. His nuclear scientists told him it would be years before they could develop something to use in the war. And Speer also knew that the outcome of the war did not hinge on one battlefield victory; the Allies had proven too determined and would eventually march into Berlin, *no matter what!*

Speer felt alone in his comprehension that this war and its conclusion would not be the same as the first Great War. In the Great War Germany kept most of its borders, and her cities were not incinerated. Speer sensed that at the conclusion of the current war, Germany would cease to exist.

The society which his parents and grandparents helped to establish would be brought to its lowest point. This war was a high stakes gamble where the winner would take all; and at the present, Albert Speer realized there was no possible way for Germany to win.

There was no secret weapon.

There would be no decisive battle.

Their leader was not another Frederick the Great.

With the amount of tanks and airplanes the United States was able to manufacture, the loss was inevitable and the change to Germany unimaginable. Speer often ended his nights with a strong drink, despondent at the thoughts of the future.

In June, events occurred which solidified his thinking on this matter. The Allies had already succeeded in capturing Italy and using Italian air bases as bombing platforms to hit German cities. The destruction of many of Germany's manufacturing plants was devastating. However, the Allies had not stepped foot into Western Europe yet.

Months earlier Hitler had directed Speer's ministry to construct thousands of pill boxes and bunkers along the French, Belgium and Dutch coasts. These defensive positions were heavily manned around the larger ports. It was believed that the Allies would certainly have to take a large port in order to enter the mainland, so precautions were taken to mitigate that possibility. Hitler had designed the pill boxes and bunkers down to the last detail. He insured that Speer and his subordinate architects carried through with the plans for Germany's defensive fortifications on the coast. Hitler believed those details could mean the difference between winning and losing.

The completion of this massive defensive project took a full two years and cost nearly four billion Deutschmarks. Over seventeen million cubic yards of concrete were utilized as well as one million metric tons of iron. It became known as the Atlantic Wall, and Hitler hoped the project would make it impossible for the Allies to penetrate the mainland without massive casualties. He also hoped that the defenses would slow down an Allied invasion long enough for Germany to win the war in the East. Even though there were already 50-60 divisions near the Atlantic Ocean, Hitler wanted to reposition more troops west once Russia had surrendered ... but the Battle of Stalingrad clouded this option. Now, Russia was actually on the move toward Berlin.

On Monday, the 5th of June, Speer visited the Berghof in Berchtesgaden. He had a conference with the Führer because of a labor dispute he was having with Himmler and his SS. In many of the factories throughout the empire — which Speer and two of his four deputies, Sauckel and Milch, worked so hard to supply with laborers — the SS were fundamentally stealing workers to send them to concentration camps.

SS guards would repeatedly name trivial infractions to remove large numbers of foreign workers. The Industrialists in turn complained to Speer about the lack of manpower. Speer estimated that the number of workers removed by the SS was approximately 35,000 per month throughout Europe. It appeared that Himmler had his men working overtime to disrupt Speer's workforce, and Speer was determined to stop this counter-effort. *How could he help win the war with so many workers being exported?*

Speer met with Hitler that day to explain how this massive exodus of personnel was greatly disrupting necessary production. Whenever Hitler praised Speer on the production numbers, Speer would remind him that it was vital to have workers to keep up with demand. In the two years since Speer had taken office since Todt's death, he raised aircraft production from 1,000 up to 3,000 fighters a month. In addition, he had organized production facilities and repair depots all across Europe to meet the needs of the military. Some of his bomber factories were completely underground and his work was praised as genius. But the one constant for Speer was that he absolutely had to have laborers to work in the factories. Success hinged on this point.

Adolf Hitler affirmed to Speer that he would speak to Himmler on these matters, but Speer wanted a stronger response. He spent hours with the Führer, trying to convince him to restrict any interference from the SS in Speer's factories. Hitler finally gave Speer the assurances he was after.

"It has to be done!" exclaimed Hitler, provoked by Speer's persistence. "Now leave me alone regarding this matter."

***

The next morning, June 6th, Speer and his wife, Margarete, drove from their modest mountain residence to the luxurious Berghof to lounge on the terrace and visit with friends. A few of the wives of Hitler's personal staff were already there taking sun, like Maria Below and Anni Brandt, Dr. Karl Brandt's wife. Eva Braun joined the ladies as they lounged in wicker reclining chairs on cushions covered with red and white gingham. Some of the younger children toddled around them on the large wooden, open deck.

The morning hours were usually very lighthearted at the Berghof because Hitler was a late riser. His routine was to stay up until two or three in the morning and then spend much of the morning in bed. Most days he would not receive his first report until noon.

Whenever Hitler would arise, one of his adjutants tipped off the visitors that the Führer was having breakfast and would join them soon. The lighthearted conversation and eruptions of laughter would cease and a quieter tone would ensue until their leader arrived. Though Hitler loved to laugh and hear funny stories, it was protocol to allow him to be the life of the party and not to be seen having too much fun without him.

Hitler loved to be near to the wives of his favorite staff members. He would frequently grab the arms of Margarete, Anni or Maria, and sit next to them at mealtime. What Speer could not understand was how Hitler would speak down to his consort, Eva Braun, in front of others. Sometimes he would mock Eva in an embarrassing way, but Eva pretended not to notice. Hitler was playful and adroit with other men's wives, but seemed awkward and belittling around his own companion. Speer felt sorry for Eva.

It was ten o'clock that morning when one of Hitler's military adjutants eyed Speer's arrival on the terrace. He quickly made his way over to Speer, intent on reporting the bad news from the front. Leaning over to whisper in his ear, he informed Speer that the U.S. and British invasion started early that morning on the coast of France.

"Has the Führer been awakened?" Speer asked.

"No, we are not to disturb him with reports until after he is up and has finished breakfast," the officer answered.

"Well, I think this day is an exception."

"No, sir, he is not to be disturbed."

Speer found this petty rule absurd. He spoke to his friend Nicolaus von Below, a bright Air Force pilot, who confirmed the Führer's order not to be disturbed. He also confirmed the invasion news and told Speer that Army Command West reported that three Allied airborne divisions had dropped into northern France during the night. When the Channel became visible at dawn, German soldiers reported to headquarters that it was filled with thousands of vessels. Everyone believed this was the much anticipated invasion, but Speer and the rest of the Berghof group had to anxiously wait for Hitler to have his eggs.

Finally at noon Hitler was ready to meet with his staff. To Speer, the Führer sounded like a broken record as reports of the invasion flooded in from the west, "This is a decoy; this cannot be the Americans' main attack. It would not make sense. Do you recall that we received a report indicating the exact location and hour of this invasion? They would not be so careless. Mark my words, this is a decoy. The main attack will be at Calais. I won't be deceived by this."

Speer noted that there was a discrepancy between what Hitler believed and what was actually happening. Every report arriving at the command post that day sounded more and more like a full-scale assault from the enemy. But Hitler continued to dig in his heels and say that the main attack would be elsewhere. He was reluctant to issue any order until he knew for certain that the Normandy Beach invasion was the main attack from the Allies.

General Erwin Rommel was perhaps the most frustrated with German High Command because there was an order that not even the Commander-in-Chief in the West could deploy the Panzer divisions; only Hitler could authorize an offensive action. Rommel wanted to deploy the tanks and engage them at Normandy but had to wait, patiently, all morning for the Führer to be notified. Then, because of Hitler's suspicions of an Allied decoy, he continued to delay his order to attack.

All of Berchtesgaden was buzzing with the news of the attack, including the foreign diplomats and dignitaries who had traveled to the mountain retreat area to visit with Hitler that week. The Berghof received more communique from the western generals that thousands of enemy aircraft were flying unhindered over German airspace.

As reports came in of bridges and airfields being destroyed, the Führer was increasingly frustrated at his Luftwaffe commander. "Where is the Luftwaffe?" Hitler asked. "Are they intimidated? Göring's planes have failed to keep the invaders out of the sky! I need to know why!"

Göring himself was not to be seen that day. He had departed the area to retreat at his Veldenstein castle. When notified of the invasion, he made arrangements to meet with Himmler and Ribbentrop, Germany's Foreign Minister, at another castle in Salzburg.

After it was reported that an estimated one hundred thousand troops had landed, and that the Americans and British were moving several miles inland to establish a secure beachhead, Hitler finally gave the order at 4:55 in the afternoon stating, "The beachhead must be cleaned up by no later than tonight."

The tanks Rommel was finally able to send into action were massacred by the low-flying American bombers unhindered by the inactive Luftwaffe stationed in

France. Allied planes forced the tanks to wait out the remainder of the day in the trees and hidden from the air. In the evening they were able to move toward the coast and the advancing enemy, but the darkness retarded the movement. The counter attack became mired with inadequacies and failed to gain traction.

All of Hitler's entourage had worried for months about when and where the attack would happen, and now it was finally here. Strangely, Hitler did not let it interfere with his reception of dignitaries, and he even walked out on the terrace to visit with the staff families. What Speer could not comprehend during those initial days was how Hitler continued to declare that the main attack would be somewhere else; that the present invasion was a feint. The other item Speer noticed was how calm Hitler seemed. In fact, it was as if he was relieved. His extraordinary calmness was terrifying to those who knew what was truly happening.

<hr />

Two weeks later in the East, the Russians launched their summer offensive against Germany on four fronts with over two million infantrymen and 2,700 tanks. Fear from this eastern invasion now gripped Germany.

CHAPTER 18

Auschwitz-Birkenau

The Architect reviewed a report from his SS kommandant at Auschwitz regarding the Hungarian Jews. Auschwitz was the Architect's favorite facility. Not simply because he had personally designed the construction plans of the gassing chambers and crematoria, but because the operation there was the most elaborate and efficient of all the camps. There was not only the main facility, but also Auschwitz-Birkenau and Auschwitz-Monowitz, where the former was used for gassing operations, and the latter for factory work production for I.G. Farben, a nearby chemical corporation. Some of the smaller camps like Riga and Minsk were still performing their exterminations by shooting, but not Auschwitz. Auschwitz-Birkenau became the primary gassing operation in the Reich and the kommandant was supportive and helpful.

The kommandant at Auschwitz — chosen personally by the Architect — reported he was able to gas 6,000 people per day. This by far exceeded exterminations at other camps because the Auschwitz gas chambers could hold up to 2,000 Jews at once. In comparison, the chambers at Treblinka could only hold 200 at a time.

The kommandant reported that with Zyklon-B it usually took three to fifteen minutes to kill the prisoners in the death chamber, depending on weather conditions. Under colder weather the gas degraded swiftly, but in hot weather the lethality of the gas endured longer. The guards knew when everyone was dead because the screaming stopped. However, in the summer they would wait an additional thirty to forty minutes before opening the door to remove all the bodies. Once the bodies were removed from the chamber, the large room was hosed down and cleaned so the next group could enter without suspecting anything.

The individuals who performed most of this important work were Jewish prisoners enlisted by the camp guards to help with the bodies. These Jewish prisoners were organized into detachments called Sonderkommandos, special commands, who would do their work with gas masks, rubber boots and a hose to wash off blood and defecations. The Sonderkommandos then used pliers to remove all the gold fillings and to pull gold rings off fingers. Then they would cut the hair and drag the corpses either to a lift or a pit. Sometimes when the operation was overcrowded, such as it was that summer, the Sonderkommandos would have to load the corpses on a wagon to be hauled to a nearby crematorium.

The Architect read that those in charge of dealing with the clammy corpses reported that the victims' lips, fingers, toes, and ears were often purple. The Architect knew this was because of the way Zyklon-B worked. Molecules from the gas bonded with red blood cells preventing cellular respiration because oxygen could no longer be carried through the body. The cellular make-up of the blood would immediately starve because of it, causing immediate death. Once fully inhaled, the crying in the chambers abruptly ceased because the gas deprived the cells of oxygen and rendered the victims unconscious without the pain and violent choking that comes from asphyxiation. The bodies would struggle to save the vital organs and spontaneously cut off blood flow to the extremities; thus the purple ears and toes.

The Architect went back to an earlier section of the report he had previously skimmed. When the transports of Hungarian Jews arrived at Auschwitz that spring and summer, the railway cars took a newly constructed spur line directly into Birkenau for gassing. The unsuspecting Jewish passengers — 3,000 per shipment — would exit down the unloading ramps, with families being separated and placed into three lines. The men would be in one line, the women in another, and the children in a third line. These lines would then be inspected by two SS medical doctors who would make a spot decision to determine who was strong enough to work either in the Farben Chemical Works Plant or the Krupps factory.

Alongside the railroad line that led into Auschwitz-Birkenau, the separated Jewish families would often run between the lines in an attempt to reunite, especially the mothers with their children. Some days it would take much work for the guards to keep prisoners in the correct lines. However, the kommandant utilized an orchestra of young, pretty girls dressed in white blouses and navy blue skirts to play lively pieces, like *The Merry Widow,* to calm the mass of prisoners marching toward the gas chambers labeled with signs reading 'Bath Houses.'

The line with children and the lines with adults not selected for work were led through the camp and marched across a meadow of fruit trees named section B-II of Birkenau. Then, if the crematoria buildings were full, they would enter into a large farmhouse called Bunker I and were told to undress. The Sonderkommandos would be there to help their fellow Jews undress and to keep them calm. The kommandant wrote that he had selected Sonderkommandos from Hungary that summer so they could speak to the arriving Jews in their own language to put them at ease. If some of the Jews became suspicious and began to talk about being gassed, the Sonderkommandos would try to relieve them of their fears. If they failed and the prisoners kept disrupting the process, the SS would take those agitators out of the building and shoot them in back of the neck with a small caliber pistol so it would not be heard by those in the house.

The kommandant reported that the Sonderkommandos were especially good with the children. After convincing the mothers to call the smaller children out from where they were hiding in some piles of heavy clothing, the children were then encouraged to play with each other. Some of them clutched a toy as they walked wide-eyed into the gas chamber. Occasionally a mother would realize what was happening and try to thrust their child back outside of the large gas chamber door before it closed, but the Sonderkommandos would reopen the door and gently lead the child back to the mother.

Once the amethyst-blue crystals of hydrogen cyanide did its work in the chamber, the Sonderkommandos would have the job of finishing the task so that bodies did not pile up and slow the exterminating process. The burning in crematorium 1 was halted a year ago, but Kremas 2, 3, 4 and 5 were fully operational. Each building held five triple furnaces and two electrical elevators for lifting the corpses from the gassing room to the ovens. Once lifted to the large oven room, the bodies would be placed on carts with wheels and quickly delivered to one of the cast iron furnaces. No caskets were needed, the bodies were simply shoved into the ovens kept hot by coal. In a few moments, what once was a human body was nothing but ash.

The Architect continued to read in the report that despite the intense efforts by the Sonderkommandos, the ovens were not able to keep up with the gassings. Due to the increased load of Hungarian Jews coming into Birkenau — sometimes over 12,000 per day — the corpses were beginning to pile up in large, outdoor collection pits. Kremas II and III could burn 5,000 bodies per day, Kremas IV and V could handle 3,000 bodies per day. The large pits outside the crematoria buildings had to burn the remaining 4,000 bodies.

Therefore, besides working the ovens all day, the Sonderkommandos also worked the pits, which was a labor-intensive activity. It involved keeping a fire stoked in the pits so the bodies would be completely consumed. They also had to pour off the accumulated fat and continue to poke holes in the scorched bodies so that oxygen could enter and continue the burning. When finished with the burning pits, the kommandant reported, they were forced to cover over the charred remains with dirt using bull dozers. Guards in the surrounding camps complained about the hideous smell.

One item the kommandant of Auschwitz wanted to communicate in his report to the Architect was his regard for the Jewish Sonderkommandos. They went about their work as ruthless as a loyal National Socialist. The kommandant could not understand their eagerness, providing care and comfort as they escorted their fellow Jews to the gas chamber, all the while knowing that eventually they would suffer the same fate as their countrymen. Not once did the kommandant hear about the Sonderkommandos alerting the Jews to the fate that awaited them. In fact, they helped to console them. Strangely, the kommandant was made aware that the Sonderkommandos would sometimes have to lead friends or family members into the chambers, yet they still served as the perfect host, acting like the prisoners were indeed going to a shower house.

One time the kommandant noticed a Sonderkommando pull a body out of the masses and then stop and stare a moment as if thunderstruck. Then the man went about his business and continued to drag bodies to the furnace. When the kommandant inquired as to the reason, he learned that the Sonderkommando had discovered his wife's body that day. The kommandant wondered where these Jews received the superhuman strength of will to do this work. Did they believe that the harder they labored they might be afforded the opportunity to escape their doom?

The Architect finished reading the report that concluded with a note of congratulations from the kommandant stating they had been successful in taking good care of all the Hungarian Jews transported to Birkenau that summer. The total number of Jews deported from Zones I through V in Hungary was over 437,000, and over 250,000 of them were already exterminated.

Success! Rejoiced the Architect. *Now I must turn my attention to the approaching Russians.*

CHAPTER 19

Reunion

Corrie sat on her cot with her head against the cold, stone wall. She was still alone, with only the ant and her thoughts to keep her company. Her mind would often drift to events from her childhood and she would close her eyes in concentration to picture every last detail.

Corrie remembered traveling with her father on a trip to Amsterdam when she was only ten years old. Every Monday, Casper ten Boom would travel by train to the Naval Observatory in Amsterdam to synchronize his watch with the official accurate time. Corrie delighted in going with him on these trips so she could spend time alone with her dad.

On one particular trip, Corrie decided to ask her father about something she had heard that was troubling her because she did not know what it meant. As they rode the train home one Monday evening Corrie gathered the courage to ask her father the question.

"Father, what is sexsin?" Corrie asked.

The older Ten Boom turned and looked at Corrie's young face. He was smiling, but there was some seriousness in his eyes. He did not answer her question. Corrie immediately regretted the decision. Perhaps she should not have asked him the question.

She knew what sex was; whether you were a boy or a girl. And she knew sin was bad, because it made her Tante Jans very unhappy. But Corrie had no idea what the words sex and sin together meant. She had heard the word in class when her teacher read a poem about a young man whose face was "not shadowed by sexsin." Corrie was too embarrassed to ask her teacher in front of everyone, and her mother's face turned scarlet when she asked her at home one day. Corrie knew her father would not let her down, but she was puzzled by his hesitation to answer. *It must be very bad indeed*, thought Corrie.

After a few moments the train stopped safely back in Haarlem. Casper ten Boom stood up and turned to retrieve his traveling case from the overhead storage rack. He placed the heavy case on the floor and looked at Corrie.

"Will you carry it off the train, Corrie?" he asked.

Corrie stood up and grabbed the handle of the case but it would not budge. She tugged at it a moment but both of them knew it was pointless. The case was filled with watches and spare parts, mostly metal, and it weighed too much.

"It is too heavy for me," said Corrie.

"Yes, and it would be a pretty poor father who would ask his little girl to carry such a load. It is the same way, Corrie, with knowledge. Some knowledge is too heavy for children. When you are older and stronger you can bear it. For now you must trust me to carry it for you."

Corrie was satisfied with this answer. It made her at peace. There were answers to all of her questions, but at that point in time she was satisfied to leave them in her father's keeping.

A letter dropped through the small opening in Corrie's door and lay on the floor in her quiet cell. She hesitated to pick it up. She had not received a letter while in prison. *Perhaps it was bad news.* Corrie looked at it a moment and then stood from her cot and walked over to retrieve the letter.

It was from her sister Nollie. How comforting to see her sister's beautiful script. Corrie peeled apart the top part of the envelope, opened the thin paper, and read the words on the page.

Will you be brave, Corrie? I have news that is very hard to write to you. Father survived his arrest by only ten days. He is now home.

Corrie read and reread the short letter several times. A severe blow. The words melted and became unreadable as Corrie's eyes filled with tears and she began to sob. She heard someone walking outside in the hallway and she shouted for them to stop and help her, that she had received some bad news.

"Wait here," the person answered. "I'll be right back."

The young woman soon returned with a sedative to give to Corrie to help soothe her nerves.

"I don't want that," Corrie moaned from deep inside. "I just need someone to sit by me a while."

"Listen, it's your own fault," the female guard said. "If you had obeyed the laws you would not be in here."

Corrie felt a sudden detachment from this person in the room with her. She repented at reaching out for human comfort instead of praying to her Heavenly Father. The person next to Corrie now could never understand how hard this was for her; to have to say goodbye to her father in such an awkward way, in such a brutal place.

"I will be okay," Corrie finally said, and the woman departed.

Corrie sat on her cot a long while, thinking of the last moments with her father and the words that were shared between them. *"God be with you, father." "And with you, my daughters."* She smiled when she thought of her father trying to wind his clocks when the SD men were ushering them out into the street. *Did he really think that was important just then?*

The times had so changed them. She thought of the quiet days before the war. Her family was entirely different now. If she was released from prison that day she would return to the shop and have only Betsie to live with.

<hr />

One day shortly after receiving the letter, the head officer entered Corrie's cell. She was the new leader and was the fiercest looking woman Corrie had ever encountered.

She had worked in Berlin before coming to Scheveningen and now she was making a lot of changes. *Fresh linens every two weeks!* Corrie had never had any sheets to begin with. *Prisoners will go outside for fresh air every other day!* Corrie had been outside once while incarcerated. *Showers twice a week!* Corrie had one shower in all the months since her capture.

Corrie jumped out of bed and stood at attention when the woman entered the room. Corrie thought she looked like a general. She was tall, with erect shoulders and cold, piercing eyes. Corrie was sure she had never seen a more evil-looking woman in her life. Immediately the new prison leader went to work on Corrie's cell to make sure it was in regulation.

The red paper Corrie received from Nollie and had fashioned into a shade for her one light bulb was ripped off by the General. The last package she had received from home was turned upside down onto her small table dropping cookie crumbs, vitamins, and sandwich spreads in a heap. The General ripped Corrie's blanket off her cot to see if there was anything else in hiding. She then took Corrie's glass jar in which she had some apple butter. Corrie was forced with trembling hands to empty the remaining contents onto some toilet paper.

Then, with her last act, the General scooped her hands under Corrie's mattress, searching for something, anything, hidden. Corrie gulped; it was where she kept her Gospels.

Nothing.

Thank you Father.

Without a word the new head matron abruptly turned an about face and went to the next cell. Corrie could hear her ripping things off the wall and emptying another prisoner's container of goodies. Eventually the fear of this woman left Corrie and she was at peace again, alone in her cell.

⬤

On another day, Corrie's door opened and a sharp looking lieutenant entered into her small living space to talk with her.

"Goedemorgen, ma'am," spoke the lieutenant.

"Guten Morgen, Lieutenant," answered Corrie.

They both smiled at the attempt to use each other's language.

In perfect Dutch the man continued, "I am Lieutenant Rahms. And you are Miss Ten Boom?"

"Yes, sir. That is my name."

Corrie noticed the brilliant colors of the man's uniform. There were stars and ribbons and a white skull and crossbones on his cap. He looked every bit the model officer. Corrie then thought of her own appearance, lying on her smelly cot in her thin dress with her slender, bare arms and long, unkept fingernails. Corrie knew she looked poor, perhaps the poorest person the lieutenant had ever laid eyes on.

The lieutenant looked rich, well-groomed and powerful. Corrie had to force herself not to stare. But what was more attractive than his looks was that he was being kind to her.

"You were arrested with your family in Haarlem, is that correct?" he asked. There was a caring, gentle manner about him.

"Yes, sir. We were all together when the SD came and took us."

"Were others there also, with you?" he asked.

Corrie did not know exactly what he meant. Did he mean the Jews, or did he mean the Beje workers? She knew that she must continue to protect those who were involved in the underground.

"Yes, sir. There were workers from my father's shop who were arrested with us."

"I heard there was a whole house full of people, almost like..." The lieutenant cut off his sentence and did not finish.

Corrie's visitor took a stool from the corner of the cell and sat down on it next to Corrie's bed.

Corrie gathered her wits and said as bravely as she could, "Will those who were arrested with me be released since they had nothing to do with my case?"

Lieutenant Rahms smiled, "We can discuss this further in the examination room. Do you feel strong enough to come and have your hearing?"

There it was, then. Corrie knew that she would be interrogated as those in the neighboring cells had been earlier that month. They had warned her of the nice lieutenant who was kind but often direct and to the point. "Don't trust him," they would say.

"Yes, of course I am," Corrie answered the man.

He at once stood up and turned to leave.

"You will be brought to my office so we can talk."

Soon after the encounter Corrie was escorted through several corridors, down some steps and out to the interior courtyard of the prison. There were several small huts along one side of the massive brick wall. The guard she followed walked along the gravel path up to the fourth hut that had beautiful flowers planted outside, and then knocked on its door and pushed it open.

Inside was Lieutenant Rahms. "Bring her in."

The guard escorted Corrie through the door and then snapped to attention and raised his right arm, "Ja, Herrein!" Then departed.

The lieutenant looked into Corrie's eyes. "You are shivering," he said. "Come here while I stoke up the fire."

It was the kindness that struck Corrie so hard. After months of harsh treatment and nary a soft word, she felt her heart warm to this man even though he was in a Nazi uniform. Then she remembered what others had said about him. *Lord, please help me not be gullible and endanger another person's life,* Corrie prayed.

The lieutenant grabbed a chair and set it down for Corrie to sit.

Set a watch, O Lord before my mouth, prayed Corrie.

Corrie noticed Lieutenant Rahms pick up some coal out of the coal scuttle with his bare hands and thrust them into the fire.

"You should ask for a shovel for your next birthday," offered Corrie.

The lieutenant smiled. Corrie complimented him on his flowers that were planted outside the hut. He spoke of the irony of growing Dutch bulbs as a German.

Corrie was relaxed. It was as if she was on a social call back in Haarlem. Then Lieutenant Rahms got to the business at hand.

"I would like to help you Miss Ten Boom," he said. "But you will have to tell me everything."

Corrie stiffened. The bluntness was startling. There it was, the cold reality of why she was there — her hearing.

Lieutenant Rahms looked deep into Corrie's eyes, "Tell me now, exactly what you have done."

"Which activities would you like me to discuss? Our clock making activities or my work with children?"

"The activities that got you arrested. Miss Ten Boom, I may be able to help you, but you will have to be completely honest."

He quizzed her for an hour. Thankfully for Corrie, Lieutenant Rahms believed that the Beje was the center of operations for *all* of the raids on the ration offices throughout Holland. Corrie could claim ignorance on how the cards were received. She thought of Mr. Koornstra but could never betray him. She avoided answering direct questions about who had helped them modify the Beje or the ration cards.

Finally, the lieutenant paused and changed the subject.

"What would you like to tell me about your other activities?" he asked. "What did you do with your free time?"

Corrie was delighted to change the subject and speak of the ministry she was leading with mentally disabled children. She spoke about the gospel and how she taught these special children about Jesus. She could see his eyebrows raising high with incredulity.

Finally he burst out, "What a waste of time! If you need converts then surely one normal person is worth more than all the half-wits in the world."

Corrie was hurt by the comment but knew his beliefs were in line with Hitler's National Socialist philosophy. Before she knew what she was doing she heard the words come out of her mouth, "May I tell you the truth, Lieutenant?"

"This hearing is predicated on the assumption that you will do me that honor," Rahms replied.

"The truth is, sir," Corrie said swallowing, "that God's viewpoint is often different from our own. So different that He had to give us a special book in which to tell us about Him."

Corrie knew that she was going out on a limb to speak so boldly to a Nazi officer about the Bible, but she felt that she must continue, no matter the cost.

"In the Bible I have learned that Jesus has a great love and mercy for all the lost and despised, and for all who are small and weak and poor. And it is possible, Lieutenant Rahms, that in God's eyes, one mentally deficient person may be of greater value to Him than a watchmaker — or a lieutenant."

She had gone too far. She could see the changed look in his eyes when she uttered her last word.

"This meeting is over," he said. Lieutenant Rahms stood up, walked to the door and shouted for the guard.

"The prisoner will return to her cell."

With that, Corrie was escorted down the gravel path, through the entryway, up the stairs and down the labyrinth of corridors until she was deposited into her cell.

When Corrie was left alone and the guard out of hearing range, the voices came to her from the other cells. "How did it go? Did you give him names? Remember not to trust him."

She decided that everything was in the Lord's hands. If she had burned her bridges in receiving help from the lieutenant then that was what the Lord wanted. She had peace thinking about her all-powerful Savior.

———

Early the next morning her cell door opened and it was Lieutenant Rahms.

Smiling at Corrie he said, "Are you ready for your second day of interrogation?"

They walked back to the courtyard where the sun was shining brightly.

"You do not get enough sun Miss Ten Boom," he said. "Why don't we have your hearing out here today, over by the wall?"

Again Corrie was struck by his kindness. Her words the day before did not seem to change his pleasant demeanor toward her.

The lieutenant looked down at the ground and thought a moment before he spoke, "I could not sleep all night. I thought constantly about what you told me about Jesus. Would you please tell me more about Him?"

Corrie thought for a moment at the turn of events. Instead of a powerful person sitting in front of her, it was a mere man who had been brought into touch with God and had learned of his own poverty.

"Jesus Christ is a light, and has come into the world in order that everyone who believes in Him need not remain in darkness. Is there darkness in your life, Lieutenant?"

There was a very long silence.

"There is great darkness in my life," he said at last. "When I go to bed at night I dare not think of the moment that I must awaken in the morning. When I awaken, I dread the day. I cannot bear the work I do here."

It almost seemed as if he would cry before he continued, "I have a wife and child in Bremen, but do not even know if they are alive. Bremen was bombed again last week. Each day I ask myself, are they still alive? Yes, there is darkness in my life."

"Lieutenant Rahms, there is One who always has them in His sight. Jesus bore your sins on the cross. Surrender yourself completely to Him, and there will be light in your life. There is no darkness so great that Jesus can't dispel it."

Corrie spoke to him at great length about eternal things. And not only that day, but two more times when he called her down for questions. There was never any pretense about the resistance activities Corrie was a part of; Lieutenant Rahms wanted to know about her papa and siblings. He was incensed that Casper had died in such a place as Scheveningen.

When their meetings were over he typed his final report and let Corrie read it.

She plans to continue in the future what she has done in the past, because she wants to help all those who appeal to her for aid, regardless of their race or creed. She is determined to do this because she is obedient to the command of Christ to love God and her neighbors.

Then Lieutenant Rahms looked up at Corrie and said, "One thing I cannot understand about God is why He should permit you, a brave woman, to be imprisoned? And what kind of God would have let that old man die in Scheveningen?"

"God never makes mistakes, Lieutenant. There is much we shall not understand until later. But these questions are not a problem for me." Then, remembering what her father told her about sexsin, she continued, "Some knowledge is too heavy for us, so our heavenly Father must carry it."

After saying goodbye, the lieutenant called for the guard to escort Corrie back to her cell. Before she left he whispered to her, "Walk slowly in Corridor F."

Corrie had no idea what that meant. Why should she walk slowly? Corrie and the guard re-entered the prison, climbed the stairs and began walking down the long corridors of cells. In Corridor F Corrie slowed her pace as the lieutenant suggested.

Corrie peered into every cell carefully. Perhaps the lieutenant was helping her to see Betsie's cell. Then Corrie was abreast of the door and peered in … just in time to see the unmistakable back of Betsie with her chestnut hair in a bun. Though Corrie saw the faces of Betsie's cellmates, she did not get to see Betsie's face. But it was her. And the cell was transformed with touches of Betsie everywhere she looked. The straw pallets were rolled and standing in the corner by the wall with each woman's hat on their pallet. Their coats were all hung neatly, and the food on the table from their packages was arranged perfectly. *Oh Betsie*, Corrie thought. *How you graced the Beje with your charming touches you have also blessed this cell in Scheveningen.*

"Schneller! Aber schnell!"
Corrie returned to reality and jumped to catch up to her escort.

———◈◆◈———

One day Corrie's cell door opened and the guard shoved in a Jewish woman to stay with her. Corrie was delighted to have company and made a special effort to make the woman feel at home in the cold cell. She had come with nothing so Corrie shared half her wardrobe from things she had received in Nollie's packages. The woman was grateful but was severely distraught about her former life.

"I had great luxury," the woman said with tears in her eyes. "I had so much in my suitcase that they stole from me. Will I ever see it again? Will I be allowed to return home one day?"

Corrie could not answer her questions on the future so they talked for hours about their families and their histories. The woman was friendly but was deeply distressed. Her husband was diabetic and she worried over him.

"He cannot get along without me. I am his nurse. What will happen to him?"

The woman cried off and on during their conversations. But Corrie was happy to share her cell with someone after months of solitary confinement, and she enjoyed having someone with whom to share meals.

After a few days, however, the woman was subjected to a brief hearing and was told to be prepared for "Transport."

"Will they torture me to death? Will they send me to the gas chambers?"

Corrie tried to tell the Jewish woman about God's love, but her misery kept her from truly understanding what Corrie was saying. Although Corrie was no longer alone, she was in the company of someone sentenced to death and who was fully given over to fear and panic. Corrie prayed constantly for her and that the Lord would reach out and save her.

The night the Jewish transport left, suddenly their lights were turned on and Corrie's guest was given thirty minutes to prepare. She departed the cell a mass of despair and Corrie prayed for her long into the dark night.

———◈◆◈———

A few days later, Corrie's door opened and it was the head matron Corrie referred to as the General. She was the tallest woman Corrie had ever seen in her life, and also the fiercest. Right behind her walked Lieutenant Rahms.

"You must come to my office," he said to Corrie coldly. "The notary has come."

With the lieutenant's icy demeanor Corrie stifled her warm greeting and prepared to depart the cell.

"Why a notary?" Corrie asked.

"For the reading of your father's will," answered the lieutenant. "The law states that the family must be present when a will is opened."

The head matron and the lieutenant walked out of the cell and began walking quickly down the corridor toward the center courtyard. Corrie ran to catch up with them. *Would she see her family?*

The head matron stopped at the doorway to the courtyard so Corrie followed Lieutenant Rahms into the bright sun and down the gravel walkway to his hut with the flowers next to the wall.

Lieutenant Rahms opened the door and stood to the side. When Corrie stepped inside she was immediately embraced by her brother, Willem.

"Corrie! Corrie! Baby sister!" Willem clutched her so tightly Corrie could barely catch her breath. Others in the room wanted to hug her as well. There was Nollie, with one arm already around Betsie; she reached out her other arm to draw in Corrie. The three sisters together again. Nollie hugged them so tight, like her strength could bind them together forever.

"Betsie! Nollie! Willem!" Corrie cried. The siblings were reunited. There were others in the room as well and Corrie was struck by their appearances. Betsie was thin and very pale; much like Corrie must have appeared to the others. Willem's face was gaunt and yellow and pained. Willem's wife, Tine, told Corrie that several of the eight men who had been crowded into Willem's tiny cell had died of jaundice.

Willem was not concerned for his own appearance but for his blond-headed son Kik, Corrie's nephew, who was apprehended by the Nazis while helping an American parachutist escape capture. The last they heard was that he was on a train to a concentration camp in Germany.

Corrie looked down to her hand where Nollie had pressed a package when they embraced. It was the entire Bible. Corrie was thrilled. She had given away her last Gospel in the shower that week.

Everyone babbled questions at once. The older siblings told Corrie that their father took ill and was taken to the municipal hospital at The Hague. There were no beds available so they laid him aside to wait to be seen. Casper died in a corridor without any records near him to testify to his identity. The hospital authorities simply buried the unknown old man in the pauper's cemetery and went about their work.

Willem quietly told Corrie and Betsie that the six individuals hiding at the Beje had all escaped. He explained that after a couple days the Gestapo guards were taken off guard duty and the Haarlem police were stationed outside the Beje. On the third night, March 1st, the chief had succeeded in having Theo Ederveen and Jan Overzet, two *inside* guards like Rolf on duty during the same shift. They found the four Jews and two resistance workers cramped and hungry but otherwise fine and stable. Then they helped them depart to other hiding places.

"They're all okay, Corrie," said Willem, "all except for Mary." Old Mary Itallie with the rasping cough had revealed herself publicly walking along a city street, and was apprehended by the Gestapo and sent to a concentration camp. The other Jews, including Eusie, were transferred and were doing well.

"The time is up," said Lieutenant Rahms. He looked to the notary who was waiting and said, "Go ahead and read the will."

Corrie finally recognized that Lieutenant Rahms had given the siblings this time to reconnect out of kindness. He waited patiently for them to catch up a little bit and then proceeded with the business at hand.

The will was short, essentially just a few sentences. The Beje was to be home to Betsie and Corrie as long as they needed it. If the home or watch shop ever needed to be sold, Casper knew they would recall his equal love for them all. He committed them with joy to the constant care of God.

In the silence that followed, all of the Ten Booms bowed their heads and Willem prayed, "Lord Jesus, we praise You for these moments together under the protection of this good man. How can we thank him? We have no power to do him any service. Lord, allow us to share this inheritance from our father with him as well. Take him too, and his family, into your constant care."

Corrie was thankful for this reunion with her family. Though her father was missing, he was present in their hearts. She returned to her cell without fanfare, sat on the bed and gently cried over the events of the day.

"*Kalte kost*," shouted a guard through her cell opening.

Corrie turned on her cot, put her hand over her mouth and continued to weep.

CHAPTER 20

Operation Valkyrie

Albert Speer finished breakfast with Margarete and put the final touches on a speech he would deliver at eleven o'clock with the Industrialists. But something else was nagging him at the back of his mind ... *the invitation to lunch that day by Colonel Claus von Stauffenberg.*

Speer had turned down the Colonel. He liked Stauffenberg, but it was too much to pack into one day. Speer had a speaking engagement with over 200 businessmen and high-ranking government officials in the late morning hours. He did not feel like he could then travel across Berlin and be prepared for a working lunch.

Speer pondered why the Colonel would be so adamant that he attend the lunch? There was a desperation in Stauffenberg's voice. It was unlike the colonel, something Speer had never noticed before. Speer decided he would have to follow up with him later that day, then reflected on the fine colonel.

Colonel Claus von Stauffenberg was a highly decorated young army officer. He was born of German nobility in a castle in the kingdom of Bavaria. Despite his military success in the field in the Third Reich, Stauffenberg never joined the Nazi party. He remained a devout Roman Catholic and emphasized love of country over pureness of blood. Speer watched with interest how the young colonel quietly denigrated Hitler's tirades against Jewish people and his moves to restrict religious liberty. Men like Joseph Mueller, a Roman Catholic priest, and Dietrich Bonhoeffer, a Lutheran minister, were imprisoned and Stauffenberg grew increasingly agitated by what he considered Nazi tyranny. When Hitler ordered that all Russian commissars were to be shot — even when surrendered — Speer heard that Stauffenberg refused to obey the order on principle.

Colonel von Stauffenberg himself was more German than most, yet he held to the ideal that Germany could be diverse, and that diversity could be a strength. Speer admired him for these thoughts, and the two had become close friends. Claus possessed a youthful charm, a quick wit and a deep love for Germany and her people. Speer loved that Stauffenberg was both poetic and precise, the true marks of a great leader.

Stauffenberg was also a favorite of Hitler's who thought him the model soldier. When the war started, Claus had thrown himself into combat with the characteristic energy of his brave family, and soon made a name for himself — first in Russia, then in Africa. In Tunisia in 1942, the colonel lost an eye, his right hand and two fingers of his left hand when he courageously maneuvered his command from the front. Any other man would have retired from the Army but not Stauffenberg. And Hitler felt that a Reich soldier with such bravery and who sacrificed so much deserved special honor.

This is why Hitler allowed Stauffenberg to play an instrumental role in the development of a homeland defense plan, and as such, to serve as deputy under a highly regarded army commander, General Friedrich Fromm. The plan was to use a reserve army for continuity in running the government and to protect Berlin in case of a disaster. It was code-named Operation Valkyrie.

General Fromm, commander of Germany's replacement army and a recipient of the Knight's Cross of the Iron Cross, was in charge of Operation Valkyrie and Colonel von Stauffenberg was appointed his deputy. The importance of the job required that one of these two men would meet with Hitler at the Wolf's Lair regularly to report on the progress of replacement armies to support the Eastern front.

Speer was good friends with both General Fromm and Colonel von Stauffenberg and usually welcomed the chance to meet with them when he was in Berlin. He recalled how Stauffenberg told him that it was absolutely essential that Speer meet with him and General Fromm for lunch that day, July 20th. Speer could not imagine why this lunch could be so important to the colonel, yet the colonel was insistent. When Speer declined for a third time that morning, he sensed the immense dejection Stauffenberg swallowed over the phone.

Speer packed his briefcase, kissed his wife Margarete goodbye, and left the house, still wondering about the need for the lunch meeting and the tone in the colonel's voice. Speer, driving through Berlin in his white Mercedes, thought more about the luncheon he would miss, and his last interaction with the handsome and almost mystical Stauffenberg. *Come to think of it, the conversation was unusual*, Speer thought.

A few days earlier Speer encountered Stauffenberg at Obersalzberg. Hitler had summoned his chief advisors for a conference at the Berghof, and the typical people were there: Himmler, Göring, Keitel, and Bormann. Stauffenberg sat next to Speer, placing his massive briefcase next to Speer's chair. Hitler monologued for hours on why the generals should trust his judgment in Russia, and he received continual affirmation and head nods from Göring and Keitel. This same, small group of men had endured these speeches time after time. But it was Stauffenberg's words after the meeting that caught Speer by surprise.

Once outside the Berghof, the two men walked down the front staircase, then stopped and looked at the majestic mountains before them. It was the military man who spoke first.

"All the other men in the room besides you are psychopaths and opportunists," said Stauffenberg. "No one actually dares to open their mouths in contradiction to what the Führer is expressing."

Speer simply smiled in assurance.

"With you I'm still very glad to talk, but there is no longer any point with these other idiots!"

Though he absolutely agreed with Stauffenberg's assessment, Speer was shocked at the blatant disrespect and that the colonel trusted him with his contempt for their leadership. Speer did not respond and he decided right then to not divulge it to anyone for fear that Stauffenberg could suffer retribution. All of Speer's closest friends like Milch and Fromm thought similarly, but never verbalized their thoughts as bluntly as Stauffenberg had done that day. The colonel certainly possessed the virtue of candor.

Speer arrived early at the Berlin conference and made sure things were prepared for his address to the businessmen and government officials. Goebbels arrived and conferred with Speer on when he would give his remarks. They agreed to end with Goebbels but give Speer the lion's share of the time.

Speer began speaking at eleven o'clock to over two hundred men, using numerous graphs to explain the present state of Germany's armaments. When finished, Goebbels took to the stage and addressed the crowd for a few minutes. After the conference concluded with the usual questions and answers at the front, the two men waited for most to disperse, then Goebbels and Speer departed to the Propaganda Minister's office for a drink. Speer had not thought of the lunch he was missing with Stauffenberg since his drive into Berlin that morning.

Soon after their arrival at the Ministry, the telephone rang and it was an urgent call for Goebbels.

"What?" Goebbels said alarmed. "Who did it? Is the Führer injured?" He turned to Speer and shrieked there had been an attempt on the Führer's life!

Goebbels went on to ask several questions before he hung up the receiver. Speer looked on from the sofa, wide-eyed and dazed.

"It happened this morning at Rastenburg. The Führer is okay, thank God, but he is injured and there were several others critically wounded. They believe it was one of your construction workers," Goebbels said to Speer with a little sneer in his voice.

"My workers?" exclaimed a worried Speer. He realized he could be incriminated if it truly was the work of men Speer hired to build the bunkers in northeastern Poland.

"Yes, they are conducting an investigation. Mussolini is on his way there right now. What kind of security checks do you make on the workers you assign to the Wolf's Lair?"

"Well, there are hundreds working there," replied Speer. "I can't tell you exactly what the methods are for securing the workforce. That's what I trust Sauckel to do."

"Good God!" exclaimed Goebbels. "That bunker is supposed to be the most restricted site we own. How could you leave the task of securing it to a subordinate? Your hiring methods have left what should be the safest place on earth vulnerable to any enemy of the Reich!"

The telephone rang again and this time Goebbels listened without asking questions. He set down the receiver, turned to Speer and said, "The stenographer, Berger, had his legs blown off, and there are several military officers severely wounded, not to mention the Führer's injuries. He can barely walk and has large splinters in his leg from the wooden conference table where they were working. Many of the others are a bloody mess."

"Who are the officers?" asked Speer.

"Brandt, Schmundt and Korten."

"General Schmundt and Colonel Brandt?" asked Speer. "Oh my."

Soon, Goebbels was on the phone with Hitler himself. He took the call in private so Speer could not hear what was being said. When nothing more could be done, the two men parted ways and went back to their ministerial duties.

Speer drove to his ministry office and met with a front line general. Then he visited with a Foreign Office official about petroleum reserves. During this meeting it came to Speer's attention that his ministry building was surrounded by soldiers, and the report was that they were not letting anyone in or out.

Speer's office telephone rang. It was Goebbels and his mood had turned very sour.

"I want you to come to my residence at once," the propaganda minister demanded tersely. "This is extremely urgent and I need you to interrupt your work and come immediately."

"Can you tell me the reason, and why the urgency?" asked Speer, now a little shaken.

"Not over the telephone," responded Goebbels. "We can talk once you get here. But be careful, there are soldiers guarding my door."

Speer hung up the phone and looked outside at the soldiers who were guarding his own entrance. He decided to call General Fromm at the Army headquarters buildings (the Bendlerstrasse) to see what was going on. The Bendlerstrasse held several high military command posts, including the headquarters office of Germany's replacement army headed by Fromm and Stauffenberg.

"May I speak to General Fromm, please?" he asked. "This is Albert Speer."

"I'm sorry, sir," came an anxious voice over the phone. "General Fromm is unavailable to take your call."

What does that mean? Speer wondered.

"Then let me speak to General Olbricht," Speer said.

"One moment, please."

"General Olbricht here," answered the voice on the other end of the line.

"General Olbricht, good to hear your voice," said Speer. "I wanted to tell you there are soldiers here guarding my ministry and I hear they are not letting people in or out. Can you tell me the meaning of this? I have an appointment I need to attend and I don't want to be detained. I also hear they are at the propaganda minister's office as well."

"Well, in your case it is a mistake," answered Olbricht. "I apologize and I will have your office free so you can go about your business at once."

A mistake! In my case?

Speer felt his head draining of blood and he knew he had to sit down. *Breathe man, breathe.*

"What do you mean a mistake? Where is Fromm?"

"He is being detained," answered Olbricht. "I cannot offer any more information. I will set it right with those guarding your office momentarily."

Speer hung up the receiver and thought about what all this could mean. What was unnerving to him was not that the highest levels of the army were actively moving about Berlin and taking control of the city, but that the guarding of his ministry was a mistake. *Does this mean they think I am in with them?* Speer wondered.

Speer's mind turned to all the conversations he had had recently with Fromm, Olbricht, Stauffenberg and others. *Could it be that they were in charge of the bombing at the Wolf's Lair? Is this why they wanted me to meet with Fromm for lunch today, so I could join in some kind of conspiracy? Is this why Stauffenberg so callously called the men meeting with Hitler all idiots?*

Speer did not like the tone in General Olbricht's voice. He had never heard him sound so stoic before. *And where now was Fromm?* As his mind rushed with memories of past conversations, he was suddenly gripped with the reality that Goebbels was waiting for him and he did not sound like he would be patient. *Perhaps he thinks I am one of the conspirators and he wants to arrest me at his office?*

Speer knew he had no choice but to drive over to Goebbels' ministry and meet with him. When he left his office the soldiers were walking away, obviously tipped off by General Olbricht. He jumped into his Mercedes and fled toward Goebbels' office. Though Speer was heavily distracted, he still noticed the warm summer air and the smell of the flowering trees in the Teirgarten.

When Speer arrived he was allowed to pass through the small group of soldiers guarding the entrance. He was escorted by Goebbels' staff up to the second floor where the Minister was waiting for him. It was five o'clock and the building was abnormally quiet.

"I need you by my side," said Goebbels coldly as Speer entered the room. "I've just heard word from headquarters that a military putsch is going on throughout the Reich. In this situation I'd like to have you with me. I sometimes go at things too hastily and I don't want to make a mistake; you can balance that out by your calm demeanor."

Speer did not know quite what to say. It seemed he was ordered to be here, but now it seems he was being used merely as a sedative. If what Goebbels was saying was true then both of their families were at risk as well. Speer instantly thought of the Allied invasion in the west and the progress Eisenhower had made in securing a strong beachhead and moving toward Germany. He also thought of how fast the Russians were moving toward Berlin; a speed which horrified the bravest German.

Had the generals finally had enough of Hitler's commanding from the Wolf's Lair, that they would take his life to run the show for themselves? Speer wondered. *Were they aligned with one of the Allied powers?* There were many unanswered questions at this point and real fear began to creep into Speer's soul.

The two men looked out the window facing the street and saw more and more battle-ready soldiers in steel helmets and with hand grenades scurry into position around the Goebbels' residence. They watched the soldiers set up machine guns near the front entrance and point them toward the street. Speer thought there must be a full platoon if not a company in and around the large estate. Two large soldiers took to Goebbels' front door and posted guard, their massive presence alone would prevent someone from slipping through. It was obvious they were serious.

Goebbels walked out of the room for a moment and returned with a small metal tin of what appeared to be cyanide capsules. He opened the container, took out two pills, and gingerly deposited them into his coat pocket.

"Just in case," he said, patting the pocket for good measure. "Help yourself," he said encouragingly.

Speer froze. He could not believe Goebbels thought the war had come to this, but he knew he wanted nothing to do with those pills.

The men sent an adjutant to the guards at the front door to glean as much information as possible. All they learned was that no one was allowed to enter or leave.

Goebbels got on the telephone and made numerous calls all over Germany to find out what was going on. The most disturbing report was that troops from Potsdam were already on the march to Berlin. Another alarming reality was that no one could get in touch with Himmler. He had seemingly disappeared from the city and from all communications. This in itself was worrisome. As the leader of the Gestapo, he was in charge of units which could have been engaged immediately in Berlin to stop the rebellion.

While Goebbels was on the phone, Speer thought of Fromm and Stauffenberg. He wondered where they were at that hour. *Why did Fromm not seem to be aligned with Olbricht? Had he too disappeared like Himmler? Surely Fromm would have been part of the putsch as the leader of the replacement army, wouldn't he?* Speer could see Stauffenberg's young face in his mind, his beautiful wife and children, then wondered how all this was going to end. *This stupid war!*

During his phone calls, Goebbels found out that the troops which had taken over the government quarter were in the command of Major Otto Ernst Remer. He located Major Remer by phone and convinced him to come and talk to him at his residence. Albert Speer was in the same room when the major entered Goebbels' second-floor office.

Speer noticed that although Goebbels was in control of his voice and actions when he began to speak, there was a hint of nervousness about him.

"Major Remer, thank you for coming so quickly on this oddly disturbing night. You remember that you have sworn an oath to the Führer?"

"Yes, sir," responded Major Remer. "I am loyal to Adolf Hitler and the party, as long as the Führer is alive. But the Führer is dead."

"No, that is not true. The Führer is alive!" shouted Goebbels, as if relieved to finally be getting to the conclusion of a struggle.

Both Speer and Goebbels noticed that Remer was taken back and visibly shaken. Goebbels sized up the man who was given the task of securing the Bendlerstrasse that evening. As one of the leaders of the replacement army under Fromm, Remer was told the Führer was dead, the military was taking over, and this was not a drill.

"Hitler is alive, major," said Goebbels. "I just spoke to him on the phone. An ambitious little clique of generals has begun a military putsch. A filthy trick. The filthiest trick in history. But this is a historic hour and the safety of the country now depends on your actions. Are you going to side with a few treasonous men who are betraying their own country and lying about the well-being of Germany's leader? Or will you do your duty and go down in history as someone who helped save Germany? Rarely has destiny afforded a young man like yourself such a chance. What will you do with it? Step up? Or throw it away?"

Speer knew that Goebbels was playing to the man's emotions and using rhetoric to strong arm the young major into doing his bidding. Speer could see Remer's disillusionment with the day's events. The major thought he was following orders by protecting his country after a true tragedy. Now he was told that he was tricked and being used as a pawn by some unpatriotic generals. Speer recognized by the look in Remer's face that Goebbels had already won. Remer would side with the propaganda minister. Goebbels could surely see it too.

"I am going to talk to the Führer right now," said Goebbels. "And I will let you speak to him personally. He can certainly give you orders which will rescind your general's orders, can't he?" Goebbels asked in a sarcastic tone.

Goebbels dialed up the Führer's headquarters in Rastenburg. Once Hitler was put on the line, Goebbels gave him some introductory comments about Major Remer and why he was in the office. Then he handed the receiver to Remer.

Major Remer accepted the receiver and placed it next to his head. With one word from the other end Remer immediately recognized his Führer's voice and snapped to attention. As Hitler talked, all Goebbels and Speer could hear were the same responses coming from the major, "*Jawohl, mein* Führer. Jawohl!"

After allowing the major to have a moment with the Führer, Goebbels took back the receiver and spoke to Hitler again. Goebbels later told Speer what Hitler told Remer — that his superior officers would soon be put under arrest but he needed Remer to take decisive action now and stand loyal to the Nazi party. Hitler told the young officer to crush the uprising, take all directions from Goebbels only, and that he was promoted forthwith from major to colonel.

The newly promoted colonel waited patiently for Goebbels to spell out what needed to be done. Remer exited the building to draw off the guard surrounding Goebbels' residence and rally all the troops in the surrounding area to hear the propaganda minister give a speech from his garden.

Goebbels turned to Speer and said, "Just watch how I play them!"

It was dark outside by the time Joseph Goebbels opened his balcony door and addressed the amassed guard waiting patiently for his instructions. Speer surmised that approximately 150 soldiers, many of them high-ranking officers, were present for this speech.

Goebbels did not raise his voice or go into a tirade such as Speer had heard from him before. Instead, he appealed to their loyalty in a personable manner. Speer noted that some of the men looked almost mesmerized by Goebbels' words. The act worked, and the soldiers departed to secure Berlin and prevent any more illegal maneuvers against the government.

After the speech and back in the second floor office, Goebbels and Speer heard that the Bendlerstrasse was retaken. General Fromm —previously detained by the conspirators — was going to conduct an immediate summary court martial of General Ludwig Beck, General Olbricht and Colonel Claus von Stauffenberg. At sixty-four, General Beck was the former Chief of the German General Staff and a wizened man, full of compassion and inner strength. Beck reminded Speer of Stauffenberg, and was not surprised to find out they were working together in the conspiracy.

Speer knew a quick court martial would not be in the best interest of General Fromm, nor what the Führer wanted. All conspirators were to be rounded up alive and investigated to ascertain as much information as possible before they were executed. If Fromm took matters into his own hands, then not only would the Reich be denied the privilege to interrogate Beck, Olbricht and Stauffenberg, but Fromm himself would be looked upon as a sympathizer.

It was midnight by the time Speer decided to take action himself. He took Colonel Remer in his Mercedes and drove over to the Bendlerstrasse. The July night air was cool and refreshing. The men drove through a totally blacked-out city and approached the government complex where the replacement army headquarters was located. There was a frenzy of activity with soldiers running around and tanks present in one of the center courtyards. The Bendlerstrasse itself was illumined with searchlights, almost as if to signal the British bombers to hit that single set of buildings.

A guard stopped the Mercedes and asked the visitors what their business was that night. Speer explained that he was on a mission from Minister Goebbels and he was accompanied by a commander of the replacement army, here to restore order to Berlin. He wished to speak to General Fromm.

Speer and Remer were told to wait by the car for a moment while the guard checked with his superiors. While they waited, out of the shadows of the trees came a large man in full uniform.

"At last, an honest German!" said Fromm, recognizing Speer.

"General Fromm," said Speer somewhat startled by the general's sudden appearance. "What is happening?" Speer could tell from Fromm's face that he was very displeased and unsettled.

"The deed is done," Fromm replied. "The putsch is finished."

"No! What did you do?" asked Colonel Remer, having exited the white luxury car.

"I've just had some criminals executed," answered Fromm.

"I wouldn't have done that," Remer responded.

"And are you giving me orders now, Major?"

"No, sir," answered Remer. He then hurried off into the shadow with an SS officer.

Fromm looked at Speer, exhausted and tense.

"I had no choice. They locked me in my office and prevented me from exercising my command."

"But you killed them?" asked Speer.

"As their appointing authority, it was my duty to hold a summary court-martial immediately of all participants of the rebellion. General Beck, General Olbricht, and my chief of staff, Colonel von Stauffenberg, are no longer living."

Speer looked at the downcast and deflated man before him. Having been a friend to the general for a long time, it seemed odd that tonight Speer could barely recognize him. There was obviously something else stirring in General Fromm's mind and heart and it manifested itself in the general's face and demeanor. Speer was appalled that he took matters into his own hands without waiting for higher guidance.

"I want to speak to the Führer," said Fromm. "Can you help me?"

"Yes, I can take you back to Goebbels' residence where he can connect you with him," replied Speer. "But please, tell me what you know of the events of today. I have not been privy to all of the Minister's conversations and am seeking to figure out what happened."

General Fromm told Speer that at 12:42 p.m. a bomb exploded in the Wolf's Lair conference room. It was emplaced by Colonel von Stauffenberg who escaped the meeting before detonation. Several people had been critically wounded, but it was obvious that it was an attempt on Hitler's life because Stauffenberg slid the large briefcase next to the Führer before he departed the room. Stauffenberg then drove past several guard posts, explaining to the junior enlisted men that he was on a special mission to see a general — purportedly Fromm — who was waiting impatiently for him on the runway. His bluff worked, and the guards let him escape.

Colonel von Stauffenberg's plane departed Rastenburg at approximately 1:00 p.m. and late in the afternoon he arrived at Fromm's headquarters and reported that Hitler was dead.

"That's impossible," said Fromm to the colonel. "I just spoke to Keitel on the phone and he has assured to me that Hitler is alive."

"Keitel is lying, as he always does," replied Stauffenberg. "I, myself, saw Hitler's body being carried out."

Then Colonel von Stauffenberg asked, "General Olbricht, what is your news?"

"The code word 'Valkyrie' has been sent out," replied Olbricht.

Fromm sprang to his feet and shouted, "On whose authority? No one can activate the homeland defense but me!"

"On the fact that the Führer is no longer alive," responded Olbricht.

"This is rank insubordination," growled Fromm, putting his hand on his holstered pistol.

"General, I myself set off the bomb and killed Hitler," said Stauffenberg, still trying to convince his boss that Hitler was indeed dead. "The impact in that conference room was as if a fifteen millimeter shell had hit it. No one who was in that room is still alive."

"Well, Count Stauffenberg," said Fromm, "your plan has failed. Hitler is alive and all heck is breaking loose. You must do the honorable thing and shoot yourself at once."

"No thank you," Stauffenberg declined.

"You are all under arrest!" Fromm barked.

"You deceive yourself," exclaimed Olbricht. "It is you who are under arrest."

"Then, they *attacked* me," an incredulous Fromm told Speer. "I managed one hard blow to Stauffenberg's face but there were too many for me. They tackled me down to the ground and put me under arrest. I was locked up the entire day. They called Paris and all over the occupied area putting hundreds, if not thousands, of Himmler's SS under arrest. Commanders all over Europe were involved in the putsch, so there will be heck to pay when all is said and done.

"This evening, when the Gestapo finally came in to put things in order and freed me I was able to take back control and deal with the perpetrators. Stauffenberg had already been shot in his only arm trying to escape. General Beck was there in civilian clothes because he was going to take over as head of state. I am sure they thought I would be their top general but I could not side with them against the Führer; I have taken an oath."

Speer finally had a chance to speak. "That is because you knew the Führer was not dead."

"That's right," replied Fromm.

"But what if Hitler had indeed been killed?" asked Speer tentatively.

"Well, that would have…" Fromm stopped short, then looked hard at Speer as if trying to read his mind. "You know how I feel about things," he said. "But it is not the case."

"No, it is not the case," said Speer.

"When things had gotten under control I told the men to lay down their arms and that they were all under arrest. Of those present there was Stauffenberg, General Olbricht, General Beck, Colonel Mertz, and Lieutenant Haeften who had accompanied Stauffenberg to the Wolf's Lair.

"General Beck said to me, 'You wouldn't make that demand of me, your old commanding officer?' I watched him as he reached for his revolver, so I told him to make sure he kept it pointed to himself. Then Beck said, 'At this moment, it is the old days that I recall…' But I cut him off and said, 'We don't want to hear that stuff now. I ask you to stop talking and do your deed.'"

Fromm continued, "Beck fired but it wasn't a fatal shot. It grazed his head and he began to bleed as he slumped in his chair. I told a young officer to go ahead and help the old gentleman, but Beck opened his eyes and insisted that he be given another chance. I relented and he failed even after a second shot and fell down unconscious. I allowed the other men to write a note home to their wives and I left for a few minutes."

Speer was aghast at the details of this story and could not believe what he was hearing. Beck was one of the most distinguished men in all of Germany. Speer wanted to know the rest so he looked intently at the general so he would finish.

Fromm went on, "When I returned I told them that in the name of the Führer I had called a session of a court martial and that it had pronounced death sentences to Colonel Albrecht Mertz, to General Friedrich Olbricht, to the colonel *whose name I no longer know*, and to Lieutenant Werner von Haeften.

"I had a sergeant drag Beck into another room and put the grand gentleman out of his misery by shooting him in the neck. Then I escorted the others down to the courtyard where we blindfolded them and lined them up against the wall. Just before I ordered the execution I heard Stauffenberg shout out, 'Long live our sacred Germany!' After the shot, they were all dead, crumpled on the ground where they once stood."

Looking exhausted, Fromm turned toward Speer and beseeched him, "It has been a terrible day and I need to speak to the Führer! Please drive me to Goebbels' now so I can make that call."

Speer could hardly believe what he had just heard. He felt terribly conflicted pondering the valor and dignity of those who failed. He and Fromm climbed into Speer's Mercedes and drove away from the Bendlerstrasse. They raced back to Goebbels' residence where the Minister was still busy making phone calls, but he received them both into his office. Fromm made his request to speak to the Führer but Goebbels declined. He informed Fromm that he would speak to Hitler himself and enlighten him of Fromm's request.

Goebbels left Speer and Fromm together while he spoke to the Reich Chancellor. Speer noticed that the general was very agitated by being put off, but there was nothing he could do. Both the men knew that Goebbels disliked and distrusted Fromm.

Heinrich Himmler finally arrived with several of his SS officers just as Goebbels ended his phone call with the Führer. Himmler told Speer and Goebbels that he had purposely taken his time to enter Berlin because that is what you are supposed to do when there is an uprising.

Goebbels bragged to Himmler how he had single-handedly stopped the uprising with quick wit and charm. He also told Himmler that although soldiers guarded his residence, the idiots allowed him to keep making phone calls to the Führer and to others. Goebbels continued to call the conspirators 'children' and said they botched the entire operation with their clumsiness. They never even took over his radio station to spread their lies to the German public.

Speer noticed that both men were in good humor at the results of the failed putsch. It sickened him at how callous they were both acting.

Then Goebbels looked up and saw General Fromm still in the corner of the room. He ordered the SS men to arrest Fromm as a conspirator and told Fromm he would never be allowed to speak to the Führer again. The SS removed Fromm at once. Speer felt for Fromm who tried to do the right thing, but he took too much power into his own hands and it ultimately backfired on him.

Promptly, both Himmler and Goebbels looked at Speer.

"Herr Speer, there are several things I would like to speak to the Minister about in private, so if you don't mind," suggested Himmler in his usual calm containment. He seemed hopeful that Speer would take a hint.

"But before you go," Himmler added, "I thought you would like to know that when my men opened the conspirator's safe at the Bendlerstrasse there was a list of names on it regarding who would run the new government. None of the current cabinet members were listed … except for you. They planned on keeping you as Armaments Minister."

Speer swallowed hard and tried to maintain a calm demeanor. He looked both men in the eyes. Looked at the floor. Tried to think of something to say but his mind was blank. *Breathe man, breathe.*

"Isn't that interesting?" asked Himmler.

Goebbels smiled, put his arm around Himmler and the two walked over to the sofas to sit down. Speer knew this was his cue to leave them. He pondered his current situation. *What will Hitler say when he finds my name on the conspirator's list?* Speer wondered.

As he drove home he turned on his radio in time to hear Hitler's speech from the Wolf's Lair to the German people regarding the attempt on his life:

> *"My German comrades!*
>
> *If I speak to you today it is first in order that you should hear my voice and should know that I am unhurt and well, and secondly, that you should know of a crime unparalleled in German history.*
>
> *A very small clique of ambitious, irresponsible and, at the same time, senseless and stupid officers have concocted a plot to eliminate me and, with me, the staff of the High Command of the Wehrmacht.*
>
> *The bomb planted by Colonel count Stauffenberg exploded two meters to the right of me. It seriously wounded a number of my true and loyal collaborators, one of whom has died. I myself am entirely unhurt, aside from some very minor scratches, bruises and burns. I regard this as a confirmation of the task imposed upon me by Providence.*
>
> *The circle of these usurpers will be destroyed without mercy. This time we shall settle accounts with them in the manner to which we National Socialists are accustomed…"*

Speer turned off the radio. He arrived at home, walked into his dark house and straight to his bedroom. Margarete was sleeping so soundly, innocently. Speer tried to sleep but his mind would not shut down. All night long he could hear in his mind Himmler asking over and over again, *"Isn't that interesting?"*

Part III

THE CROSSING POINT

CHAPTER 21

Volleys at Vught

Corrie heard shouting down the prison corridor.
"Get dressed at once!" screamed an angry guard. "Pack all belongings in your pillow case. Prepare for departure."

The pillow case. Corrie was so thankful for this one luxury. It was one of the accommodations made by the General who had also promised sheets which never came. But Corrie appreciated this one change, so she could lay her head on something soft and clean.

Corrie sprang out of bed and quickly put on her clothing. She took all of her other possessions and shoved them into her pillow case. She gently placed two crackers in a folded napkin, then sat on her cot with her hat on her head, waiting for the next order. It did not come all morning; at noon she removed her hat and jacket and held them in her lap.

It was summer of 1944, and the afternoon sun peaked through the barred window and began to crawl across the far wall. Corrie wondered if they would ever be asked to depart the cell but she was not bored; imagining the Allies retaking Holland left much to her imagination.

It must have been nearly four o'clock when the shouting began again, guards moving through the prison opening doors and telling the women to stand in ranks of five. Finally, Corrie's door opened.

"Out! *Schnell!* No talking!"

The women prisoners gathered into the corridors, all holding tightly to their pillow cases and jubilant for this drastic change of routine. They were whispering to each other about an invasion. It must be the only reason to be departing; the Allies had surely landed on the continent and were retaking Holland.

Corrie was happy to be leaving Scheveningen. However, she was hoping they would not go too far from home. She shuddered to think about transport to Germany. Her thoughts went to Betsie; Corrie wondered where she might be.

The great mass of women finally all departed the prison and, after a short wait outside, loaded into a row of waiting busses. The busses had the seats removed and the windows painted over so no one could see inside. Corrie was marched into the third bus and stood closely packed with a group of women, all gripping their coats, hats and pillow cases.

The convoy moved forward, then wound through the streets of The Hague for several minutes until at last it stopped on the outskirts of town. The guards shouted at the women to depart the vehicle and form into lines.

Corrie stepped down out of the bus and saw they had arrived at a train yard. They were to be transported somewhere. *Oh please, may it not be Germany dear Lord,* Corrie prayed.

As the women all huddled together in large groups in the rail yard, Corrie looked around for Betsie again. Her eyes scanned the rows of women all lined up anticipating their next movement. The guards were roving around them telling the group to keep still and to stop talking but there were not enough guards for the job.

Corrie noticed one woman about her sister's height with the same chestnut bun as Betsie's. *Could it be her?* Corrie wanted to push through the crowd and maneuver toward that woman but dared not because of the intense yelling of the guards.

"Keep your heads forward! Eyes to the front! No talking!"

Corrie knew the sun would be down soon and then perhaps the darkness would grant her the opportunity she needed. A gentle sprinkle started as the last rays of sun hit the rail yard. The train finally arrived; it kept moving forward and backward until it was completely dark outside, and that is when they were ordered to board.

Corrie courageously made her move to find her sister. As the crowds of women pushed forward, Corrie elbowed her way to the left and moved diagonally through the crowd toward the direction of her beloved sister. Just before she got to the boxcar she came alongside the woman with the chestnut bun and grabbed her hand. The woman turned and gave Corrie the most delightful smile. *It was Betsie!* They hugged and interlocked arms as they boarded the train on iron steps and made their way to seats in the crowded compartment. They wept as they talked and retold the stories of their separate adventures in Scheveningen.

The train did not move until late that night but the Ten Boom sisters did not mind because they were reunited. Betsie shared with Corrie about her cellmates, Corrie shared with Betsie about her ant. Corrie was not surprised to learn that Betsie had given away everything she ever received from Nollie including her Bible which she tore up to distribute books of it to everyone she encountered.

Finally the train lurched ahead and began making its journey. Rumors spread among all the women as to where the train might be destined. At 4:00 in the morning the train stopped, the doors were opened and bright searchlights were aimed at the railcars.

The guards shouted in an attempt to control a mass movement out of the train and into the dense forest a few feet from the tracks.

"*Schneller! Aber Schnell!*" yelled the guards. "Out of the trains, form in ranks, move down the path. March! *Schnell!* Double-time!"

Corrie and Betsie stepped down from the train and were herded onto a road that entered the thick woods. Corrie noticed the mounted machine guns pointed in the prisoners' direction. There would be no argument from her. Though she was hungry and tired, she interlocked arms with Betsie and propelled both of them down the dark path with hundreds of other women.

For not quite an hour the women marched on the trail in the wooded darkness, five abreast while agitated guards yelled their threats. If a woman did not keep up with her line she was butted in the back with a rifle. Corrie made sure this never happened to her or Betsie. The terror march seemed to never end.

It is funny the things one thinks about when forced to march a mindless journey in the dark. Corrie ten Boom's thoughts turned to memories of the only relationship with the opposite sex she had ever experienced. It was several years earlier with a young man named Karel. He was a friend of her brother Willem. To a young girl — when Corrie and Nollie would visit their brother in college — Karel was someone who made Corrie's heart flutter when he seemingly took interest in her and delighted in her presence.

A few years later when Corrie finally finished secondary school, the relationship blossomed. They would take long walks down a country road and speak of their future together. Corrie imagined her life with Karel, but her dreams of marriage were interrupted by Willem telling her that Karel could never marry her.

"Karel must marry into money," said Willem. "His family would never allow him to marry a Ten Boom. Only someone with riches and a proper society upbringing would be acceptable to them."

This news broke Corrie's heart. And sure enough, though they continued to write for months, one day Karel showed up on the Beje doorstep with a proper Dutch fiancée beside him. How awkward that day was for Corrie! It was such a heartache and she had a hard time understanding why God would put her through this pain.

As she lay sobbing in bed that evening, her father, with that sweet cigar smell about him, came up the wooden steps and to her bedside to speak to her. Corrie wondered if he would say those empty words, how someday she would find someone else, but her father spared her the embarrassment.

"Corrie," Casper started, speaking gently, "do you know what hurts so very much? It's love. Love is the strongest force in the world and when it is blocked that means pain. There are two things we can do when that happens. We can kill the love so that it stops hurting. Or, Corrie, we can ask God to open up another route for that love to travel. Then perhaps God will give you His own love for Karel, a love nothing can prevent or destroy. Whenever we cannot love in the old, human way, Corrie, God can give us the perfect way."

Corrie was grateful for her father's reassuring words. They had unlocked the secret to understanding a very hard moment in her life. This key would be comforting to her again, she was sure, in darker moments like the one she was in now. When Corrie could not love others with her own love, perhaps she could love them with God's love, even if the moments were full of heartache.

The night of her father's talk Corrie prayed to God, "*Lord, I give to you the way I feel about Karel, my thoughts about our future — oh, you know! Everything! Give me Your way of seeing Karel instead. Help me to love him that way. That much.*"

As Corrie marched through the dark forest beside her sister where all around them were the harsh shouts from the guards, she thought of her prayer and the only earthly love of her life — Karel. She hoped he was doing well with his wife and that he was far away from the terror Corrie was experiencing that evening.

The group of prisoners finally arrived at a row of wooden barracks surrounded by barbed wire. The women were escorted through the fence and allowed to enter the wooden structures to rest just as the first rays of daylight began to reveal their surroundings. There were no beds in the buildings so the women lay on backless benches and had thoughts of food every time their stomachs started to rumble.

When they awoke, the bright, late-morning sun flooded into the windows. Yet the guards were no longer present to yell at them or give them directions. They were alone and allowed to talk at leisure for the first time in many months.

Eventually, three male guards came into the barracks building and shouted, "It is shower time. We need twenty of you at a time to undress immediately and come with us."

Twenty women near the door began to undress in front of the barking guards. Corrie was thankful she and Betsie were near the back of the building that housed 150 of the women. It would be a while until the guards came for them. Corrie watched the male guards walk around the naked women at the front. The ladies were made to stand and line up but they did not take them immediately out, obviously for the guards' enjoyment. Corrie thought it a cruel punishment to endure and was fearful for her moment to shower.

Soon, the next twenty were shouted at to undress. Corrie could see the smirking guards as they studied the naked women being led in and out of the barracks.

Twenty more were ordered to undress. Corrie felt so vulnerable, but before it was their turn, the guards ceased the shower drill. Apparently they had run out of gowns so they ordered everyone else to stay put, and they would receive showers at a future time.

Corrie breathed a sigh of relief. Before the sun went down a prison crew arrived with great vats of porridge. The women ravenously devoured their portions and then waited again for instructions. None would come.

They slept in the barracks that evening. Roll call in the morning came with more shouting from the guards. An outside march around the barracks followed, then they waited around with nothing to do. Corrie was very thankful to be near Betsie. It made the hours pass more pleasantly. A sweet young Jewess came to Corrie and asked if she would pray for her.

"Can you comfort me?" she asked. "I am so frightened."

Betsie prayed for the woman while Corrie held her hands.

On the third day, a female guard entered the barracks with a clipboard. Corrie recognized her as the General; the tall, stern guard from Scheveningen. The General took immediate charge of barracks life. She told them they were outside the main gate of a concentration camp established by the Third Reich, named Vught after the nearby town. Soon the women would be dealt with on a case-by-case basis. The General described how most would remain and work at the Vught factory, but some would be transported to another work camp.

The General made them stand at attention, sometimes for hours. Her cruel face and sarcastic comments made the time she was with them pure misery. Corrie was conscious of her constant fear of the General.

Crack!

The volley of shots pierced the normal sounds of the camp. Every few days shots were heard coming from outside the camp. Corrie was not afraid of the noise but it created panic in the barracks. Every woman who had a husband in the male area wondered if he was one of those killed each time they heard the firing squad.

With nothing to do during most of the day many of the women began to complain and grumble. Betsie decided to make a special society to help with the boredom and overall mood of the women around them. To be a member one had to pray and say encouraging remarks throughout the day. Membership required not speaking ill of anyone or being grumpy but living a quiet life of prayer instead.

Several of the women signed up for Betsie's club and prayed regularly for things to be better at Vught. *That was so Betsie!* Corrie thought.

Finally, after two weeks in the wooden barracks outside Vught, Corrie and Betsie, along with a dozen others, were called out by the General. They were given pink slips of paper and told to report to the general administration building at 9:00 a.m.

"Those pink slips mean that you will be going home," one man told them. "Those are your release papers."

"No. Are you telling the truth?" Corrie asked.

"Yes," said the man earnestly. He was one of the long-term prisoners there and a member of the food crew.

He should know, thought Corrie.

Betsie and Corrie grabbed each other and hugged in immense joy. They returned to the barracks to retrieve their few personal items and they were soon surrounded with friends wishing them well. Corrie felt bad for leaving the others at Vught. Some of the women with whom Betsie roomed at Scheveningen were crying for Betsie's good fortune. The sisters decided to share their belongings with the others to help ease their stay a little bit. Soon, their pillow cases were empty but their hearts full of hope.

"Surely the war will be over soon and you will all be released as well," encouraged Corrie.

They walked with two other women and ten men through the main gates and across the yard to the administration building. They waited in line until 9:00 a.m. when the door opened and they were officially processed. Their papers were examined and stamped. They were fingerprinted and questioned at one station and then led down the hall to another station where they were questioned again. Their papers were scrutinized at several stations. To Corrie it was a tedious process but she did not mind since the joy of her release still flooded her heart.

The group was led outside and brought to another building where they were met by a woman behind a desk. When Corrie's turn arrived her papers were looked at and she was given a brown envelope. Corrie opened it, turned it upside down, and out of the envelope slid several personal treasures: her Alpina watch, her mama's ring, and paper guilders. *Money! Perhaps to buy a rail ticket home?* Corrie wondered.

Corrie was shocked. She had not seen these items for many months and it finally convinced her that they were indeed going to be leaving soon and going home. *O Lord, thank you!*

The group was marched around again to different offices and held in line outside by the main gate of Vught. One member of their group was discovered to be a Jewess. She was separated from the group and forced to stand pitifully by herself and face the outer wall. She was scantily clad and Corrie thought she had never seen a more desolate human being. *Have mercy on Your ancient people, O Lord,* Corrie prayed.

When the group was left alone, one of the Dutchmen standing next to Corrie said, "If any of you have faith to pray then I would do it now."

"Yes, we can pray," said Betsie. "But we thought we were going to be released. Is this not so?

"No, it is not so," he replied with sympathy in his voice. "You are going to be brought into those nearby torture bunkers." He pointed across the yard at some cement bunkers with small barred windows.

This news iced the group's countenance. Betsie decided to sing a hymn. No one stopped her for no guards were near them.

After a long delay, the group was marched into yet another building where they were told to give up all of their valuables.

"Watches, money, purses, jewelry; please deposit everything at window C," said the man in charge.

"But we were just given these items," protested Corrie. *Are we not to be released?* Corrie thought but did not ask out loud. She could not bear the answer.

They were paraded from office to office and then led into the main courtyard again in sight of where the cement bunkers were located. The sun was setting by this time. They had marched around and waited in lines the entire day.

The group was close to the bunkers when a female guard in a military cape stopped them and shouted, "Halt!" The group stopped and she screamed to her counterpart nearby, "Please explain to these newcomers the function of the bunkers."

"These bunkers are for prisoners who fail to cooperate with the camp rules," the woman said. "The rooms are very small, about the size of a large footlocker. Hands are tied above the head all day, and not everyone appreciates this treatment," she said sarcastically.

Corrie watched as two guards helped transport a very skinny man outside from one of the cement bunkers. His eyes were sunken and rolled back in his head; he appeared alive because he was moving, but Corrie could not detect consciousness.

Corrie knew what atrocities had been committed in those bunkers. They all knew. People were essentially smothered to death. Such cruelty was too hard to grasp. *Father, please carry this for me,* Corrie prayed.

Corrie grabbed Betsie's arm and heard her sister whisper, "Corrie, if people can be taught to hate, then they can be taught to love. That is our mission here. We must find a way, you and I, no matter how long it takes." Corrie pondered Betsie's words as they were marched back to the barracks.

Corrie was selected to work at the Phillips factory located in Barracks 35. Betsie was told that because she looked frail she was allowed to stay in the barracks with the sick and elderly and sew camp uniforms. Corrie put on her blue worker overalls with a red stripe on the leg and reported for duty at the factory.

In the building there were rows of long plank tables with people sitting at stations tinkering with tiny radio parts. Corrie was assigned to sit near the front of the building and given the job of measuring small glass rods and arranging them in piles according to lengths. There were thousands of radio parts spread across the tables and each worker was assigned a special role in their assembly.

Corrie was amazed at how diligently every worker performed their task. She would have loved to get to know others working around her but it seemed that no one was allowed to talk. Everyone looked so serious about their work.

The Nazi officer in charge walked around the factory studying the workers, then he exited through the front door. At once the atmosphere changed. Everyone stopped working and the quiet, studious environment transformed. People pulled out paper and books from underneath their work benches. Some began to knit. People stood up and walked over to have conversations with friends. Several people gathered around Corrie to welcome her and find out who she was.

This social interaction was much appreciated. People were taking the time to get to know her. Corrie felt funny about not working but after a half hour the prisoner-foreman who was watching out the window for the workers began to whistle.

"We have a quota to fulfill today," he said pleasantly. "Back to work everyone."

Corrie learned that at noon each day the prisoners were given a gruel lunch of wheat and peas followed by a full half hour to walk around the grounds of the factory. She could not go to see Betsie because the living quarters were on the other end of the camp. Some of the women with husbands in the work camp would go to the fence to scan the yard for a glimpse of their spouse. Corrie would walk in the sunshine and think about Karel.

As the days progressed, Corrie learned that the foreman who looked out for everyone was Mr. Moorman. He was a former headmaster of a Catholic Boy's School. Corrie watched him go from station to station and encourage each worker. One day he came by her side and struck up a conversation.

"You are from Haarlem, is that correct?" Mr. Moorman asked.

"Yes sir," answered Corrie.

"I noticed that you have been curious about the work we do here," Mr. Moorman said. "I believe you are the only female worker who has followed her parts down the entire assembly line to see what happens to them."

"Yes, it is interesting to me," said Corrie. "I am a watchmaker."

"Really?" asked Moorman. "Well I can find you a more technical job then."

Mr. Moorman took her to the other end of the building where the final assembly of relay switches was done and said, "I think you will enjoy this work more. It is harder and more intricate but it will make the day go faster for you." He then sat her down and showed her exactly what needed to be done on the switches to get them operational.

Corrie was not used to this degree of kindness in prison. The man was like an older brother who had taken special interest in her. She was thankful for this encounter and for being offered a better task.

"I won't let you down," Corrie said before Mr. Moorman left.

Crack!

A volley of shots was heard throughout the entire camp. Several women in the Phillips factory screamed, hoping it was not their husband who had just been executed. Soon, everyone knew what was to follow … smoke would rise from the crematoria buildings nearby.

During the weeks that followed, Mr. Moorman continued to check up on Corrie. One day he noticed a row of assembled relay switches in front of her. They were all perfectly assembled and in ready-working condition. Corrie was proud of her work but was surprised when Mr. Moorman gave her a lecture.

"Dear watch lady! Please remember for whom you are making these switches. These will be used in German fighter planes!"

Mr. Moorman reached in front of Corrie and pulled a wire out of one of her completed parts. Then he grabbed another switch and twisted a glass tube from its assembly. "Now, solder them back together wrong, and don't let me catch you working this hard again," he said with a slight wink.

Corrie did not know whether to laugh or cry. She was berated for doing too good of a job. She decided to take it in the spirit it was given. Mr. Moorman was a smart man who looked out for all his workers. He risked having defective parts leave his plant, which made him brave, but Corrie felt for the man. She learned recently that during the very week she and Betsie arrived at Vught, Mr. Moorman's twenty-year-old son had been shot at the camp. What pain he must feel, but never showed. *Lord, please help him,* Corrie prayed.

———◆◆———

As the summer of 1944 labored on, Corrie counted down the days to September 1st. She had heard that people in prison for stealing ration cards were to spend only six months in confinement. She talked to Betsie about this when she would return from the factory, hopeful that this rumor would hold true for them. But Betsie did not appear to care much about leaving and seemed content with the ministry work of prayer and Bible studies they held in their barracks. Corrie was amazed at her sister's peacefulness in confinement, as if being at Vught was just as good as being at the Beje.

Corrie always looked forward to the end of the work day and returning to the barracks from the factory. She would tell Betsie all about the people she worked with, including an intense communist woman named Floor. Mrs. Floor was eight months pregnant yet would never eat her ration of bread each morning. She would slip it through the fence to her husband during lunch break or the morning march.

Corrie watched the undernourished expectant mother and knew she needed strength for her baby. She gave Mrs. Floor her morning bread but that bread also ended up going to Mr. Floor. August brought an increase in the sounds of the firing squad. At the end of August, Corrie noticed a full piece of breakfast bread on Mrs. Floor's empty work station one day. Mrs. Floor's baby had been born early that morning and died within a few hours. Mr. Floor had died the night before.

Betsie would also update Corrie on what she learned from those who stayed in the barracks with her. One day she told Corrie a very disturbing story. A woman in her sewing group had been betrayed by a man named Jan Vogel. The woman was from the city of Ermelo and told Betsie that the man, also from Ermelo, had sided with the Gestapo there and betrayed many people working in the underground, including this woman and her entire family. When he was exposed to the other residents in Ermelo as a traitor, he moved to Haarlem and began to work with Willemsen and Kapteyn.

The name was starting to jostle in Corrie's mind and the story was helping put together pieces of the puzzle. The man who had betrayed the Beje operation was named Jan Vogel. He had visited the Beje the day of the raid, and Betsie had woken up Corrie to speak to him when she was sick in bed. Corrie remembered his shifty eyes that never met hers and his lack of confidence; her gut told her not to trust the man, and she was proven right. *Why hadn't she trusted her instincts?*

Corrie had a terrible time receiving this news. Her mind raced to her father suffering in the hospital on the day of his death without family or friends by his side, and of Mary Itallie who had escaped from the hiding place in the Beje but then was soon after arrested on a city street. Corrie had no doubt that if Jan Vogel stood before her right now she could kill him with her own hands. Little did she realize how these feelings would set her off in a downward spiral of emotions.

That evening Corrie could not read her Bible, could not pray, and could not lead the prayer meeting.

"You lead the prayer meeting tonight, Betsie," said Corrie. "I have a headache."

Corrie's entire body ached with violent feelings against the man who had betrayed her. She could not sleep that night because her mind fumed with anger. She tossed and turned in her tiny space on the bunk all night.

Corrie was tired the next day but forced her way through her work. She did not sleep the next night either. By the end of the week she was a physical and emotional wreck. Her supervisor, Mr. Moorman, stopped by to see what was ailing her. Corrie unloaded her pain and frustration about Jan Vogel, yet it did not make her feel better.

What Corrie could not understand was why Betsie was not angry. There was no rage or irritation in her life. She slept soundly and led the Bible study of women as if nothing was wrong. This began to fester in Corrie's mind and it bugged her to the point that she had to bring it up with her sister in the small hours one night.

"Betsie, you have certainly heard me toss and turn each night, haven't you?" asked Corrie. There was no way Betsie could avoid it. Because of overcrowding, three prisoners shared one cot.

"Yes, I am aware that you have not been sleeping soundly," answered Betsie.

"Betsie, aren't you angered with knowing about Jan Vogel?" asked Corrie to her older sister. "Doesn't it bother you?" Corrie knew she was being indignant because she could not control her angry tone, but at that point it did not matter to her.

"Oh yes, Corrie," replied Betsie. "It bothers me terribly. I have felt for him ever since I knew. I pray for him whenever his name comes to mind. How dreadfully he must be suffering!"

How dreadfully he must be suffering? Corrie could not get that comment out of her head. Who was her sister? Was she human? This was not the response Corrie expected. Corrie laid awake for some time thinking about what Betsie said. How could she care so much about how *he* was suffering? What about *our* suffering? What about what that man did to our family and friends?

It took a long while before Corrie finally realized in her soul that she had destroyed Jan Vogel over and over again with her thoughts. *Was Betsie gently telling me that I am just as guilty as he is before our all-seeing God?* Corrie certainly knew that her health had been affected by her thoughts ever since she knew her betrayer's name. *Could God be reproving me that I have murdered Jan Vogel with my heart and tongue?* Corrie wondered.

"Lord Jesus," Corrie began in a whispered voice to herself, "I forgive Jan Vogel as I pray that You will forgive me. I have done him great damage. Bless him now, and his family."

That night, for the first time since she learned of Jan Vogel, Corrie felt at peace and slept deep and undisturbed until the morning whistle summoned the prisoners to roll call.

Crack!

More rifle volleys outside the camp. Then, an earlier than usual 3:30 a.m. roll call because a prisoner was late to evening check-in. Corrie's back ached as she stood at parade attention for nearly two hours. It was followed with black bread and coffee, then the march to the Phillips factory to work for twelve hours.

Evening check in. A meager supper of more bread and gruel. Bible study and prayer with Betsie and the other women. Roll call at 5:00 a.m. Then the march to the Phillips factory for another long day of work. Daily life was becoming routine and monotonous. There seemed to be little hope for change, until one day when distant explosions to the west caught everyone's attention.

"It is the Allies coming to rescue us," one said.

"Perhaps it is the Princess Irene Brigade," said another of the prestigious Dutch Army unit that had escaped to England during Holland's five-day-war.

"We will be rescued by the end of the week," said a third.

It was hard for Corrie not to get her hopes up. One thing that kept everyone sober was the continual sound of the firing squad. The prisoners knew exactly what that meant. Another factor foreboding change was the increased testiness of the guards. More and more prisoners were beaten for not remaining at attention or falling behind during a march. The elderly and the ill were treated mercilessly.

Mid-September rolled around and the misery continued. One day, however, the camp awoke to explosions closer than ever before. The guards shouted. The prisoners emptied out of the barracks for formation. It was a chaotic day. And still, the work at the factory was supposed to get done but no one could concentrate on anything except the possibility of being freed.

Right after lunch the factory was emptied and the prisoners were told to go back to the barracks and wait. Rumors were flying. Hope was held in the hearts of the camp workers as they rejoined their friends and family members who stayed behind each day and sewed. As the afternoon progressed there was wild anticipation of the Allies storming in to set them free. Optimism was high; the question was when would the troops arrive? But then everything changed.

Over the loud speaker on the men's side of the camp, a monotone voice began to read names. The recent surge of hope was replaced with dread. Some of the women feared their husbands may not live to see their freedom. A wild fright went off inside each married woman who heard her husband's name. Name after name was called and then the loudspeaker grew quiet.

In the eerie silence that followed, many women clutched each other in desperation. No noise came from either camp. The women exchanged panicked glances with each other. One could cut the air with a knife. Fear gripped everyone.

Crack!

Rifle fire; the first volley.

Crack!

The second volley.

Crack!

The rifle volleys lasted for two hours. Two hours of torture for the women of Vught who wept for their loved ones. The prisoners lost count, but certainly hundreds of men were going into the afterlife, and perhaps just hours before they were all to be freed. It was too much for the human mind to endure. *Would they be taken outside and shot as well?* Corrie wondered.

At 6:00 a.m. the guards woke the prisoners and told them to grab their things, they were leaving Vught. As if in a fog the women scurried around the barracks and filled their pillow cases with everything they possessed. Then they formed in ranks on the camp yard, marched through the concentration facility and past the rows of barbed wire outside the Vught gate. The women found themselves now marching through the woods on the same path they had taken that first night of dread when they arrived.

"March! *Schnell!* No talking!" the guards yelled.

In less than an hour they arrived at the train tracks. There were boxcars lined up as far as they could see in each direction. More yelling! The women were ordered to immediately step up into the cars.

Corrie helped Betsie into a boxcar that had a machine gun mounted on top, and they maneuvered near the back where there was a large pile of stacked bread loaves. Corrie tried not to think of what the bread meant; they were in for a long trip. She could not allow herself to think of going into Germany but there could be no other explanation for the bread.

The guards kept forcing the women into the car. Even when the Ten Boom sisters felt there was no more room, more women were added. The car could hold thirty and there were at least sixty squeezed into the small space. Still more women. The ones in the back began to shriek in terror.

"Stop! Stop! You are crushing us!" they screamed.

Incredibly, the guards still forced in more women. There must have been over eighty inside the dark boxcar before they slid the heavy door closed and clanged the iron bolts into place. It was miserable with so many women wedged into the small space. Some of the women wept and a few fainted, but because they were standing so close to each other they did not fall down. There was no extra space to shift around. Some were still screaming at the guards. Panic set in quickly.

Corrie prayed, *Please Lord, allow us to endure this hardship.*

Then she heard Betsie whisper to her, "I am thankful that father is in heaven today."

"Yes," replied Corrie. *Thank you Father, for sparing Papa this agony.*

Some of the women in the middle began to suffocate. There was no moving air. The train remained still. Women clawed at the walls finding nails to wiggle free. Using the sharp points they made the tiny holes larger. Soon there were several small holes in the wood of the boxcar and a little bit of fresh air entered the foul-smelling cabin.

It took hours for the train to depart. Women were relieving themselves right where they stood. The train moved a little then stopped. Moved a little more. Lurched to a stop. Someone near one of the small holes looked outside and saw men walking around with railroad track parts. They were fixing the line as they traveled.

When the train was moving again, the boxcar was suddenly being pummeled with what sounded like hail. *Takka, takka, bratatat,* the sharp staccato noise hit all around them. A moment later more hail. After the third onslaught on the car, the machine gun above their roof opened fire. The women then realized it was not a hailstorm but bullets hitting their rolling chamber. Some of them cheered for the Princess Irene Brigade. Others moaned, miserable and wondering what they were in for next.

The train kept moving. At last someone looking out a small gap of the side paneling shouted out, "We're going through Emmerich!"

The women wept at the news, for they were now in Germany.

CHAPTER 22

Scorched Earth

During the days immediately following the failed putsch against Germany's Chancellor, thousands of people were either arrested, disappeared, fled, committed suicide or were shot. Entire families — wives and children of military and government leaders — were taken into custody and sent to concentration camps without a trial. Violent acts of retribution against anyone suspected of disloyalty were mostly hidden from the public.

In the cellars of the Gestapo's Prinz Albrechtstrasse headquarters in Berlin, military officers and civilians were interrogated. Many high-ranking officers appeared before the People's Court — where evidence seemed irrelevant — then hanged for treason. Once hanged, the bodies were hauled by meat hooks and pictures were taken to show the Führer. This went on for months until an Allied bomb fell directly into the court, killing the corrupt judge and incinerating the piles of papers of the current docket of defendants.

For Albert Speer, it was the day after Operation Valkyrie when he realized his relationship with the Führer had irrevocably changed. Finding Speer's name on the conspirators' list of future leaders created a black cloud surrounding not only him, but his Armament Ministry work associates. He could not concentrate on his Ministry work as fear gripped Speer's thoughts for his family who could be collected by Himmler's Gestapo at any moment.

On July 21, 1944, Adolf Hitler called a celebratory meeting at his Wolf's Lair bunker. All his important Cabinet Ministers were invited to meet with Hitler to offer their congratulations at surviving the assassination attempt. Speer arrived in Rastenburg and waited to shake the Führer's hand inside the windowless bunker with cement walls that were sixteen feet thick.

While standing in line, not one person would speak to Speer. A few men even hissed at him. When it was Speer's turn to speak to Hitler, he shook the Führer's flaccid left hand — Hitler's right arm still in sling — but cut his remarks short, noticing the Reich Chancellor was not paying attention to him.

Immediately after Speer stepped off, Hitler welcomed Speer's two deputies, Karl Saur and Xaver Dorsch, with inflated cordiality. Speer sidled into the reception room and took a seat. Those sitting nearby instantly stood up and moved away from him. Speer could not shake the nervous impulse that all eyes were on him and judging him.

Finding himself alone and uncomfortable, Speer then moved to a side room where, upon his entrance, the conversation immediately ceased. Everyone stood and exited the room, passing Speer without a hello.

The last person to leave, one of Hitler's adjutants named Julius Schaub, walked by Speer and said coolly, "Now we all know who was behind the assassination attempt." Then he walked out, leaving Speer alone.

Albert Speer was dumbfounded. Then, he learned that his two deputies were invited by Bormann to the afternoon tea with Hitler, but Speer, unsummoned, spent the time alone. He decided to work on an updated armaments report and figure out a strategy for how to survive current perceptions. He could not simply nurse a bruised ego, the events made his rejection something deeper, more personal.

The next morning attitudes were somewhat less tense. Hitler greeted Speer with forced cordiality, saying he looked forward to his report later on that day. Speer realized that being on the conspirators' list of future cabinet members cost him dearly. The only thing that prevented his arrest by Himmler's SS was the question mark someone had written next to his name.

Speer thought this ironic; that he was indeed a question mark. He had questioned himself many times with where he stood. Would he have sided with the conspirators had he been approached? Was that what was to be asked of him at the lunch with Colonel von Stauffenberg? Or would he have turned them in? He did not know the answer and it was this mind angst that gnawed at him. *Can't I stand for anything, one way or the other?* Speer wondered.

One thing Speer found amusing when it was relayed to him was how an argument among Hitler's staff just after the bombing had quite embarrassed the Chancellor. The dislodged Italian Prime Minister, Benito Mussolini, was scheduled to visit the Wolf's Lair the afternoon of the bomb blast. Even after all the damage to the bunker and the injury to the Führer himself, Hitler decided to keep the visit, much to his later regret.

Hitler walked and talked with the Duce as if on tour, showing his guest the wrecked conference room where the bomb blew, and pointing to where the charred wood was still smoking. Hitler also showed Mussolini the pants he had been wearing that were torn to shreds. With singed hair, burned legs, and his right arm badly bruised, the proud Führer told his guest that this was the climax of all the assassination attempts against him; yet he survived.

Mussolini was horrified that something like that could happen at the highest headquarters. But the Führer was emboldened. Having escaped death a third time, Hitler was convinced that it was a sign he was promised victory. "Fate," he said, "was surely preserving me for a special assignment."

The humorous part, Speer thought, was what transpired when Hitler sat with Mussolini for tea with some of his cabinet members. In the room was Admiral Karl Dönitz, Chief of the Navy; Reichsmarschall Göring, Chief of the Air Force; General Keitel, Chief of the Army; and the German Foreign Minister, Joachim von Ribbentrop. The men began to yell at each other when they learned that the putsch was still in play in Berlin. Without sensitivity to their Italian visitor, their voices grew louder and louder.

"It is the Army who is at fault for our losses in the East," Admiral Dönitz exclaimed. "And now, with this plot, they are trying to take over the government!"

"Do not blame the Army," argued Keitel.

"Why not?" asked Göring. "Isn't it Army officers who are right now taking over operations in Berlin? You don't see my Luftwaffe officers involved in this sort of coup."

"Unfortunately, we don't see the Luftwaffe in the *air* either," answered Keitel.

"Hear, hear," shouted Dönitz. "If the Luftwaffe could keep away a third of the Allied bombers we would be in much better shape. As it is, it seems we don't even have an air force these days. The navy, on the other hand…"

"That's enough out of you," Göring interrupted. "I'll have you know I flew with von Richthofen in the last war and I won't have you denigrate our brave fighters. Besides, if our foreign minister could do a better job at diplomacy we wouldn't be in this mess."

"Don't blame me for your failures," shrieked Ribbentrop. "I had nothing to do with this plot, and it was certainly a military putsch if anything."

"Shut your whimpering mouth, Ribbentrop!" yelled Göring. "You dirty little champagne salesman."

At this point, Speer heard that Göring raised his field marshal's baton as if to hit Ribbentrop, but Keitel and Dönitz maneuvered between the two.

"Treat me with respect!" cried Ribbentrop. "I'm still the Foreign Minister, and my name is *von* Ribbentrop."

The ambassadorial milieu Hitler hoped to achieve was incurably destroyed. Though his right ear was deaf and in pain, the disturbance greatly unnerved him. The fidgeting Führer began to chew on multi-colored pills as the arguing increased.

Then he chewed at his bomb-blackened fingernails with his teeth, biting them down to the quick.

"Traitors in the bosom of their own people deserve the most ignominious deaths — and they shall have it!" the Reich Chancellor exclaimed. "Exterminate them, yes, exterminate all of them!"

This outburst sobered the room. An aide opened a side door to let in a breeze. Hitler gripped the sides of his chair. Mussolini put on his coat. For a moment the two leaders sat still in silent reverie. Tea time was over.

───※───

As the days passed, and more evidence was gathered, the Gestapo learned that it was not a small band of disgruntled Army officers. It was a widespread assassination attempt by German generals from Russia to France, and leading officials from varying positions within government who wanted the Führer dead. Ringleaders who led bands of resistance followers were killed immediately or imprisoned to be sentenced at the People's Court. Chief conspirators were dealt with severely and extended family members were spared no mercy, including at least a dozen women over seventy.

These new discoveries revealed wide-spread sentiment against the Führer. Thinking he was beloved by all of Germany, this news sent his ego and mood into a tailspin.

"My life is full of sorrow and so heavily laden," Hitler told one of his secretaries. "Death itself would be a salvation for me."

Bormann brought the dog he had given the Führer as a gift three years prior.

"Look me in the eyes, Blondi," said Hitler. "Are you also a traitor like all these generals?" The Alsatian wagged her tail with endearment for her master.

Goebbels helped the Führer's feelings of persecution with a radio speech soon after the assassination attempt. He portrayed the failed putsch and Stauffenberg as a crazy effort by a satanic leader of a small clique of military officers, and that it did not represent the Wehrmacht as a whole. He cited that these few rebels were in union with the English to overthrow the government and end the war.

Speer knew that Hitler had long been terrified of an assassination attempt. One time, before the war, the two were on a touring adventure in a large open-top Mercedes sitting side by side. Hitler turned partially to Speer and said, "I feel safest from assassins in the car. Even the police are not told my destination before I leave. An assassination has to be planned long in advance; driving time and the route all have to be known. But speaking engagements are different. I'm afraid that someday I will be killed by a sniper while delivering a speech in a meeting hall. There's no way to dodge that sort of thing. The only thing to protect me is the crowd's enthusiasm. No one would venture to raise a weapon because my admirers would knock him down and trample him to death."

Speer pondered several episodes of Hitler saying he feared that he would one day become a victim by a close associate or friend, that this would keep him awake sometimes wondering who it would be. Ironically now, Albert Speer was the one kept awake wondering when an SS agent would come for him in the middle of the night because he was believed to be one of the conspirators. Perhaps some new discovery would implicate him further as a friend of the wrong person, or because of something a tortured conspirator might say under duress. The other troubling aspect was that the gains Speer had made just months before as a Third Reich Minister were quickly reversed.

Because of his faithfulness to the Führer during the July 20th attempt, Joseph Goebbels was given extraordinary new powers. As such, it seemed that everyone reported to him, including Speer.

In September, Speer wrote Hitler a letter regarding the factories he oversaw. He explained that the Industrialists were upset with intrusions at their work sites. They wanted an immediate cessation of the SS interfering with work production and for their factory managers to be the ones overseeing operations. Hitler needed to emphasize that the chain of command must be followed stringently for work production to be maintained. Speer pressed the issue that labor given to him for arms production must be kept in the factories working, and not diverted to other efforts.

When Speer handed his letter to the Führer in person, he glanced at it without a word. Hitler pressed the signal button, and when the adjutant arrived he was handed the document and ordered to give it to Bormann.

When the adjutant departed, Hitler said to Speer, "Goebbels and Bormann will decide together what to do."

Speer was mortified.

Now there is a two man super-Cabinet above the regular Cabinet?

Soon, Bormann called Speer into his office. Goebbels was already there waiting for him. Both looked anxious to receive Hitler's Armaments Minister.

Goebbels declared, "Listen Speer, as of July 25th I am the Reich Trustee for the Total Mobilization of War. Hitler decreed it himself. I am going to make full use of this new authority to command you and your contributions to the war effort, including factory production."

"Yes," said Bormann. "Speer, you need to understand that Hitler wants it this way. You shouldn't bother him with these petty worker requests any longer. Everything should come through us first. Production will be fine, you'll see. With the doctor and me in overwatch, we will bring new efficiencies to armaments production."

Goebbels gave Bormann a knowing look, stood, and walked to the other side of the room and then turned to face Speer again.

"Here is the new reality, Speer," said Goebbels. "You will no longer go to the Führer to try to influence him directly. Everything must come to us first, and we will decide if the Führer should be bothered with it. You see how his hand shakes. The attempt on his life changed him. He needs us to filter everything for him now."

Speer glanced at Bormann, noticing his ghoulish grin. This was the moment Bormann had waited for since Speer's recovery from his illness. Speer was now put in his place, in the back of the line behind Bormann and Goebbels.

Speer had an odd feeling that crept over him; he remembered that it was just a few months ago when he, Göring and Goebbels were in union against Bormann,

Keitel and Lammers. And now, because of the assassination plot in which he was not involved, Speer was left out of power and at the hand of Bormann. It was precisely this quickly shifting sand of power that aided Speer's feeling of frustration and defeat. He felt in freefall, not knowing where he would land next.

After more lecturing, the two Nazis concluded with a stern warning for Speer about his grumbles. They would tolerate no more attempts at sabotaging the war because of petty labor issues. And with that, Speer was promptly dismissed.

In the weeks that followed, Albert Speer decided to throw himself into his work to get his mind off the current politics within the Reich. His family, who had hardly seen him since the assassination attempt, would have to take a temporary back seat. Speer promised himself he would make it up to them when the war concluded. For now, he needed to work on Hitler; convincing him to agree to more fighters was Speer's top priority in aircraft production.

As such, Speer decided to align with General Adolf Galland, the fighter commander and highly decorated flying ace who had flown over 700 combat missions during the war. Perhaps the two of them could convince Hitler to produce more fighter planes, and they were desperately needed. The Allied bombings had not subsided. In fact, since the Americans were now in the south and the west, their air attacks had increased and Göring's Luftwaffe had done nothing to deter them. Both Galland and Speer knew Germany needed to step up fighter production to make a difference in the air war.

"Bombers, bombers, bombers!" shouted Hitler whenever the subject came up. The man was singularly focused.

Speer knew that Hitler did not understand the importance of the smaller and sleeker fighters, and perhaps it was because of his limited understanding of current warfare. Messerschmitts and the newer Focke-Wulf 190 fighters were drastically improved even since 1941. Their strength, ability for high-altitude combat and many additional enhancements made them essential to modern warfare. German fighters were necessary to keep the Allied bombers in check. Even if the Reich lost two or three fighters to every bomber the Allies put up, it would greatly reduce the ground damage to the factories and logistics routes.

In addition to the thousands of bombers, Speer was producing more fighters in 1944 than had been achieved in all the other years of the war combined. The Reich started the war with only 770 fighter planes. Now, Speer had over 2,000 fighters a month rolling off the assembly line. But the Luftwaffe needed even more.

General Galland and Speer flew to Rastenburg to see Hitler at the Wolf's Lair. They needed to speak to him about an order just decreed whereby all aircraft were to be redirected to the western front. These two men knew that the planes were needed to protect the factories inside Germany and the eastern regions. If sent to France, the planes would be systematically wiped out because of the air superiority of the Americans and British. This was an unacceptable outcome to Speer and Galland.

Hitler agreed to meet the men and hear them out. Even while producing as much evidence as he could to promote his position, Speer noticed that Hitler was growing increasingly tense. The Führer chewed his fingernails, fidgeted his hands, and kept folding and unfolding his arms. Near the end of Speer's presentation, the Führer was red in the face and could contain himself no more.

The Reich Chancellor interrupted Speer's concluding remarks by shouting, "Operative measures are my concern! Concern yourself with your armaments! This is none of your business!"

Then, just as suddenly, and with great energy, the Führer hissed at the men as they further tried to convince him. In a rage Hitler screamed, "I have no more time for you!" And he motioned his hand for them to leave.

Speer was dumbfounded. He could not imagine why Hitler was being so adamant on this point. Speer felt he presented a thorough case stating that every available fighter plane should stay inside Germany's air space to combat the bombers and not be sent west. *What had inspired such wrath and obstinacy?*

The next morning Galland and Speer were set to depart headquarters when Julius Schaub, Hitler's adjutant who had recently snubbed Speer, informed the men they were to report immediately to the Führer. *What now?* Speer wondered. He quickly found out as they walked into the Chancellor's office only to be barked at again.

In a wrathful tone, Hitler declared, "I have decided that no more planes will be produced at all. The fighter arm is to be completely dissolved. Stop aircraft production! Stop it at once, understand?"

Looking directly at Speer, Hitler snarled at him, "You're always complaining about your lack of skilled workers and party interference. Now you will have plenty for production of bombers and anti-aircraft guns. I want you to take all the materials now used for fighters and produce additional bombers and flak, then you will have plenty of workers and raw materials. I will hear no more complaints from you. Fighter production is finished. This is an order! In the future, send me your deputy, Saur, to speak on these issues, not you! Now I want you two to depart at once!"

Their meeting instantly concluded, the dismissed men were escorted from the bunker. They went into the tea room and took a hard drink. Galland was beside himself with anger. The fighter corps he led had just been disbanded by Germany's Chancellor. He could not believe his Führer would sabotage his own war efforts with such an irrational decision.

Speer retained his composure. He had seen Hitler make decisions in anger many times. Usually the Führer's mind would change the next day when he had calmed down. "Don't worry too much about what was said in there. Saur and I will keep producing fighters."

"How are you going to do that?" asked Galland.

"We will convince him when he calms down," answered Speer. "It might take some time, but leave that to us. For one thing, the industrial facilities we use to make fighter planes cannot be applied to the production of anti-aircraft guns. We have plenty of guns, we just need more ammunition for them. He will understand all this one day soon."

Somewhat hopeful, Galland relaxed a little. The men, thrown out of Hitler's office moments earlier in humiliation, left the tea room in more positive spirits. They would return to Berlin and resume their duties. Nothing would change at the factories.

Karl Saur reported to Hitler the next day. Hitler's message to him was the same. Speer decided to travel with Saur on a future visit to try and convince Hitler out of his absurd demands. When Speer approached the topic of fighter jet production he was rebuffed again.

"Maybe I have not made myself clear," said Hitler. "I want more flak production and less fighters being made."

Back in Berlin, Speer decided to flagrantly disobey the Führer for the first time working as one of his Cabinet members. He called his staff together and told them, "For the good of Germany, for the remainder of the war, we are going to send fighter jet production soaring. With increased fighters we can make headway against the greatest threat Germany faces. We will send their bombers to the ground when they seek to torment us from the air." But in the back of his mind, Speer wondered about the consequences he would face for his blatant defiance.

As fall began, Speer was given an ominous warning from a Nazi leader friend who worked in southwestern Poland. His friend strongly advised him not to accept an invitation by the party to inspect the concentration camps around Auschwitz.

"Do not, under any circumstances go visit there," Speer's friend said. "You have to promise me this."

"Why, what is going on?" asked Speer.

"I cannot say. In fact, I do not want to think of it ever again. I have been exposed to something there that I am not permitted to describe. In fact, I wouldn't even know how. Just promise me, Speer that you will never go to those camps. This is important."

"Okay," Speer promised, confused as to what could be so horrible there. It was a simple agreement and Speer tried to put it out of his head.

The discussion led him to remember a time when Hitler, looking out a window in Berlin, said thoughtfully to those standing behind him, "The bridges behind us are burnt."

What was eerie was in how he made the statement, quietly, calmly and resolute, as if Germany had intentionally committed an unforgivable sin. A sin which would unite the world against them.

Speer laid awake that night wondering if the sin Hitler spoke of had something to do with Auschwitz.

The American and British armies continued to steamroll through Western France toward Germany. Hitler decided to take action to slow their progress. Making an irrational decision that would affect Germany for a generation or more, the

Führer issued orders for the complete obliteration of all industrial installations on the western edge of his Reich empire. It was a policy of destruction called scorched earth used to prevent the enemy from utilizing Germany's own resources during their advance. Hitler did not want the Americans to reinforce with supplies found on the occupied land.

But it was more than just military supplies to be destroyed. Something sinister embered in Hitler's mind when he decided that if portions of Germany were too weak to hold off the Allies, they needed to be punished and left to their own defenses. It was for the greater good.

Banks, grocery stores, gas stations and government buildings were scheduled to be razed. All railroad switch houses were to be destroyed, the tracks torn up and twisted, and the bridges demolished. The electrical systems were to be bombed, fuel burned, gas and water lines anihilated, essentially total doom. There would be no telephone communications available, and no fuel or electricity except for what the Allies brought with them. The demolition of all mines along with the steel industry was to be carried out as well. This scorched earth principle was to be viciously applied in the Ruhr, Germany's western frontier.

Albert Speer knew that this would bring about the long-term ruination of the German people. When the war concluded it would take a generation to be able to rise up and produce again. People could not work at factories if they were all burned to the ground. If Hitler had his way, there would be no basic amenities for those fellow countrymen unfortunate enough to live in the broad swath of the advancing Allies.

Not only would basic necessities be eliminated for millions of people, but for historical purposes, all public records in society would be burned as well. There would be no more ration cards, birth certificates, marriage licenses, property records, bank accounts or death registries. Churches, libraries, banks, museums, theater houses and shopping stores — all were to be burned and flattened. The historical significance would be vast and permanent. This was now the dark desire of Germany's Chancellor and protector.

"Not a stalk of wheat to feed them, not an ounce of oil to speed them; they will find nothing but death, annihilation and hatred to greet them," Hitler dictated to the German press chief.

Speer was furious. He met with the Chancellor at his headquarters to see if he could talk some sense into him.

"Mein Führer, the people are being forced to evacuate from their homes and towns," informed Speer. "Many have only the clothes on their back; their children are starving on the journey."

"Don't interfere this time," came Hitler's stern reply. "You do not know what is going on. I am working to *save* the German people."

"They are being ruined!" pleaded Speer with uncharacteristic emotion.

"That is my concern!" barked Hitler. "If I take all the butchers, bakers and cheesemakers from the west I can put these men in the army, or have them work in the armaments factories. You do not understand, this is total war. I need to shut down operations in the west so we can use the manpower elsewhere."

"Sir, we cannot cease production in the Rhine-Westphalia factories," said Speer, followed by a sharp glare from Hitler. "These armaments plants must continue until the last moment or we will surely lose the war…"

"Do not make predictions on the outcome of our struggle!" shouted Hitler. "That is my concern."

"Forgive me, I'm not trying to be a strategist," said Speer apologetically. "I implore you to understand the position we are in with our factories. If we destroy them prematurely, not only will we cease to have the benefit of their production, but our own people will surely suffer as well. We must keep the hospitals supplied with medicine and power or the loss of life will be staggering."

Hitler sat in his chair and rubbed his trembling right arm. "Here it is, Speer, the one who has lost everything has to win everything. The people out west have the enemy at their front door. They will fight fanatically to win. It's the man who can be ruthless, not the coward, who wins. Only great individuals decide the course of history."

Hitler then leveled his head at Speer with his cheerless eyes and in an icy tone said, "I will not tolerate any more opposition, Speer. Anyone who disagrees with me from here on out is going straight to the gallows, without question. I hope this is clear. My dear Speer, don't worry about the destruction and stop letting the people's whining bother you."

The conversation was over. Speer was escorted by Bormann from the room and out of the building.

The Lion of Germany had spoken. However, Speer could not abide by this policy of destruction. He could not sit idly by and watch the suffering of his fellow Germans, it was morally wrong. Speer realized his split with Hitler had come. He did not want to be a question mark any longer but he did not know what to do next.

He decided to speak to Göring, the commissioner for financing the war. Perhaps Göring would have some insight on this lunacy and provide advice for Speer on his intent to disobey. He drove to Carinhall, not knowing what the Reichsmarschall might say, or how he would receive Speer.

Despite past differences, Göring greeted him warmly, "Herr Speer, it is good to see you. Ride with me."

The two were escorted in a carriage around the extraordinary property. Göring, wearing his green jerkin, looked more like a hefty Robin Hood in the leather sleeveless jacket than a cabinet minister to the Führer. He also sported a preposterous blade that was half sword, half knife.

Speer passionately explained his dilemma, "The people of the Ruhr are going through Hades, and it's only going to get worse. Hitler wants to cease all shipments of goods to the area because he believes it will soon be lost to the Allies. I am not going to obey this order. I cannot obey it. It would inflict unnecessary mass suffering on hundreds of thousands of our countrymen."

"Well," said Göring thoughtfully. "You have to obey the Führer. You don't have the option to disobey."

"Well, I'm not obeying!" countered Speer. Knowing this was perhaps the most courageous conversation he had ever had, Speer realized he was placing his future in the Reichsmarschall's hands.

Göring shook his head, "But surely you cannot pocket your Minister's salary and disregard the Führer's orders?"

Speer remained silent. *German people are suffering, why can't you see that?*

Göring then smiled, "Report sick! Take your family abroad! I would be prepared to transfer money for you to flee to Spain by way of Bernard. You can leave the Armament work to me."

"I can't do that," replied Speer. "I'm staying here, but I'm not obeying Hitler's order. It is our duty as leaders in the Reich to provide for the sustenance of our people."

The conversation stopped for a moment while Göring appeared deep in thought.

Eventually, the wealthy Nazi responded, "Well, then, do what you must. Nobody is going to hear about it from me. I'm no informer."

Their carriage rolled to a stop at a wooded park near the mansion. The two exited and began walking through the magnificent forest. Neither said anything for a while, both deep in thought about the war and their country.

Finally, Speer broke the silence. "I appreciate what you said about not informing."

Göring continued to walk. "Of course. You don't need to worry about that from me. You will have an easier time breaking from Hitler. I, however, must remain loyal."

Speer started to speak about loyalty to country but then swiftly changed his mind. The two walked a trail thickly covered with fallen leaves from the dense woods around them.

Göring continued. "Until the fighting ends I must stand alongside the Führer. But after the war, well that is a different matter. I suppose I will be treated with respect by the Americans since I tried to prevent this war at its beginning. Also, my ties with General Motors ought to help me."

Speer did not respond. He thought of the Russians in the East, making their way rapidly toward Germany. It would be just a matter of weeks before they crossed Poland and Speer shuddered to think of what would happen once they reached Berlin. The way Hitler treated Soviet POWs did not give Speer hope for any mercy.

He felt that the war was crashing down upon Germany ... and him. He had to do something, even if it was speaking to one of the most corrupt men he knew. Nonetheless, Speer appreciated the camaraderie shared with Göring that evening. It felt like one last pleasant time before the storm. He set his mind to do everything in his power to countermand Hitler and help save his fellow Germans from starving. He had no more doubts and was no longer a question mark.

In every man's life there is a fountain, one spring entirely his own. When he uncovers that rare opportunity to offer himself as a ransom — no matter how foolish or dangerous it might seem — he must act on it, or be rendered morally obsolete. The split had come; Speer's affections for Hitler had been silently and deeply sapped for months. He was now on a separate path, a perilous course where he jeopardized not only his own life, but the lives of his family and work associates.

CHAPTER 23

The Desert Fox

The Architect's mind raced with the recent reports given him regarding Albert Speer's contempt for Nazi order. Unfortunately, he had more pressing matters, like taking down a highly respected general.

During the chaotic days after the assassination attempt on Hitler's life, the Architect was instrumental in using his agents to round up those who were part of the Valkyrie conspiracy. Even merely the threat of the Architect coming to one's home in the middle of the night led several high-ranking generals to attempt suicide. Those who were captured alive were brought to the Gestapo dungeon in the basement of the Prinz Albrechtstrasse building in Berlin where the People's Court met. They were tortured and often induced to provide names of other high-ranking officers who were, even in the slightest bit, sympathetic to the conspiracy. If they survived, they were brought before a corrupt judge, then executed.

Two tortured generals implicated Erwin Rommel, a battle-tested general who was one of Adolf Hitler's favorites. The news sickened the Führer, but there would be no doubting the information the Architect had received from these two sources.

One high-ranking officer, General Carl-Heinrich von Stuelpnagel, the military commander in charge of German-occupied France, came under question. On the day of the assassination attempt, he incarcerated all the SS leaders in his region, desperately hoping Stauffenberg would be successful in his attempt to kill Hitler and implement Valkyrie. Immediately after the failed attempt, Stuelpnagel was recalled to Berlin for questioning. Knowing what awaited him, and with no intention of allowing himself to be interrogated, he drove to Verdun, a small city in northeastern France. Alongside a canal he pulled out his revolver and attempted to shoot himself in the head.

When his aides waiting in the car heard the shot ring out they ran to discover their boss floundering in the water with one eye shot out. At the Verdun hospital his other eye was removed because it was severely damaged as well. Blind and hopeless, Stuelpnagel was escorted to the People's Court. As he lay on a cot before the judge, he was pronounced guilty and taken to the cellar to be strangled to death. During the torturous interrogation before his death, the delirious Stuelpnagel shrieked out a name ... *Rommel*.

This was not the first time General Erwin Rommel's name was mentioned. The other officer to implicate Rommel under torture was Lieutenant Colonel Caesar von Hofacker. Hofacker was made of the same ilk of Stauffenberg and rebellious until the end. Standing before the judge at the People's Court he defiantly said that his one regret was not having carried out the assassination attempt himself. Hofacker was sentenced to be hanged. Before his execution, during his intense struggle with the Gestapo, he was tortured and drugged to such an extent that before he breathed his last, they extracted from him the name of Rommel. With more torture the Gestapo heard from Hofacker that General Rommel sided with the conspirators in Berlin and said they could count on him if Operation Valkyrie was carried out.

This was all the evidence the Architect needed. He sent his men to stakeout the Rommel residence. As soon as he received a definitive answer from the Führer he would make his move.

On a pleasant fall day in October, Rommel was home on convalescent leave. He had been wounded again, this time by the Allied advance in France. His skull sustained shards of shrapnel and was fractured at both temples. The Desert Fox, as he was called because of his fox-like sneak attacks, recklessly fought near the front lines as a means to encourage his men. He had escaped death on several occasions, yet always managed to return to the front, more emboldened to fight for his beloved Germany. While home on this occasion, the general went for a walk in the woods with his fifteen-year-old son, Manfred, and noticed they were being followed. With top generals around him disappearing after Valkyrie Rommel knew he was under suspicion. Now he realized his life was in danger.

The Architect finally received the news he needed; he had been given permission to seize Rommel at his home. He planned everything to the last detail. At noon, on October 14, 1944, Rommel's home was surrounded by the SS with five armored cars and snipers in the woods. The Architect sent word ahead of time to the Rommel family that these men were coming, on orders from the Führer, to discuss his next assignment. Two highly trusted and loyal SS generals drove up the driveway to execute the mission. In their possession they had some cyanide capsules to offer to Rommel if he chose.

When the men arrived they spoke to General Rommel alone in his study. It quickly became apparent they were not there to discuss his next mission. They explained to him that he was being charged with high treason against Hitler. Since Rommel was a national hero held in high esteem by the people, it would not be fitting to usher him to the People's Court to be made a public spectacle. If General Rommel decided to take his own life and save the Führer the embarrassment of the trial, he would be given state funeral honors and his family would remain unmolested.

After looking at the evidence against him, Rommel asked if he could take a few minutes to speak to his family and it was granted him. The general walked upstairs and into his bedroom where his wife, Lucia, was waiting. He gave her the news that he had been accused of high treason and the options the SS gave him. When he told Lucia the decision he had made, the two embraced and kissed, then Rommel walked to Manfred's room where he delivered the same verdict. The Desert Fox further told his son that the poison he would be given would kill him in just a few seconds so Manfred was not to worry. The father and son hugged tightly, Rommel pushed himself away, executed an about face and left the room.

Lucia was told by the SS that her phone would ring from the hospital in Ulm to explain that General Rommel had been victim of a brain seizure caused by his injuries and had died on the way to a conference. General Rommel put on his Afrika Korps leather jacket and grabbed his field marshal's baton. He joined the two men, departed his house, and was never seen alive by his family again.

The three men drove down the driveway and out of the village for three miles, then slowly veered to the side of the road beside a forest. The gravel crunched under the tires just before the car stopped, the gear put in park, and the engine turned off. The driver exited the car. The man in the back seat with Rommel gave him a cyanide pill and told him that this was the time to follow through with his duty. Rommel obliged and within three minutes, the highly decorated general and skilled commander was slumped over with his head supported by the leather upholstery of the front passenger seat. The general officer beloved by the Führer and revered by the masses had been eliminated by the Architect due to the threat to Hitler's ego.

Frau Rommel received the expected phone call stating that the General suffered a cerebral embolism as a result of his war wounds. There would be no autopsy. A hero's funeral was planned in Ulm, not Berlin, as had been stipulated by Rommel before his forced suicide. One last strategic maneuver for the military man.

A day of mourning was proclaimed in Germany, for one of the greatest commanders in the nation's history. Frau Rommel received a wire from the Führer stating, "Accept my sincerest sympathy for the heavy loss you have suffered with the death of your husband. The name of Field Marshal Rommel will be forever linked with the heroic battles in North Africa."

On burial day, the funeral belied Rommel's true loyalty. At a private viewing with the family, the facial expression on Rommel's corpse was that of colossal contempt. But during the solemn ceremony, the German officer presiding looked over the swastika-draped coffin in front of him; then, to the family as he spoke of Rommel said, "His heart belonged to the Führer!"

The Rommel family would receive the customary military pension, the nation would grieve for the General for months, and the rest of the officer corps would mind their business and express deeper loyalty to their Führer. The Architect laughed to himself. Because of the swift retribution to the Wehrmacht generals, it was as if rigor mortis had set in. All the generals acted as if benumbed and were henceforth all the more eager to grovel at Hitler's feet.

Manfred Rommel was one of the few who knew the truth about his father's death. He also knew that his hero father believed Hitler was a liar, and it grieved him to serve a leader who shunned the advice of his highest generals. As a young teenager, Manfred did not care about the battles and military strategy. He did not care about Third Reich politics. His father was taken away from him and forced to die. There was still so much he needed to learn from him. His father would never come back to Manfred or his mother for the Desert Fox was no more.

CHAPTER 24

Ravensbrück

T he stench was all around. Corrie could barely stand the smell. The train continued for two more days without allowing the women any opportunity to relieve themselves except at their own feet. Occasionally, a loaf of bread would be passed to those in hunger, but most could not stomach the food. They hoped and prayed every hour that the train would come to a stop and allow them to depart it and stretch their legs. Their lips were cracked and they were desperately thirsty and fatigued. Their minds and bodies ached and above all they were terrified of plunging deeper and deeper into the land of their enemy. *Would they be taken to a Polish death camp?* Corrie wondered.

A few days before, her hopes were high that she and Betsie would be released. Now she hoped they would survive a few more hours in that terrible tomb of a train. *Will it ever end?*

The train was slowing, then came to a stop. The heavy door opened a few inches and a bucket of water was passed inside for the women to drink. Those near the door gulped the entire pail, much to the anger of those farthest from the door. The door then shut, the women screamed, the train moved forward again.

Once again the train stopped and some water was passed inside. The dire situation caused the impatient women to act like animals, clawing at it causing some to spill. Betsie wept at the misery of it all. Corrie held her. The train moved forward.

Finally, on the morning of the fourth day, after such misery, fear, and foul air, the train stopped and the boxcar door was opened all the way. The women covered their eyes from the bright autumn sun, then staggered to the opening and lowered themselves to the ground. The floor of the train car they departed was a filthy mess and they were relieved the trip was over.

There was a beautiful, blue lake before them. Some of the prisoners were sent to fetch water for the thousand women clambering down from the train. Desperate, Corrie and Betsie hobbled down to the lake and drank through stinging lips. They had survived. *But where were they?*

The train had less cars than when they started. Many of the women were saddened to learn that the rail cars with the men in them had been detached somewhere on the journey. This did not upset the Ten Boom sisters as much as it did those women whose husbands had survived the firing squads at Vught.

Corrie and Betsie, slightly revived by the refreshing water, were forced to stand in columns with the other women and march around the lake. If they had not been prisoners who were barely able to stand because of muscle aches, it would have been a beautiful morning to stroll through the lakeside forest. Corrie allowed Betsie to put weight on her arm to help her in the march up a slight hill.

The blue sky and greenery looked surreal, as if made for another time and place, with the straggling herd of women an interruption to an otherwise idyllic narrative. There were villagers walking on the trail and Corrie noticed that the children would stare as if in amazement, but the adults turned their heads toward the road or the opposite direction from the women.

The prisoners marched five abreast in neat columns going as far back as one could see. When they topped the hill and saw ahead to the place they were marching, the columns slowed and a moan of horror echoed out from the group. It was a concentration camp, but not just any other concentration camp — the many rows of barracks, the crematorium in the center with its line of smoke rising into the clear, blue air; this was unmistakably the Ravensbrück death camp.

The women whispered the name Ravensbrück all the way to the back of the marching columns. This camp was notorious even in Holland as a women's extermination camp. Its intimidating guard towers and tall, electrified fence gave no doubt as to the identity of the compound. The women, in their blue Vught overalls, were marching toward one of the most feared places in Germany.

Corrie witnessed that the guards seemed to enjoy the rampant fear spreading through the women as word passed through the masses about the camp. These young, female guards marched alongside the Dutch prisoners with Alsatians, guard dogs who were trained to growl at those in camp uniforms. They finally reached the gate and saw the black signs with yellow painted skull-and-crossbones hanging on the large fence. The woman in charge of the prisoners handed several ruffled papers to the gate guard. The women were counted and allowed to enter through the massive iron gates of Ravensbrück.

While marching into the concentration camp, many of the women began to sing with pride and defiance:

> *"We never let our courage lag,*
> *We hold our heads up high;*
> *Never shall they get us down,*
> *Though they be ever so sly.*
> *O yea! O yea! You Netherlands women,*
> *Heads up, heads up, heads up!"*

The guards did not stop them. Ravensbrück prisoners stared at them in disbelief. *Did they not know what kind of place they were marching into?* No one smiled. Fear and a grimness filled every inhabitant.

The group of women continued to march down the main avenue of the camp. As they passed one of the barracks, emaciated women with skeleton-like arms and hands reached out to them, begging for food. Some of the new prisoners dug into their pillowcases and handed those reaching out something to eat. One of the newcomers asked, "How is it here?"

"It is horrible! They starve us!" came the reply. Glancing up at the intense blue sky, Corrie wondered if Ravensrück could indeed be that bad.

The prisoners marched until they reached a wide, open-sided canvas tent that covered over an acre of straw-covered dirt. The women were told to go under the canvas and wait. Corrie and Betsie sat down but sprang immediately back up. *Lice!* The straw was swarming with lice. *What could they do?* Eventually, the women all sat back down on the lice. Several pairs of scissors were passed around and everyone began cutting each other's hair. Looking at Betsie's beautiful hair, Corrie at first refused, but she quickly realized long hair was a folly in this place. With great sorrow, she cut off Betie's chestnut waves and wept. They buried their hair in the dirt beneath the straw.

After a while the women were told to leave the tent area and stand in a line on the hard cinder ground next to the camp wall with the high electric fence. Evening came and most of the women laid down. Corrie and Betsie hesitated but realized as it grew darker that they were to remain out there in the open all night. They placed one blanket below them and used the other blanket for a cover. Around midnight the thunderclaps began. Pouring rain soaked all the blankets and formed puddles underneath the tired women. It was the end of their first day at Ravensbrück.

<hr>

The sun broke on the chilly morning. The prisoners were left alone the entire day to wait. Again they slept outside, under the stars, but on this clear night it was cold. The blankets were still damp from the night before but at least it was not raining. There was coughing, and crying, and the Ten Boom sisters tried to keep their calm. They were never given a reason. They just had to wait.

Sometime during the night Betsie started coughing from the chill and could not stop. Corrie reached into her pillowcase and pulled out the blue sweater Nollie had sent her at Scheveningen. She wrapped it around Betsie and gave her some vitamin oil. Betsie developed painful intestinal cramps and had to use the ditch beside the wall several times. Finally, they made it through the night.

The third day was exactly the same as the two before. They were to stand at rigid attention, enduring the sun all day. The only breaks were for some coffee and black bread in the morning, and a ladle of turnip soup and a small potato at night.

At the end of the third day they were approached by screaming guards and barking Alsatians. *At last, they would be processed!* The women were marched to the administration building for new arrivals. Their names were recorded, their photographs taken, and then they were ushered into a massive reception room and ordered to place all of their belongings in a pile. Much to the horror of Corrie and Betsie, they saw at the front of the line women completely undressing and waiting for the bath house. *They are taking all our belongings? They are stripping us bare?* Corrie shuddered at the thought as she watched the male SS guards roving around the naked women.

A young woman next to the Ten Boom sisters quietly protested to Corrie, "This is worse than when they took everything out of my home, including my grand piano. Now we will have no blanket or extra clothing. Everything is being taken."

After the first fifty women bathed, Corrie saw them all come out with nothing but a thin dress, an undershirt, and a pair of wooden shoes. *There is no way Betsie could survive the winter nights in that,* thought Corrie. *What about the blue sweater?* Corrie decided she must take a chance to keep the blue sweater for Betsie.

Before the women reached the mound of clothing and possessions the prisoners were discarding, Corrie asked a guard if she could use the toilet.

"Over there!" he yelled. "Hurry up!"

Corrie grabbed Betsie's hand and escorted her into the latrine area. She eyed some moldy wooden benches crawling with cockroaches. *Perfect!* Corrie told Betsie to take off her woolen sweater and she used it to gently wrap around her Scripture and the vitamin bottle, then hid it under one of the nasty wooden benches. Corrie said a prayer, asking God to protect their precious items.

The two women returned to the line, threw the rest of their possessions on the pile and watched the women ahead of them strip naked to prepare for the shower room. A white silk blouse was thrown to the top of the pile, and Corrie watched as it rolled down until one of its sleeves ended up in another prisoner's discarded jar of apple butter. An aged woman stood beside the pile silently weeping.

"I can't do this, Corrie," whispered Betsie as she and Corrie arrived at the point to undress.

Corrie noticed that her sister was shivering and said, "Betsie, God will see us through. Are you prepared to offer this sacrifice if God should will it so?"

At that moment, a guard with a cruel face, noticing Betsie's hesitation to undress marched toward them, "Do you have any objections to surrendering your clothes? We'll soon teach you Hollanders what Ravensbrück is like."

Corrie quickly put her arm around her sister and led her to the far side of the pile. Corrie undressed quickly while the guard stared approvingly.

"I can't do this Corrie," said Betsie again.

"I will pray for you," said Corrie. "Lord, if you ask this sacrifice of us, give us the strength to make it."

It took another moment until Betsie's shivering arms began to scratch off her dress and undergarments. Their old clothes were left behind and the two women walked into the next room. Female guards stood with scissors, ready to cut the hair off anyone with lice.

One young Belgian girl with beautiful golden hair just in front of Corrie walked to the guards for inspection. There was no lice but they cut off her hair anyway, just for spite. The women proceeded into the bathhouse and let the cold water wash over their lice-eaten skin.

They were attended to by several female prisoners dressed all in white who had a small triangular patch of cloth on their arm. Corrie would learn later that each color indicated their status: lilac for Jehovah Witnesses, red for Politicals, a red and yellow star for political Jews, black triangles for Asocials, and green for Criminals.

Once out of the flow of water the women gathered around a heap of thin prison dresses and held them up to check for appropriate sizes. Corrie found one that would fit loosely on Betsie to cover the blue sweater, then handed it to her. She found another one for herself and put it on quickly. Then, Corrie grabbed Betsie and maneuvered back to the toilet area and retrieved their special bundle. Corrie took the blue sweater and wrapped it around her waist, then put her pouch of Scriptures and vitamins around her neck and under the top of her dress. The sisters proceeded back to the line to exit the building with the other women, but they did not feel poor, but rich. Rich in this new evidence of the care of Him who was God even of Ravensbrück.

Just then, however, they discovered a new danger before them. Each woman was searched, not once but twice. Once by the male guards at the corridor door, and once by the female guards at the outside door. The SS men ran their hands over every prisoner: front, back, and sides. Other women trying to conceal extra clothing underneath their dresses were forced to strip again. Each woman was searched copiously by more than one male guard. Corrie feared that the blue sweater and her special pouch of vitamins and Scripture would be taken from her. She prayed to God that she would be allowed to pass.

The woman in front of Corrie was searched three times. Corrie calmly walked past as the guards waved her on, then Betsie was stopped for a thorough search. It seemed to Corrie at that moment that she was invisible. A small victory.

There was one more obstacle — the female guards at the exit door. Each woman walking out the door was searched again. Corrie prayed another desperate prayer. When she got to the door one of the guards shoved her shoulders and yelled at her, "Move along! You're holding up the line."

Unbelievably, she and Betsie were suddenly thrust into the dark courtyard with all of their secret belongings. Corrie, with this sudden reminder of the power of God, prayed, "O Lord, if this is how you answer prayer, I can face even Ravensbrück unafraid."

It was late when the Ten Booms finally stumbled into their quarantine barracks. New prisoners were made to be quarantined for a specified time upon arrival. The sisters were assigned a bed that already had three women sleeping on it. Corrie gave Betsie her sweater to put on and then the two tried to lay down on the edges of the straw sack mattress.

Thankfully, the other women were kind enough to shift so that all five could fit on it, but they were squished together and it was not easy to get to sleep. For one to turn, all had to turn. It was a chore but it was better than being outside. These women had two thin blankets and shared the ends of them with the sisters. Betsie shivered uncontrollably for a long while, then finally warmed from other's body heat and fell asleep. Bits of straw and filth drifted down from the beds above them but Corrie, thankful for the roof over her head, dozed off while watching the sweeping searchlights and hearing the guards on patrol outside. It was much past midnight and their third day at Ravensbrück had concluded.

Roll call at Ravensbrück began at 4:30 a.m. The women prisoners were made to stand in the pre-dawn chill at rigid attention from the time they entered the courtyard until long past sunrise. They stood in blocks of one hundred, ten prisoners wide and ten prisoners deep. Sometimes, after they returned to the comfort of the barracks they were yelled at again to return back outside and stand at attention. It was harassment and hard on the human heart. Once, a camp guard struck Corrie hard on the side of her neck in anger as they passed each other. The cruelty hurt Corrie worse than the blow.

The tedium of roll call was also a test of endurance. One roll call would end and they would return to the barracks where they were to stand and wait for the next roll call. Each roll call lasted several hours. All the prison numbers were called out to ensure no one had escaped. Betsie was prisoner 66729, and Corrie was prisoner 66730. When roll call ended, the women were left to stand in agony until the guards decided they could be dismissed back to the barracks.

Betsie wasted no time making their sleeping area a home, and began knitting and mending things for other women with a needle and some borrowed thread. Corrie became acquainted with the other women in the barracks and read Scripture to them as they huddled around her and Betsie. One day, Tine, an older sickly woman they knew from Vught, crawled through the barracks window to rejoin the Netherlanders. She was sick with tuberculosis but had escaped from the hospital.

"Did you leave without permission?" asked Corrie, who always admired Tine's bravery.

"Yes, I had to," said Tine. "Things are simply unbearable in the hospital. On three different occasions already, my bedfellow died in the evening and I had to lie abed all night beside a corpse. They do not remove the bodies until morning. It is a terrible practice and I can't tolerate it any longer."

Corrie and Betsie welcomed their friend back into the barracks. During the days when not senselessly ordered to stand outside at attention, the Ten Boom sisters taught the Bible to more and more of the women. A group of spiritually hungry souls stood around while either Corrie or Betsie read words of hope to the women of Ravensbrück.

"Who shall separate us from the love of Christ?" Corrie read to her fellow prisoners. "Shall tribulation, or distress, or persecution, or famine, or nakedness, or peril, or sword?" Corrie looked up at the thin faces of her fellow travelers, having survived the horrific train ride from Vught they had a bond and a collective triumph. "We are being put to death all the day long, and considered as sheep to be slaughtered. No, in all these things we are more than conquerors through Him who loved us, and nothing will separate us from the love of God in Christ Jesus our Lord."

Yes, we are conquerors, Corrie knew. *Dirty, frightened, cold, hungry, sick and abused externally, but conquerors because of our internal and unseen faith in God.* Though their bodies were wasting away, their spirits were growing like a flourishing garden.

The quarantine barracks where the Ten Boom sisters were housed was located next to the Punishment Block, a barracks building where prisoners were punished for breaking any rule. Prisoners could be kept in the Punishment block for a day or even up to a month. The sounds coming from the building were horrific.

Corrie knew that it was no mistake to house the new inmates next to the Punishment Block as a warning of how to behave. The newcomers were far from home and in a strange place. The Punishment Block was a powerful tutorial for their future stay at Ravensbrück. The shouts, screams and cries from the torture were sometimes heard all through the night. Blows to the body were heard in rhythm with the cries of the one being beaten. The women tried to muffle the sound and press their hands against their ears but it did not help. The abuse emanating from the Punishment Block was a constant reminder to the prisoners that they were at war with an enemy driven by evil.

A medical inspection for each prisoner was performed on Fridays. The women were lined up and marched to the hospital to be inspected by the doctors and nurses. The women were made to stand on the cold cement floor and strip naked while they waited to be seen by the camp physician. One day, as Corrie and Betsie stood in their humiliation, Corrie grabbed some clothing to cloak her naked body, only to be reprimanded by a guard.

"Come now, we understand what you're trying to do," the guard said. "Now put that down, and stand in line like you are supposed to. Stand erect. Hands at your sides. Your turn is coming. Be patient."

Corrie waited in line while grinning guards looked up and down the long corridor filled with naked women. She felt for her older sister Betsie, how much harder it must be for her to bear. Corrie was strong and could take the cruel punishment if she must, but she feared for her sister's frailness.

The frustrating part of the whole ordeal was that when they finally reached the doctor it was obvious they did not have to be naked. He looked at their throat and between their fingers. The dentist looked at the teeth. Why they had to be naked Corrie could never figure out. The women were paraded back to where they left their dresses and returned to the barracks.

As Corrie thought about the experience she realized that Jesus Himself was naked on the cross, and the humiliation He must have felt to be stripped of his clothes in His dying hours. One day in line, shivering and naked, waiting to be examined, Corrie mentioned this thought to her struggling sister, "Betsie, they took His clothes, too."

Betsie spun around and gasped, "Oh, Corrie. And I never thanked Him…"

One day in October 1944, the women were given a half hour of leisure and several of them walked by a different barracks building and wondered what was inside. They looked through the window and were startled by what they saw. Inside the concrete-walled room stood a small, barefoot girl with short dark hair, and without a stitch of clothes on except a short vest. Emaciated, and with a vacant look in her eyes, the skeleton-like girl leaned against one of the hard walls. Corrie studied the gray-faced little girl and her environment and wondered why she was in the room and all alone.

A woman sidled up next to Corrie and whispered, "Can you understand how human life can be so tenacious? That child is mentally deficient and has been living here for weeks on half rations; she sleeps at night on the concrete floor, without a mattress or blanket; yet she can still stand upright."

The group of women moved on but Corrie could not get the image of the girl out of her mind. She wanted to open a home for children like her when the war was over, where they would receive love and good care. She prayed for the girl, that the Lord would take her home soon and save the world from the oppressive Nazi regime.

Soon after this experience, the day came for the Netherlanders to move to their permanent barracks. The women had to stand at attention in the courtyard for four hours. Then, they were marched ten abreast down the wide avenue to the multiple rows of regular barracks. Ravensbrück was set up in blocks from north to south, and each block had a row of barracks set alongside the main avenue. Corrie's group marched to the southernmost block in front of Barracks 28, across from the Siemens work factory.

Again, the women waited patiently for each number to be called.

"66728, 66729, 66730….," the block leader called out.

Corrie and Betsie dismissed themselves from the formation and walked into the barracks to discover their new home. The place was horribly filthy and reeked of human waste. The plumbing had backed up and was never fixed. Many of the windows were broken, with rags and trash attempting to cover them. The beds were soiled and rancid. The bunks were tiered and many of the slats were missing. When a few of the newcomers crawled to their designated upper bed, some of them broke the thin slats and fell through to the next level, creating a cloud of straw and dust. There was hardly any ventilation and the stench was awful, but this crevice would be their new home.

As Corrie and Betsie crawled up the pier to their own assigned beds, nausea hit them from the rancid straw. Still, they carried on, but they no sooner found their spot when something bit Corrie in the leg.

"Fleas!" Corrie cried. "Betsie, this place is crawling with fleas!"

The two looked around their new bed and discovered an infestation of the tiny insects. "What are we to do?" asked Corrie of her older sister. "Oh Betsie, how can we live in this place?"

"Show us," said Betsie, "show us how."

Corrie realized that Betsie was praying and not speaking to anyone other than God.

Suddenly, Betsie exclaimed with excitement, "Corrie! He's already given us the answer."

"What do you mean?" asked Corrie.

"Remember that passage you read this morning from Second Thessalonians?"

Corrie took her Scriptures from the pouch around her neck and opened them up to the mark, "Do you mean, rejoice always, pray constantly, give thanks in all circumstances; for this is the will of God in Christ Jesus?"

"Yes, that's it," interjected Betsie. "That's His answer. *Give thanks in all circumstances!* That's what we can do. We can start right now to thank God for every single thing inside this new barracks."

Corrie stared at Betsie, then looked around the dark, foul-smelling chamber.

"Such as?" asked Corrie.

"Such as being assigned here together," answered Betsie sweetly.

"Okay, thank you Lord for this," said Corrie.

"Such as what you're holding in your hand."

Corrie looked down at the Scriptures which were truly a gift from God in a place like Ravensbrück. "Yes, thank you Lord, for allowing Your word to pass through inspection and for all the women who will get to meet You in these pages."

"Yes," said Betsie, "and thank you for the overcrowding here because that many more women will get to hear Your word when we read it." Betsie looked at Corrie expectantly and prodded, "Corrie!"

"Oh, all right. Thank you for the jammed, crammed, stuffed, packed, suffocating crowds."

"Thank you," Betsie went on serenely, "for the fleas and for…"

The fleas? This was too much. "Betsie, there is no way even God can make me grateful for a flea!"

"Give thanks in all circumstances," Betsie quoted. "It doesn't say in pleasant circumstances. Fleas are part of the place where God has placed us."

And so the sisters sat between multiple piers of bunks with countless women and gave thanks for the fleas. But this time Corrie was sure Betsie was wrong.

<hr />

Corrie looked out into the dark October night and saw that the sky was aglow behind some distant camp bunkers. She had not noticed this before and it drew her curiosity. *Perhaps it was a bonfire the guards were having that night? Or perhaps it was something else?* Corrie wondered what it might be, then turned once again to face her new roommates … and the fleas.

CHAPTER 25

Trouble in the Ardennes Forest

Albert Speer did not have to sit and ponder what to do with his new resolve to fight for his countrymen; the needs were all around him. Events were overtaking the Reich and moving Germany rapidly toward its end. Coal was not being delivered because the Nazi Gauleiters were confiscating the rail cars when they passed through their territories. Berlin remained unheated even though winter was closing in and the weather was turning cold. Oil plants were on the verge of shutdown, gas and electricity were used on a restricted basis, and even hospitals were running low on the drugs they needed to treat pain.

Speer crisscrossed the country countermanding Hitler's orders of total destruction as best he could. He entrusted himself with few men, only those who realized that Hitler's scorched earth policy would bring mass destruction on Germany and on its citizenry. Hitler wanted all the western bridges destroyed. Speer sent orders to spare them from demolition. When plants were bombed by the Allies, Hitler wanted them abandoned, but Speer was there to oversee the rebuilding so that supplies could continue to flow. Speer sent trains with fuel to the front lines, rail cars filled with food to the people of the Ruhr, all of which were in direct disobedience to the orders of the Führer.

One day, in early fall of 1944, Speer observed what his separation with Hitler was costing him. Speer, still the Führer's Armaments Minister, walked across the heavy, handwoven rug in the Chancellery and joined the other men in the tapestried map room. The massive situation table was a single slab of Austrian marble; it was blood-red, striated with beige and white cross sections of an ancient coral reef. Speer sat across from Hitler and watched him intently as the Chancellor spoke to his marshals and generals.

"We have the good fortune to have a genius in our armaments ministry," said Hitler. "I mean Karl Saur. All difficulties are being overcome by him."

One general officer put in the tactful word, "Mein Führer, Minister Speer is here."

"Yes, I know," Hitler replied snappishly, visibly annoyed at the interruption. "But Saur is the genius who will master the situation for us."

Speer swallowed hard and looked straight ahead at the large window. Hitler had obviously heard of some of Speer's rogue activities and was intentionally trying to humiliate him in front of others. Oddly enough, the insult did not bother him like it might have a year before. Speer had taken his leave of Hitler.

━━◆◆◆━━

A few weeks later when the trees were exploding in autumn color, Hitler called Speer aside and said, "You mustn't say a word to anyone, but I am preparing a great offensive; one that will wipe the Americans and British from the continent." Hitler's hands were shaking and he continued to rub his right elbow.

Speer's interest in the plan spiked, though he knew from his own accounting Germany did not have the fuel to pull off an offensive that autumn. They were losing more and more ground and barely able to put up a good defense to the Allies on both fronts. He wished Hitler was bluffing to use this idea as a decoy for redoubling their efforts against Russia, but deep down Speer knew it was no bluff.

"I am going to concentrate all our forces to the west," said Hitler quietly while he massaged his right arm; a constant, painful reminder of the July 20th assassination attempt. "I need you to organize a special corps of construction workers. I want them sufficiently motorized to be able to carry out all types of bridge building even if the rail transportation should be halted. Remember the western campaign of 1940?"

"It is thrilling to hear," stated Speer as politely as he could under the circumstances, "however, we do not have enough trucks left for such a task, nor the fuel to make them run." Speer was baffled at how the man's brain worked; there were absolutely not enough logistic components in place for this endeavor. He scrutinized Hitler's pale and puffy face. He was repulsed, just as he had been when in the hospital months before. *How could this man be the leader of Germany?*

"It doesn't matter," countered Hitler. "Everything else must be put aside for this counterattack to work." Then the Führer looked off and declared forcefully, "No matter what the consequences, I am staking everything on this offensive. This will be the great blow which must succeed."

<hr />

While Speer refused to carry out Hitler's orders to raze German villages in the Allies' path, he did organize a group of construction workers as he was instructed. The Russians bolstered their advance in the East, with speedier access to Germany since Hitler removed divisions from their path. Speer knew that Hitler's gamble would more quickly bring about the end of the war so he was somewhat in favor of the new endeavor, because he was sure of its failure.

In November Hitler again declared to Speer, "A single breakthrough on the western front! You'll see! It will lead to collapse and panic among the Americans. We'll drive right through their belly and take Antwerp. Then they will have lost their supply port. A tremendous pocket will encircle the entire English army and we'll gain hundreds of thousands of prisoners for our labor camps."

When Hitler unveiled his daring plan to the Wehrmacht generals for the first time, one of them verbalized their collective thought: "This plan doesn't haven't a leg to stand on."

Hitler sarcastically replied, "Apparently you don't remember Frederick the Great. At Rossbach and Leuthen he defeated enemies twice his strength. How? By a brazen attack. Why don't you generals ever study history? History is going to repeat itself. The Ardennes will be my Rossbach and Leuthen. And as a result, another unpredictable historical accident will take place; the alliance against the Reich will suddenly split apart. You'll see."

Hitler's eyes shone, but the generals remained unconvinced.

<hr />

In an attempt to persuade his military commanders, Hitler and his entourage boarded the Führer's personal train at the Wolf's Lair rail station, embarking to the western front.

The day was November 20th, and the train was outfitted with two heavy locomotives followed by an armored car equipped with anti-aircraft guns. After this came Hitler's personal car, possessing a large salon with walls paneled in rosewood. The car also had a kitchen, a private bedroom, a bath, a wardrobe and servants' quarters. The following car was the Command Center equipped with a map room and a place for officers to meet. This car was a mobile headquarters for the Führer as he continued to lead the war while away from the Chancellery, the Berghof or the Wolf's Lair.

The next car held Hitler's escort consisting of twenty men. Then came a car for each of his ministers, including Albert Speer who joined the entourage in Berlin. After several guest cars and a baggage car, the caboose was a highly reinforced armored car equipped with lethal artillery pieces.

During the train ride from Poland to Germany, Hitler's physician performed on him a much-needed throat operation, which kept the Führer in seclusion for several days. When the locomotives reached Berlin and Speer stepped onto the train, he discovered a staff weary with the war effort. They were sitting around killing time waiting for Hitler to rejoin them for meals in the salon.

Speer took some time alone in his compartment as well and reflected on another trip in which he participated with the staff when they departed from the Berchtesgaden rail station two years before. They journeyed to the city of Linz in Austria, about 100 miles away. Hitler went on and on about the building projects he was going to launch there including new museums, a new opera house, a new stadium. It was the Führer's hometown, the city where he grew up, and he desired for it to become a cultural center rivaling Budapest and Vienna. Everyone was enraptured by the stories about his childhood and also about the future of Linz. It was an exciting time for all involved.

Speer cogitated on how personable Hitler could be when he wanted. People who sat beside the Führer at mealtime had the sense that he really cared about them. Hitler would ask questions about their family, then follow-up with a story about his own history. He had a remarkable ability to tell anecdotes and speak about people he had met in an interesting way. When looking at his own personality, Speer always felt like there was a screen between himself and others, but Hitler had no barrier. He could look people in the eye, listen, and relate to them personally. In fact, he was a master at relationships, which is why he could play his staff against each other so easily.

Yet Hitler was hard to go deep with. In a way, Speer believed that he and Hitler shared something in common, their inability to let anyone truly know them. Hitler stayed closed even while opening up others. Speer stayed closed and struggled to relate to others. Perhaps that was why Hitler liked Speer, his inner core was similarly isolated and detached.

Speer recognized that he himself typically related to others in a pragmatic sort of way in order to accomplish something, like quid pro quo. Speer proffered a 'how are you' merely so he could get to the subject at hand, not because he truly cared. When he did attempt some type of concern for others, his efforts were too clumsy and usually parried. One of his own staff told him that he was the world's most inhibited man, and another friend confessed that he often felt Speer was closed and hard to get to know. Speer thought of his wife, Margarete, and how he wished he could prove his love to her and show her something demonstrable to let her know he cared. But it was impossible when he hardly ever saw his family. Whatever words he spoke to Margarete now were hollow.

The war had become a wedge in their relationship, fracturing the old feelings of endearment. Also weighing heavily on Speer was the knowledge that the impending defeat would ruin their dreams of a future together. Lately, Speer had a hard time looking at Margarete in the eyes, afraid she might use the moment to ask him to stay home with her and the children. Or worse, flee to Denmark.

A whistle blew and the wheels began moving after what seemed to be several hours. The train finally departed, heading to the western front ... with Speer watching from the station. Absent-mindedly, Speer had stepped off his rail car and was standing back on the platform of the station in Berlin. He watched the stately train move slowly away from him until it was out of sight. He would go home and spend a day or two with his family before joining the others at the front.

———◆◆———

Several days later, on December 12th, Adolf Hitler called together his division commanders deep inside his bunker at Ziegenberg, the site of a medieval castle in the Taunus Mountains. The generals and their staffs were stripped of pistols and briefcases by the Gestapo —thanks to Colonel von Stauffenberg— and were ushered into a room where they were forced to swear on their life they would not reveal what they were about to hear.

With hands twitching Hitler explained to them his blueprint for an assault on the Americans. "Never in history was there a coalition like this of our current adversaries. It is essential to deprive the enemy of his belief that victory is certain. We must allow no moment to pass without showing the enemy that, whatever he does, he can never reckon on our capitulation. Never! Never! The battle must be fought with brutality and all resistance must be broken. In this most serious hour of the Fatherland, I expect every one of my soldiers to be courageous and again courageous. The enemy must be beaten — now or never! Thus lives Germany!"

In preparation for the attack, Speer traveled to Bonn to visit Field Marshal Model's headquarters; a hunting lodge set in a narrow wooded valley in the Eifel Mountains. It was the perfect venue to observe how the upcoming offensive would progress. Speer had done his work as Armaments Minister to help ensure the machinery was battle-ready. In the last few days he had personally overseen the transport of nearly ten million liters of fuel from working plants to the front lines. He was not convinced this new scheme of Hitler's had any legs to stand on, but he was not going to thwart the war effort while still serving on the Führer's cabinet.

And so, on December 16th, in the densely forested region of Wallonia in Belgium, France and Luxembourg, the Ardennes Offensive began. Hitler desperately wanted to catch the enemy off guard and he succeeded. On that first day there were encouraging reports from all sectors as 200,000 men attacked a weakly defended section of the Allied line. The low-lying clouds hampered all enemy air activity. The German divisions broke through and separated the dispirited Allies away from each other. The offensive took the Allied High Command completely by surprise. For several days it seemed that the German Army had succeeded in breaking open the American and British line which could lead to a rout.

Speer tried to follow in his automobile behind the advancing German units but found there was too much traffic on the road and he progressed only two miles in several hours' time. His construction teams did not fare any better and were unable to arrive at a blown-up bridge on the main route to aid the armored advance. The engineering supplies the army needed and many of the workers were stuck in traffic East of the Rhine. Also, because the main body of the attack had advanced so quickly, fuel and ammunition supplies for the front were swiftly exhausted.

After a few days the weather cleared and American fighters and bombers were all over the skies. This made travel during the day impossible for the German support elements. Supply trains were bombed and the trucks in long convoys were delayed in traffic. Unfortunately for the Third Reich, the German advance stopped and the divisions of soldiers marching forward were fiercely counter-attacked.

Speer traveled as best he could under the cover of pine trees to oversee several of the divisions and how they were doing, but he kept hearing the same story. The Americans were relentless fighters, and without additional fuel and ammunition making its way to the German front, the advance could not continue. By Christmas Day the generals knew that the Ardennes Offensive had failed, but Hitler would not yet admit defeat. As Speer navigated through the war zone he observed in many places the snow blanketing the Ardennes Forest was red with blood.

One of Hitler's advisors pleaded with him, "Mein Führer, we must face the facts squarely. We cannot force the Meuse. The offensive cannot go on."

Hitler heard several reports like this from all of his generals. Eventually he replied, "We have had unexpected setbacks because my plan was not followed to the letter. But all is not yet lost."

Göring, still the second man of the state, arrived in a flourish hoping to speak some sense to the lost situation, "Mein Führer, we must seek a truce. The war is lost!"

"If you do anything behind my back like Hess I will have you shot!" shouted Hitler, referencing his former deputy who deserted early in the war effort. "At this time my generals do not need to hear cowardice, they need to hear about courage."

Göring cowered at the threat. "Mein Führer, I would never do anything behind your back."

Hitler did not respond; he departed the room leaving the Reichsmarschall sulking at his rebuke.

Speer continued to do everything he could to aid the war effort, despite the ominous foregone conclusion of defeat. He telephoned orders to the gasoline plants in the Ruhr area and had them utilize improvised tankers to transport fuel to the front. However, his efforts went largely unnoticed; the setbacks and despair across the entire front were too great.

On New Year's Eve 1944, Speer made the arduous journey to report to Hitler's bunker at Felsennest, but he was delayed due to low-flying American fighters. It was two hours past midnight when Speer arrived at the bunker after a full day of travel. He found the Führer's doctors, adjutants, secretaries and Martin Bormann gathered around Hitler, giving toasts and drinking champagne. Though the atmosphere seemed subdued because of the stall in the offensive, Speer noticed that people were generally positive.

Hitler seemed the most enthused of anyone, possibly because of the new year with its fresh opportunities. Though not a drinker, he appeared drunk that night. Speer reflected that the nation's Chancellor always delighted in celebratory occasions so he could recount past stories of glory and fortune in the Reich.

Speer stood near the back of the room next to his friend, Nicolaus von Below. He could discern the anguish in a few faces even while they raised their champagne glasses again and again. Most put on a convincing show of true happiness while they listened to their enigmatic warlord.

Discounting the gloomy reports of defeat from every sector, Hitler trumpeted optimistic forecasts for 1945 while Bormann seconded every prediction. Hitler again made the parallel between himself and Frederick the Great who overcame tremendous odds in the Seven Years' War. Speer was present to show his support to the leader of the organization he had pledged his life to support, but deep down something incredibly important was missing — *reality*. Speer knew that not only was the battle lost, but also Germany's last hope at restraining the western invaders in an effort for a truce.

As Speer stood in the back with Below, a general officer arrived from Poland, his black leather boots still caked with dirty snow. The general was on an important mission, and he whispered to Speer that he would quickly need to report to Hitler that a few hours ago the Soviets launched a massive army in the East. Their goal was to reach Berlin by March. The officer was waiting, however, so as not to interrupt the Führer's victory speech. Speer was thunderstruck.

CHAPTER 26

Barracks 28

The quarantine barracks where Corrie and Betsie were initially held was a tight fit for so many and they did not think the crowding could get any worse. Soon, they discovered that their new life in their permanent barracks would be worse. Although Barracks 28 was designed for four hundred women, it now quartered over fourteen hundred. There was no room to maneuver or move around in any way. Legs hit other legs and elbows often dug into women's backs by accident. There simply was not enough room for that many people to attend to the basics of daily life.

When a woman had to use the toilet, she would have to crawl over others on the same level, hoping the slats would hold. Often they would bump their head on the wood above, or catch their dress on a bed post. Sometimes there would be a loud crash in the middle of the night followed by screaming and coughing from the straw dust. Instead of being in a barracks made up mostly of other Dutch women, Barracks 28 had many nationalities and different languages were spoken all around the Ten Boom sisters that they did not understand.

Besides the language difference there was also none of the camaraderie they shared with their fellow countrymen. The women screamed at each other in anger whenever someone acted selfishly. Those who slept near the windows were cold and tried to cover them up. Those in the center felt suffocated by the stuffy air and threatened to have the windows opened again.

One night when the emotional intensity had risen among the residents, Betsie grabbed Corrie's hand and prayed, "Lord Jesus, please send your peace into this room. There is too little praying here and the very walls know it. But where You come, Lord, the spirit of strife cannot exist."

Soon after Betsie's prayer Corrie noticed a gradual change in the attitude of the women. They began to accommodate each other and laugh.

"Let's make a deal, we will open the window half way..."

"So all of us will be miserable?" laughed one.

"I can swap beds with you, so you can be closer to the window," said one with a thick German accent.

"And swap your fleas for my own, no thanks."

More laughter.

Corrie smiled. God was at work, and Betsie was right. The barracks needed more prayer.

Although prayer was raising their morale, a nasty SS guard was lowering it whenever she was in their presence. Their tormentor was nicknamed "the Snake" because of the shiny dress she wore and the way she performed her duties. Often she would hide so she could catch the women doing something forbidden. Her vicious manner kept the prisoners constantly on edge and in fear. The women were getting along better but they had to keep a watchful eye out for the Snake every day.

———⊰•◆•⊱———

At 4:00 a.m. the whistle blew for the women to fetch their breakfast so they could be ready by the 4:30 a.m. roll call. As she stood outside in formation, Corrie looked down the row of Ravensbrück barracks and saw literally tens of thousands of women standing at rigid attention, the steam from their breath filling the night air above them. As far as the eyes could see, women gathered in one mass formation while prisoner numbers were called out in each respective courtyard. This routine lasted for hours. After roll call the work crews exited to the factories.

Corrie and Betsie were assigned to the Siemens factory. For eleven hours they would push a heavy handcart to a railroad siding where they unloaded large metal plates from a boxcar and wheeled them to the receiving gate at the factory. The iron was so cold that it hurt their hands. Corrie put wood chips in Betsie's hands to keep them from freezing. At noon the prisoners were given a boiled potato and some thin soup. The work was hard and Betsie struggled to keep up the desired pace of the taskmasters.

The large Siemens factory complex was over a mile from the main camp. The prisoners enjoyed the view of the lake and changing colors on the trees as they marched to the mills and railroad buildings. The women were usually too tired to notice their surroundings on the march back to Ravensbrück. Their arms and legs ached, and all they wanted to do was to collapse on their bunks. However, they were forced to stand in line for a ladle of turnip soup.

As soon as they received their supper, Corrie and Betsie would go to the back of Barracks 28 and underneath a single, dim bulb conduct a Bible study for the women who were interested. At first only a few came, but every few minutes, more and more women wandered over to their area and crowded around the bunks on that end of the barracks. Some sang hymns, the Roman Catholics recited the Magnificat in Latin, and others gave liturgy. Betsie would read the Bible in Dutch, Corrie would translate it in German, then others would continue the translation in French, Russian, Polish and Czech until everyone was satisfied. It was amazing to have that many nationalities, all crammed into one room worshipping God together.

This went on for weeks. What the Ten Boom sisters could not understand is why they were never threatened by the guards. It seemed that the guards either did not notice or did not care to come to the barracks to tell them to cease their religious activities, not even the Snake. In every prison up until then, there were always guards present with the women, making them keep rigid adherence to all the rules. But not at Ravensbrück, thankfully. There were so many women who wanted to be part of the service after a few days that the sisters decided to have two services, one before evening roll call and one right before lights out.

It was November 1944 and the cold nights turned into increasingly cooler days. Everyone was issued a coat but it was thin and did not keep them warm during early morning roll call.

The bombing raids came frequently now. The women knew that at Vught the danger for the camp officials came from the Americans and the British. At Ravensbrück the danger was from the approaching Russians. As at Vught, rumors swirled through the barracks every evening with news of the Allies approaching Berlin, and hope for freedom for the prisoners. It was obvious that the camp was growing in number. Every day new shipments of prisoners from the East were unloaded from the railroad cars and marched to the quarantine area of Ravensbrück. As the Russians moved closer to Germany, the concentration camps were shutting down in Poland and sending their prisoners west.

Betsie was growing weaker by the day and Corrie worried for her. Corrie herself had a hard time keeping up with what the screaming guards wanted. Then one day the work at the Siemens plant ceased unexpectedly. Corrie wondered if it had been bombed in one of the air attacks.

The women were assigned a new work project, to level some rough ground just inside the camp wall. Betsie could only manage tiny shovelfuls; she would scoop up a small amount of dirt and stumble over to the discard pile. The guards noticed her laughable effort, and they began to imitate and yell at her.

"Loafer!" one screamed. "Lazy swine!"

Betsie did not look up but continued to dig up her next clump of dirt.

"*Schneller!* You must move faster."

Corrie began to feel heat in the back of her neck. She was so angry with these guards. *Couldn't they be decent for once?* She fumed.

A female guard walked up and snatched Betsie's shovel from her hand. She held up the pitiful amount of dirt that represented what Betsie could lift, and walked it around to the other work crews. All the guards laughed in derision, scorning Corrie's sister for her lack of strength.

"Look what Madame Baroness is carrying! Surely she will overexert herself!"

All the guards and even some of the prisoners laughed. The one with Betsie's shovel began to imitate how she walked back and forth, stumbling as she went and spilling some of the dirt on purpose. More laughter. More heat encompassed Corrie's neck and face.

Suddenly, to Corrie's astonishment, she saw that even Betsie was laughing with everyone.

"That's me all right," she admitted. "But you better let me totter along with my little spoonful, or I'll have to stop altogether."

The guard's cheeks flashed crimson with anger, "I'll decide who's to stop!" Grabbing the leather crop from her belt, she slashed Betsie across the cheek and neck.

That was too much for Corrie. A murderous anger rose in her heart for that guard. Without considering the consequences, Corrie grabbed her shovel with both hands and stormed toward the guard. At just the right moment, Betsie stepped in front of Corrie and whispered to her, "Corrie, it's not worth it. Please keep working."

Before Corrie realized what was happening, Betsie took Corrie's shovel out of her hand and shoved it down into the mud. No one had seen Corrie's rage. Betsie had blocked the guards view.

The guard threw Betsie's shovel at her in contempt then rejoined the other guards. Corrie noticed the welt on Betsie's neck turning red and puffing up. Betsie noticed where Corrie was looking and put her hand on the spot to block Corrie's view. "Don't look at it, Corrie. Look at Jesus only."

She drew away her hand.

It was sticky with blood.

The days at Ravensbrück dragged on, but not without its brutality and contempt for human life from the guards. The Snake was the worst guard for dolling out punishment of any kind. One day Corrie was struck in the back by the Snake's whip. Another day she was taunted for not doing enough work. Betsie was derided several times for the measly labor she could provide. Some of the guards verbally assaulted her with venomous words and torments. Yet Betsie kept her sense of humor.

When fiercely mocked by one of the guards as to how little she was shoveling that day, Betsie turned to Corrie and said with a twinkle in her eye, "God can shovel without a shovel."

Corrie smiled, instantly recognizing that Betsie was referring to an incident with one of Corrie's feeble-minded girls in Haarlem years ago when she made an accidental statement about God and creation. The Dutch word for creation — *scheppen* — also means shoveling. Corrie taught the girls that to make a house humans need a lot of supplies like stone and wood and tools, but God made the world out of nothing. A week later the girl told the class, "When we shovel we need a shovel; but God can shovel — *scheppen* — without a shovel." Betsie's comment was a testament to Corrie that Betsie was somehow undisturbed at the evil around her. But it was the harsh physical demands that began to take their toll.

For an entire week in November a special roll call time was held at 3:30 in the morning instead of the usual 4:30 a.m. as punishment for some of the women not exiting Barracks 28 soon enough. After roll call was finished, the women were to stand in the frigid cold, silent and motionless, for an extra hour as punishment. Finally, the siren gave the signal to fall out and the numb women returned to the barracks to get warm. However, one day they were not allowed to enter.

The guards, on orders from the Snake, stood in front of the doors to the barracks with whips glaring at the freezing women. One woman tried to go into the building through the window but she was beaten back mercilessly with a whip. Corrie winced at the sound of each lash and the resulting screams from the one persecuted.

Another young girl pleaded that she had to use the latrine, but the guards just smirked and stared at her. After forty-five minutes the girl relieved herself in front of them. She too was whipped without mercy and her wild shrieks pierced the camp. An older woman begged to go inside but when refused, collapsed and fell hard to the ground. Hours went by and some of the women began to moan at the torture.

Corrie wrapped her arms around her sister who was shivering from the cold. Thinking about Betsie, she usually seemed in another world, where God reigned supreme and no one would dare to treat another human being without dignity. She scarcely noticed the abuse of the guards and the vicious things being said and done. But on this day, Corrie noted that it was one of the few times Betsie noticed the evil in the camp. In the midst of the extreme misery of those around her, Betsie whispered, "Oh, Corrie, this is Hades."

And yet the torturous treatment continued. During another early morning roll call that same week the women were standing outside in the cold and dark. Most of them stomped their feet continually in an attempt to keep warm, but it was difficult due to the heavy mist falling from the sky. Usually when it rained the women would be drenched for days, and barely able to raise their body temperature. They were forced to stand at attention in ankle-deep puddles and were punished when they tried to avoid them. The only noise for hours in the dark night was the stamping of thousands of feet continuously hitting the ground.

On this particular night, as the women stood with soaking feet, and their bodies enduring the persistent wind, they heard a low rumbling coming toward them. Eventually, trucks drove up and parked across the road in sight of the women of Barracks 28.

There were several flat freight trucks without a canvas canopy on top. Suddenly, the door from the hospital opened and a nurse came out with a feeble woman leaning on her arm. The nurse helped the woman up onto the truck and laid her down. Others came behind them in a straggly procession and the nurse in the truck helped each one with the big steps into the bed of the truck. The hospital seemed to be emptying out many of its sickest patients.

Corrie knew they were not supposed to be watching this sight. The terrifying words, "Sick transport!" were whispered among the women. Horror stricken, the stamping of feet had ceased and the prisoners watched with wide eyes as a hundred of the sickest patients were taken out the door of the hospital and loaded onto the trucks. The nurse on top proficiently helped each woman to either lay down or sit up until every person had a spot. There was no protest on that misty night. Soon, the hospital door closed and the trucks drove toward the brick building beside the crematorium.

Early that morning, before daylight invaded Ravensbrück, Corrie saw that the sky behind the bunkers was aglow. She now knew for certain what this meant; the crematory was working at full blast.

The horrible stench in the bedding.

The lice constantly invading their skin and clothing.

No privacy.

Constant abuse from the guards.

This was Ravensbrück. Prisoners never had the opportunity to be alone. In formation and work details they existed among thousands of other prisoners all trying to survive. In the barracks building they were crammed next to so much flesh it was unavoidable to bump into others constantly, all day and all night long.

When the call came for the evening meal, Corrie and Betsie had to push with throngs of other women to get their place in line and wait for their supper: soup, black bread, or the small piece of sausage they received once a week. Corrie ironically craved solitude and thought of her time in Scheveningen prison where she was alone all the time. Betsie somehow seemed to embrace the crowds, her face always shining with peace and serenity.

One day, in the throes of 1,400 humans pushing against each other attempting to maneuver through the barracks building, Betsie once said to Corrie, "I am beginning to love the multitude." Corrie stared at her in bewilderment, as she had done many times before.

The cold and wet November was hard on the health of many of the prisoners. Standing for hours in thin striped dresses, legs, hands and noses turned blue with cold by the time the command came to be released. Whenever there was a miscount at roll call, the entire list of numbers would be read again to ensure everyone was there. If someone was missing, the women could be forced to stand for hours until the missing woman was found.

If someone refused to attend roll call, disobey a command, or strike an SS guard, they would be sent to the Punishment Block. For any infraction women could be sent to the Punishment Block where they would be left standing outside for three days without food or water. Depending on the offense, some were not housed in the Punishment Block Barracks, but put into the Bunker.

The Bunker was a two-story rectangular cement building with few windows. The upstairs held an examination room and a whipping room. Shoes were confiscated, heads were shaved, and prisoners had to sit on cold, filthy floors, being served only a small portion of bread daily. They lived in absolute darkness and isolation. The downstairs was where punishment, or torture, was administered. Prisoners were strapped naked to a rack and they were caned, with the prisoner ordered to count each hit whacked upon them. After a period of time, sometimes weeks or even months of physical and mental abuse, the women were released back to the barracks.

Corrie and Betsie often tried to help the women who would return from the Punishment Block. These pitiful waifs came into the barracks with hands over their eyes, barely able to see, and with welts on their thighs and buttocks. They were walking skeletons and some of them would perish within a few days. Many had to be immediately taken to the infirmary. It was whispered that fifty to a hundred women died every day in the camp and this did not include the gassings. As winter approached, many women in the Bunker froze to death, and their corpses would be stuck to the cement floor the next morning.

With death all around, the Ten Boom sisters worked hard to share the love and hope of God to those around them. They continued their Bible studies and chapel services. Some of the Nazi guards called the Bible the "Book of Lies" and said it was forbidden in Ravensbrück; but this did not dissuade Corrie and Betsie. Prisoners came to them from all directions and listened as they shared Bible stories in between bunk beds three tiers high. One day alone, Corrie was invited to teach nine different times to various groups of women who needed encouragement.

One of the women influenced by Corrie was a Hollander named Mrs. De Boer. The desperate woman came to Corrie one day full of fear. "Corrie," she asked, "could you help me? I've just seen a woman cruelly beaten to death. It was terrible. When will my time come to be killed? I am afraid of death. Perhaps you can tell me something from your book that will take away this terrible fear. Can you help me?"

"Yes, indeed, I can," Corrie replied. "This book has the answer in John 1:12, 'As many as received Him, to them he gave power to become sons of God.' If you are a child of God you need not fear death, Mrs. De Boer. Jesus said 'In my Father's house are many mansions, and I go to prepare a place for you.' You see, children of God are at home in the Father's house. To them, death is the gateway to heaven."

"That means nothing to me," answered Mrs. De Boer. "I'm not religious, and I've never read the Bible. When you say I must accept Jesus I simply don't know what you mean."

Corrie prayed for wisdom on how to answer her, then suddenly an idea popped into her mind, "Do you remember years ago when Mr. De Boer proposed to you? How did you answer him?"

"I said yes," she said with a smile before sadness came to her eyes.

"Exactly! And when you had spoken that one little word you belonged to one another, you to him and he to you. Today, Jesus asks you, 'Will you accept Me as your Savior?' If you say, 'Yes Lord,' then you belong to Him and He belongs to you."

"Is it as simple as that?" she asked.

"Yes. To become a child of God you need only to accept Him, like a gift. A very important day was your wedding day when your life changed, and you joined one another. The day you accept Christ's gift of salvation is another important day. Then, all the promises of the Bible are yours for you to claim and trust. You can cast all of your sins on Him, all your fears, all your doubts. God is the only one in the world who can wash away our sins. Isn't that wonderful."

The two women sat for a moment in silence as Mrs. De Boer thought over Corrie's assuring words. Finally, she bent her head over, and together they prayed as Mrs. De Boer said the word, "Yes," and that was all.

When the two met up the next day, Mrs. De Boer was truly happy and full of peace. She told Corrie, "I am well aware that they can do anything they please with us, even cruelly murder us, but I know also that no one can take out of my heart the peace and happiness I have found now that I know Jesus lives in my heart. I am forgiven and saved and so happy." Even in her awful surroundings, Corrie felt a moment of joy and a sense of purpose for why God had placed her there.

That same day Corrie met with Mrs. De Boer's friend, Mrs. De Goede. "Why not take the same step your friend has taken," Corrie asked her. "See how she has been changed? You too can have the same peace."

Mrs. De Goede's face hardened, "That's not for me. You know nothing of my past. I'm too wicked to be a Christian. Oh, no. Being a Christian is all very well for noble souls like you but not for me. I'm far too wicked."

"Just one moment," Corrie said. "When you read the Bible there is just one type of person Jesus couldn't help — the Pharisees. In their own eyes they were so perfect they didn't need a Savior. But sinners were never rejected by the Lord Jesus. To them He said, "Whoever comes to me I will never cast out.' Do you know what the Bible tells us about sins we confess? That God drowns them in the depths of the sea; and as far as the east is from the west, He removes our sins from us. John says, 'If we confess our sins, He is faithful and just to forgive our sins and cleanse us from all unrighteousness.'"

Then, Corrie read to Mrs. De Goede the parable of the Prodigal Son. After they discussed this, Mrs. De Goede also made the decision to accept Christ like her friend.

It was near the end of November when Betsie took to coughing through the night. Corrie tried to tend to her, but Betsie began to spew blood. Corrie finally decided she must take Betsie to the infirmary.

CHAPTER 27

Evacuation

The Architect perused several calendar updates from the kommandant of Auschwitz, Rudolf Höss, regarding the final days at Auschwitz-Birkenau. The Architect had sent word to destroy the crematoria buildings and move people out of there in haste because of the fast-approaching Red Army. With the rapid advance of the Russians in July, Majdanek, the concentration camp near Lublin, was overrun before all the incriminating evidence could be destroyed. The Soviets reported to the world what they found there — an intact extermination camp. The Architect was fixated on preventing this from happening with Auschwitz. The bad press it could bring the Reich would be devastating.

Kommandant Höss gave a written update of the latest events leading up to the evacuation.

September 25, 1944

After the destruction of the Hungarian Jews, we were instructed that the Sonderkommandos who worked to burn the bodies in the ovens of the crematory and during the open-pit cremations should themselves be killed. This would eliminate the only witnesses who were in a position to tell what happened. Though the kommandant was fond of these Jewish workers, he obeyed the orders and two hundred Sonderkommandos were transferred from Birkenau to Auschwitz where they were gassed in the chamber used to disinfect clothing.

October 3

Eleven new transports from Theresienstadt in Czechoslovakia arrived to Auschwitz totaling 22,000 Jews. Over 18,400 men, women and children were gassed, the rest were deemed strong enough to live as workers.

October 7

A camp resistance movement acted against the Gestapo at Crematory IV. Also, at Crematory II and III prisoners began firing rifles at the SS guards. Two SS guards and a German Kapo were killed at Crematory II. After those in the resistance cut through barbed wire and fled on foot, they were surrounded in the woods and recaptured. Approximately 750 resistance fighters fell in battle and 212 were shot that evening for participating in the uprising. Fourteen additional prisoners died as a result of torture during their investigation of the uprising.

October 27

Another group of prisoners organizing an escape were betrayed by their driver, SS Corporal Johann Roth, and sent to the cells in Block 11. They took poison and died rather than face interrogation.

November 25

Per the Architect's order to destroy the crematories at Auschwitz-Birkenau, wrecking Kommando units were formed to help in the operation. One hundred female prisoners destroyed Crematory III. Another crew began cleaning and covering the earth with turf over the open-pit burning areas where the Hungarian Jews had been cremated.

December 12

A large shipment of three thousand Jewish women departed Auschwitz and were sent to Ravensbrück concentration camp.

December 26
Soviet airplanes bombed Birkenau and five SS were killed.

January 6, 1945
Four Jewish women were hanged at Birkenau during roll call in full view of the assembled women prisoners as a warning.

January 17
The last evening roll call took place at Auschwitz. Over 67,000 prisoners were present. The SS began to burn camp registers and files from the hospital block. Dr. Josef Mengele packed up his research on twins and fled for Berlin.

January 18
The evacuation of Auschwitz began in the early hours of the morning. Columns of five hundred women and children were marched out of camp guarded by the SS. Columns of men from Birkenau began leaving in the afternoon. The last groups departed just after midnight. Along the route the SS guards shot those who were weak and not able to keep up. In twenty-three mass graves along the way 510 men and women were buried. Those who survived were sent to concentration camps in Germany, namely Buchenwald, Dachau and Sachsenhausen.

January 19
The sick, the weak, and the children were left at Auschwitz, in all over 7,000 prisoners. Soviet aircraft bombed the town of Oswiecim and destroyed the power station. The sick prisoners were left with no light, no food, and no water.

January 20
The SS led 200 sick women who could still walk away from the camp and shot them all to death. They also set explosives to some of the crematories, blowing them to shreds.

January 23
The SS set fire to a pile of corpses near Crematory V then set fire to the barracks that housed all the remaining goods that was plundered from the Jews and not yet sent to Germany.

January 25
The SS shot all the prisoners who were too sick to march away. As they formed columns of the remaining prisoners the SS were informed that the Soviet Army was so close that Auschwitz would soon be encircled. They left the columns of prisoners standing out in the open and the guards quickly disappeared in their cars.

January 27
In the afternoon, Soviet troops entered the town of Oswiecim. A small firefight took place at the front of Auschwitz. Two Soviet soldiers were killed in battle in

front of the main gate of the camp. At 3 p.m. small groups of Soviet soldiers safely entered into Auschwitz and Birkenau. Approximately 600 bodies of men and women prisoners lay on the ground having died from the cold, starvation or being shot. Close to four thousand more are presumed still alive but should not be able to survive the next few days, even with restored electricity and Soviet rations.

—◆—

    The Architect put the report down on his desk and mulled over the last few entries. There had been plenty of time to dispose of all the infirmed prisoners and to bury them before the Soviets came. He did not understand why his orders were not quickly and fully carried out. The kommandant should be commended for dealing well with a wretched situation, but the Architect regretted the work left undone and what the Soviets could still find at Auschwitz.

    His hope was that the prisoners would be destroyed, the buildings leveled, and no trace left to reveal that the camp was used as an extermination center. But now he realized that this would not be the case. Even though most of the crematories were destroyed, the Soviets will surely put the puzzle pieces together with the leftover evidence.

    This was not good news. The Architect needed to immediately report to Hitler the status of the Polish camps and what the Soviet media would relay all over the world. He looked at the map of Germany on the table in front of him and realized the Russians would not be stopping their advance. His eyes fell on Ravensbrück. He must begin evacuation procedures there at once or the same situation might occur.

CHAPTER 28

Sisters

Betsie was in the hospital for her cough and Corrie could not bear being without Betsie for very long. They were best friends and helped each other get through the torturous days by being brave when the other was weak. Corrie felt alone all day and needed to see her sister.

    Corrie decided to do something desperate.

    The next morning a heavy fog covered the camp making it hard to see very far. Corrie decided to use this opportunity to slip away and see Betsie. Prisoners were not allowed to enter the hospital to visit others, so she needed another way to enter, a secret way. She had been told by Mimi, a friend who worked at the hospital, that behind the building where the latrines were located there was a window too warped to completely shut. Corrie quickly walked to the back of the hospital, careful not to be seen by the guards.

Sure enough, the large window slid open when Corrie pushed it upward. The smell coming from the latrine made her hold her breath, but she climbed up and through the sill. She found herself in a room with a row of lidless, doorless toilets, standing in a pool of their overflow. As Corrie swiftly moved to the door to leave, she glanced at the opposite wall from the toilets and found a dozen, naked corpses lying side by side on their back. Some of the eyes were open with a blank look staring toward the ceiling. Corrie shuddered, knowing these were real human beings, deeply cared for by their people somewhere.

Afraid to be caught there in the latrine, Corrie stepped foot into the corridor and walked briskly down the hall, trying to get the picture of the bodies out of her head. *Now, where to go to find Betsie?*

The hospital barracks held a maze of passageways and Corrie tried to find one that would lead to where her sister was kept. She walked into a room filled with cots of sick patients and looked from face to face to find Betsie. She guessed right, there was Betsie with a pleasant smile. Corrie walked through the room toward Betsie unafraid of the nurses who might interdict her.

Betsie was lying on a narrow cot side by side with a French girl. She told Corrie that the French girl repetitively kicked her until one time it knocked Betsie out of bed.

"There is such darkness in the heart of this poor sick child," said Betsie. "I have told her about the love of our Savior, and though she kicks me, I know it is no accident for the two of us to be placed together. Jesus is victor, and He will win in the end!"

"Have the doctors treated you any?" asked Corrie.

"Not yet," smiled Betsie.

"No medicine?"

Betsie shook her head. Just resting helped her feel much better.

"I can't believe they just leave you in here without helping you. Are you coughing much?"

"Oh, some."

"Have you seen much misery?" asked Corrie.

Upon hearing the words of the question, Betsie gave Corrie the sweetest expression without words, reminding Corrie that her sister lived above the wretchedness around her. They clasped hands, Betsie thoroughly satisfied as if they were at the Beje, Corrie troubled at the suffering around her.

A nurse entered and walked up to them, standing behind Corrie when she said, "What are you doing here? Who are you?"

"Prisoner 66730. I am Betsie's sister."

"You need to leave now, and if I see you again I will report you."

Corrie departed, back through the washroom window to rejoin her crew before they departed for the day. Suddenly, as Corrie walked, rebellion against God began to flood her heart. *How can You do this to my sister? What did we do to deserve all of this? Why should that horrid French child kick her out of bed? Why do You leave us here in this misery?*

Against the backdrop of her wordless anger, Corrie heard three words as if spoken aloud, *"Rempli de tendresse."* Corrie looked around but no one had spoken to her. She realized this was God reaching out to her in her desolate state. *"Rempli de tendresse."* There it was again, three simple words. Oh, she did not deserve this mercy and felt deeply ashamed. "*Rempli de tendresse.*" Tears of sorrow filled her eyes, but also tears of gratitude. She had been sustained even when rebelling. She deserved His wrath but received only His comfort. God was there for her, and those three French words whirled over and over in her mind, "*Rempli de tendresse*, filled with tenderness."

He loves me, and I am not alone. Corrie returned to her fellow prisoners with new resolve. Thinking of the pleasant smile of Betsie and the love of God filling her heart, she was renewed and able to make it through this day and the next.

On the third day Betsie returned to her. She was assigned to the knitting brigade and would stay in the barracks while Corrie and the others departed for work. With her Bible in her lap, Betsie read from the Scriptures to those around her. When her quota of socks were completed, Betsie would move from station to station and read the Bible out loud for all to hear.

The women who slept immediately above the Ten Boom sisters were prisoners punished for prostitution and known as "Red-light Commandos." They were too ashamed to join Corrie and Betsie's evening worship services, but Corrie noticed the women would listen from a distance. Corrie decided to speak to them in private and encourage them to seek the Lord, as she had done with Mrs. De Boer and Mrs. De Goede.

Corrie learned that a few of these women were pregnant, and desperately wanted to change their lives when they returned to Holland.

"When I return to my home I am going to change and live for God," one of them told Corrie.

"Well, you can live for Jesus now," exclaimed Corrie, and she read to her the story of the Prodigal Son.

"Yes, I want this but it is so hard to believe in this camp."

"Half-way measures are no good," said Corrie. "Jesus wants your entire heart."

One day these young women were sentenced to the Punishment Barracks for stealing. As Corrie and Betsie passed by the fence separating their block with the Punishment Block the three young ladies shouted out to them.

"Tante Betsie, Tante Corrie, are you there?" they asked.

"Yes, we are here," answered Betsie. "How are you getting along?"

"Badly, it is awful here. We work so hard and we are so homesick. If we could only be back in the barracks with you."

"The Lord Jesus is everywhere and with you also," answered Betsie. "You know what he asks of you."

Suddenly, a guard shouted at the "Red-light Commandos" to move away from the fence and to quit speaking. Corrie prayed for these young women that they might find Christ and that He would change their lives as surely as He had changed hers and Betsie's. Corrie knew they were all sinners and it was only by God's grace that eyes were opened enough to receive forgiveness of sin and accept eternal life.

One day Corrie returned with her work crew from gathering firewood outside of the Ravensbrück gate. When she came up to Betsie, Corrie noticed an especially chipper demeanor on her sister's face with her eyes a'twinkling.

"You're looking quite pleased with yourself," said Corrie to her sister.

"You know we have never understood why we have had such freedom in our barracks allowing us to openly read from the Bible. Well, today I found out the reason."

Betsie explained that there had been a disagreement among the knitting brigade about sock sizes needed from them. They sent for a supervisor to come in and sort everything out for them but the supervisor would not enter into the room. The guards would not come either. No one in authority would step foot near them.

"And do you know why, Corrie?" Betsie asked with triumph in her voice. "It's the fleas! That's what they said, this place is crawling with fleas and they didn't want to come inside."

Corrie's mind flashed back to their first hour in the building when they bowed their heads and Betsie thanked God even for the fleas. Corrie could see no use for them, but now, looking into Betsie's beaming face, she could only smile and thank God for the miserable little creatures again.

The Ten Boom sisters had several run-ins with the Snake, the ferociously brutal woman who they sought to avoid at all times. But occasionally coming into contact with her was unavoidable.

Two women the sisters had known from Vught had died and Corrie was encouraged to lead a memorial service for them. Everyone stared at the ground as Corrie commemorated their lives, even the Polish women who did not understand the German language stood reverently because of the solemn occasion.

The Snake, hiding in the back of the crowd violently shouted, "Enough! Stop this at once." She was furious at Corrie. But Corrie, calmed by a supernatural presence, continued to speak.

The Snake moved toward Corrie with her whip outstretched and continued to shout for silence.

Corrie bravely went on with her eulogy, "May I ask you all to remember the dead in a moment of reverent silence?" Corrie closed her eyes, expecting the blows from the whip to fall on her back, but inexplicably the silence remained unbroken.

A moment later, the ceremony concluded, Corrie glanced over to see the Snake, whip in hand, staring fixedly before her.

Another medical inspection.

Another wait for hours in a long line without a stitch of clothing on, hands to the side, back erect.

Another fierce volley of wind whipping through the barracks yard area making everything intolerable.

December rolled in and the temperatures continued to drop well below freezing. Betsie was still sick and getting worse. Mimi gave Corrie and Betsie an old newspaper she had swiped from her work site. Corrie carefully stuffed it inside Betsie's blue sweater to help her withstand the bitter cold.

The women were repeatedly forced to stand outside in the morning air for hours. Some did not make it. One girl, two rows in front of the sisters, soiled herself and when the Snake found out she rushed at the girl with her thick leather crop raised above her head. The young woman shrieked in pain and terror and the Snake beat her mercilessly, over and over again until the screaming stopped and the girl lay, unmoving, in a clump at the feet of the Snake.

When the Snake walked away Corrie felt such remorse for all these women who were suffering at the hands of such evil. She whispered, "Betsie, what can we do for these people when the war is over? I would like to make a home for them so they can be cared for and loved, and shown the love of God."

"Corrie, I pray every day that we would be allowed to do this. To show them that love is greater."

It was later in the day, as Corrie gathered wood outside with her crew, when she realized she had been thinking of a home for prisoners and Betsie for their persecutors.

That very week, Betsie received her vision from God. She told Corrie about a house they would have, one much larger than the Beje, where they would care for people after the war.

"It's such a beautiful house, Corrie!" Betsie exclaimed. Even though she was growing so weak, her voice was strong with excitement. "The floors are all inlaid wood with statues set in the walls and a broad staircase sweeping down. The windows are tall and beautiful, letting so much sunlight into the home. And with gardens, Corrie, beautiful gardens all around where they can plant flowers. It will be so good for them, won't it, to be able to care for flowers?"

Corrie stood and stared in amazement as her sister went on and on about the place they would have after the war was over. It was as if Betsie could see it in her mind, as if the place already existed, and she was describing it to Corrie who for some reason could not see it. It seemed to Betsie that the beautiful house with the bright gardens was reality and the filthy barracks they were living in was a dream.

It was now the week before Christmas and Betsie was having trouble with her legs. The frigid morning roll calls were only tolerable when able to stomp the feet hard enough to keep blood circulating. Betsie was so weak that she could not stomp her feet any longer. When they returned to the barracks after morning roll call, Corrie spent time rubbing and massaging Betsie's frozen legs. But it was not just the legs that frightened Corrie; Betsie seemed strangely lethargic and her speech labored. Corrie noticed Betsie's emaciated appearance and realized that her condition is what happened to all the ailing women before they took the downward spiral to death.

The next morning, Corrie tried to help her sister prepare for morning roll call by helping with her shoes when she noticed that her sister's legs were paralyzed. Corrie went to the block captain and asked if Betsie could remain behind this morning.

"The commander has ordered that even the dying must report for roll call," was the cruel response.

Corrie, and their friend Mimi, carried Betsie through the dark to formation and sat her on a stool. Betsie survived morning roll call, however, later in the day Corrie noticed that Betsie's face was ashen and she looked deathly ill. They spent the night in Barracks 28 and Corrie nursed her sister as best she could, rubbing her legs and feet and speaking to Betsie to keep her coherent. *If only she had something warm to sip on.* Their wretched poverty was never as acute to Corrie as that night.

The next morning Betsie woke up and was unable to move either arms or legs. Corrie shoved her way through the crowded aisles to find the guard on duty. To her horror, it was the Snake. Corrie proceeded anyway, unafraid and desperate to find help for Betsie.

"Please!" Corrie begged. "Betsie is ill! Oh please, she's got to get to the hospital this morning."

"Stand at attention!" the Snake barked. "State your number."

"Prisoner 66730 reporting. Please, my sister is sick!"

"All prisoners must report for the count. If she's sick she can register at sick call."

Corrie and Mimi formed a cradle with their arms and carried Betsie out of the barracks and over to the hospital, then stopped. In the light of the street lamps, the sick-call line stretched to the end of the long building and around the corner. So many desperate people, huddled together, trying to stay warm as they waited for the hospital doors to open. In the snow beside the line lay three bodies where they had fallen.

Without a word, Corrie and another friend, Maryke, turned and carried Betsie back to roll call. The three patiently waited for the roster to be read so they could return to the barracks and put Betsie back in bed.

As Corrie cared for her emaciated sister that day, she would catch whispered phrases about the house they were to have. "The house is ready and waiting for us, such tall, tall windows, and the sun is streaming in." Then she was interrupted with a coughing fit.

Later, Betsie spoke of another place, this time in Germany, where they were to care for people. "A concentration camp where we are in charge. The barracks are gray now, Corrie, but we'll paint them bright green, like springtime!"

We'll do this together Betsie?" asked Corrie. "We're doing all this together, you're sure about that?"

"Oh yes! Always together, Corrie. You and I, sisters, always together."

When the siren blew the next morning, Corrie and Maryke carried Betsie to roll call but were stopped by the Snake just outside the barracks door.

"Take her back to the bunks," said the Snake sternly.

"I thought all prisoners were to…"

"Take her back!"

Corrie and Maryke replaced Betsie back to her bed, wondering what the Snake might be plotting. During roll call, Corrie worried about what would happen to her sister. *Was it possible that the Snake had some sympathy for Betsie?* The thought seemed too good to be true. As soon as roll call was over, Corrie raced back to her barracks building and there, looming over the bed, stood the Snake. Beside her were two orderlies from the hospital placing Betsie on a stretcher.

The Snake straightened up, almost like a guilty child, as Corrie approached. "The prisoner is ready for transfer," she declared.

Corrie stared in disbelief at the Snake who had risked fleas and lice to spare Betsie the sick-call line. Corrie followed the stretcher out of the barracks without a word from the Snake to stop her.

It was sleeting outside when Betsie, the orderlies, and Corrie all traveled across the yard and up to the front of the hospital. Corrie noticed the large line of sick people, all waiting to enter and be seen by the doctor. They moved through the entryway and into a large ward of patients. The orderlies set the stretcher down to the ground. Betsie was whispering something, so Corrie bent over and put her ear near Betsie's mouth to hear her.

"We must tell people what we have learned here," implored Betsie in her feeble voice. "They must know that there is no pit so deep that He is not deeper still. They will listen to us, Corrie, because we have been here."

Corrie stared at her sister's wasted form, "But when will all this happen, Betsie?"

"Now; right away! Oh, very soon, Corrie. We will be out of prison by the first of the year." Corrie could not believe what she was hearing. *Could it be true?*

A nurse caught sight of Corrie so she backed away, toward the outer door. She watched as they put Betsie on a narrow cot next to the window. Corrie left the hospital and ran around to that same window. She looked in and saw her sister. Finally, Betsie caught sight of her standing there in the sleet, and the sisters exchanged momentary smiles.

At noontime, Corrie bravely walked up to the Snake and said, "Prisoner 66730 reporting. Request permission to visit the hospital."

The Snake glanced up, then scrawled out a pass and handed it to Corrie. Corrie raced to the hospital but the nurse would not let her enter Betsie's room. Corrie ran around the hospital to the window where she had stood that morning. When Betsie looked up and saw Corrie she smiled sweetly, faintly.

Corrie mouthed the words, "Are you all right?"

Betsie nodded. Corrie stood there a moment, then said, "You must get good rest."

Betsie mouthed something Corrie could not follow so she placed her ear to the window and was able to make out a few of Betsie's words, "So much work to do." Then one of the camp police shouted at Corrie to move along.

Corrie walked back to the barracks. That evening the Snake was off duty and the guard in charge would not allow Corrie to go to the hospital.

The next morning after roll call, Corrie ran to the hospital without waiting for permission. She approached the window and looked forward to seeing Betsie's encouraging smile as she had nearly every day of their pre-war life. But when she looked inside her view was momentarily blocked. There were two nurses, each holding the sides of a sheet at its four corners. On top of the sheet was Betsie's naked and emaciated body; Corrie's beloved sister now nothing but a skeletal waif, unmoving, and with eyes shut. Corrie could see the indentation of every rib, joint and even the outline of teeth through the thin parchment of skin wrapped around her. It took Corrie a moment to recognize Betsie and to realize what was happening.

"She is dead," Corrie moaned out loud. *Gone! But we had so much to do together!*

The nurses lifted the corpse and left the room with their bundle as they did every day with the patients who died overnight.

Where are they taking her? Corrie wondered frantically. She turned from the window and ran around the side of the building toward the main entrance, her chest burning as she breathed. Then Corrie remembered the washroom where she had snuck in before. *That window!* She maneuvered to the back of the hospital complex, to the small building used as a latrine. She pushed up the warped window and crawled through it. *What if Betsie is there on the floor?*

Corrie counted eleven dead bodies lying on the floor, none of them Betsie. People using the reeking washroom had to step over the corpses. *The regime has no respect for the dead,* thought Corrie. She departed and walked around the camp awhile, occasionally walking by the window and peeking in.

Suddenly, as if being awoken from a dream she heard her name, "Corrie! Corrie! I've looked for you everywhere." It was her friend Mimi, the hospital worker who had helped with Betsie during her last few days. She pulled on Corrie's arm as if to take her back to the hospital.

"I know, Mimi," Corrie said defeatedly and wrenched her arm free. "I already know."

Mimi pulled again, "Come, Corrie. Please come."

Corrie allowed Mimi to lead her back to the hospital. They went to the same washroom window and Mimi helped Corrie through the opening to where the dead bodies lay. When Corrie glanced up she saw a nurse standing in the room bringing instant fear of being reported.

"This is the sister," Mimi told the nurse.

Corrie decided not to look at the bodies lined up behind the nurse, but Mimi had another idea. She put her arm around Corrie and maneuvered her past the nurse to where the bodies were lying.

"Do you see her, Corrie?"

Corrie could not look at first, but finally raised her eyes to the face of her sister in disbelief. There Betsie lay dead, her eyes closed, but with the sweetest expression of peace on her face. Corrie could not believe what she was seeing. She had not seen her sister look this way since they were together at the Beje. The grief, the fear, the hollows of hunger were all simply erased and replaced by contentment. It was Betsie; stronger, radiant, and free. *Thank you Lord Jesus!* Corrie knew her sister was in glory. This was a gift from God to quiet the storm of sorrow in Corrie's heart.

The nurse said softly to them, "You can leave through the hall."

Corrie took one more look at her sister's serene face, then she and Mimi walked out of the washroom. In the hallway there was a mound of clothing heaped alongside the wall. Corrie noticed Nollie's threadbare blue sweater at the top, stained with newsprint, and she instinctively reached for it.

"Don't touch it, Corrie!" Mimi said sharply. "Black lice. That pile is to be burned."

Corrie pulled her arm back from the last physical tie she would have with her sister. She consoled herself that it was better this way; what tied Corrie to Betsie now was the hope of heaven.

CHAPTER 29

The Tent

T he Architect looked over a narrative confiscated from one of the SS guards
at Ravensbrück. The pitiable guard had sought to deliver it to the Red Cross
but he was intercepted and the report sent to Berlin. The Architect read the
gory details with relish, thankful it would never reach the Red Cross.

———◆———

*Nearly three thousand Jews from Auschwitz entered Ravensbrück
and marched toward the tent set up as a makeshift holding cell for
those arriving at camp. The difference for these Jews is that it is not a
temporary station for them. Unfortunately, since it is winter, the tent
does little to protect its residents from the cold. Many of the women do
not have blankets and were not issued one upon arrival at the camp.
Ravensbrück is simply overrun with prisoners. There is no more space.
The women in the tent are forced to remain there unsheltered.*

*These Jewish women who escaped Auschwitz and its gas chambers
are dying like flies. The starving women, huddled together and sitting
on their own excrement in the urine-soaked straw, are not permitted
to depart the tent. The SS guards who patrol the tent are instructed
to keep everyone inside and not allow visitors to enter.*

*Other female prisoners housed in the barracks nearby could hear
the shrieks and moans from the dying women inside the tent but are
not permitted to help them. Each day, nearly forty dead women are
carried out of the tent in two-wheeled carts pushed by other prisoners
and then hauled by lorries to the Ravensbrück crematorium. The
stench has infused the entire area and everyone around can smell the
suffering and agony happening inside the tent.*

*The women nearby — barely able to survive themselves — are
filled with shame because of the tent. They are not allowed to help
those inside under pain of death. It was Heinrich Himmler's orders,
"All women who are either sick or incapable of marching are to be
killed," and the women inside the tent were deemed too sick to live.*

*The crematorium in Ravensbrück worked overtime but could
not keep up. The glow of the furnace illuminated the dark around
it all night long. Daytime brought a haze of ashes created by the
burning flesh. As with the Hungarian Jews at Birkenau, a burning pit
outside the crematorium is used to accommodate those who could not
be squeezed inside the over-worked ovens. Prisoners managed these
open-pit carcass fires and then were gassed themselves. This operation
of death and cover-up is now a well-oiled machine.*

The bodies piled up throughout the camp. Some of the bodies sent to the burn pile were found to be chewed on and partially eaten by starving inmates. Prisoners' belongings are not returned to families. Death notices are no longer sent to the next of kin. The administration is collapsing under the weight of the misery of death. The camp officials cannot keep up; it is much easier to kill and dispose than to feed, heal, or provide notifications to family members.

———◆◆———

The Architect set the report down. Despite Ravensbrück's efficiency for dealing with undesirables, he knew it was time to evacuate the camp. The Soviets would be there within a few weeks.

CHAPTER 30

A Clerical Error

Alone.

Alone in Ravensbrück.

Alone in Barracks 28.

No more conversations with Betsie.

No more desire to pray and lead Bible studies.

Betsie's absence left a terrible void in Corrie's heart. She was reassured by her last memory of Betsie, serene and full of joy. But now Corrie would have to go through the misery of Ravensbrück on her own.

The very first night, Corrie was in bed thankful to have a few moments to herself before falling asleep. She looked down into the aisle beneath her and saw a Russian woman looking hopelessly about for a place to sleep. Everyone turned her away and a hunted look of desperation came into the poor woman's eyes. Corrie knew that Betsie's place beside her was vacant but her heart craved this moment by herself to deal with the grief of the day's events. Corrie gave it thought, then motioned down for the woman to come join her in bed. She pulled the blanket back and waved her arm again.

The Russian woman gratefully crawled up to Corrie and slipped in beside her, relieved. Their two heads were right next to each other as the woman looked up at the slats of rotted wood where other prisoners slept above them. Corrie did not want to be bothered but felt she should speak to her. She did not know Russian but said the words, "*Jesoes Christoes?*"

At once the woman smiled, made the sign of the cross and kissed Corrie on the cheek, thankful to find a faith friend. Betsie was gone, but the Lord replaced her spot with a woman who also loved Jesus. Corrie was somber but knew that God was in control and had a plan for her life. She thought of 1 Corinthians 15 and the triumphant words, "The body that is sown is perishable, but raised imperishable; it is sown in dishonor, it is raised in glory; it is sown in weakness, it is raised in power; thanks be to God who gives us the victory through our Lord Jesus Christ."

Two days after Betsie's death, one of the fourteen hundred women of Barracks 28 had failed to appear for roll call. The women were left standing at attention in the bitter cold from 5:30 in the morning until noon. The women were counted again and again, then checked off one by one against the guard's record book. They deciphered the name of the one who was missing and eventually found her, a little Polish woman, dead in her bed in the barracks. The prisoners had been punished because of the absence of a dead woman.

When Corrie walked back to the barracks one of the "Red-light Commandoes" called out to her through the Punishment Block fence, "Corrie, are you there? Tante Betsie, how are you?"

"I am here and I am fine," answered Corrie. "Betsie is dead, however."

Corrie heard sobbing from the other side of the fence. *How those three loved Betsie*, Corrie thought.

"How are you, Corrie?" one of them asked through tears.

"I am okay, much comforted and thankful Betsie is at home in heaven. How are you?"

"Well, we wanted you and Betsie to know," one of them said at last, "that we have all three been converted. We are Christians now."

⬤◆⬤

The next morning during roll call in the courtyard, Corrie received a shock when an announcer called over the loud speaker, "Ten Boom, Cornelia! Stand to the side!"

For a moment Corrie stood where she was. She had been known as Prisoner 66730 for so long, the sound of her name came as a startling surprise and momentarily paralyzed her. *What would happen next? Had someone reported her Bible?*

The siren finally blew, and when the mass of women marched back to the barracks, Corrie saw a guard signaling for her. The two marched through the camp, Corrie's legs still painfully swollen from the six-hour roll call the day before. They made their way to the administration building where Corrie and Betsie had first checked in upon arriving at Ravensbrück. Once inside, they entered a room with a line of prisoners waiting behind a large desk where a man was signing a woman's paper.

"*Entlassen!*" said the officer seated at the desk when he stamped a piece of paper for the woman in front of him.

Released? Corrie wondered what this could mean. Was the woman standing there with the piece of paper free to leave Ravensbrück? *It couldn't be.*

The next woman moved up to the desk and the same thing happened.

"*Entlassen!*" said the officer when he handed the woman her signed paper.

"*Entlassen!*"

"*Entlassen!*"

Corrie slowly made her way to the front of the line. She noticed that the others stood around, waiting for someone to tell them what to do. At last, she was next.

"Ten Boom, Cornelia."

Corrie stepped up to the desk but wobbled so she steadied herself with her hands. The officer in front of her did not look up. He signed the paper with her name on it, then shouted, "*Entlassen!*"

Corrie held up the paper to read it, saw her name and birth date and the words CERTIFICATE OF DISCHARGE written at the top in bold, black letters.

Stunned, Corrie moved over to the small group of women who were being led out the door. In the next room they were handed a rail pass for transportation through Germany to the Dutch border. *Could this actually be happening?* Corrie knew women who had been prisoners at Ravensbrück for years, much longer than she was made to endure it.

Trying not to get her hopes up, she maneuvered down a hall to another room where the women in front of her were taking off their dresses.

"*Entlassen* inspection," a prisoner said to her with a big grin as she pulled her dress over her head and threw it on the other dresses.

Corrie braced herself to endure another medical inspection, took off her Bible from around her neck along with her dress and rolled them together before laying them down, underneath another dress. She stood beside the row of naked women waiting to be examined one last time by the doctor, their backs and buttocks against a rough wooden wall. Corrie and Betsie had endured this abuse many times, but the thought of freedom being so close made this inspection more shameful.

Finally, the medical doctor arrived, a freckle-faced boy in a soldier's uniform who looked at the women with contempt. One by one the women had to bend, turn around and spread their fingers.

When the doctor reached Corrie, he looked down her body to her feet and said with disgust, "Edema! You have to go to the hospital. Prisoners have to be released in good condition."

The women were told to put back on their clothes. Corrie was one of two who were told to go to the hospital.

"Does this mean we're not released?" she asked one of the guards.

"No, it just means you have to get better before they release you."

The two dejected women made their way across the camp to the hospital. The sick call line wrapped around the building but they walked straight through the front door. They were escorted to a sick room crammed with double-decker cots. Corrie found an open one by the window and she immediately laid down and elevated her feet so she could get the swelling to go down in her legs.

The hospital was a horrible place to be on regular occasions. Today, however, it was unbearable. Most of the patients around Corrie were survivors of a bombed prison train and in severe pain and anguish. The nurses walked around and mocked those who screamed out, imitating the sounds from the mutilated patients and then laughed at each other. The jeering from the staff was an appalling form of mental abuse. Corrie thought she was having an evil nightmare.

Four of the hospital staff worked on a woman who screamed loud shrieks of pain and suffering. They treated her for hours and the screaming continued. Another young woman, thin as a skeleton, walked around the ward with nothing on but a shirt, calling out for the staff to help. Her eyes bulged out in horror and she could barely walk or hold herself up, yet not one of the staff seemed to notice or care; it was a scene from Hades.

Darkness came and all night the screaming continued. Several women called out the word, "*Schieber!*" a German word Corrie did not know.

"*Schieber! Schieber!*" the word came out over and over again, often from rasping throats, but there were no staff to aid those in need. Some of the women tried to help themselves down but were not strong enough to get out of the bunk by themselves and crashed to the floor. Three of those who fell died by morning.

The next night Corrie realized women were calling for bedpans. She knew these women would never make it to the filthy, bitterly cold latrine next to the hospital, the one filled with dead bodies. Corrie crawled out of her bunk, found the two bed pans, and went from woman to woman, doing the chore as best she could.

"Why are you doing this?" one asked.

Corrie smiled and rubbed her hand.

"You're a good person," the woman said.

The hurting prisoners looked at Corrie with deep gratitude. She made sure everyone in need was taken care of and did not notice the breaking of the dawn.

It was Christmas morning.

"Edema!" the doctor said to Corrie. "Hospital."

Corrie had her legs checked every morning at the clinic in front of the hospital. For days she was turned back to her cot, her legs barely better from the day before. She knew the edema in her feet and ankles was keeping her from being released from Ravensbrück. She prayed each day that the swelling would go down enough to be released.

On her sixth night at the hospital both bedpans had mysteriously vanished. Corrie had a thought as to where they might be. On the top bunk in the center aisle two Hungarian gypsies often laughed and conversed by themselves about the other patients. One of them had a gangrenous foot and would thrust it in the face of anyone who came near, so Corrie never walked by their bunk.

Sure enough, someone screamed out that the two gypsies had both bedpans hidden under their blankets to save them from a trip to the latrine. Corrie decided to go to their cot and plead with them as best she could, because she did not know Hungarian, and they did not know German.

Suddenly in the dark something wet and sticky wrapped around Corrie's face. The woman had taken the bandage off her foot and threw it at Corrie's head. Corrie ripped off the foul bandage and ran to the latrine sobbing as she went, then ran water on her face over and over again from the wall spigot.

Corrie vowed never to go down that aisle again. *What did she care about the whole mess? It wasn't her problem!* She laid in her bed with a sense of loathing and fear of infection. After she prayed, Corrie knew she did care and would go back and deal with the issue.

She had changed since leaving the Beje and was a different woman now. There was no more fear. She had strength to move forward in love despite her circumstances. Ravensbrück had given her evil but God was already turning it into good.

With courage and determination Corrie walked back down the aisle toward the gypsies. When the women saw her coming, they were astonished. Instantly both bedpans were tossed out from the covers and clattered on the floor in front of Corrie.

The next morning Corrie ten Boom heard the words she had waited to hear for months.

"Approved!"

Corrie was brought to a room in the administration building and given extra clothing for the trip. Her old leather shoes, held together by threads were put aside and she was given almost-new shoes, along with a woolen skirt, a silk blouse, a hat and an overcoat. She was handed a form to sign stating that she had never been ill at Ravensbrück, never had an accident, and that her treatment had been good. Corrie signed.

She also received one day's bread ration and food coupons for three additional days. Corrie's watch was returned, along with her Dutch money and her Mama's ring. She was then escorted to the front gate and waited with a dozen others for the massive iron doors to open.

Mimi came running to the gate to say goodbye to Corrie before she left Ravensbrück.

"Did you hear that Mrs. De Boer and Mrs. De Goede both died this morning?" Mimi asked.

"No, Mimi, I hadn't." Corrie looked again at the gray concentration camp and thanked God for the opportunity to share about His love with these women before they died. *Perhaps that was the reason I was sent here!*

Presently, the gates opened so Corrie said goodbye to Mimi and walked out of Ravensbrück on the road leading up the hill to the train stop. She realized that Betsie's words had come true ... they were both free before the new year.

Later, Corrie learned she was released because of a simple administrative error by a low-level clerk. Corrie was supposed to have been taken to the gas chamber.

Spring 1945

The Fall of Berlin

"The Fall of Berlin"

Part IV

PEACE AND PUNISHMENT

CHAPTER 31

Notes from *Mein Kampf*

" Y ou know I ordered everything in France to be destroyed!" exclaimed Hitler with a stern tone. "Then how is it possible that French industry is already approaching its prewar production only a few months later? I need an answer!"

Speer looked at Germany's leader for a moment before responding. He knew the true answer was because he had countermanded Hitler's orders at every opportunity. Speer worked deals with the Industrialists and Gauleiters, twisting Hitler's wishes and spawning opportunities in spite of the Führer's scorched earth policy of destruction.

Speer recognized he could not answer the truth, it was too banal, treasonous. Hitler had called for the immediate death to anyone disobeying his orders. Therefore another answer must suffice. "It's probably a propaganda report," Speer replied calmly.

Hitler knew about false propaganda reports because he ordered Goebbels to utilize them extensively.

To Speer's relief, his answer was accepted and the affair was dismissed.

Several days after the New Year's Eve celebration Hitler decided that the only way to win the war now was mass conscription. If Germany drafted every male available for war there would be enough men to continue the fight for several more months, if not a year or two; enough time for secret weapons to be made.

"Does everyone see the necessity of this plan?" asked Hitler of those in attendance.

Of the few men present, Bormann, Keitel and Goebbels nodded their heads enthusiastically. It was those three who felt most empowered around Hitler, and thereby did most of the agreeing. Also present were two members from the Armaments ministry, Speer and Saur. As was common during the last few months it was Speer's deputy, Karl Saur, who Hitler turned to again and again for armaments decisions thus circumventing Speer.

Hitler noticeably ignored Speer and deferred to Saur whenever an armament decision surfaced. It did not rattle Speer too much for he knew the war was lost. However, he could see that Hitler's treatment of him visibly shocked some of the other ministry leaders and they wanted Speer to do something about it. Speer realized the failure of the Ardennes Offensive meant the end was near. There was no need for turf wars now or to try to win the Führer's affections again.

Yet Speer could not sit by and allow this last decision take root. The disruption to all armaments production across the Reich would be significant. If tens of thousands of men were to depart the factories, then production of arms and ammunition would come to a grinding halt. Speer knew that only the healthiest would be selected leaving the sick and dying to the industrial work. But even with fresh recruits to fill empty spaces in brigades, sending them to the front would not make much of a difference. Untested draftees sent to fight a war against battle-hardened soldiers would be tantamount to slaughter. Though Speer preferred to remain silent and let Saur puppeteer his ministry, he felt it his duty to speak up.

"Mein Führer, if I could," started Speer.

All eyes turned to Albert Speer in anticipation of what would surely be his objection.

Hitler glared at Speer as if to threaten him with merely a penetrating look. *Speer would not speak against the Führer, would he?* Speer could almost read the faces of those around him. But he had to follow the leading of his heart.

"If we move forward with this levée en mass and mobilize everyone, then our current programs will grind to a halt," Speer reasoned with them. "This plan could lead to the total collapse of our industry. I cannot support this, we must have laborers for our factories to continue the war."

Though Hitler's dark stare bore a hole through Speer, it was Goebbels who was most irate at the dissent and began screaming. The Propaganda Minister eyed Hitler while saying, "Herr Speer, you will bear the historic guilt for the loss of the war due to the lack of a few hundred thousand soldiers! Why don't you say yes for once? Consider it! Your fault!"

No one moved or dared say a word, they were all waiting for their Führer to comment. Finally, Hitler nodded to Goebbels. Germany would follow through on the mass conscription plan. Speer lost another argument but he was not surprised. His advice had not been adhered since the assassination plot of July 20th when he was officially diminished among the cabinet ministers.

Another week.

Another meeting.

Another battlefield loss.

Another snub from the Führer.

Speer felt it useless to give his opinion in cabinet meetings because Hitler seemed to always do the opposite from what Speer suggested. The Führer refused to meet with Speer alone because he knew Speer would only report the negative aspects of the war.

In mid-January the western Allies effectively ended the Ardennes Offensive with one great bite when they encircled 20,000 Germans north of Bastogne. It was as Speer had predicted.

In early February a meeting was called in which Hitler wanted to speak to Speer and Saur about a memorandum Speer had prepared concerning the war. In the memo Speer had discussed Upper Silesia, the region rich in minerals and natural resources cherished by Poland before the 1939 invasion. The potential loss of this region to the Red Army would bring such a tremendous reduction of tanks and ammunition, war production would be severely impacted. In fact, Speer began with the words "The war is lost," and he went on to report that the Silesian mines produced sixty percent of Germany's coal.

There would be no way to replace what was lost. The Third Reich currently had only two weeks' supply of coal for the German railways, power plants and factories. Speer stated that he could now only supply one fourth of the coal and one sixth of the steel that Germany had been producing in 1944, just the year before. He concluded his report by writing "there would not be enough to supply the front lines any longer, and these losses cannot be made up by the bravery of the soldiers."

This last sentence was the part Speer knew would inflame the Chancellor. Hitler always proclaimed that the unique patriotism and bravery of the German fighter would outweigh any disadvantage he might have against a Russian soldier.

Speer and Saur traveled to the Chancellery in Berlin where they were escorted into Hitler's private study. They were offered seats and a drink as Hitler began to discuss with the men the ammunition and ordnance position. The Chancellor kept his eyes on Saur who was much more optimistic than Speer. Speer sat in silence while Hitler purported a positive spin on current events and Saur agreed that things were not all bad, that Germany would probably be just fine for the next several months.

After a few moments of pleasant banter between Hitler and Saur, the Führer finally turned to Speer with a noticeable change to his demeanor. Coolly he said, "You are perfectly entitled to let me know your estimate of the armaments situation, Speer, but I forbid you to convey this information to anyone else. You are not permitted to give anyone else a copy of this memorandum. As for your last paragraph, you cannot write that sort of thing to me."

Hitler spoke softly and in a measured tone, remaining calm and collected, "You might have spared yourself the trouble of such conclusions. You are to leave to me the conclusions I draw from the armaments situation."

It was the way he said it.

Because the Führer did not yell nor show any emotion it unnerved Speer more than at other times. Speer was convinced the manner in which Hitler communicated that day was much more dangerous than if he had shouted at him in anger. This was, most definitely, Hitler's final word on the subject. The two men were dismissed at once; Hitler's goodbye cordial with Saur, but curt with Speer.

<hr />

After the meeting with the Führer, Speer decided to visit Hermann Göring once again at Carinhall. Göring was terrified of losing his vast estate to the oncoming Russians and had positioned his own parachute division in defense of the property. The Reichsmarschall was probably the only German who could get away with using a military division to protect his own hide. *Poor Hermann!*

Over the past few weeks, though Speer had endured neglect from Hitler, it could be said that Göring was Hitler's punching bag. Göring suffered more verbal abuse than any of Hitler's other generals and often in a public setting. He was routinely made the scapegoat for the failures of the Luftwaffe and Hitler consistently denounced Göring in the most violent and hate-filled language whenever a major Allied bombing campaign occurred.

Ironically, these episodes made Speer appreciate Göring more, if for no other reason than he felt sorry for any man in his position —deserved or not — and shared a certain camaraderie with him as one who was out of Hitler's good graces.

"I cannot support Hitler or his policies any longer," said Speer in a private meeting room deep inside the labyrinth of Carinhall. "He has become my greatest disappointment."

It was extremely quiet as Göring poured Speer a drink from his magnificent Rothschild-Lafite brought up from his wine cellar. The only sound in the room was the wood crackling in the fireplace; the servants were told not to disturb them. Emmy, Göring's second wife, was ordered by Hitler to depart the premises in January because of the approaching Russians. Many of the servants had left with her. Speer noticed upon his entry to the great hall that the paintings and statues had been taken down. Göring shipped many valuables to his retreat home in Berchtesgaden.

"I understand how you feel," said Göring, sipping his exclusive wine. "But it is easier for you than for me, dear Speer. Since you joined Hitler much later in his life you can be free from him all the sooner. It is not so easy for me. I have been through much with him and it is not as easy to seek separation. Many years of common experiences and struggles in those early years of establishing the Nazi Party has bound us together and made us inseparable."

"But the way he berates you in public?"

"He doesn't mean it. He just gets angry. I know him, Speer, where you do not. He calms down and our old relationship is still in place. Though he yells at me publicly, I know he is still loyal to me. Loyalty is important for each of us."

Göring went on to speak of how easy it would be for Speer to leave Germany now and to separate from Hitler, though he did not see the same opportunity for himself. He tried to convince Speer he should flee with his family and Göring again offered to help.

The two men said goodnight and Speer felt a new closeness had developed between them. Göring acted the gentleman and Speer decided he could trust him again.

Two days later, Hitler commanded that Göring's parachute division be deployed away from Carinhall and positioned in southern Germany. *So much for Nazi Party loyalty*, thought Speer.

■◆■

Albert Speer was not entirely sure what to do now. After his conversation with Göring, he thought about fleeing with his family. He knew Germany had lost the war. But the other fact gnawing at him was that his homeland would no longer exist once the Allies divided up the country. The press reported how the Allies sought to divvy up the goods, once in possession of their prize. Speer was sick in the soul with this reality, yet he chose to continue to perform his duties for the sake of his country.

However, his nights were becoming more restless. He was haunted by the warning he received from his friend regarding Auschwitz. *What was the meaning behind the warning? What was going on in Poland? Was he serving an evil regime?*

Speer reflected on the statement Hitler made long ago when he told Speer quietly that the bridges behind them were burned. Speer knew he should have questioned this but he failed. He failed to question his friend about Auschwitz, and he was failing now at getting the Führer to acknowledge him.

It was with all of these thoughts swirling in his mind when a friend of his, an Industrialist named Dr. Friedrich Lüschen, chose to stop by Speer's Ministry office in Berlin late one night in February 1945. Dr. Lüschen was head of the German electric industry and chief of research and development for Siemens. This man, who was now 70-years-old, was as close to a mentor Speer had ever experienced. Speer treasured their friendship and wished they had more time to spend together.

After a drink and catching up on family and the war effort, Dr. Lüschen handed Speer a slip of paper from his pocket and said, "Are you aware of the verses in Hitler's *Mein Kampf* that are most often quoted these days?"

Speer opened the piece of paper and read, "The task of diplomacy is to ensure that a nation does not heroically go to its destruction but is practically preserved. Every way that leads to this end is expedient and a failure to follow it must be called criminal neglect of duty."

Speer was spellbound with these words. *The angst in his heart originated in no other place than Hitler's own book!* Before he could collect himself and respond to his friend, Dr. Lüschen handed Speer another slip of paper and then quickly put on his overcoat.

Speer read, "State authority as an end in itself cannot exist, since in that case every tyranny on this earth would be sacred and unassailable. If a racial entity is being led toward its doom by means of governmental power, then the rebellion of every single member of such a *Volk* is not only a right, but a duty."

Speer was flabbergasted. He glanced up into the face of Friedrich Lüschen, a German patriot and hero of industrial society. Without a word the man locked eyes with Speer for a moment, executed an about face, and silently drifted out through the door.

Speer paced anxiously around the room holding the two slips of paper from Dr. Lüschen. Seeing these thoughts written by Hitler years before the present situation; such clear answers to the vexing problem ... *a failure to follow it must be called criminal neglect of duty.* This is precisely what Speer needed to hear, though it did not improve his situation. Hitler himself wrote — with such succinctness — what Speer tried to get across to the Führer for the past eight months. Hitler himself was deliberately committing high treason against his own people. Hitler himself was the one who must be rebelled against, as was Speer's duty, according to Hitler's own words.

Speer sank uneasily into a wooden chair in his Ministry apartment. He was agitated, and at a turning point. At that moment, Albert Speer decided, for the good of his country, to assassinate Adolf Hitler. He knew that to let the Führer live would equal the death of the German populace.

It was startling at first, for Speer to consider murder. Though he had lived and worked around those who made life and death decisions for thousands without batting an eye, Speer was never forced to consider if taking another life was necessary or even moral. But now, he wanted to exact a victory for the German people.

Once he got over the why, he now considered the how. How could he effectively eliminate the Chancellor? As he contemplated this, the thought of poison gas kept entering his mind. On previous walks in the Chancellery gardens Speer noticed the ventilation shaft to Hitler's bunker. Camouflaged only by a small shrub, the air intake shaft to the most important bunker in Germany was exposed to the public with only a thin filter protecting it, which could easily be penetrated by the poison gas called tabun. Speer loved the idea. If he was able to pull it off, the gas would not only kill Hitler but also his close-knit advisory team of Goebbels, Bormann and Ley at the same time. Speer made a mental note to speak to the head of his munitions production team, a man named Dieter Stahl, as soon as possible.

Speer went to bed that night feeling rejuvenated. He was embarking on something that could positively impact the war and it energized him. His mind refused to think of the downside, just the goodness his act would create by doing away with Hitler and those closest to him. He would sleep well that night, he thought, and he closed his eyes and fell asleep. One hundred miles away from him in Dresden the bombs started dropping.

———◆———

Dresden was the seventh largest city in Germany and the capital of the German state of Saxony. It was a defensive stronghold and a major manufacturing center with over one hundred factories. Its importance to the region centered on being the central hub for telephone communications, utilities, railroad junctures and banking operations. The surrounding region was supported by Dresden with supplies moving in and out of the city day and night.

During four bombing raids between February 13th and 15th, British and American bombers dropped nearly 1,400 tons of explosives and over 1,000 tons of incendiary devices into the city. The impact demolished city structures and ignited an intense firestorm. More than 20,000 residents were killed and the entire city center was burned. Over 1,600 acres of old town Dresden were destroyed in a massive blaze where no one could survive. All that remained was anguish, rubbish and colossal finger-pointing.

When Hitler called a cabinet meeting to discuss the raid, Goebbels was quick to blame the absent Göring, bellowing, "What a burden of guilt this parasite has brought on his head for his slackness and interest in his own comfort!"

Hitler was so irritated at both the Reichsmarschall and the Allies that he could barely speak. His white, doughy face pinched with menace as he spit in between nail-bitings.

Speer received the news with calm. He knew the Propaganda Minister would use the loss of civilian life to assert to the world evidence for Allied war crimes. Speer deeply regretted the casualties but knew Germany had caused the trauma and feared events would get much worse.

Göring did not respond to the accusations or to the bombings and the failure of the Luftwaffe. He did not hear about them until later. While the Dresden buildings and citizenry burned, Göring had embarked on a shooting expedition in the Schorfheide Forest.

⬤━◆━⬤

Near the end of February, Speer met with his munitions chief, Dieter Stahl. The two discussed the war and the policy of "leave the Allies a desert," Hitler had been purporting. Stahl thought it was terrible what Hitler was doing.

"I was wondering," Speer began to probe, "if there was any chance I might be able to get my hands on some of the new poison gas, I believe it is called tabun?"

Stahl did not blink at Speer's unusual question. He simply nodded assuredly that yes, Speer could acquire some.

Speer thought a moment before making his next comment. He was taking a step of faith and trusting the individual sitting next to him with his life.

"It is the only way to bring the war to an end," Speer continued. "I want to try to conduct the gas into the Chancellery bunker."

Dieter Stahl did not act alarmed in the slightest, a gesture comforting to Speer. He told Speer he could get him some gas and never once gave the impression that Speer was doing something out of the ordinary, nor denying his own loyalties.

In a few days Stahl met with Speer and communicated to him that he was able to secure some of the tabun but that his experts told him the gas is only activated after it exploded. This would not work on the bunker air shaft because if the ventilation shaft exploded the gas would not be able to transfer down into the living area.

Speer did not give up and asked Stahl for another type of gas that could do what he needed. Stahl affirmed that he could retrieve for him a more traditional type of gas, like the pesticide Zyklon-B.

Speer grew increasingly anxious that his plot would be uncovered and harm would come to his family. *What if Stahl asked the wrong person and was taken prisoner and tortured? What if Speer's name came out as someone who wanted to assassinate Adolf Hitler?* He decided to walk around the Chancellery gardens one more time to look at the shaft in question and see where he would have to execute his assassination work. It had been at least three months since he had last walked in the garden.

Speer vigorously walked along the sidewalk leading to the central garden. As he stepped down, ice crunched under his leather shoes. To his astonishment things had changed from his last visit. There were now armed SS sentinels patrolling the rooftop and surveying the garden. There was also a series of searchlights installed around the entire property. Worst of all, the ventilation shaft had changed dramatically. Instead of being at ground level, where Speer could have easily dropped the gas, a ten-foot chimney had been installed which would prevent anyone from doing what he was proposing, almost as if by design to thwart such an attack. At first Speer feared that he had been found out, then he realized the bunker had assuredly been updated on account of the July 20th plot.

Speer remembered how Hitler discussed with the staff about the fact of gas being heavier than air, and that he did not want to be poisoned again as he had been in the First World War as a corporal. He was constantly taking extra precautions, doubling security at every level. The impenetrable Wolf's Lair was a prime example of his paranoia.

In a way, Speer was relieved. His plan would not work. He could either find another plan or give up the idea completely. He chose the latter. He told Stahl to forget about his request for the gas. Speer's frustration was still present but his anger was soothed by the gripping reality the war was almost over due to the rapid advance of the Russians. In a few days, possibly weeks, all would be lost. He knew that instead of taking matters into his own hands, he would wait and allow the surrounding Allies to eliminate Hitler. Speer himself would direct his efforts back into trying to save as many German people as possible.

———◆◆◆———

In March, General Patton's forces converged on the Rhine River, while the Russians took Hungary and were poised to enter Austria. Millions of Russian soldiers slammed across Poland and the Oder River into a position just 50 miles from Berlin.

Speer composed a final armaments report that he knew would infuriate Hitler. To entice Hitler to read it, he began the document like his other reports, speaking about coal supplies and mining goods. Then he went a step forward and spoke about the necessities needed by the German populace such as food, gas and electricity. He concluded this section by saying that the final collapse of the German economy could be expected with certainty within four to six weeks.

Then, appealing directly to Hitler, Speer wrote, "No one has the right to take the viewpoint that the fate of the German people is tied to his personal fate. Our primary obligation of leadership is to help the people wherever possible. At this stage of the war it makes no sense for us to undertake demolitions which may strike at the very life of the nation. A total destruction policy means eliminating all further possibility for the German people to survive."

Speer was fearful at what might happen to him once the report was read by Hitler. He was so unpredictable, he could order Speer shot at once. Therefore, Speer decided to hand deliver it to him and at the same time ask for a picture of the Führer for Speer's 40th birthday on March 19th. He knew this was a bit duplicitous but it seemed a matter of etiquette, and could keep Hitler from knowing the true state of things inside Speer's heart.

Speer entered the Situation Room at the Chancellery and found the usual members present: Bormann, Goebbels, Ley, Keitel and several other general officers. The men discussed the impending takeover of the western Saar region by the American Army. Several of the villages in the area pleaded with the German Army not to enter, knowing the inevitable destruction that would follow. Some of the German commanders acquiesced and allowed the town to be taken by the Allies without a fight. This infuriated Hitler's cabinet.

During the meeting, Hitler turned to Keitel and told him to compose an order to the Commander-in-Chief and the Gauleiters to forcibly evacuate the entire population at once in the threatened areas. Without a moment of hesitation Keitel sat down and wrote the order.

One of the generals contended with Hitler that it would not be possible to evacuate the hundreds of thousands of affected people without trains and buses, and Speer agreed with him.

"There are no vehicles available to evacuate them," the general said. "And even if there was transportation there is no fuel."

"Then let them walk," Hitler replied.

"But it is still cold, they will freeze," reasoned the general. "No preparations have been made. Where will they go?"

"It doesn't matter, they must evacuate."

"This cannot be done!"

"It will be done!"

"How?"

"By my command!"

And per protocol, Hitler got the last word.

Speer bit his lip until it nearly bled. He wanted to scream.

Keitel read the order forcing the evacuation of all German residents west of the Rhine, demanding they leave their homes and walk east without any support from the government. No one voiced any objections.

Hitler concluded, "We can no longer afford to concern ourselves with the population."

During a short break, Speer left the meeting in anger. *Could he not see? Did he not care? Why didn't the entire room rebel against this?* Yet Speer acknowledged that he too had remained silent. Speer considered the memorandum he held, intending to personally hand it to Hitler once the conference concluded.

It was well past midnight when the meetings were over and Speer approached Hitler asking if he could meet with him privately.

With a quick nod, Hitler turned toward an orderly and shouted, "Bring that picture I've signed."

When Hitler handed Speer the red-leathered case stamped with the Führer's emblem he looked into Speer's eyes and divulged, "Lately it's been hard for me to write even a few words with my own hand. You know how it shakes. Often I can hardly complete my signature."

Speer received the birthday case and read Hitler's inscription to him, speaking of lasting friendship. Speer then handed Hitler his memorandum. He knew it was anything but cordial and would surely sever what friendship that remained.

Hitler received it without a word.

They said goodbye and Speer walked toward the door.

Hitler stood stoically still and said to Speer, "This time you will receive a written response to your memorandum." After a brief pause Hitler continued in a severe tone; all warmth from the previous moment had evaporated. "Speer, if the war is lost the people will be lost also. It is not necessary to worry about what the German people will need for elemental survival. On the contrary, it is best for us to destroy even these things. For the nation has proved to be the weaker and the future belongs solely to the stronger eastern nation. In any case, only those who are inferior will remain after this struggle, for the good have already been killed."

Speer departed the Chancellery feeling resentful about everything he had just encountered. He traveled westward to the command headquarters where General Walther Model and others were directing the war effort against the Allies approaching the Rhine.

The next day, a response came from Hitler regarding Speer's memorandum. It stated, "All military, transportation, communications, industrial, and supply facilities, as well as all resources within the Reich are to be destroyed. All food stores are to be destroyed so they do not fall into the hands of the enemy. All directives opposing this are invalid."

Speer swallowed hard. This was surely the death sentence for the German people. If carried out they would have no electricity, no water, no gas, no coal, no phones, eventually no food and no method for any shipment of resupply.

The message from Hitler continued, directed more at Speer, as it stripped Speer from all his authority. It stated that every one of Speer's orders given to the Commanding Officers of the Military and to the Gauleiters had been revoked. A new policy was in place; Speer no longer stood in charge of industry.

Speer recognized that the spineless mole Bormann was responsible for the last part, not that it helped. Speer was officially out of favor with Hitler and stripped of all of his powers. The next day Speer learned that his friend, General Fromm, who was a part of the July 20th assassination plot, was executed. Speer worried what the general might have said under duress.

CHAPTER 32

I am Corrie

The weather — *beautiful!* Everything was covered with snow. The small group of released prisoners walked up the slight ascent toward the train station and looked around when they reached the top. Near the entrance of Ravensbrück several prisoners were being forced to march into the forest to chop wood, another group worked near military trucks unloading potatoes and coal.

Mixed feelings of sadness yet pleasant relief overcame Corrie. She was free. She would not be ordered to work anymore, or forced to stand at roll call for hours. Soon she would board the train and depart for her homeland. What grief she had experienced here but it was a beautiful place this morning. A resplendent sun reflected off the castle rooftop in the distance. The frozen lake and the snow-laden pines picturesque, thought Corrie. At another time she would have enjoyed visiting the area. For now, however, she needed to depart and end this chapter of misery.

The train transported the released prisoners to Berlin. After many hours of boarding and deboarding trains to accommodate troop movements, Corrie was hungry. She reached inside her coat pocket for the bread and ration cards she had been given for her journey but they were not there. *Stolen!*

Corrie waited in Berlin for hours. She did not leave the station but looking out at the bombed city, Corrie could not help thinking that the war must surely come to an end soon. Everywhere the eye could see there was ruin and rubble.

Eventually she boarded a train for Uelzen located 300 kilometers northwest of Berlin. When the train reached Uelzen, Corrie was forced to depart the station and find the building of the political police. Once inside, she sat at a table while the clerk stamped her paperwork. Several teenage Dutch Nazis were moving in and out of the building.

One 16-year-old girl took an interest in Corrie and asked her, "So, you just came out of a concentration camp, huh? I don't suppose you had too jolly of a time there? Awkward, isn't it, to be a prisoner?"

Corrie stared at her in disbelief. The girl had no idea what evil was happening in German concentration camps. Corrie did not have the heart nor strength to say anything in response.

"It must be pretty nice, seems to me, to be free again?" the girl said to Corrie before she left her alone. Corrie pondered at how many teenagers voluntarily associated with the Nazi regime, not understanding the cruelty and hatred. They worked in an atmosphere of naiveté and untruth. How uncaring these people seemed to Corrie.

Waiting for a train into Holland, Corrie sat at a table near the Uelzen station, trying to stay awake so as not to miss her train. When once her head slipped and rested on the table, a furious blow to her ear sent her sprawling on the floor.

"These tables are not for sleeping!" shouted the scowling attendant.

Trains came, trains went. Most were occupied by soldiers and civilians were not permitted to be on them. Even when Corrie was told to enter a train, she sometimes had to debark because of a change of load plans.

Early the next morning Corrie climbed aboard a train that took her across the border of Holland. She was back in her native country. How good it felt! She arrived in Groningen, a city in the northern part of her homeland. Still in the occupied part of Holland, the tracks were torn up after Groningen and only government travel was permitted beyond the city. She was stuck.

Corrie walked to a Christian convalescent home located not far from the station. She waited for her evaluation and walked down the main corridor where she could see most of the patients. How neat the beds were. How clean the sheets, pillowcases and floors. It was as if Corrie had entered a dream, she had not seen such order and cleanliness for months.

After being evaluated by the superintendent, she was escorted by a nurse to a room where she would spend some time to recover.

"So where are you headed?" asked the nurse.

"To Haarlem," answered Corrie.

"Oh, Haarlem? Do you know someone there named Corrie ten Boom?" asked the nurse.

Corrie looked into the nurse's face and recognized her. She was one of the Y.W.C.A. leaders with whom Corrie had worked.

"Truus Benes!" Corrie exclaimed in delight.

"Why yes, that is my name," she responded. "But I don't think I know you."

"I am Corrie ten Boom!" exclaimed Corrie excitedly.

The nurse gave her a pleasant frown, pitying the deluded woman walking beside her.

"I'm afraid that is impossible," said the nurse. "For I know Corrie very well, and you are not her."

"Oh Truus, truly, it is me!" shouted Corrie.

The two women stared at each other for a moment.

"I *am* Corrie."

Then, Truus smiled and with wide-eyed amazement said, "Corrie, it is you! I am so sorry." Then both of the women hugged and laughed together.

Truus brought Corrie to a table where she was served a meal of potatoes, vegetables, meat and gravy. Then for dessert, pudding with currant juice and an apple. Corrie savored every bite. She could feel the food rejuvenating her malnourished body.

Corrie then went into the bathing area to take a hot bath. When she looked at herself in the mirror she understood why Truus had not recognized her; hollow eyes, thin face, hair in thick clumps dropping all around her face — *I barely recognized myself!* Corrie's skin was damaged by lice and her clothing filthy after several days of travel and sleeping on the floors.

The bath was ready so Corrie undressed and entered the warm water. What pleasure! Corrie relaxed and felt her body begin to heal. She was so overcome with joy, the nurses had to coax and plead with her to leave the water.

"Just five more minutes?" Corrie asked repeatedly.

Finally she got out and allowed the nurses to help her get dressed, they fixed her hair and gave her night clothes and slippers. Corrie laughed out loud with sheer joy at their kindness. Everything was wonderful now. The people attending to her were loving and kind, so unlike the cruel and evil guards at the camps.

The nurses gave her a special bedroom, one that was used by a nurse who was away on leave. Corrie had departed a gray existence and entered into a bright glow of warmth and friendship. The thoughtful staff took good care of her, aware that she had survived a horrific trial. The beautiful sound of Bach down the hall, the colors in her bedroom, the thick woolen blankets, an extra pillow tucked down by her feet for comfort; each another reassurance to Corrie that she was finally free and no longer a prisoner. *Would she ever have to leave?* It was all so wonderful. On the shelf were books to read for leisure, outside the sound of a boat and of children laughing. Farther away, in the distance, Corrie could hear singing. Tears wet her pillow. She was now far away from the gray monochrome of the Ravensbrück barracks, the dirty cinder streets, the moaning and shrieks from the prisoners, the screaming and scolding of the guards.

Corrie was in a place with harmony and music, care and thoughtfulness. She always loved her homeland, but Holland was beautiful beyond words. She would never again speak bad of a fellow countryman. Netherlanders forged a unique way of life, of appreciation, of helpfulness, of caring. They were not Germans and could never be content with such tyranny. They had survived the war and would rebuild; first human hearts, then the buildings.

———❖———

Corrie stayed in Groningen for ten days. It was an essential time of restoration for her. She was damaged not only physically but also emotionally. The caring staff helped Corrie recover much of what she had lost from her months in prison. To trust a person in authority over her, to be treated with respect, to be valued and cared for — all areas Corrie had taken for granted before, but were deprived when the concentration camp nightmare began.

She departed the convalescent home to visit her brother Willem. Corrie ached to be with family again. She had not seen Willem and her sister Nollie for many months and she had so much she needed to share with them about Betsie and Ravensbrück.

Since it was illegal to travel south of Groningen, Corrie had to be smuggled on a food truck one night. They did not use their headlights for fear of the Germans. The truck twisted and turned over the bomb-blasted roads, trying to avoid contact with other vehicles.

The truck stopped in Hilversum where Willem ran a nursing home for the elderly. Corrie thanked the driver and departed the vehicle, then walked up the sidewalk which led to her brother's residence. She knocked on the door of the large brick building, just as the night was fading away into the gray morning. A tall, broad shouldered nurse answered the door. Corrie explained who she was and the nurse ran down the main corridor to find Willem.

Soon Willem came hobbling down the hallway. Corrie embraced her older brother and told him of Betsie's death. Both Ten Boom's wept at their reunion. Willem's wife, Tine, joined them and two of Corrie's nieces. The family was worried for Kik, their tall, blond son who was deported to Germany and had not been heard from since.

Corrie recalled Kik coaching her with the practice raids on the Beje. "No, Tante Corrie, you have no Jews here, remember?" he exhorted her. Willem feared Kik had been sent to Bergen-Belsen, the concentration camp in northern Germany.

Her reunion with family was wonderful and healing, but Corrie yearned to return to Haarlem. Willem had multiple phone conversations with resistance workers still operating in Holland and finally arranged a transport for her.

After two weeks spent with Willem, the two hugged and said their goodbyes, then Corrie was on her way to Haarlem. The vehicle moved quietly over the bridge spanning the Spaarne and across the Grote Markt. Corrie noted the absence of the Bride of Haarlem tree, cut down for firewood long before. She suddenly yearned for spring and to feast her eyes on some tulips, knowing that time would come in a few weeks. The car finally stopped in front of the wonderful and familiar old building Corrie grew up in. She opened her vehicle door, sprang out of her seat and ran down the narrow alley. Corrie turned the handle of the unlocked side door, then stepped into the Beje. She was home!

Nollie was there with her daughters sweeping and washing the windows for Corrie's return. The sisters hugged and cried for a long while, reminiscing on their father, Betsie, Eusie, and the Frisian clock Casper wanted to wind the day the SD men forced them out of their home. Finally, after several hours of catching up, Nollie and her daughters left Corrie alone in the Beje.

The youngest of the Ten Boom family who grew up in the Beje was home again. With quiet filling the hallways, Corrie walked upstairs to her father's room and leaned against his empty bed. She ran her fingers over the smooth wood and thought of Haarlem's Grand Old Man.

Corrie remembered a time when she was in primary school and visited a poor family's house with Nollie. In the upstairs bedroom lay a dead baby girl still in her cradle. Corrie was horrified at the thought of death, yet before leaving the home she bravely touched the girl's small curled hand, icy to the touch. This experience deeply troubled her the rest of the day so when Casper walked up the wooden staircase to tuck her in and say good night, Corrie burst into tears.

"I need you," young Corrie cried to her father. "You can't die! You can't!"

Nollie, who laid next to Corrie, explained to her father what had happened and that Corrie had not said a word all day or eaten her supper.

Casper sat down on the edge of the bed next to his youngest daughter. He touched her cheek with the back of his hand and stared into her soft brown eyes.

Her father gently consoled his youngest daughter, "Corrie, when you and I go to Amsterdam, when do I give you your ticket?"

"Why, just before we get on the train father," Corrie responded, wiping her eyes.

"That's right, and our wise Father in heaven knows exactly when you need things too. Don't run out ahead of him, Corrie. When the time comes that some of us will have to die, you will look into your heart and find the strength you need — just in time."

Corrie appreciated that her father always brought their conversations back to God. It was exactly what Corrie needed to hear at the time.

But now, standing alone in that big empty house, the reality set in that the two people Corrie had lived with her entire life were no longer going to be at the Beje with her. It was an overwhelming realization, and Corrie stood by the bed and wept. Although she was deeply saddened, oddly, her tears became tears of joy. She knew that her father and Betsie's experience with their Savior was now unlimited. Heavenly music filled their ears and hearts while Corrie stood alone in the shadows.

She was happy, but there was something in her heart now yearning for heaven more than ever before. When she was a prisoner of Ravensbrück, every night she yearned to be set free. Now she was finally home, but not yet fully free like her loved ones. Just as her father's story taught her about God's perfect timing, Corrie could sense God telling her there was still much more work for her to do.

"Yes, Lord. I am your servant. Use me how You see fit."

CHAPTER 33

The Führer

A fter the Führer's response to his memorandum, it was with trepidation that Speer continued to meet with the generals and Gauleiters. They were aware he was no longer acting in an official capacity, but Speer pleaded with them to spare Germany's infrastructure for the sake of its people. He raced throughout the Ruhr convincing men in power not to destroy bridges and factories. He used the logic that when the war turned and Germany needed the supplies from the Ruhr factories, the Gauleiters would be at fault if they were no longer producing goods to meet the needs of the nation.

The Gauleiters protested and mentioned the Führer's orders. Speer continued to talk, argue, reason — whatever he could do to prevent them from ordering nearly a million people into the streets. The urban centers would be the most hard-pressed to survive. They were poorly fed and scantily clad; any attempt to move them east toward Berlin would be disastrous. Disease and death would greet the multitudes at every intersection. Also, if the bridges were destroyed then how would the populace travel to Berlin?

Thankfully for Speer, General Walther Model, the field marshal in charge of Army Group West, agreed not to purposely destroy any industrial sites. Speer continued to stay in touch with Model as the battlefield moved toward the East.

The Allies had taken Mannheim and were fast-approaching Frankfurt and Heidelberg. Speer noticed that small patches of German soldiers continued to march east and away from the front. The Americans found little resistance. Speer encountered many anxious mayors in agreement with his plan to thwart Hitler's orders for a scorched earth. By working with the general in charge of the district Speer immeasurably helped the Heidelberg mayor to declare the city a hospital zone and surrendered without a fight.

This had special significance for Speer as his parents were residents of Heidelberg. He took the opportunity to visit his folks, and spent a moment catching up. When the younger Speer prepared to leave, his father followed him to his car. The two were never close nor showed physical affection but Mr. Speer grabbed his son's hand for a moment and looked intently into his eyes. Both accepted the realization that this was their last goodbye.

Speer moved on and continued to speak to any leader who would listen to him. He received aid in his plan from an unsuspecting source. Thanks to General Patton, the Allies were advancing so fast the Nazi Party leaders were unable to demolish much infrastructure before their city capitulated. A few factories and bridges were destroyed but nothing on the scale of what Hitler had projected in his memorandum. The German populace would survive — albeit in the hands of conquerors — but would not perish on foot, marching away from their homes during the coldest months of the year.

When Speer finally returned to Berlin after his tour of the west, he found the situation there had changed dramatically. As his first act of business, he was ordered to report to the Chancellery and sign over his leadership of aircraft production. Hitler issued an edict that both Göring and Speer were to relinquish their responsibilities and agree to serve as deputies under an SS officer named Hans Kammler.

Additionally, all armaments production were removed from Speer and given to Saur, Speer's deputy, with the overarching idea that Heinrich Himmler would eventually take over the Cabinet position for War Production. And a final sting for Speer, his staff informed him that another order was issued from Hitler stating that all post offices, railway stations, telegraph relay offices and antenna and broadcasting offices were to be destroyed by fire, explosion or dismantlement.

The first two items regarding Speer's relinquishing of power were infuriating and humiliating for Speer to stomach, yet not unexpected. However, the latest edict of Hitler was inexcusable and went too far! Speer met clandestinely with several high-ranking SS officials and generals in Berlin who agreed with him that this latest, desperate attempt to impair the enemy would destroy Germany more than its conquerors and immensely retard the rebuilding process. They promised they would not act too fast to carry out the latest orders.

The phone in Speer's office rang. He was to report to Hitler's Chancellery bunker immediately for a meeting with the Führer. *What was this about?* Speer wondered. The SS agent who delivered the message was particularly unfriendly in his request, leaving Speer quite apprehensive. *Did Hitler want to shoot him for insubordination?* A few members of Speer's staff gave him a startled look. His secretary's eyes glistened as he departed. Annemarie had worked with Speer throughout the entire war and Speer knew that her life was on the line as much as his. That was how Hitler operated.

On the walk over to the Chancellery building Speer thought of his confidant, Fromm, who had survived the great purge of those participating in the July 20th plot. Sadly, Fromm was no longer around, recently executed by Hitler's order. *Am I next?* Speer wondered.

Speer made his way down the numerous bunker steps and reported to Hitler's suite. When he was escorted into the underground office, the Führer did not welcome him nor shake his hand. The contempt on Hitler's face was palpable and his disposition overwhelmed Speer, making him more nervous with every step. There would be no cordiality, no pleasantries in this encounter and Speer knew he would have to choose his words very carefully.

"Bormann informed me on your conference with the Ruhr Gauleiters," Hitler bluntly began. "Did you think I wouldn't find out? You pressed them not to carry out my orders and declared that the war is lost! Are you aware of what now must follow?"

Speer's mind exploded. This was the meeting he dreaded ever since he started acting independently to subterfuge Hitler's plans of destroying Germany. Speer knew that only death for him, his family and his staff could follow; he would depart the way of Stauffenberg and Fromm.

Speer tried to swallow but his mouth turned dry.

He could not breathe.

His eyes moistened.

Was this the end?

Then, the unthinkable happened. Hitler's tone softened. With a mournful expression he declared, "If you were not my architect, I would pursue the matters that are called for in such a case."

Speer was astonished.

Hitler's left hand steadied his trembling right forearm. He glanced at the floor, then turned his brooding eyes back onto Speer's face for a response.

Without taking the time to think about the follow-on effects, Speer said, "Take the measures you think necessary, and grant no consideration to me as an individual." It seemed like the right thing to say at the moment, but he immediately felt he was too hasty with his bravery.

Hitler's pallid face had neither a sour nor friendly expression when he made his next statement, "You are overworked and ill. I have therefore decided you are to go on leave at once. I will have someone else run your Ministry."

Speer did not like this weaseling. *If I am to be punished then punish me, but let's not sweep this under the rug!*

"No, I feel perfectly well," Speer replied resolutely. "I am not going on leave. If you no longer want me as your minister then dismiss me from my post." As he said the words he remembered that Göring had rejected this proposal over a year ago. It was not the way the Führer conducted his business.

Hitler continued, "I do not want to dismiss you, Speer. But I insist that you begin your sick leave immediately."

The conversation regained its original intensity as each man dug in his heels. Speer stubbornly continued, "I cannot keep the responsibility of a minister while another man is acting in my name."

"You have no choice!" Hitler growled. "It is impossible for me to dismiss you. For reasons of foreign and domestic policy, I cannot spare you."

"It's impossible for me to go on leave!" Speer rebutted. "As long as I am in office I must conduct the affairs of the Ministry. I am *not* sick!" Speer's boldness shocked both of them.

The two men sat down. Hitler appeared to be deep in thought and remained silent for a while. Finally, he declared, "Speer, if you can convince yourself that the war is not lost, you can continue to run your office."

"You know I cannot be convinced of that," Speer replied. "The war *is* lost."

Hitler launched into a monologue of recollection of other trials through which he had successfully maneuvered. Speer had heard all of the stories before and could repeat them verbatim if Hitler gave him a chance. Speer sat for hours at the Obersalzberg teehaus listening to the man relay past situations in his life repetitively. Hitler labored on and on regarding the difficulties he had overcome by mastering them purely with his wit and boundless energy.

On this day it appeared Hitler wanted to lecture so he droned on, one story after the next. Speer was terribly bored by the familiar monologues but tried not to show it. Finally, Hitler wound down and continued the conversation at hand.

"If you would believe that the war could still be won, if you could at least have faith in that, all would be well."

Speer noticed that Hitler was now almost pleading with him. The Führer seemed desperate for Speer to be able to say something which gave hope for their present difficulty. Speer realized for the first time that the Führer needed him and that his loyalty and friendship were critical assets Hitler desired. This illumination empowered Speer and made him think twice about what was the most important issue.

Usually, Speer would have given in to the Führer's wishes by now but considering the destructive plans to all of the community services he currently held his tongue, hoping for some leverage to press his advantage. He despised men like Bormann and Keitel who too quickly agreed with their leader and had no self-respect.

Hitler waited for Speer to reply, edgy.

"I cannot," answered Speer. "Mostly because I do not want to be one of the swine in your entourage who tell you they have faith in Germany's victory without truly believing in it."

At first Hitler did not react, sitting in stony silence. He then began telling more stories and drew comparisons of himself and Frederick the Great. *Did he not understand what I just said?* Speer wondered.

Eventually Hitler implored, "If you could at least *hope* that we have not lost! You must certainly be able to hope? That would be enough to satisfy me."

Speer did not respond and there followed another long, awkward silence.

Finally Hitler stood up rather abruptly. "You have twenty-four hours to think over your answer! Tomorrow let me know whether you have hope that the war can still be won." His tone was frosty. The meeting ended as it had begun with the same icy interaction.

"You're dismissed!"

Speer quickly stood and departed the room. As he walked through the underground offices he heard talk about a teletype coming through from the Chief of Transportation stating that all locomotives, passenger cars, and freight cars were to be blown up. All barges were to be burned, and all canals and rivers were to be blocked by intentionally sinking ships in them. This was precisely why Speer had taken mental leave of Hitler and refused to acquiesce. *He is a criminal!* Speer thought.

But what does one do when a criminal possesses absolute power? You can reject him and suffer the consequences liken to Colonel von Stauffenberg, or, you can appease the ruler and serve in conflict with your own integrity.

Upon returning to his office after meeting with the Führer, Speer met with his staff who eagerly awaited his return. Annemarie Kempf wanted to know every detail. Speer accepted that his Ministry staff was fully conscious that not only was Speer risking his own life with his endeavor to save Germany but all his colleagues could be implicated as well. He was walking a tightrope and risking the lives of his family and staff in a high stakes gamble.

Speer explained the conversation in the bunker to his leadership team and that he did not have any idea as to how he would answer the Chancellor. After saying goodnight to Annemarie and the others, Speer fell into the bed in his Ministry apartment, exhausted and worried. There was no good solution for him. He could not stand for what Hitler was demanding — this total destruction policy. But could he reject it and lose everything he held dear? Hitler was giving him a way out with the illness excuse. *Perhaps I should take his offer?*

After resting, with many ideas flooding his mind on how he could respond to Hitler's ultimatum, Speer took some coffee and wrote a response by hand. It was partially an answer and partially a treatise in an attempt to make Hitler see reason. He described how it seemed that Fate had turned against Germany: the cold in Moscow, the fog in Stalingrad, and the blue sky during the Ardennes Offensive which aided the Allied air campaign. He wrote that he believed in a Providence that was just and inexorable, and thus he believed in God. In his final lines Speer pleaded with Hitler to see the futility of continuing his policy of destruction. *The foundation of our national existence is being destroyed.*

Speer tried to send the letter to Hitler's office in hopes that the secretary, Traudl Junge, would type it out on the special typewriter with the oversized letters. However, she telephoned back and said, "The Führer has forbidden me to receive any letters from you. He wants to see you here and have your answer verbally."

Shortly after her call, Speer was summoned to appear at the bunker and meet with Hitler at once. He washed himself, changed his clothes and said farewell to his associates.

His pensive staff stood around with anxious expressions on their faces. Speer turned to face them all and said, "Well then..."

It was all Speer could get out before his throat suddenly felt dry and hardened. He walked out the door. He realized that their destiny was tied to his, and this burden was too much for his mind to comprehend.

It was midnight when Speer arrived at the Chancellery. The twenty-four hours were up. He still did not know exactly what he was going to say. He decided to leave his final decision to the moment of confrontation.

Hitler held still beside his desk, without expression, without movement, as if trying to detect a clue from Speer's face to what his answer would be. He looked weary rather than tense and he asked tersely, "Well?"

For a moment Speer stood there anxiously. He did not have an answer. He did not know what to say. Finally, something came to mind which Speer knew could be parsed multiple ways.

Speer spoke formally, "Mein Führer, I stand unconditionally behind you."

With those few words, Hitler's eyes brimmed with tears and he held out a trembling hand to Speer. After a quick embrace — the warmth of their old friendship restored — a thought entered Speer's mind and he subsequently blurted it out in a moment of emotion, "But it will help if you immediately reconfirm my authority from your March 19th decree."

Hitler complied at once, still visibly moved, and told Speer to draw up a document for him to sign immediately. Before the first word hit paper, Speer felt a slight moral twinge that he was deliberately lying to Hitler; he had no intention whatsoever to carry out any further destruction. But Speer knew this lack of candor and integrity was actually a truth fighting its way out of his heart in a tough situation, a truth stronger than sentimental words, a truth bound for personal victory. Hesitations aside, Speer quickly wrote:

> *No measures may be taken which would impair our own fighting strength. Production must be continued up to the last possible moment, even at the risk that a factory might fall into the enemy's hands before it can be destroyed. Total destruction of particularly important plants will be ordered only on my instructions as the Minister of Armaments and War Production.*

Speer outlined several procedural steps whereby making himself again the sole authority through whom the demolition of any factory building would have to come first. Hitler looked it over and signed the decree without question. The Chancellor, weary from this personnel conflict and the tolls of running the war, sat down on a sofa and faced Speer.

Speer felt that Hitler knew he was conceding a great deal to his architect. But for some reason Hitler valued the restored friendship and trust more than a few burnt buildings.

"You know, Speer," Hitler began, "the scorched earth idea had no merit in a country of such small area as Germany. It can only fulfill its purpose in vast spaces such as Russia."

Speer was astounded to hear these comments coming from a man who, the day before, was signing documents to destroy every part of Germany's infrastructure! But it did not matter. Speer departed with resolve, and new authority, to thwart all the destructive policies he could.

"Annemarie, it's me," said Speer to his secretary on the bunker telephone.

"Oh, my goodness! You survived!" Annemarie Kempf exclaimed. "We've been worried sick about you!"

"You should be in bed," said Speer.

"None of us could sleep. We thought we would never see you again. We didn't know…"

"I need the crew to mobilize tonight; this is urgent."

"Anything!"

"Tell the entire staff to gather all the motorcycles, automobiles, and orderlies they can find," said Speer quietly and confidently. "Get everyone up and fully staff the Ministry's telephone and teletype offices. Also, assemble people over at the printing presses and get them operational at once."

"Whatever for?" asked Annemarie.

"I'll explain when I get there and describe my meeting word for word. I just need to know you understand the urgency of all of this."

"You've done it, haven't you?"

Speer paused, smiled to himself, then said "Annemarie, get everything going. I'll be back soon. Tell Edith to get the coffee on, it's going to be a late night."

"It already *is* a late night."

"I know, I will see you soon, and … thank you."

In a few hours' time, the printing press provided hundreds of copies of Hitler's new order restoring Speer to his former position. In the middle of the night every command throughout Germany received the communique of Speer's reinstatement.

Long before the breaking dawn Speer made phone calls and sent telegraphs to safeguard all industrial installations, power plants and water works operations. That morning Speer sent a dozen trains stocked with food blindly into the Ruhr area to those inhabitants who were encircled by the Allies. He drew up orders which authorized the Wehrmacht's stockpile of food and clothing to be delivered to those people fleeing from Czechoslovakia and Poland. Speer knew that by the time Bormann found out, his actions would already be in play. If Bormann attempted to thwart him now, it would cause mass confusion throughout the Reich.

Speer cleverly looked over all new teletypes coming out of headquarters to the field generals; whenever there was one issuing a decree of destruction, Speer would send a follow-on message stating that only he alone was in a position to authorize demolition of a factory. Speer knew he would never issue any such order but made it sound that demolition decrees would be proceeding forthwith. Using these methods he saved numerous bridges, plants and public utility operations.

Speer's staff had survived to live another day. But no one knew what the next day would bring. Hitler's birthday was fast approaching. The significance of the day was not lost on those around him. His staff targeted the date as the approximate time when the Russians would storm Berlin's Tiergarten.

In April 1945, Albert Speer clandestinely moved his family out of Berlin and located them in western Germany. It was a region he knew would be assigned to the British once Germany was divided. Speer felt the British would be kinder to prominent Nazi families than the Russians.

Shortly after he accomplished this safety measure, Speer discovered that Dr. Brandt, Hitler's personal physician, had consummated the same act, moving his family to Thuringia, only to return to Berlin a traitor. Hitler ordered a summary court martial of Dr. Brandt, then acted as both prosecutor and judge, giving him a death sentence. When Hitler asked Speer where his own family was, Speer lied and said that they were visiting a friend's estate near Berlin.

Also at this time, Eva Braun, Hitler's longtime paramour, left Munich and moved to Berlin, declaring she would not leave Hitler's side again. Hitler scolded her at first, then was proud that Eva had decided to join and not abandon him when several of his close associates were leaving. Speer tried to arrange for her to depart Berlin on one of the few planes still available, but Eva repeatedly refused him. She would die with Hitler and this made the end suddenly more tangible to those still working for the Führer.

But it was not until Magda Goebbels, Joseph Goebbels's wife, brought her six young children to the bunker did death settle on the place.

CHAPTER 34

Death March

The Architect knew the war was coming to a close. He recalled a biblical parable he once heard in mass and decided he should follow it now. It was the story of the shrewd servant from the Gospel of Luke and it made an impression on him as a youth and became his favorite biblical story. Its essence was how an unrighteous servant — about to be fired — contacted the people who owed his master money and cut their debts in half. Those who owed the master money paid the reduced fare immediately, thankful for the opportunity to expunge their debt. When the master saw all the money coming in he changed course and praised the unrighteous servant for being shrewd because the servant now had many places where he was welcome.

The Architect believed he, too, should try to make friends now while he was in power in order to receive help later. He had several valuable bargaining chips still available to him. When he decided to shut down operations at Ravensbrück, his first call was to the Red Cross. The organization had pestered him to let them visit the concentration camp and evacuate the sick and dying. They believed there was a humanitarian crisis there and requested permission to send a train with medical supplies and rail cars for transport. They had no idea how deteriorated the conditions had become or how late in the game they would be arriving, but the Architect decided to take advantage of their good will anyway. Perhaps for his compassion and decency *today* the Red Cross would advocate on his behalf *tomorrow* if he was ever charged with war crimes.

He then called the Ravensbrück Kommandant, Fritz Suhren, instructing him regarding the Red Cross visit. The Architect further ordered him to immediately destroy the gas chamber and use the crematoria to burn all camp documents. *This was not going to be another Auschwitz!*

The Red Cross sent a large train to transport thousands of sick passengers and take them to Denmark. However, there were still tens of thousands of prisoners left stranded at Ravensbrück. In the distance, cannon fire could be heard from the Russian artillery. The prisoners had hoped to be liberated by the western Allies, not the Soviets. Fear spread among those left behind by the Red Cross transport, so Kommandant Suhren called the Architect to ask him what to do.

"March them out of there, immediately!" the Architect snapped. "Soon your guards will defect and leave the prisoners alone. Who knows what stories they will tell their liberators. Get them out of there, to the woods in the northwest towards upper Mecklenburg, then wait for further instruction." The Architect knew he could use them later as a bargaining chip with the Americans.

The gates of Ravensbrück opened and thousands of female prisoners departed in a northwestern direction, hoping to make contact with the Americans before the Russians caught them. The Soviet forces were just miles away, rapidly approaching the area on their trek to Berlin. Long columns formed and the women were forced to keep up the pace. Though out of the camp, they were constantly harassed by SS guards with guns.

"Keep moving," the guards shouted. "Any who hesitate now and slow us down will be shot on the spot."

Some of the prisoners used the chaos of the march to try and escape but most were captured and shot by the wary SS. If prisoners could not keep up with the pace they were shot. If a prisoner fell — too sick or weary to continue — they were shot. The SS left them beside the road, littering the German ground with dead bodies. The Architect later received word that many of the SS guards also used this time to escape, their uniforms, patches and name tags reportedly strewn through the forest en route toward the Americans.

On the second night of the forced march, a numerous group of mostly French women broke off from the main group and fled to a nearby town, hiding in a large barn in the woods. They had high hopes they had avoided the SS and earned their freedom. However, just before sunrise they were surrounded by advancing Russian soldiers who, instead of liberating the emaciated women, repeatedly raped them — every last one — even the old and sick. Some of the women weighed no more than 70 pounds but were still used as fodder for the ravenous Russians.

"Please," begged one prisoner. "We have survived five years of torture in Ravensbrück concentration camp, only to be freed a few hours ago..." But her words were incomprehensible. Some of the women — now too weak to continue their journey of freedom — died in the barn.

The three thousand women abandoned and left to die at Ravensbrück were trying to hide when the Russian soldiers invaded the compound and mercilessly attacked them sexually. Some of the women disguised themselves to look diseased and contagious before the soldiers arrived but it did not matter. All of the women and children were raped multiple times, even the old and feeble. As the camp was ravaged, more Russian soldiers poured into the nearby town with its five thousand residents and raped every woman there as well. It was a matter of policy.

The women in the long SS columns fleeing west kept moving. Rumors sometimes spread down the line that the Russians were just a few kilometers away. At one point the SS guards broke ranks and ran on ahead, leaving their charges to fend for themselves. Those SS still with the main party changed into civilian clothes so they would blend in once they too escaped for freedom. There were no more gunshots, just stragglers who stopped to die beside the road.

Approximately one third of the women from Ravensbrück perished on the westward journey. Some fortunate enough to escape from the march and enter a surrounding town only suffered the fate of the women in the barn. The core group of prisoners who kept marching forward finally made it to Allied lines and pleaded for sanctuary. The Americans immediately took them in to feed them and nurture the wounded, providing impenetrable protection from the vengeful Russians.

The Architect was despondent the prisoners were now in American hands. He could no longer use them as leverage to assist his own chance for survival. He would have to think of another plan.

CHAPTER 35

The Final Hours in Hitler's Bunker

Down a long flight of stairs was a large, steel-reinforced door guarded by two SS men. Once through the door there was a narrow corridor and another steep staircase which led down to a platform unpleasantly wet as it sat below the water table. Through another door was a short, damp staircase leading to the upper rooms of the bunker. There was a central vestibule which served as the mess hall, then twelve smaller rooms all opening up to the dining area.

Continuing the descent down, another curved stairway led to the Führer's bunker area comprised of eighteen rooms, a waiting area and a conference room. Adjacent to the conference room was a small map room, a powder room, and the six-room suite of Adolf Hitler and Eva Braun. Beyond these rooms was an emergency exit — four steep flights of concrete steps which led up to the Chancellery garden area.

It was in this underground fortress that Hitler learned the news of the death of Franklin D. Roosevelt, the American President. Roosevelt, in the Führer's mind, was a criminal. Hope sprang from this news which would surely bring about a reversal of fortune and lead Germany to the victory Hitler was to accomplish. It did not matter that the Russians were crossing the Oder River to the east and were now less than 45 miles from where Hitler was hiding. The Führer wanted to share this triumphant news with all his staff but could not find his Minister of Armaments, Albert Speer.

The date was April 13th, and high above in the streets of Berlin, Speer was helping organize the final concert of the Berlin Philharmonic. That afternoon, the Philharmonic Concert Hall was filled with Berlin residents alongside Speer and several other dignitaries listening to Germany's finest classical musical. There was no heat in the hall so everyone sat in overcoats. The concert was performed when electricity was usually turned off to the residents of Berlin but Speer ordered the current to stay on so the beautiful hall could be lit and appreciated.

Some of those listening were deeply moved at this oasis in the midst of war. They momentarily sat in bliss while bombs dropped nearby, and the outskirts of the city was being invaded. The irony was palpable, as if the Berliners in their furs and felts, were acting out a final scene from Shakespeare.

When the concert attendees stepped back onto the street following the concert, Hitler Youth members in uniform handed them petite baskets with cyanide capsules inside. Nazi Party functionaries had organized this macabre behavior and it disgusted Speer. He was then approached by a courier and told that Hitler wanted to see him at once.

When Speer arrived into the lower level of the bunker, Hitler, Goebbels and Bormann shared the news they celebrated of Roosevelt's death on April 12th. They also shared their opinion that Providence must be assisting the Reich. Speer was more circumspect.

"Why can't you ever celebrate with us?" asked Bormann. "This is surely a sign from heaven that the war will turn and fate is on our side."

"No, I am not so sure about that," answered Speer.

Hitler was ecstatic as he held up the article, "See this newspaper clipping yourself. This is the miracle I predicted. You never wanted to believe but here it is! Who was right, Speer? The war isn't lost. This will be the turning point. You'll see!"

Goebbels was more blunt, "Admit it, Speer, you were wrong — again!"

Speer felt that the national leadership team was rubbing the Roosevelt news in his face, as if this information proved that Germany would win the war. Hitler was convinced this was another sign that compared him to Frederick the Great. But Speer did not see it this way. He was convinced Harry Truman would continue where Roosevelt left off as president, plus it was only a matter of time before the Russians would overwhelm Berlin, including the bunker where they currently met.

———◆◆◆———

On April 20th, Hitler celebrated his 56th birthday in the Berlin bunker with the usual Party members: Himmler, Göring, Goebbels, Bormann, Ribbentrop, Admiral Dönitz, General Keitel, Speer, Eva Braun and the Chancellor's staff members who cooked, cleaned, typed and drove for him. The short-lived optimism from Roosevelt's death faded due to continued reports of Russian advances into Berlin. Therefore Hitler decided to say goodbye to those who had worked for him and impart final instructions. The Führer dispatched one admiral to the Berghof to destroy all the official papers there. He mobilized the Hitler Youth from ages 14 to 16 for the defense of Berlin street by street. He had several of his long-serving secretaries depart for the retreat in Berchtesgaden.

Hermann Göring — absconding from his beloved Carinhall — was now in Berlin. After loading up the last of the large vans with treasures from his massive estate, Göring surrounded the residence with mines and ordered his SS minions to blow the palace to ruins. Carinhall had been a symbol of Göring's power and personality and he could not tolerate the idea of it falling into the hands of his enemies. After several tremendous explosions, he watched the buildings split apart, fall asunder and burn before he departed. Göring, traveling in a long caravan with the remaining cache of his priceless collections, was destined for Berchtesgaden. On the way he decided to stop his cavalcade of cars and trucks in Berlin to wish Hitler a happy birthday.

Hitler received his guests with affection; even Göring, at whom Hitler had lashed out only days before because of the Luftwaffe's failures. Week after week, insidious insults were lobbed at Göring behind his back due to the perpetual bombing campaigns against Germany. Current reports showed the Russians moving just south of Berlin so they were close enough now to bomb the city with their field artillery.

Those visiting that day feared they would get trapped in the bunker if they tarried too long to say goodbye. Despite the rush, Göring took time to change from a silver blouse to the olive-drab of an American uniform topped with elegant shoulder epaulettes with his Reichsmarschall eagle woven into them in gold.

Hitler was in uplifted spirits and said to everyone, "The Russians will suffer their bloodiest defeat of all before Berlin." The generals present smiled but did not nod their heads enthusiastically like Bormann and Goebbels.

With Bormann snickering in the background, Göring walked up to the Führer and shook his hand warmly. He wanted to get on the road with his goods before the capital city was completely surrounded.

"Happy birthday, mein Führer," said Göring with a wide grin. "Will you not depart with me to a safer location? The north-south route through the Bavarian forest is open but shall be blocked off at any moment."

"How can I call on the troops to undertake the decisive battle of Berlin if at the same moment I withdraw myself to safety?" Hitler asked him.

Göring's fat face instantly broke into a sweat as he asked, "Would you prefer for myself or General Koller to stay here with you in Berlin?"

Speer could see in Göring's eyes that the Reichsmarschall hoped the answer would be Koller.

"You go; Koller stays here," said Hitler.

Relieved and grinning like a Cheshire cat, Göring quickly said, "Goodbye, mein Führer," and exited the room. The hefty Reichsmarschall clambered up the fifty steps from the lower bunker, taking a break in the upper chamber to catch his breath. He left the cement structure, climbed into the lead vehicle of his caravan and headed south for Berchtesgaden.

One by one the Nazi Party members cordially shook Hitler's hand and said their adieus. They all told the Führer where they were going and how they would continue working for him. Each one knew it was the last time they would see him, except for Speer. For some strange reason, Speer felt he would see Hitler again and this would not be his final farewell.

Hitler retired to his quarters unusually early while Eva Braun led a group of party goers above ground to the partially bombed out Reich Chancellery. They toasted each other with champagne and danced in the drawing room until late into the evening. Several drank to Germany, some to the Führer. While those from the bunker partied, the buildings on the outskirts of Berlin were shelled and splitting to shreds.

<hr/>

After having a drink with Hitler's staff, Speer traveled to Hamburg to dismiss his own staff and disband what was left of the Armaments Ministry. His team was set up in two mobile homes they had procured from Speer's construction section.

Annemarie Kempf was there making sure everything was in order. Again, she wanted to know all the details from Hitler's birthday party.

Two days later on April 22nd, Speer experienced an intense restlessness with how he had left things with Hitler. He decided to return to Berlin to say a proper farewell. Annemarie advised against it; besides, how would he even get there? Panic had hit the streets of Berlin and thousands of automobiles were fleeing the city taking the full width of the road. The Americans and British were approaching from the west; the Russians were fighting their way through the eastern and southern parts of the city.

Yet it was something Speer had to do. He may not make it back out. He may never see his family again. But he felt compelled to speak with Hitler one last time and be forthright with him regarding the recent past. Speer reflected on how hard he had worked against Hitler, disobeying him at every turn over the last several months. It made no sense to see him again. But emotions are often nonsensical and Speer felt internally prompted to speak with Hitler one more time before the end. There was an intimacy with Hitler that Speer could not deny; they were akin to two sojourners, artists, who were caught up in something so vast and destructive it destroyed all their dreams.

Speer remembered their early days at the drafting table, planning the future of Berlin. Speer remembered times at Obersalzberg, where Hitler graciously hosted his family and bounced Speer's children on his lap. He remembered their walks in the snow to the teehaus, and the times Hitler stopped and wanted to talk only with Speer. This overpowering desire to see him one more time probably stemmed from when Speer idolized Hitler and wanted nothing more than to be praised by him. Perhaps it was something Speer missed in his childhood but he was no psychologist. As absurd as it seemed, Speer simply wanted to say goodbye to the man; *he must go and do this final act!*

Speer wrote his wife a few lines telling her he did not intend to join Hitler in death. Then he said goodbye to his staff and left Hamburg for Berlin. It was a desperate trip that started out with a setback. Fifty miles from the city the route was impeded by vehicles of every type — tens of thousands of them — furiously trying to leave Berlin. Speer decided to maneuver over to the Reichlin airfield in Mecklenberg where he knew the kommandant.

Together they studied the maps of Berlin to determine the Russian position. Thankfully, Berlin was not completely surrounded yet. Speer and his escort flew in an Fi 156 Stork at three thousand feet to Gatow in southwestern Berlin. They landed right on the broad avenue which led through the Tiergarten at the Brandenburg gate. Then they hailed an army vehicle to take them to the Chancellery.

When Speer arrived at the upper chamber of the bunker, those present were glad to see him. Eva Braun and Rochus Misch, one of the few aides Hitler allowed to remain in the bunker, both gave him a warm greeting. Misch told Speer about Magda Goebbels who had recently taken up residence in the bunker with her six children. Frau Goebbels was having chest pains, and Misch was worried for the entire Goebbels family.

It was not long after Speer's arrival when he was summoned to see the Chancellor. "The Führer will see you now," Hitler's adjutant informed Speer.

Speer walked down the last fifty steps to the lower bunker. The first person he saw was Bormann, smiling like he had swallowed the proverbial canary. It was obvious the calculating man sought a favor from Speer.

"When you see the Führer, you'll persuade him to fly out, won't you?" inquired Bormann. "We need to get to Bavaria as soon as possible. It's getting desperate and I do not want to remain here."

Speer gave a noncommittal reply. He was content that, at the very end, Bormann was imploring Speer to do something because he was too weak to accomplish it himself.

Speer left Bormann and walked into Hitler's chamber. There was the man. Speer had not thought of what he would encounter once he was in the Führer's presence again but he hoped there would be a friendly handshake and a smile. Neither appeared. Hitler was lifeless, emotionless. There was neither friendliness nor animosity; his countenance was simply devoid of expression. Speer sat in a comfy upholstered armchair.

"What do you think of Admiral Dönitz as my successor?" asked Hitler listlessly.

"I think he is a better choice than others," replied Speer. He knew Hitler would recognize which *others* he was speaking about: Göring, Bormann, Himmler or Goebbels.

In a lethargic, almost burned out tone Hitler asked, "What do you think? Should I stay here or fly to Berchtesgaden? They tell me that tomorrow is my last chance to leave."

"I think you should stay here," replied Speer. "It seems better to me you should end your life here in the capital as the Führer, rather than in your mountain retreat."

Weakened and seemingly without will or purpose Hitler said, "I have resolved to stay here. I only wanted to hear your view once more."

For a moment, the room was completely still as each man sat motionless. Hitler appeared to Speer very anemic and tired. Speer could not help but stare at him as he waited for Hitler to speak.

"I shall not fight personally. There is always the danger that I would only be wounded and fall into the hands of the Russians alive. I don't want my enemies to desecrate my body. I have given orders that I be cremated. Fräulein Braun wants to depart this life with me and I'll shoot Blondi beforehand. Believe me Speer, it is easy for me to end my life. A brief moment and I'm freed of everything, liberated from this painful existence."

Speer did not know what to say. The scene was playing out like a classic Greek tragedy, the last act in a twelve-year relationship. Speer decided he would tell Hitler about all he had done behind his back, and come clean. Yet it did not seem like the Führer was himself nor possessed the energy to relive their past struggles.

Suddenly, before Speer started, the men were interrupted by an announcement that a general had arrived with the daily situation report. For this conference, only Hitler, Bormann, Goebbels, Speer and some lower ranking officers would be present.

Though the report was grim, with the Soviet offensive nearing the Chancellery at every angle, Hitler showed optimism and believed there could still be a turnaround with a last minute offensive.

The meeting over, Speer was approached by Goebbels. "Yesterday the Führer made a decision of enormous importance. He stopped the fighting in the west so the Anglo-American troops can enter Berlin unhindered."

Speer remained silent.

Goebbels continued, "My wife and children are here with me now," the Propaganda Minister said with a smile. "We will all end our lives at this historic site."

Speer was repulsed and did not hide this emotion from his face. "I hear Magda is sick. May I visit her, please?"

"Certainly, follow me."

Speer spent several minutes at Magda's bedside, wishing Goebbels was not hovering behind him. Before the war, Speer and Magda Goebbels had been close; he always appreciated her dignity, despite being married to a man he greatly disliked.

Speer took Magda's hand. He was sick to his stomach that Goebbels was imposing a death contract upon the entire family. Their children were beautiful, especially the youngest one, Heidi, who was not even five yet. He just could not fathom doing something this drastic, especially to innocent children. Speer's visit with Frau Goebbels was cut short by a commotion in the situation room.

⊶•⊷

"Is Hitler still alive?" asked Göring of his second-in-command, pacing back and forth while on the phone. The Reichsmarschall was in Berchtesgaden, wondering what was happening in the bunker.

"Yes, he is still alive," responded General Karl Koller, the man stuck underground in Hitler's bunker so that Göring could flee with his goods.

"What is his state of mind?" Göring asked, glad to be at his luxurious estate in the mountains.

"He has decided to remain in Berlin and fall here," said Koller. "This means the responsibility of the State now belongs to you."

"What do you mean?" asked the Reichsmarschall.

"Hitler is effectively just the kommandant of Berlin, not the head of the Army. That power belongs to you now."

Göring smiled. This was the news he had waited years to hear. *Could it be true?*

"I am sure if I act now Bormann will call me a traitor and seek to kill me," said Göring. "This would be seen as betrayal."

"I don't think so," answered Koller. "Essentially he has made you the supreme commander of the Wehrmacht. Listen, I need to leave from here before I am caught by the Russians and hanged. It is intolerable and I do not want to stay in the bunker." Then Koller had an idea which would cater to Göring's ego, "In your first official act as Chancellor would you summon me to leave Berlin and join you in Berchtesgaden? I've got to get away from here."

Koller's words hit the bull's-eye; it was the exact opium Göring's ego craved.

"Of course you can come! Depart at once. No need to ask anyone's permission there; you are leaving on my new authority as head of state."

As soon as Göring hung up the telephone, those around him brought out a copy of Hitler's decree from June 29, 1941, that stated, "*Should I have my freedom of action curtailed or be somehow removed, Reichsmarschall Hermann Göring is to be my deputy or my successor in all my offices of State, Party and Army.*"

Göring's advisors assured him that the decree was still valid and legal.

"But this is too much of a risk," said Göring, hoping they would not agree with him.

"If you want to make absolutely sure, why not send Hitler a message that puts the matter to bed quite clearly?" one of his associates asked.

Göring sat down and drafted his message.

> *Mein Führer! In view of your decision to remain at your post in fortress Berlin, do you agree that I, as your deputy, in accordance with your decree of June 29, 1941, assume immediately the total leadership of the Reich with complete freedom of action at home and abroad?*
>
> *If by 10 p.m. no answer is forthcoming, I shall assume you have been deprived of your freedom of action. I will then consider the terms of your decree to have come into force and act accordingly for the good of the people of the Fatherland.*
>
> *You must realize what I feel for you in these most difficult hours of my life and I am quite unable to find words to express it.*
>
> *God bless you and grant that you may come here after all as soon as possible. Your Most Loyal, Hermann Göring.*

Göring sent the missive and then over lunch decided he would fly to see General Eisenhower in Rheims the following day and talk everything out "man to man." He would bring the Reichsmarschall baton. *That would impress anyone,* Göring thought.

———◆◆———

In the bunker, Martin Bormann was outraged. He carefully read over Göring's message and declared it treasonous. He immediately started shouting so loudly that those in the nearby rooms could hear him.

"This is an ultimatum!" Bormann exclaimed. "Göring is seeking to usurp the leadership of the Reich and wield it for his own advantage!"

Bormann rushed the typed message to the Führer's quarters; Speer and Goebbels followed close behind. Bormann read the message to Hitler and waited for a response.

Hitler simply shook his head, evoking the same apathy he had shown to Speer moments before. Soon, another message came and Bormann read it to the group.

> *To Reich Minister von Ribbentrop, I have asked the Führer to provide me with instructions by 10 p.m. April 23. If by this time it is apparent that the Führer has been deprived of his freedom of action to conduct the affairs of the Reich, his decree of June 29, 1941, becomes effective, according to which I am heir to all his offices as his deputy. If by 12 midnight, April 23, 1945, you receive no other word either*

*from the Führer directly or from me, you are to come to me at once
by air. Signed Göring, Reichsmarschall.*

Bormann, filled with agitation, blasted out, "Göring is engaged in treason! He's
already sending telegrams to members of the government and announcing that on the
basis of his powers he will assume your office at twelve o'clock tonight, mein Führer!"

"That traitor!" shouted Hitler, finally shaking off his former lethargy. "He has
failed me for the last time! I have known of his failures and covered over his weakness,
the drug addict. But this is it. This is treason!"

Others in the bunker also bemoaned the Reichsmarschall's actions. Hitler
gave an order to Bormann, "Here is what I want you to write to the man; tell him
that he has committed high treason. On this basis I am stripping him of his right
to succession. He has not only been treasonous to me, but to National Socialism.
However, I will exempt him from all punishment if the Reichsmarschall promptly
resign from all his offices for reasons of health."

While Bormann left to transmit the message, Hitler looked up at Ribbentrop,
Goebbels, Speer and Misch and stated, "I've known it all along. I know Göring is
lazy. He let the air force go to pot. He is corrupt. His example made corruption
possible in our state. Besides, he's been a drug addict for years. I've known it all
along."

These were words Speer never thought he would hear Hitler say. *How could he
acknowledge this now? If he knew all of these things about the number two man in the
state, why would he let him continue to serve? This was preposterous!*

Speer knew Hitler turned a blind eye toward Göring but never for once thought
Hitler was aware of the depths of Göring's corruption and drug use. Speer looked
intently at the Führer. Hitler had stopped talking and sat, wilted in a chair, utterly
exhausted by the latest crises. It appeared that Hitler's apathy returned and he looked
listlessly around the room.

In a half hour, Bormann returned with Göring's reply. It stated that because
of a severe heart attack Göring was resigning all his powers. Speer looked into the
face of the Führer's gloating secretary. Finally, Bormann had achieved victory over
Göring and, in essence, had the Reichsmarschall permanently eliminated. It took
the entire war, but Bormann won in the end and Göring was forced to forfeit all he
had gained in the last decade.

Speer remembered the meeting at Obersalzberg the previous year when Bormann
paid off Göring to keep him from gaining an advantage with the Führer. Speer
remembered other times when Bormann worked behind the scenes to keep people
from acquiring too much power; power Bormann thought would intrude on his own
standing within the Reich's highest office.

The time was getting late and Speer decided he should leave Berlin. He wanted
to approach Hitler to tell him he would soon depart but the Führer had withdrawn
to his quarters. An SS orderly cornered Speer and gave him a message that Eva Braun
wanted to see him in her suite before he exited the bunker.

Eva's bedroom was decorated nicely for an underground lair. She had brought
some of the expensive furniture Speer had designed for her before the war started

when she possessed an apartment at the Chancellery. Her bunker room was small, but homey and when the door closed Speer and Eva began talking honestly at once.

"How about a bottle of champagne for our farewell?" Eva asked. "And some sweets? I'm sure you haven't eaten anything for a long time." An orderly brought them a bottle of Moet et Chandon and some cake, then left the two alone to continue their meeting.

"You know, Speer, you almost came too late. Yesterday the Führer heard that the Russians had entered the city and were closing in all around us and he went into a rage like I had never seen before. I thought it might be our last day. But he calmed down and was glad that you came today to show your support and friendship. He liked what you said about not leaving Berlin. He tried to get me to leave and return to Munich, but I refused. I've come to be here until the end and I know you know what that means."

Speer asked her about her health and how she liked living in the bunker with mostly all men in such a confined space.

"It is okay for the most part. I do not like Bormann's constant scheming. You know he does not like the lot of you who hold important positions in the Reich."

"Yes, I know."

"Besides this, the Führer needs me now," said Eva. "I am happy to be here to support him. This is where I shall stay until the last hour."

The two talked from midnight until 3 a.m. Speer conveyed how he was disgruntled that Goebbels stayed in the room during his entire visit with Magda. Speer told Eva that all Frau Goebbels had to do was to say the word and he would ensure the Goebbels children were brought to safety. Eva slowly nodded, then gave him a knowing smile; it would never happen.

When they were notified that Hitler was awake, Speer sent word that he wanted to say goodbye to the Führer. Albert Speer and Eva Braun said their goodbyes and Speer left feeling awful that she ever got involved with Adolf Hitler.

When at last Speer was by the Führer's side, there was absolutely no intimacy when Hitler said, "So you're leaving? Good. *Auf Wiedersehen.*"

Speer — quite underwhelmed with the brevity of it all — stood in silence for a moment. No regards for his family, no warmth, no thanks for a job well done; the end had come and with a coldness that slapped Speer in the face.

Hitler became distracted with something else, the farewell was over and Speer was dismissed from his presence. Within ten minutes Speer had ascended the bunker steps and linked up with his pilot who was waiting for him outside in the Chancellery gardens.

Speer could hear the detonations of Russian shells and remembered they were completely surrounded. He knew there was absolutely no time to spare or he and his pilot would be captured. The small aircraft used the road between the Brandenburg Gate and the Victory Column as a runway despite its many potholes. Soon, the two men were back in the air and quietly flying over Berlin, dodging artillery fire. They arrived at Rechlin airfield, some 100 km north of Berlin, at five o'clock in the morning and Speer heard that Himmler was nearby and wanted to visit with him. *Is this some kind of sick joke?*

Four-year-old Heidi Goebbels ran down the concrete steps in her nightgown to the lower bunker reception room. She turned left and ran right into the tall legs of Rochus Misch, Hitler's aide and telephone operator.

"Hey there, sweetheart, where are you going so fast?" asked Misch.

"Can I hold the puppies please?" asked Heidi.

"May I?"

"May I hold the puppies please?"

"Why certainly sweetheart," responded Misch with a grin. He had taken to the adorable girl from the first moment they met. When introduced, Heidi grabbed his hand and traced some of the lines on his palm. Then, with bright eyes looked up at him intently and said, "Misch, Misch, you're a fish!" At which, Magda scolded her youngest daughter at the protest of Misch. Heidi then jumped into Misch's lap, put her arms around his neck and whispered, "Sorry" into his ear.

Misch was mesmerized by her. He remembered that he could barely speak at her age and was terrified of adults. Yet Heidi seemed comfortable around everyone.

Misch took Heidi's delicate hand in his and brought her over to Blondi so she could play with the puppies.

"Say, Heidi, does your mother know you're down here?"

Heidi turned around while holding one of the furry pups and gave Misch a wide-eyed suspicious look.

"That's what I figured," said Misch with a grin.

The staff had taken to all six of the Goebbels children as soon as they were brought into the bunker. At first, the children were extremely polite with the bunker workers. Nine-year-old Helmut Goebbels would bow when introduced. All of the girls except the youngest were good at curtsying. Heidi often tipped over, then laughed hysterically, making everyone laugh with her. Soon, formalities forgotten, all the children ran through the bunker and played as if they were on holiday.

Just as Misch suspected would happen, several of the other Goebbels children trickled into the reception room looking for Heidi. They all played with Blondi's puppies for a while, then sauntered back up the stairs where breakfast was waiting for them.

Later that day, Adolf Hitler walked into the area and sat next to Misch on a bench outside the switchboard room. An important dispatch was being transcribed regarding secret negotiations Heinrich Himmler was making with Sweden. Soon, Bormann was by Hitler's side, then Goebbels. Misch knew something significant was happening but he did not know what.

The transcriber handed the note to Hitler who was sitting with one of Blondi's puppies on his lap. Immediately after reading the radio dispatch, Hitler's face turned completely ashen and he slumped over, putting his head into his hands. The puppy on his lap slid off and hit the floor with a thud and a slight whimper. Hitler handed the note up to Bormann and Goebbels who quickly read it.

The radio listening post at the Propaganda Ministry had picked up a BBC broadcast from London. There was a Reuter dispatch from Stockholm stating that Heinrich Himmler had participated in top-secret meetings with Count Bernadotte, the Swedish diplomat who was negotiating for the release of prisoners from German concentration camps. Himmler negotiated with the Count by acting as Germany's new Chancellor to surrender the entire Western forces over to Eisenhower.

Bormann and Goebbels shrieked at the news. Others began to moan and cry. Misch picked up the puppy and brought her over to the box with Blondi. Helmut Goebbels ran down the stairs to see what the adults were yelling about but he was shooed back up by one of the secretaries.

Hitler, crimson-faced, finally recovered from his shock. He stood up and angrily ripped into Himmler for this treasonous attempt. Himmler, the Reichsführer and SS Chief, had contacted the enemy behind Hitler's back and tried to make negotiations to end the war. This was a worse betrayal than Göring, who had at least asked for permission.

"This is the most hideous kind of treachery!" hollered Hitler. "My loyal SS servant, who was supposed to be true even if all else failed me, has done this wicked thing! This is the worst act of betrayal I have ever known! Can no one be faithful? First Röhm, then Hess, then Göring, and now Himmler!"

Another report came in that the Duce, Benito Mussolini, along with his mistress, had been assassinated by Italian partisans while trying to escape into Switzerland. Their bodies were brought by a truck to Milan where they were dumped out onto the piazza. The following day they were strung up by the heels and hung from lampposts. After a while, they were cut down and allowed to lay in a gutter for a day so that loyal Italians could defile their bodies.

This news unnerved Hitler and the others in the bunker. The missive about Mussolini was followed by a message that the Russians were now fighting one city block away from the bunker. The residents had one more day at most before they would be discovered and taken prisoner.

"We cannot be taken prisoner!" declared Hitler. "I do not want to be put on exhibition in some Russian wax museum. We must get moving now with the rest of my plans."

Hitler said his final goodbyes to the staff. Cyanide capsules were passed out to all the assistants along with a final offer to escape for freedom before it was too late. Most decided to stay with the Führer until the end, except for a few low-level staff.

Hitler called for his secretary, Traudl Junge, who would record his final will and testament. He expounded on the failure of the Third Reich generals which was, in his mind, the reason behind this embarrassing defeat. While he was dictating his final words, Eva Braun prepared herself for marriage. Adolf Hitler had finally agreed to partake in matrimony with his mistress as a favor to her.

Bormann used the time to send a note to Berchtesgaden in an attempt to settle some old scores. He ordered the SS officers there to place Göring under arrest and to keep him in custody until they received further word from the bunker. To the SS officers near Himmler's home he told them to arrest their chief and they would be rewarded later. Bormann did not want either Himmler or Göring to be in charge once the end had come because he knew that Hitler was drafting a will placing Admiral Dönitz in charge. But no one knew if Hitler's final will would ever make it out of the bunker.

In his message to Germany's next Chancellor, Bormann wrote that Admiral

Dönitz needed to immediately eliminate all traitors. He also incriminated Keitel, Himmler, and Göring. In a second note, this time to Berchtesgaden, he wrote:

If Berlin and we shall fall, the traitors of April 23 (Göring and his staff) must be exterminated. Men, do your duty! Your life and honor depend on it!

While writing, Bormann was disturbed by loud music coming from the upper level of the bunker. The staff, finally free to do as they wished, started a party and several of them danced and drank schnapps. Bormann yelled upstairs for them to shut up so he could concentrate; he had more important work to do.

The sound of exploding shells above the bunker grew heavier. There was not a doubt in anyone's mind that the Russians were battling for the Chancellery garden area, Germany's last defense! Misch and several others wrote final notes to their wives.

Hitler stripped Himmler and Göring of Party membership before concluding his will. He was also still defiant against the Jews and wrote:

Above all, I enjoin the government and the people to uphold the racial laws to the limit and to resist mercilessly the poisoner of all nations, international Jewry.

As Traudl Junge typed up the thirteen pages of handwritten notes, Hitler left her and proceeded to the map room where his bride-to-be was waiting patiently for him in her long black silk gown. Martin Bormann, Joseph and Magda Goebbels, and five others were there as guests. Eva was radiant.

A clerk named Wagner, recently fetched to the bunker just for the wedding, presided. "You come here willingly, with hearts prepared, to receive each other in marriage?" Wagner asked.

"Ja," Adolf and Eva answered together.

"Will you love each other and be loyal until death separates you?"

"Ja."

"Please join hands and affirm the vow. Do you, Adolf Hitler, take Eva Braun to be your lawfully wedded wife until death separates you?"

"I do," answered Hitler stoically.

"And do you, Eva Braun, take Adolf Hitler to be your lawfully wedded husband until death separates you?"

"I do," answered Eva smiling.

"By the authority invested in me, I now pronounce you man and wife."

Unfortunately, the rings did not fit. They were hastily procured from outside the bunker and were too big. Eva did not mind; nothing could rob her joy that day. Adolf and Eva Hitler signed the wedding certificate. Then, Bormann and Goebbels signed it as witnesses. The wedding party paraded into the study for a small wedding feast.

After a brief moment of toasting, Hitler, Bormann, and Goebbels rejoined Frau Junge who had just finished typing up Hitler's will. After Hitler signed it, again Bormann and Goebbels signed as witnesses. It was now four in the morning on April 29th and everyone went to bed.

Eva Braun slept late and spent the afternoon of the 29th fixing up her nails and hair again, ensuring everyone now called her Frau Hitler. Hitler and Bormann sent out four messengers who were to deliver copies of his final will and testament to Admiral Dönitz's headquarters, to the Army Chief's headquarters, and two copies were to be deposited in Munich for posterity and safekeeping. The most important part of the document was the naming of Germany's new Head of State, Admiral Karl Dönitz.

More reports on the Russians moving above the bunker.

More drinking and dancing by the staff.

More playing with the puppies by the Goebbels children.

Hitler's chauffer was ordered to secure 200 liters of fuel and place the containers in the Chancellery garden near the entrance to the bunker. Hitler planned to have a Viking funeral where his remains would be burned because he did not want his body defiled by the Russians, as Mussolini's was by his own people.

That afternoon, as the staff were all considering how and when they would die, Goebbels suggested to Hitler that perhaps the cyanide was defective and would not work. It *was*, after all, distributed by that traitor Himmler. They spoke to the doctor who suggested to try out a capsule on Blondi.

Hitler called over his Alsatian one more time and rubbed his hands on each side of her face. After a quick hug, Hitler had the doctor force a capsule down Blondi's throat. The two men watched as Blondi succumbed to the poison within two minutes and shut her eyes for the last time. Everyone in the bunker mourned for the dog who had been with the headquarters staff for years. The puppies were then gathered together, taken upstairs to the garden entrance and each killed with one shot in the back of the head. The Goebbels children were told the puppies were given to happy homes.

Everyone in the bunker knew the time had come. There would be no more escapes and no more errands or messages sent out. When they all went to bed on the 29th, they realized it would be their last night in the bunker.

On April 30th, Hitler had a light lunch, then told Misch that no one was to disturb him. Misch cleared everyone from the lower level of the bunker and moved all the workers upstairs. Hitler took Eva into his living area. They sat on the sofa and spoke for a few minutes. Hitler then barked at Misch to deal with the loud party noises coming from upstairs.

To Misch's surprise, Magda Goebbels, who had been distraught for days about what to do with her children, flew down the bunker steps in a rage, wanting to see Hitler. Before Misch knew what to do with her she barged into Hitler's room.

Misch heard angry shouts from the Führer ordering Magda to leave, that "*Now is not a good time!*"

The distraught woman closed the Führer's door and slumped over to a small wooden bench and sat down weeping. Then came Traudl Junge, and Bormann. Recognizing that *the* moment had come, everyone wanted a last word with the Führer but it was too late. Misch told them all that Hitler strictly ordered that no one was to disturb him.

Frau Junge looked at Magda, then thought about the six Goebbels children. It was past three o'clock and no one had remembered to feed them lunch! She raced back up the stairs where the children were sitting at the mess table waiting patiently. She made small sandwiches for the hungry children who were all mourning the loss of Blondi and the puppies. Heidi began to sing a little song and tried to get her siblings to join in but they were not in the mood for her antics that day. All of a sudden a shot rang out. Helmut, thinking it was an explosion above from the Russians yelled, "Bang on!"

Traudl Junge knew otherwise, excused herself from the kids, and walked back down to the lower bunker area. Looking over Bormann's hefty shoulders into Hitler's living area, Traudl saw that Eva was laying back against the arm of the sofa, having died with a cyanide capsule. Hitler's body was sprawled over the coffee table in front of them, falling forward after a self-inflicted shot to the side of his head. In his hand was his 7.65 caliber Walther pistol, the one he owned since beginning the Nazi Party. Those standing at the entrance to the room seemed paralyzed for a moment as they took in the apocalyptic scene of doom.

Finally, Bormann stepped in and grabbed Eva, flinging her over his shoulder like a large bag of dog food. He turned and exited the room, her upper torso and limp head with flowing hair carelessly thumping against his broad back with every step. Another two aides wrapped Hitler's body in a blanket and the three men escorted the newlywed couple to the top of the bunker steps. Adolf and Eva were placed outside into a prearranged pit filled with petrol, and then the puddle was set on fire.

Weathering the Russian artillery barrage coming from all around the burning site, the men kept adding gasoline for several hours until there was virtually nothing left of the smoldering corpses. Later that evening, the few chunks of charred remains were swept onto a canvas, wrapped up, buried into a shell hole and covered with dirt.

The Führer was no more.

The six Goebbels children were playing in the bedroom when their mother came in and told them to put on their white nightgowns.

"But mama, it's not bedtime yet," protested Heidi.

"I know dear," Magda said trying not to cry.

The older ones began undressing so Heidi followed their lead. Once everyone was in their night gowns, Magda led them to the kitchen where there was a jug of chocolate milk and six cups waiting for them. As the children drank the milk laced with morphine to sedate them, Magda combed their hair and held their hands tenderly. She wiped a milk mustache from Heidi's face and tied red ribbons in the girls' hair.

When they had all sipped their milk mixture Magda led them past the switchboard room where Misch was working. One by one the children said goodnight and started up the stairs to their bedroom. The last child to depart was Heidi, hand-in-hand with her mother, being guided out of the room to the stairs. The spirited child turned and caught sight of her friend Misch one last time and paused to say another goodbye.

Misch gave Heidi a wave and smiled at the darling girl.

The young lass held up one hand at first, then turned to go up the steps. But suddenly she turned around, smiled broadly and yelled, "Misch, Misch, you're a fish!" and laughed like it was the funniest thing ever said.

Misch frowned playfully and pointed his finger at her, "Don't be a funny bunny!"

She made small but intimidating fists at him, then turned, rejoined hands with her mother and continued her journey.

Misch heard Heidi keep saying, "Misch, Misch, you're a fish!" all the way up the stairs.

Magda said goodnight to the children, all in their bunk beds, then turned out the light and shut the door. An hour later she returned to the room with the doctor who helped her crush several cyanide tablets and place the contents into each child's mouth while they slept. The doctor helped Magda ensure that everyone ingested some poison. Then he gave the confirmation to Magda; all six of her children were dead.

Magda Goebbels left her deathly-still children neatly tucked in bed in their white nightgowns and with ribbons tied in the girls' hair. She returned to the common area where her husband was waiting. Together, they walked up to Misch and stood before him a moment. Joseph Goebbels finally said, "Good luck, Misch. We're going up top. It's easier this way; you don't have to carry our bodies upstairs for us afterwards."

Misch did not respond, but noticed that Magda was shaking uncontrollably and could barely walk.

The Goebbels couple slowly made it up the stairs that opened into the Chancellery Garden. Once outside, Joseph positioned his pistol to the base of Magda's skull and without saying a word pulled the trigger. She fell instantly to the ground. He then held the pistol to the side of his own head, fired the revolver and fell next to his wife on the ground, dead. A guard standing by drenched the bodies with petrol and set them on fire in the same pit he had burned the Hitlers.

Misch tried to focus on his solitaire game but could not. His eyes misted over when he thought of the bright-eyed girl who loved to laugh and make fun of his name. Now, Heidi and her entire family were gone forever.

Several hours later Russian soldiers stormed the bunker. Misch, one of the few on Hitler's staff not to commit suicide, was taken prisoner and deported to a Soviet Gulag where he was severely beaten, interrogated, and imprisoned.

The Russians did not capture Martin Bormann in the bunker. He had secretly escaped without anyone knowing.

CHAPTER 36

Escape

The Architect was thankful Speer had obeyed and dropped by to visit him. "You know, Speer," the Architect said thoughtfully, "I am very busy setting up the future German government so I don't have long. However, I did want to offer you a position in it. Göring and I have had a prearranged deal whereby I will be the Premier. Therefore, I am organizing my cabinet, and it would be good for you to join — probably the smartest decision you could make for your future."

Speer looked at the Nazi thoroughbred before him with bewildered pity. He could never get around the fact that this pedantic, insecure, little man could remain so cold and calculating; always speaking in quiet, measured phrases, yet carrying a large, secret club.

"I don't think that would be best for me right now," Speer answered.

The Architect did not look up from the floor when he asked, "Why not?"

"I just finished speaking with Hitler in the bunker. He is putting Admiral Dönitz in charge. If I aligned with you, I am not sure what that would do to my relationship with Germany's new leader."

"This is your only hope for survival Speer! It would be wise if you took this opportunity now, before it is gone forever. Dönitz will not be in charge, I have the SS and a political network throughout the empire."

"I believe I will pass," said Speer graciously. "But thank you. Perhaps you should go and speak to the Führer yourself, before he dies."

"That would be pointless. Besides, he is probably already dead, and I am actively engaged in working out all the details of Germany's future. You know I am too important to the Reich for such a risky trip back to Berlin. The Russians are in the Teirgarten. What if I did not make it out alive?"

Speer had no response. Soon, he departed, leaving the Architect alone to plan his future.

A few days later the Architect continued to obsess whether he would ever be Chancellor and he was upset he had not been summoned by Grand Admiral Karl Dönitz regarding his involvement in the new government. *Will I be Germany's new leader?* He knew that he *should* be, but Hitler did not set him up for success. The Architect traveled to Flensburg to visit Admiral Dönitz with six armed SS men to see what he could work out.

At the Dönitz headquarters he was shown a copy of the Führer's last will and testament naming Dönitz as his successor. This was unnerving.

"You see," Dönitz explained, "Bormann sent this over from the bunker before Hitler died. This instrument of succession is authoritative and proves that I am now in charge of the Reich."

The Architect was visibly shaken and drew a deep breath. He did not want it to come to this. In a deflated tone he said, "Then I offer my services to you as second-in-command."

There was no immediate response from an astounded Dönitz.

"Choose wisely Admiral," the Architect admonished while giving a sidewise glance at his armed cohort, "I still have two Waffen-SS divisions who can seize Berlin by force if necessary."

"I cannot accept your offer," said Dönitz decisively. "We do not need a military solution for our current crisis. And it is no longer necessary to have the SS. I want them to lay down their arms and I want the National Socialist Party dissolved."

At these words the Architect nearly fell over. If they were uttered a few days before, Dönitz would have been separated from the Navy and executed by a firing squad for treason.

Admiral Dönitz continued, "What we need now is diplomacy because we have been overrun. My only aim at the moment is to end this war quickly and then hand over the government to the Allied leaders. That is our purpose here."

"This is short-sighted! Don't you realize we still have Denmark and Norway we can use as bargaining chips? Perhaps if the two countries were forfeited to the Allies peacefully, then Germany could be left alone to rebuild. We cannot give everything away so fast; we still have some negotiating room."

"Do we?" Dönitz asked derisively. "Look around you. The few people we have here are making the necessary preparations for our capture. Our army is on the run. Our navy is finished. The British will be at our doorstep within days if not hours. You deceive yourself."

The Architect was at a loss for words. In his mind's worst case scenario he thought he would be slated as the number two man in the state. Now he had nothing.

While several naval security guards came into the room and stood behind Dönitz, the new Chancellor said to the Architect, "I am officially asking you to depart headquarters at once. This request will not be refused or repeated. In fact, you are dismissed from any responsibilities as a Reich Minister and I demand that you keep clear from the seat of government from now on. You are not welcome here any longer. Guards, please escort our friend out of the building."

With these words the Architect and his SS men were maneuvered outside and escorted through the barbed-wire gate lined with military men and machine guns. He was now on his own — and without government employment. *This is the end of the world!*

The Architect realized the time had come to prepare an alternate plan for his post-war life. He would not be able to visit his mistress, Hedwig Potthast and their two children in Berchtesgaden until the war was long over. The Americans had surrounded the entire area. Hopefully Hedwig, three-year-old Helge and nine-month-old Nanette would get along fine in Bavaria without him. His legal wife and daughter, Margarete and fifteen-year-old Gudrun, were already in the hands of American interrogators in Italy.

The Architect thought about his relationship with his lover, Hedwig Potthast. He hoped he could trust her to dispose of his secret collection of artifacts stored in their attic in Berchtesgaden. He had trusted her to safeguard the hand-made treasures presented him as gifts during an inspection at Dachau, his model concentration camp.

It was a collection of special furniture made from human skin and bones, including a lamp of a femur and a lampshade made with human skin. The Architect knew that in the wrong hands people could misjudge him and possibly not give him regard as the genius he was. He hoped Hedwig burned the artifacts in the incinerator as he requested, though lately people had a hard time following his orders. He would like to have those possessions after the war because they would surely be worth a small treasure as relics but he knew others would not appreciate their value like he did; the plague of his existence when working with others — *their lack of taste!*

The Architect again tried to make contact with General Dwight Eisenhower. *If the General would just hear him out!* He knew his hours were limited at this point and he wondered what had happened in the bunker to restrain his options so much. Hitler used to praise him continually, but it appeared the Führer simply used him. *He disposed of me when I was no longer necessary to him!*

Where to go? What to do? He had bought a favor from some friends in the Red Cross with the prisoners at Ravensbrück and issued a telegram to the Red Cross officials stating he wanted to speak to Eisenhower, but to no avail. The Architect had also worked with Count Bernadotte of Sweden and essentially surrendered Germany to the Count stating Hitler was incapacitated. However, the offer was rejected. *Bormann probably intercepted the plot and thwarted it — the slime!*

How could I not be called upon to lead the government?

He was the chief law-enforcement officer in the nation. No one identified problems, found solutions and saw matters as clearly as he did. He was usually the only one in the room knowing exactly what to do at any given moment. Not being number one for the past few years was difficult and required much self-control. The Architect maintained patience with Hitler in their conversations, hoping the former corporal would catch up before a decision was made. He knew Hitler respected him, but for some inane reason the Architect always had to have the Führer's permission before attempting new operations.

One special skill the Architect possessed was his ability to manipulate others, especially those who were weak-minded. His truism and his personal incantation was to:

Disguise personal discrepancies,
Overcome weaknesses with self-discipline, and
Exploit other's weaknesses to take advantage of a situation.

These were the only rules that seemed to work for him; his personal Sermon on the Mount.

With Dönitz being stubborn, the only thing left to do is run, the Architect finally decided. Unfortunately, his appearance was too familiar with the public here and abroad so he would have to wear a disguise. It was tough being so famous. People had no idea what challenges were associated with power. His celebrity status was always getting in the way. As a repugnant smile swept across his mustached face, there was one thing he took comfort in: *the name of Heinrich Himmler will live eternally!*

The Architect disguised himself as Sergeant Heinrich Hitzinger, with a patch on one eye and dressed in civilian clothing. He would travel by foot with his private secretary, Rudolf Brandt, and several other associates hunted by the Allies — all six men camouflaged in disguises. Their intent was to hike into the northern German mountains and hide out until the upheaval of the war and its aftermath was settled. *Then perhaps journey to Switzerland or Austria?*

The group hiked together for days, avoiding towns and Allied checkpoints at all costs. Three of the men decided to leave the group and try their luck in a small town. The Architect and two other men continued on, walking through tall wheat fields and wood lines, mostly at night to avoid detection. All the men kept a cyanide capsule either in their mouth, hand, or pocket for quick consumption should they be discovered.

After ten days of hiking, arduous evasion of human contact, and near exhaustion, the three men inadvertently stumbled upon a British checkpoint. They were stopped and interrogated for two days, during which Wehrmacht Sergeant Heinrich Hitzinger's identity as a Nazi Party leader was discovered. Soon, he would be sent to the Allied headquarters, interrogated, and charged with war crimes along with his associates. Before he departed for headquarters the British decided to give him a medical inspection.

While walking with a guard into the makeshift hospital, the Architect thought, *It is time.* He pushed the cyanide capsule into position between his teeth, ready to bite down.

"In here," the guard ordered, pointing to an adjacent room where a British physician and nurse awaited him.

Seeing the sparsely guarded facility, the Architect moved the capsule back under his tongue. *Perhaps I can escape this,* he thought.

The examination seemed routine and was almost over when the doctor paused and studied his patient. Suspecting this was the famous Heinrich Himmler the doctor reasoned he was probably hiding something. He looked directly into Himmler's dark eyes and said, "Okay now, open your mouth." Then he brought his gloved finger up for insertion.

No response.

"I said open your mouth!" The doctor pushed his finger against the Architect's closed lips but the Nazi jerked his head to the side.

This is the time!

With his last moment of manipulation, the Architect looked intently into the doctor's eyes as he crunched the cyanide capsule between his teeth.

"What have you done?" the doctor asked, horrified. "Guard! Guard! In here, quick!"

It was too late. The Nazi leader before him fell heavily to the floor, totally unconscious. The blue-tipped capsule had worked its magic. Heinrich Himmler, age 44, was dead.

Without the duty and chivalry he preached to others, the Holocaust Architect mutinied against his own country, family, and indeed, his own flesh. Though his body was buried in an unmarked grave, his words remain forever etched in human history as a tribute to his life's work:

"With regards to the extermination of the Jewish people, most of you know what it's like to see 100 corpses lying side by side, or 500

> *or 1,000 of them piled up. To have coped with this, and to have remained decent, this is what has made us tough, and it is a glorious page in our history.*

CHAPTER 37

Shaved Heads

I n the spring of 1945, Corrie, feeling somewhat restless in her new solitude, received an opportunity to help with the Dutch Resistance movement again. She was approached by someone in the national underground who asked her to carry papers to the Haarlem police station. The Resistance had someone in jail they needed to free so they had falsified papers of release. All Corrie had to do was to carry the papers into the police station and deliver them to the chief. Since the Beje was one street away from the station, Corrie felt it was a simple request.

As Corrie walked through the familiar large double doors of the station, a paralyzing fear entombed her. She suddenly felt her heart pound inside her dress. *Would she blow the operation?*

When Corrie looked up, her eyes discovered that Rolf was at the front desk. Rolf, the Ten Boom's orange-haired friend, had helped them on many occasions before the raid. She felt a level of comfort to see her old acquaintance.

"Yes?" Rolf addressed the visitor, rather coolly. "You had an appointment?"

Corrie was happy to see the young lieutenant, yet mystified he did not recognize her, much like Truus at the convalescent home.

"Why Rolf! Don't you remember me?" asked Corrie hopefully.

Rolf took a moment to study the woman standing before him. "Why, yes. The woman from the watch shop. I heard you were closed down for a while." His stiff mannerism communicated there was no affection for, nor relationship with the visitor.

Corrie was confused and hurt. Rolf certainly knew who she was. *What was he doing?*

Then Corrie recalled where she was and who was listening. There were probably a dozen German soldiers standing within earshot. Corrie all but communicated that she and Rolf held a special relationship and that they had been working on the same team. *How could I be so careless?*

Gripped with fear, Corrie realized she no longer had the courage for the work of the underground. She quickly walked toward Rolf's desk and provided him the forged papers the Resistance workers had given to her for delivery. She hoped that none of the other officers noticed how much her hands were trembling when she released the paperwork. Rolf was a statue; the perfect spy.

"These must be approved by the Chief of Police," he told her in an official tone. "Can you return tomorrow afternoon at four?"

Corrie did not answer. She turned and exited through the large wooden doors as fast as she could. She paused on the sidewalk out front to catch her breath and wait for her knees to stop knocking before she made her way home.

The underground work was no longer for her; she would have to find another way to serve God. *What now?* As she thought about her time in captivity, Betsie's words and dreams kept echoing through her mind. *"We must tell people, Corrie. We must tell them what we learned."*

That very next week, Corrie ten Boom began to tell others what she learned about God from her time in Ravensbrück. Wherever she was invited — churches, club rooms, or private homes — Corrie spread the message of God's love and forgiveness. And it was a message the people in Holland needed to hear.

"There is no pit so deep, that the love of God is not deeper yet," she told them, quoting her sister Betsie from the hospital in Ravensbrück. "Nothing can separate us from the love of Christ; not persecution, distress, hunger, nakedness or even death can infringe on the victory we possess in Christ Jesus."

Having personally experienced all these trials, Corrie powerfully communicated that people were conquerors, and in fact, *more* than conquerors through Christ who loved them. "Nothing in all creation can separate people from the love of God that is in Christ Jesus the Lord, not even the evil Nazi regime. I experienced God's love in the pit of Ravensbrück, and you who survived this war in Holland can experience the love of God as well."

Corrie's audiences devoured the spiritual truth poured out in her meetings. There was much pain and suffering in Haarlem and all of Holland as the war neared its end.

The second week of May, 1945, the Allies retook Holland. The Canadians rushed food, blankets, and medical supplies to every city center, hoping to save as many starving people as possible. There was incredible rejoicing in all the streets and market centers. The flag of Holland flew from the open windows. The Dutch national anthem, *Wilhelmus,* was played on the radio repeatedly, reminding people of the regained freedom of the government and media.

> *William of Nassau am I,*
> *Of a Dutch and ancient line,*
> *Loyal to the fatherland,*
> *I will remain until I die.*
> *A prince of Orange am I,*
> *Ever free and fearless,*

To the king of Spain I've granted,
A lifelong loyalty.

To live in fear of God,
I have always tried,
Because of this I'm driven,
From people, home and land.
But God, I trust, will direct me,
Like a good instrument,
And one day reinstate me,
Into my government.

Hold on my subjects,
Who are honest and good,
God will not abandon you,
Though you are now pursued.
He who tries to live devoutly,
Must pray to God day and night,
That he will give me power,
As champion of your right.

The sounds of laughter and blowing horns could be heard in the streets and the color of orange was everywhere. Corrie noticed scores of young men and children darting here and there, finally free after hiding from the Gestapo. Holland was held in captivity for five years and now the enthusiasm to celebrate flooded Corrie's heart. She headed to the Grote Markt along with her countrymen, noticing the few remaining Germans disappear into the alleyways.

When Corrie arrived at the city center she heard a loud commotion in the direction of city hall. *What could the disturbance be now that the war was over?* Corrie wondered.

Then, as she looked over the heads of her countrymen, she saw several strong Hollander men pull three Dutch women up the steps to a platform area with people shouting all around them. Corrie noticed the anger and fierceness of people who, moments before, were celebrating and laughing. The three women were petrified and forced to kneel down so everyone could see them. Corrie found out the girls were Hollanders who had relations with German soldiers.

Corrie remembered how she felt when Betsie told her who had informed the Gestapo about the watch shop and their underground activity; the anger, the bitterness and desire for vengeance enveloped her for a time. But she also remembered how *she* was the one who suffered for those feelings. Now she looked on at the hostile crowd taking matters in their own hands, seeking vengeance by making the girls pay for aligning themselves with the enemy.

Corrie and other Haarlem citizens watched angry men take clippers to the women and attack their heads, leaving stubs at the top and remnants at the feet.

One still had a long, black strand of hair covering her face. They were all shaved poorly on purpose.

Corrie looked into the face of one of the women, her head raggedly shaved as punishment. Anger, scorn, fierceness. The woman displayed the same malice as her captors did toward her.

A young man grabbed her arm and moved it in time with the singing of "Oranje Boven," the song sung with affection to the House of Orange. Another man thrust flowers in her hand while someone else smeared the top of her head with orange paint. The paint oozed down the front of her head and into her lap, covering her clothes.

The Dutch crowd gathered that day had suffered for five long years, being starved of food, pride, and freedom. Many were hunted down and forced to hide, some in attic rooms or secret closets for years. Finally they were able to find a release, lashing out and punishing someone else for their own personal torture. *But this is not the way*, thought Corrie.

The crowd turned its attention to two more girls who were forced onto the platform, both with waves of hair yet to be destroyed, both with tears in their eyes. Orange paint was smeared on their heads and it trickled down onto the newly-detached hair on the platform.

More flowers for their hands.

More furtive looks and weeping from the captives.

More scorning from the public.

The group of five now on display were forced to sing the *Wilhelmus* and keep time with the crowd. If they did not sing, their arms were jerked here and there to keep in time with the beat.

The battered and shunned women were forcefully exhibited to their neighbors so everyone in town could mock them. Corrie did not like to see this mistreatment in her homeland. She felt like crying out, *"Be careful! You are destroying something!"*

Corrie thought of the "Red-light Commandos" and how they were mistreated and shunned in prison. She instinctively realized that no amount of harm you inflict on others could help ease the pain you have suffered in the past. These objects of hatred were no different than Hitler's personal hatred of the Jews. He felt as though he had been provoked and unjustly wronged by those who worshipped Jehovah. These Hollanders were provoked and persecuted by the men these women loved. They felt betrayed and their recent freedom emboldened them to take action against those who no longer had protection.

Corrie decided to return to the Beje. She could not take part in these kind of perverse celebrations and the *Wilhelmus* was too sacred to her for it to be used in such a derisive manner. She shut the door behind her, still hearing the screaming and shouting outside. The crowd now marched the women down the street just in front of the Beje door. Corrie closed her eyes and prayed for the women and she prayed for their tormentors, just as Betsie had prayed for their German guards.

Corrie's thoughts returned to Ravensbrück. One night near the end, when hundreds of women died each day and their bodies fed to the ovens, Betsie could not sleep and wanted to talk.

"Corrie, are you awake?" she sweetly asked.

"I am now," answered Corrie. She could feel Betsie's bony, cold fingers gently rub her cheek as if to confirm Corrie was awake and speaking. Morning roll call was a few hours away, they had better whisper to avoid waking others.

"What do you want?" whispered Corrie.

"Corrie, there is so much bitterness," answered Betsie. Her breath came in short rasps.

Corrie laid her hand on her sister's side. She could feel no padding, just the bones of her ribcage moving up and down and her heart fluttering inside. She could not have much longer to live.

"Corrie, we must give to the Germans that which they now try to take away from us; our love for Jesus." Betsie paused and caught her breath. "This concentration camp has ruined many, many lives, and there are camps like Ravensbrück all over Germany. After the war there will be no use for them anymore. I have prayed that the Lord will give us one in Germany so we can use the camp to build up hurt lives."

Oh no, not in Germany!

"In Germany, Betsie? Must we?" Corrie was not excited about this vision.

"The Germans are the most wounded of all the people in the world, Corrie," Betsie whispered. "Think of that young female guard who swore in such filthy language yesterday. She was only a teenager but did you see how she was beating that poor old woman with a whip? What a job we have to do after the war!"

Corrie opened her eyes and looked around the Beje. Betsie had two visions, one of a home for those who had suffered because of the war, and that of using a former concentration camp to help Germans. Corrie wondered if and when Betsie's visions might come about. *What a job we have to do after the war!*

CHAPTER 38

Nuremberg

To the astonishment of Annemarie and the rest of the armament staff, Albert Speer returned to Hamburg after his final visit with the Führer in the Berlin bunker. He spent several days with them, attending to minor details and tying up loose ends. Their armaments mission was over but they needed to address how they would survive and communicate when the Allies took over.

On May 1st, while Speer visited Admiral Karl Dönitz in Flensburg, a radio message came from the bunker announcing the death of Adolf Hitler. Both Speer and Dönitz knew this event was forthcoming but still took a moment to digest the news. A second message arrived stating that in place of Reichsmarschall Göring, the Führer had named Dönitz as his successor. He was told to await further instructions from Bormann who was to link up with Dönitz and provide more guidance.

Dönitz studied the messages solemnly. He and Speer decided that if Bormann arrived at Dönitz's headquarters he would be placed under arrest.

"We could not possibly govern the Reich with Martin Bormann," stated Dönitz.

"I feel the same way," concurred Speer.

"Then what should we do with these instructions from headquarters?"

"Burn them as fast as possible."

"I agree," said Dönitz. "Nobody can work with a man like Bormann around."

"That is true."

The nation of Germany as they knew it had come to an end and the transitional government needed to be purged of the baggage of Hitler loyalists.

That night, Speer went into his room in the Flensburg headquarters building and opened his suitcase. Annemarie had placed the red leather folder containing Hitler's picture given to Speer a few weeks before as his birthday present. When Speer opened the container and saw the picture he wept uncontrollably. The fatigue and stress of the last few days had overtaken him. This moment for Speer was a climactic grasp of the death of his former master and friend ... and the end of suffering for millions of people. The war was over and Germany was utterly destroyed.

———◆◆◆———

The Dönitz government did not last long. On May 7th, there was an unconditional surrender by Germany in all theaters of war. In the next few hours, at the recommendation of Admiral Dönitz, instruments of surrender were signed by Generals Alfred Jodl and Wilhelm Keitel which included the line, *"All forces under German control to cease active operations at 2301 hours Central European Time, on May 8, 1945."* Though Admiral Dönitz led meetings and appointed Cabinet members, there was little for anyone to do. The Flensburg compound was surrounded by British forces and Speer, now the Minister of Economics and Production, felt they were all operating in a vacuum, creating work, though nothing important could be done.

One day a British officer walked into the Dönitz HQ building and, upon entering Speer's private room asked, "Do you happen to know where Albert Speer is?"

"He is me," said Speer. "What can I help you with?"

"The American headquarters is collecting data on the effects of Allied bombings and was wondering if you could come speak to them."

Speer spent three days with the Americans going over the impact of their bombing campaigns and giving an insider's report. When these interviews were completed, Speer decided to leave the British controlled Flensburg area and drive without permission to see his family. He traveled past the hamlet of Glücksburg into rural Germany where his family was staying in a country home.

Margarete and the six Speer children were delighted and relieved to see the patriarch of the family, if only for a brief visit. Albert made the secret trek several times but during one of his stays the Speers had some special visitors. A British security detail surrounded the estate, entered the home without knocking and a sergeant walked into Speer's bedroom.

"Mr. Albert Speer, you are now under arrest," the sergeant informed him. "You may have a few moments to pack your things."

Before the sergeant departed the room, he took off his belt and the loaded pistol attached to it, then placed it on a small table by the door of Speer's room.

Speer gathered his things together into a suitcase and, leaving the sergeant's pistol undisturbed, he hurried out of the room.

The former Reich Minister of Armaments and War Production was escorted back to Flensburg and placed under 24-hour surveillance. Within a few days, the entire Dönitz government was assembled into a reception room where they were forced to sit on wooden benches with their personal belongings beside them. One by one they were called into an adjoining room to be registered as prisoners. During the processing, each member of the Dönitz group was strip-searched and every orifice was examined for a cyanide capsule.

Afterward, they were marched into an open courtyard where machine guns were trained on them from the upper levels of the building. Newspaper photographers were allowed to take pictures for several minutes and then the prisoners were loaded onto trucks. The caravan left Flensburg with several trucks laden with prisoners along with dozens of armored vehicles in front and behind to escort them.

When the caravan reached the airport, the prisoners were loaded onto cargo planes where they sat on small crates. They were flown south to the country of Luxembourg and taken to the Palace Hotel where they were kept under house arrest. The former Reichsmarschall, Hermann Göring, was already there and had assumed leadership of the German contingent. There were generals and admirals and other high-level members of Hitler's staff. When Dönitz entered the hotel a feud began as to who should be in charge.

Göring thought he should be the leader. Dönitz believed he was the rightful successor because of Hitler's final will. Speer watched as the two men battled over who would be in charge. Speer knew it was a silly argument. They were all prisoners now, equal in status and position.

The prisoners chatted with Dr. Brandt, who had narrowly escaped execution after moving his family from Berlin without Hitler's authorization. Brandt spoke of the losses he had incurred because of the war when Hermann Göring cut him off and said, "Oh, come on now. What possible reason can you have to complain when you had so little? But I, who had so much; think what this means to me."

Speer tried to adapt to being a prisoner; it helped that he felt he would not be held captive for very long because he had not done anything but serve the government that lost the war. But then things grew more complicated. Former German decision-makers were being sent to Nuremburg. New and horrifying information was coming out of a concentration camp called Auschwitz.

———◆◆◆———

The city of Nuremburg was chosen by the Allies as the place where due process would be served to the highest officials of Nazi Germany. Nuremburg was considered the ceremonial birthplace of the Nazi Party with its propaganda rallies and anti-Semitic Nuremburg laws passed in 1935, and thus, considered a fitting location for the Nazi Party to meet justice for its crimes.

Nuremburg also held the Palace of Justice which had been kept intact during the bombings. This courthouse was a massive four-storied brick building containing several court rooms and a large prison as part of the facility. The Allied Control Council would meet at Nuremburg to prosecute German officials for crimes against humanity and for violating the laws of war.

Albert Speer arrived at Nuremburg in the first week of October, 1945. His jeep pulled up to the front gate after dark and Speer was led inside and taken to his cell. He was given recycled American Army fatigues to wear which were dyed black and told to change into them.

Speer's section of the prison was always dark; his cell on the first floor did not receive any direct sunlight. The only furniture was a straw pallet and three dirty blankets. There was one solitary light bulb that hung from the ceiling, only lit for two hours in the morning and two hours in the evening.

Speer was not permitted to speak to the other defendants but he could see Göring across the corridor wearing the enemies' old uniforms. *There is Hermann, reduced to one drab outfit!*

With his broad girth seen every time he crossed by the large keyhole, Göring was like a caged animal pacing back and forth in his cell — six paces one way, and six paces back.

The only other person he saw was the mess attendant who silently delivered a tray of meager rations three times a day. Speer asked for but was not granted anything to read or write. He simply sat in his cell and reflected quietly to himself.

After one week Speer was moved to another prison cell on the fourth floor. It had a window which afforded ample sunlight during the day and allowed him to view a section of the blue sky that he greatly enjoyed. It also contained a cot, a table, and a chair. He was very grateful for the new accommodations but was still not allowed to speak to his fellow prisoners. He was told that the trial would begin soon and he needed to focus on what he would say and how he would defend himself.

In mid-October, Speer was brought out of his cell for numerous interrogations by the prosecutors. One American prosecutor, a man by the name of Thomas Dodd, was fairly severe.

In one question, Dodd asked Speer about the more than four million foreign workers he had deported from the Third Reich's conquered territory, men ripped from their homes to be used as slave labor. This stung the former War Minister and made him quite nervous. *Will I be held accountable for all of their lives, their suffering?*

On October 19, 1945, Speer was served with a 24,000-word indictment for the charges against him. When the British officer who delivered the indictment to him left his cell, Speer took a deep breath. The seriousness of his situation was suddenly very real and it startled him. He would be charged with crimes against humanity along with Göring, Keitel, Ribbentrop, Dönitz and Bormann in absentia. *Why? What crime have I committed?* Speer wondered.

He had hoped that his cooperation with the British before his arrest would lead to him being exonerated and allowed to serve merely as a witness. But it seemed the prosecutors had a lot of evidence against Speer because of the labor he had provided the factories.

Speer tried to read through the indictment as thoroughly as he could. In one section it spoke of the nine and a half million Jews who lived in Europe under Nazi domination and that nearly six million of them had disappeared; most put to death by Nazi conspirators in extermination camps. *Is this what I am to be held responsible for?* Speer worried. The deportation of laborers was certainly under his jurisdiction, but not the destruction of the Jews.

With all of the crimes listed in the indictment, Speer had to face the wicked truth which shattered any doubts about Hitler and the Third Reich. It was a shock to see all of the evil in writing. Speer had disagreed with Hitler and countermanded him for months knowing that the Führer's path to victory was ill-fated and that he was annihilating the German populace. But now Speer knew the dirty little secret of the Nazi Party, the one he was warned about from his friend regarding Auschwitz. Not only had they started an unnecessary war, confiscated historic treasures, and ruined countless lives, they exterminated millions of innocent people based purely on race.

Whatever defense Speer might have put together before in order to save his neck, he now grasped the extent of the evil of the Third Reich. It was rotten to the core and he served on the national leadership team. Hour after hour, alone in his cell, Speer reasoned with himself how this tragedy could have happened and he came to realize that it was hundreds of small decisions by Nazi Cabinet members who turned the other way and did not ask questions. Speer himself also made small decisions which could have turned the course of the war. The truth was that the regime had committed horrific crimes and Speer knew that he could not utilize the defense that he was just obeying orders. The 22 Reich leaders on trial at Nuremburg were handed a valid indictment, Speer concluded, and he could not in good conscience weasel out of his responsibility.

A few days after his interrogations ended, Speer was allowed to choose a German lawyer to represent him. He decided on a man named Dr. Hans Flächsner out of several who were available because he thought Flächsner was humble and sensible; a man he could get along with. Speer told Flächsner he was thinking of taking responsibility for all the crimes of the Reich.

"Whatever for?" asked Flächsner. "If you do, you will surely hang! I cannot be much help defending you if you admit responsibility."

"It is important for someone to own up to this mess," said Speer. "There is a common responsibility for such horrible crimes, even in an authoritarian system. If we were victorious, all of us would be claiming our share of the success. How can we claim no part when it becomes a disaster?"

Flächsner sat speechless.

"I am determined that there must never be a Hitler-like figure again and whatever I can do to prevent it I will," said Speer. "You cannot change my mind on this."

"Well," said Flächsner stoically, "I guess we'll see what happens. This is your life we're talking about. If you hang…"

"So be it," finished Speer.

On October 25th, a guard whispered to Speer that the night before, Robert Ley, a co-defendant in the case against high-ranking German officials, had made a noose for himself out of stripped edges from an army towel and hanged himself from a pipe in his cell. The warden did not want the information to get out but all the prisoners heard about it. Speer thought how he himself might attempt suicide. But then he made a different decision; he would begin to attend chapel services regularly.

Of the 24 men charged who represented the government of the Third Reich, only 21 sat in the docket. Ley was dead, Martin Bormann — his whereabouts still unknown — would be charged in absentia, and Industrialist Gustav Krupp was considered too frail to stand trial. The defendants were charged with crimes on four counts:

1. *Participation in a common plan or conspiracy to wage a war of aggression in violation of international treaties.*
2. *Planning, initiating and waging wars of aggression and other crimes against peace.*
3. *War crimes, meaning a violation of the laws or customs of war, and the murder, ill-treatment or deportation to slave labor of civilian populations.*
4. *Crimes against humanity, murder, extermination, enslavement, deportation and other inhumane acts committed against civilian populations before or during the war. This included crimes against Jews, ethnic minorities, and physically and mentally disabled persons.*

On November 19th, the day before the trial would begin, all of the defendants were allowed to enter the courtroom together so they could be assigned seats. Göring received the first seat in the dock as the number two man of the state. The second seat was given to the former deputy Führer, Rudolf Hess, recently transferred from Surrey, England, where he had been a prisoner since May of 1941. The third seat was given to Ribbentrop the foreign minister, the fourth one to General Keitel, then to Admiral Dönitz and so on. Speer was seated nineteenth.

When the seating chart was completed, the prisoners were allowed to stay in the court room and visit. It was the first time they were given an opportunity to speak together since arriving in October. Speer was alarmed at how fast Göring assumed leadership and decided on how everyone should testify.

"The only way we are going to beat this," said Göring smiling, "is if we all stand together. Everything we did was for the greater German Reich. I wish we all had the courage to confine our defense to two simple words: Up yours!"

"That's not the way I see it," expressed Speer, startling everyone present.

"What do you mean, Herr Speer?" asked Göring, his arched eyebrows conveying his antipathy.

"I believe we share a collective guilt," said Speer.

"Now listen," Göring angrily replied, "we have to present a common front of pleading not guilty. That is the only way to succeed here. We must show the world that the court is incompetent and has no legal basis. Besides, during the Third

Reich, the laws of the Third Reich were the law and we were morally compelled to obey them."

"I believe that universal law representing civilized thought, supersedes national laws," responded Speer as calmly as he could, though his hands were shaking. "We *must* consider ourselves responsible and we should stand together in court as honorable men and say so. That is the common front we should strive for."

"Come now, Speer," asserted Göring, "doesn't that seem a little arrogant to say that you are responsible? I mean, you were not the Führer, now were you? You were not even loyal to him."

Keitel, Dönitz, Hess and Ribbentrop all heartily agreed with Göring. *Who was Speer to think he could single-handedly express responsibility for all these crimes?* Göring seemed to have the better strategy to beat the rap by delegitimizing the court.

Göring smiled to everyone once again and declared, "This is a bully court. The victor will always be the judge and the vanquished will always be the accused. Our great sin was losing the war."

Speer decided to remain silent and think more about his position.

It was November 20th, the opening day of the trial. At 10 a.m., the black-robed judges entered into the courtroom. Four allied countries — the United States of America, Great Britain, France, and the Soviet Union — each provided one judge, an alternate, and a prosecutor. Then, out of a side door came the prisoners from their cells. One by one they entered the courtroom where the tension was so palpable it could be cut with a knife. Dressed in business suits, Göring, Hess, Ribbentrop, Keitel, Dönitz, Raeder, Shirach, Sauckel and the other 13 defendants in order took their assigned seats.

All eyes were fixed on Hermann Göring. As the second-in-command to Hitler, as well as the most flamboyant and rumored about, he was one man the public definitely held responsible for Nazi crimes. He invoked much curiosity with his military history, lifestyle and relationship with the Führer. Göring did not speak or look at those in attendance but showed his contempt for the process with his facial expressions, hand gestures and the strategic times he whispered to those around him.

On the first day, all of the charges were read against those accused. Then the court was adjourned until 10 a.m. the following day. Speer was thankful the trial had finally begun. Now they would see what would transpire from it, who would live and who would hang.

On the second day, American judge Robert H. Jackson, read opening remarks:

> *The privilege of opening the first trial in history for crimes against the peace of the world imposes a grave responsibility. The wrongs which we seek to condemn and punish have been so calculated, so malignant, and so devastating, that civilization cannot tolerate their being ignored, because it cannot survive their being repeated. That four great nations, flushed with victory and stung with injury stay*

the hand of vengeance and voluntarily submit their captive enemies to the judgment of the law is one of the most significant tributes that Power has ever paid to Reason.

In the prisoners' dock sit twenty-odd broken men. Reproached by the humiliation of those they have led almost as bitterly as by the desolation of those they have attacked, their personal capacity for evil is forever past. It is hard now to perceive in these men as captives the power by which as Nazi leaders they once dominated much of the world and terrified most of it. Merely as individuals their fate is of little consequence to the world.

What makes this inquest significant is that these prisoners represent sinister influences that will lurk in the world long after their bodies have returned to dust. We will show them to be living symbols of racial hatreds, of terrorism and violence, and of the arrogance and cruelty of power. They are symbols of fierce nationalisms and of militarism, of intrigue and war-making which have embroiled Europe generation after generation, crushing its manhood, destroying its homes, and impoverishing its life. They have so identified themselves with the philosophies they conceived and with the forces they directed that any tenderness to them is a victory and an encouragement to all the evils which are attached to their names. Civilization can afford no compromise with the social forces which would gain renewed strength if we deal ambiguously or indecisively with the men in whom those forces now precariously survive.

What these men stand for we will patiently and temperately disclose. We will give you undeniable proofs of incredible events. The catalog of crimes will omit nothing that could be conceived by a pathological pride, cruelty, and lust for power.

We must never forget that the record on which we judge these defendants today is the record on which history will judge us tomorrow. To pass these defendants a poisoned chalice is to put it to our own lips as well. We must summon such detachment and intellectual integrity to our task that this Trial will commend itself to posterity as fulfilling humanity's aspirations to do justice.

At the very outset, let us dispose of the contention that to put these men to trial is to do them an injustice entitling them to some special consideration. These defendants may be hard pressed but they are not ill-used. Let us see what alternative they would have to being tried.

<hr />

On November 29th, the film "Nazi Concentration Camps" was screened by all in attendance at the trial. Albert Speer sat in disbelief. It was horrible — monstrous! Though he could not believe what he was seeing, he had absolutely no doubt that it was the true state of affairs and that the video had not been doctored. *But how could Germany do this?*

In the past, Speer had often felt uneasy when the subject of the concentration camps was discussed at headquarters meetings. He had worked long and hard — alongside Sauckel, who was also on trial — to make sure that the Industrialists always had enough workers. *But this, this massive killing for no apparent reason? What devilry is this?*

Speer slept uneasily in his cell that evening. He remembered that Göring and some of the others sometimes joked about disappearing Jews. He even heard some coarse remarks there at Nuremburg. But Speer himself was deeply disturbed with what he saw on the film that day.

In the final scene of the movie, footage from Belsen Concentration Camp showed over 12,000 corpses lying unburied around the camp rotting in the open air when the Allies liberated it. The captured Nazi SS guards were forced to bury the dead but could not work fast enough; 500 additional people at Belsen were dying every day from typhus, even after liberation. The British resorted to using bulldozers to move the corpses into massive graves to prevent disease and contamination. Bodies were simply scraped along the earth like rag dolls to the edge of the pit, eventually falling down into their final resting place and mercifully covered over with dirt.

Footage of subsequent camps revealed similar horror stories; padlocked train cars jammed with dead bodies, buildings used to store mounds of corpses, wooden structures locked and set aflame with living prisoners inside of them. It seemed the Nazis experimented with every possible way to massacre groups of people. Many bodies revealed torture before their death. Most were undernourished and starved. Survivors walked around the camps like living skeletons.

Speer was shaken, appalled. These masses of people he wanted to use as laborers were all under the care of the German nation and they were wholly destroyed. What was especially grievous were images of hundreds, if not thousands, of children waiting in lines to be gassed. More and more photographs of similar Nazi deathcapades from all over Germany and Poland were shown at the trial. Speer was repulsed. He decided he must stand up against Göring's effort to convince others that they were all just following orders, even if it caused his alienation.

On January 3, 1946, Otto Ohlendorf, a Nazi SS leader, testified matter of fact to the execution of 90,000 Jews by the Nazi Party in Ukraine. He told the court the Jews were brought by truck out to a field where they lined up, shot in the back, then quickly buried. Eventually the women and children were excluded from the outdoor shootings; instead they were gassed in special trucks designed to kill those in the cargo hold.

During Ohlendorf's testimony, Speer signaled to his attorney that it was time to present to the court his attempted assassination of Hitler. Flächsner asked Ohlendorf if he was aware that Speer had planned to kill Hitler in February. With this bombshell the dock of defendants went wild. At the break, Göring charged over to Speer.

"How dare you make such a treasonable admission in open court!" Göring exclaimed. "You are disrupting our united front!"

"You and your united front are a load of manure," Speer replied angrily. "You need to take a look at what has happened!"

Göring, confounded by Speer's contempt, hardly knew what to say. He turned his back to him and began to speak with someone else about a totally unrelated matter.

On January 28th, Marie-Claude Vailant-Couturier, a captured French Resistance worker who was a prisoner in Auschwitz for 18 months, testified to the gas chambers and burning pits that killed hundreds of thousands of Jews and Gypsies during her stay there. She spoke of the orchestra composed of pretty girls with white blouses and blue skirts who played gay tunes like the *Merry Widow* and *The Tales of Hoffman* on a raised platform surrounded by flowers. Whenever the trains arrived the music echoed throughout the camp, occurring several times a day. This made the new arrivals less suspicious when the able-bodied men strong enough to work were separated from the elderly, women and children who the Nazis herded directly to the gas chambers.

That evening, following Ms. Vailant-Couturier's testimony, Speer racked his mind to remember what might have been said in cabinet meetings he attended about the concentration camps in Poland. It seemed that most of the camps had been discussed, but those operating in Poland — Chelmno, Belzec, Sobibor, Treblinka, Aushwitz and Majdaneck — were seldom brought up. Only on one or two occasions could Speer remember the Polish camps discussed and each time he was sure that Himmler was present.

Speer could understand now why it was so difficult to keep laborers in his factories. Hitler preferred to exterminate the Jews, even the males, rather than allow them the chance to survive the war. Until they disappeared altogether in 1943, Jewish workers were systematically pilfered out of Speer's work camps by the SS in order to be gassed.

The more Speer thought about the images he saw from Poland, the more he asked himself the hard, honest question about his knowledge of the exterminations. He then painfully recognized that deep down he knew this was happening — everyone did. It was the ultimate expression of Hitler's anger toward the Semites. But for some reason it did not cause him alarm when it was happening. *Did I not care? Was I that self-absorbed?* Most people tried to ignore the stories and believe that it was not as bad as the rumors. *Was I as selfish as most people?* Speer wondered, yet he knew the agonizing answer. He, perhaps, was the most selfish.

In March, Hermann Göring took the stand and evaded all responsibility. In essence, he declared that the trial was a farce. One item that stung Speer in Göring's testimony was when he told the court, "We never should have trusted Speer."

In April, Rudolf Höss, took the stand as a witness for the prosecution. Höss, the former SS kommandant of Auschwitz, described in detail to the court how the mass execution of the Jews took place in the gassing chambers and how the bodies were burned in the crematoria ovens and burning pits, all worked by the Sonderkommandos.

"After their arrival, the victims were stripped of everything they had?" asked Dr. Kauffman, the lawyer for the defense. "Did they have to undress completely and surrender all their valuables?"

"Yes," replied Höss.

"And then they immediately went to their death?" asked Kauffman.

"Yes," replied Höss.

"I ask you, according to your knowledge, did these people know what was in store for them?"

"The majority of them did not, for steps were taken to keep them in doubt about it. For instance, all doors and all walls bore inscriptions to the effect that they were going to take a shower."

"And then the death by gassing set in within a period of 3 to 15 minutes, is that correct?" the lawyer asked.

"Yes," replied Höss.

"And you also told me that even before death set in, the victims fell into a state of unconsciousness?"

"Yes. From what I was able to find out myself, the time necessary for reaching unconsciousness or death varied according to the temperature and the number of people present in the chambers. Loss of consciousness took place within a few seconds or a few minutes."

"Did you yourself ever feel pity for the victims, thinking of your own family or children?"

The courtroom grew very quiet after this question was asked. *Was Höss a monster? Or was he just like everyone else in the room?*

"Yes," replied Höss.

"How was it possible for you to carry out these actions in spite of this?" the lawyer asked.

Again, utter quiet in the courtroom, Speer noticed.

"In view of all these doubts which I had, the only one and decisive argument was the strict order and the reason given for it by the Reichsführer Himmler."

"Did Himmler ever inspect the camp and convince himself, too, of the process of annihilation?"

"Yes. Himmler visited the camp in 1942, and he watched in detail one group of Jews processing from beginning to end."

<hr />

As the weeks and months progressed, Speer had seen and heard enough about the atrocities of the Third Reich. He knew that any position of innocence by his co-defendants was absolutely indefensible. Speer would take responsibility for his part in the crimes — in a general sense — by sharing in the total responsibility for all that happened. He might not have been fully aware of the scope of extermination but decided that at least one leader on trial at Nuremburg should own up to the images and testimonies relentlessly thrust before them each day. Speer decided that leaders hold a unique burden that the citizenry does not own. *There is a collective responsibility the leadership shares with the actions of the organization they belong to, whether they were actually the ones committing the crimes or not.*

What bothered Speer now was thinking he was possibly being too prideful. *Had any individual in legal history ever declared himself guilty in principle, even though he did not share in the criminal acts? Do I have the right to bear this burden, making the other defendants vulnerable to be accused of similar guilt? And what of my family? Am I selling them out as well? What would Margarete say?* These were the questions keeping Speer awake at night. And oh, how he tossed and turned on his tiny cot.

◆•◆

On June 20th, 1946, seven months after the start of the trial, Albert Speer was finally called to the stand. The days leading up to his turn at testifying brought him increased agitation. Speer discreetly swallowed a tranquilizer pill given to him by a German doctor right before his testimony.

All eyes in the courtroom were locked onto the 41-year-old man in the pressed suit silently walking toward the witness table. Everyone wanted a closer look at the former architect who had declared there in Nuremberg that if Hitler had had any close friends, he would have been his closest friend.

Speer's hand felt leaden as he reached for the glass of water to prepare for his testimony. Even being slightly sedated, Speer was wildly anxious and his heart pounded inside his shirt.

Judge Jackson began to question the former Armaments Minister, "Will you tell me whether you were a member of the SS?"

"No, I was not a member of the SS," answered Speer.

"You filled out an application at one time and you never went through with it?" asked Jackson.

"That was in 1943 when Himmler wanted me to get a high rank in the SS," answered Speer.

"And why did you not want to be a member of the SS?"

"I became well known for turning down all these honorary ranks," said Speer. "I did not want them because I felt that one should wear a rank only when he had responsibility."

"And you did not want any responsibilities in the SS?" asked Jackson.

"I had too little contact with the SS and did not want any responsibility in that connection."

Jackson changed the subject, "Now there has been some testimony about your relation to concentration camps and, as I understand it, you have said to us that you did use and encourage the use of forced labor from the concentration camps."

"Yes, we did use it in the German armament industry," answered Speer.

"And I think you also recommended that persons in labor camps who were slackers be sent to concentration camps, did you not?"

"Workers who did not get to their work on time or who pretended to be ill, severe measures were taken against such workers during the war and I approved of these measures," answered Speer.

Judge Jackson pulled out a sheet of paper in front him and continued his interrogation, "Did you not say once in October 1942 that there is nothing to be said against the SS and police taking drastic steps and putting those known to be slackers into concentration camp factories? There is no alternative. Let it happen several times, and the news will soon get around. Are these not your statements?"

"Correct."

"In other words," continued Jackson, "the workmen stood in considerable terror of concentration camps, and you wanted to take advantage of that to keep them at their work, did you not?"

"It is certain that concentration camps had a bad reputation with us," said Speer.

"It was known throughout Germany, was it not, that concentration camps were pretty tough places to be put?"

"Yes, but not to the extent which has been revealed in this trial," answered Speer.

"You also knew the policy of the Nazi Party and the policy of the government towards the Jews, did you not?" asked Judge Jackson.

Speer looked directly at the judge and said, "I knew that the National Socialist Party was anti-Semitic and I knew that the Jews were being evacuated from Germany."

"In fact, you participated in the evacuation, did you not?"

"That is correct. We managed to keep Jews on at our factories until 1943 but then our resistance gave way and we were forced to get the Jews out."

"As I understand it, you were struggling to get manpower enough to produce the armaments to win a war for Germany," the judge stated. "And this anti-Semitic campaign was so strong that it took trained technicians away from you and disabled you from performing your functions. Now isn't that the fact?"

Speer looked at the two Russian judges who were frowning. He could not help but think that Judge Jackson liked him and he was bringing the questions about in such a way that Speer would somehow be separated from Hitler and his anti-Jewish policies. Despite being on trial and incarcerated, Speer liked Judge Jackson since he heard his opening remarks several months before. He seemed a fair and honorable man.

"That is a certainty," answered Speer. "If the Jews who were evacuated had been allowed to work for me, it would have been a considerable advantage to me."

Judge Jackson again changed the line of questioning, "Now I want to ask you about the recruiting of forced labor. As I understand it, you knew about the deportation of 100,000 Jews from Hungary for subterranean airplane factories and you made no objection to it. That is true, is it not?

"That is true, yes," answered Speer.

"And you told us also, quite candidly, on that day that it was no secret to you that a good deal of the manpower brought in by Sauckel was brought in by illegal methods. That is also true, is it not?"

"I confirmed that I knew that they came against their wishes."

"As a matter of fact, you did not give any particular attention to the legal side of this thing, did you? You were after manpower, isn't that the fact?"

Again, Speer reflected, another softball from the judge, "That is absolutely correct."

"And whether it was legal or illegal was not your worry?"

"I considered that in view of the whole war situation and of our views in general on this question that it was justified. The workers were brought into Germany largely against their will and I had no objection to their being brought to Germany against their will. On the contrary, during the first period, until the autumn of 1942, I certainly also took some pains to see that as many workers as possible should be brought to Germany in this manner. It is well known that Russia did not sign the Geneva Convention statement."

After a break, the judge persisted to ask Speer about the factories and the harsh treatment at them, then about the breakout of diseases that killed many of the workers. Speer took responsibility in a general sense but denied that the minister in charge of such a large ministry would have specific knowledge about everything that happened in each camp.

Judge Jackson continued, "Your statement some time ago that you had a certain responsibility as a Minister of the Government for the conditions, I should like to have you explain what responsibility you referred to when you say you assume a responsibility as a member of the Government."

"Do you mean the declaration I made yesterday that I..."

"Your common responsibility, what do you mean by your common responsibility along with others?"

"Oh, yes," said Speer. "In my opinion, a state functionary has two types of responsibility. One is the responsibility for his own sector and for that, of course, he is fully responsible. But above that I think in decisive matters there is, and must be, among the leaders a common responsibility. For who is to bear responsibility for developments, if not the close associates of the head of State? This common responsibility, however, can only be applied to fundamental matters, it cannot be applied to details connected with other ministries or other responsible departments, for otherwise the entire discipline in the life of the State would be quite confused, and no one would ever know who is individually responsible in a particular sphere. This individual responsibility in one's own sphere must, at all events, be kept clear and distinct."

Judge Jackson summarized, "Well, your point is, I take it, that you as a member of the Government and a leader in this period of time acknowledge a responsibility for its large policies, but not for all the details that occurred in their execution. Is that a fair statement of your position?"

"Yes, indeed," answered Speer.

"I think that concludes the cross-examination."

Back in his cell, Speer threw himself on his cot. The persistent knot in his stomach began to loosen a little. He buried his head in his pillow, mentally extinguished, and hoped, somehow, for a good result from all of this; but he had an overwhelming sense that his life was at an end.

On July 27, 1946, Sir Hartley Shawcross made the summation speech for the British prosecution delegation. He read to the court an affidavit written by Hermann Gräbe, on an extermination event he personally witnessed near Dubno, Ukraine in October 1942.

Gräbe relayed that he watched men, women, and children of all ages ordered off the trucks by an SS man holding a riding whip.

"Undress, and put your clothes in the piles over there," the SS man shouted. He pointed to several massive mounds of clothing articles that looked peculiarly out of place in the open field.

The large group of Jews slowly undressed themselves, glancing sidewise in shame to be exposed in this manner. They carried their clothing in a heap between their arms. Then, upon reaching a shoe depository — which already held at least 800 pairs and was over eight feet high — they threw their shoes onto the massive pile of leather and strings. They flung their underwear on the large undergarment pile, and their clothes on the third pile.

While they walked away from this last pile, a loud volley of rifles cracked behind a large mound of dirt. The SS man shouted for the first twenty people to walk around the mound to the side of a large pit. The adults still waiting began to quietly weep, and speak tenderly to each other. The children looked up and into their eyes, wondering why everyone was crying.

Crack! A loud volley of rifle fire echoed throughout the large field. A family of eight gathered around each other and lovingly embraced. A Jewish father held the hand of a boy about ten-years-old who was fighting his tears. The father pointed to the sky, stroked his child's head, and seemed to explain something to him. The boy tried to smile at his father. A thin, young woman with black hair — apparently alone — stood near to them, overhearing what the father explained to his son.

"Okay, the next twenty will walk around the mound," the SS man with the whip shouted. He then counted off twenty people, including the large family, the boy and his father, and the young woman. He marched the naked victims around a large dirt mound.

As the bewildered Jews walked toward the gunfire area, the slim, black-haired girl looked at Gräbe and pointed to herself. "Twenty-three," she said.

No response.

The group marched to the edge of a tremendous grave, filled with a countless number of bodies. People were tightly wedged on top of each other, most with blood coming out of their heads. Some were still moving and moaning, turning their heads upward to show they were still alive. Several SS men stood alongside the edge of the pit with rifles. One, a particularly forbidding sort, sat on the edge of the pit with a tommy gun on his knees, his feet dangling into the grave. He held a cigarette in his mouth and a grim look on his face.

The twenty Jews, completely undressed, were ordered to march down the clay steps carved into the steep wall of the pit. Then they clambered over the arms, legs, torsos and bloody heads of Jews who had gone before them, trying to avoid disturbing those who were still moving.

"Now lay down, all the way down, and lay still," the SS man with the sleek machine gun shouted.

The father and son laid down, and the son hugged his father, seeking comfort from the slithering pit of death. The family of eight spread out as best as they could while trying to hold hands on the swarming mound. The girl laid down by herself, trembling, without anyone to comfort her. She found a large woman to lay upon who was still breathing. The young girl spoke to her and tried to comfort her.

Crack! Several guns fired down into the pit. Most who had just entered the pit now bled from their necks and heads, their bodies momentarily twitching. Then, a minute later, the following group of twenty marched into place and were ordered to walk down into the pit and lay on top of them.

The father and son, still clinging to each other, no longer moved. The girl, with eyes bulging and black hair matted with blood, was dead.

On and on the shootings continued until the large earthen cavity was completely full. The SS man with the whip mentioned to Gräbe that the lower layers of half-killed Jews were eventually suffocated by the weight of bodies and the drenching blood. Soon, bulldozers would cover the pit with dirt, and another massive ditch would be prepared for more shootings. Day after day it continued, until tens of thousands were killed, and hundreds of lorry-loads of clothing were brought to nearby towns to distribute among the poor.

Sir Hartley Shawcross finished his remarks by sardonically asking, "What special dispensation of Providence kept these 21 men from seeing these things? It is like Goethe who said that one day Fate would strike the German people because they submit to any mad scoundrel who appeals to their lowest instincts. What a voice of prophecy! For these are the mad scoundrels who did these very things. You must remember when the time comes to give your verdict the story of this mass execution, but not in vengeance — in a determination that these things shall not occur again. The father — you remember — pointed to the sky, and seemed to say something to his boy."

<hr />

On October 1, 1946, the individual verdicts were pronounced to each of the 21 defendants. First Göring, then Hess, then Ribbentrop, all the way down the seating chart until it came to the Armament's Minister.

An American soldier in a white helmet appeared at Speer's prison door to escort him. Together they walked down a basement corridor and entered a small elevator. As the elevator ascended the soldier said nothing: he merely stared at the closed door. When the door opened, the soldier led Speer down another corridor, opened a door and allowed Speer to walk through where he found himself standing on a small platform.

A guard handed Speer a pair of headphones which he hastily put on. When he heard a lone voice in his earphones, Speer looked up and into the faces of eight men who sat in judgment over him. In an abstract and mechanical tone, as if lecturing about outer space, the voice declared, *"Albert Speer, to twenty years' imprisonment."*

Speer glanced at his lawyer, Dr. Flächsner, who stared back in wide-eyed bewilderment. Both men were shocked. Though Speer hoped for freedom, he knew he could also get execution. The cold announcement and reality of twenty years in prison at the moment seemed worse than dying. He would be 61 when he left prison, all his children grown and gone from the home. *Would Margarete wait for him?*

Speer gave a slight bow to the judges before him and then the American soldier led him back down the corridor and returned him to his cell. A little later, an American lieutenant arrived and ordered Speer to grab his bedding, table and other possessions and to follow him.

Speer was moved to another part of the prison. While lugging his belongings up a flight of stairs he encountered Rudolf Hess, Hitler's former deputy, also moving his belongings.

"What sentence did you receive, Herr Hess?" Speer asked the man who, during the trial, had feigned insanity and memory loss.

"I don't know, I wasn't listening," replied Hess. "Probably the death penalty."

After Speer arrived at his new room, he was visited by the court psychologist who told him the verdicts for the other men on trial. All but ten of the men were condemned to death by hanging. Three of them — Schacht, Von Papen, and Fritzsche — were given their freedom. Admiral Dönitz was given ten years imprisonment, the former foreign minister Neurath fifteen years, Speer and Shirach each twenty years; Hess, Funk and Admiral Raeder were given life imprisonment. Göring, Ribbentrop, Keitel and the others would be hanged there at Nuremberg on a still-to-be-determined date.

The psychologist wanted to know Speer's reaction to his verdict. After a thoughtful moment Speer replied, "Twenty years. Well, that's fair enough. They couldn't have given me a lighter sentence, considering the facts, so I can't complain."

Speer waived his right to an appeal. Deep in his heart he tried to accept his sentence. *Any penalty would weigh little compared to the misery the regime brought on the world,* he reasoned. *I am guilty and cannot offer excuses. The scale of the crimes are so overwhelming; any human excuse pales in comparison.*

Speer silently sat on the cot alone in his cell. While millions of concentration camp victims were liberated and starting new lives, Speer was starting a new life as well — as an inmate doing hard time.

CHAPTER 39

Prisoner 66730

As life settled down a bit for Corrie back in Haarlem, she enjoyed the simple things she once did but were denied to her while imprisoned. Corrie walked along the Barteljorisstraat at night without fear of guards catching her and giving her a beating. The war was over and there were no more Germans in uniforms prowling the streets.

Corrie was, however, still speaking to others of the love of Christ. She traveled to meetings wherever anyone would have her speak. At the end of one of her meetings a surprise occurred.

As Corrie concluded her story about Ravensbrück, she relayed Betsie's vision of the house with inlaid wood, large gardens and tall windows.

"This house," Corrie explained, "is to be used to help victims of the war, of those who have suffered. They are to work in the gardens, and relax on the grounds. Perhaps sharing stories with other survivors will allow them to be healed, as Christ does a work in their heart."

Corrie also spoke of the second vision Betsie had of the concentration camp in Germany. "My sister Betsie also wanted to do something for those who were unfortunate enough to work for the Nazis. I could not understand Betsie's logic at first, nor the compassion God placed in her heart for our tormentors. But she was very clear when she said to me, 'Corrie, it is a concentration camp where we are in charge. The barracks are gray, Corrie, but we'll paint them bright green, like springtime!'"

The meeting ended and an aristocratic woman approached Corrie to ask her a question. Corrie remembered her name, and that she was the owner of a large home in Bloemendaal.

"My dear, Cornelia," the lady began, "do you by chance remember me?"

"Yes, ma'am," answered Corrie. "You are Mrs. Bierens de Haan." Corrie remembered someone saying that the Bierens de Haans owned one of the most beautiful houses in Holland.

Mrs. De Haan smiled at Corrie's good memory. "Do you still live in the watch shop house on the Barteljorisstraat?"

"Why, yes ma'am."

"My mother used to tell me about your lively home. She went there frequently to visit an aunt of yours involved in charitable work."

Corrie smiled, wondering where the conversation was going. "Yes, ma'am, I remember. She came to see my Tante Jans when I was a little girl. Sometimes I would let your mother in the door."

Mrs. De Haan returned the smile. "I live in a very large home in Bloemendaal with flower gardens all about it, but I am a widow now, and my five sons are working in the Resistance. Four of my sons are alive and well, but one of my sons I have not heard from. While you were speaking just now a voice came to me and said that my son Jan would return alive and well, and then in gratitude I would open up my home for the vision of Betsie ten Boom."

This offer took Corrie's breath away. She did not know what to say at first. If she recalled correctly, Mrs. De Haan's home would fit the description of Betsie's large house. *How much like God it would be to provide His answer so soon, and so miraculously.*

"By any chance, does your home have inlaid wood floors, statues set in the walls and a sweeping staircase?" asked Corrie, cautiously in awe of Betsie's vision.

"You've been there, then?" asked Mrs. De Haan curiously.

"No, but I…"

"Heard about it from someone who has seen it?" Mrs. De Haan finished for Corrie.

"Yes," Corrie answered. "From someone who has seen it."

———◆———

Two weeks later a letter was delivered to the Beje with only one line of text: *Jan is home.*

As Corrie toured the 56-room mansion of the Bierens de Haan estate, she could not keep her eyes off the large windows, the statues and the floor.

"Have you observed how beautiful the woodwork is?" asked Mrs. De Haan as she escorted Corrie through the mansion.

"Oh, yes, ma'am, I noticed," Corrie replied with a twinkle in her eye.

Corrie and Mrs. De Haan walked outside through the gardens where Mrs. DeHaan explained how the former prisoners could work them and keep them up. Corrie could hear in her mind, *And with gardens, Corrie, beautiful gardens all around where they can plant flowers. It will be so good for them, won't it, to be able to care for flowers?*

Corrie made preparations right away and by summer those tortured by the Nazis began to come to the Bierens de Haan home soon after Holland was liberated. At first it was just a few who trickled in, but it did not take long for all the rooms to fill up. Corrie worked as hard as she could to help the people who needed healing.

Over the months to come, many hundreds stayed at the Bloemendaal house under Corrie's care. Most of them were prisoners in Germany during the last two years of the war like Corrie. All of the visitors needed a similar healing to take place in their lives, that of forgiveness. Each person had been wounded and hurt by someone they needed to forgive. For some it was the neighbor who betrayed them. For some it was the concentration camp guards. And for some it was a fellow prisoner who had been especially cruel.

Everyone had their own aches and scars from the war. At Corrie's care house there was singing, much eating, and retelling of stories of persecution on the porches and walkways. But Corrie noticed that it was in the gardens, which Betsie had described in detail, where visible change often occurred. When flowers bloomed, or vegetables ripened, people began to look toward the future and away from the past. *It was as if Betsie had known all along.*

———◆———

The cost to keep up Bloemendaal took a tremendous amount of support, so Corrie decided to travel and speak. She crisscrossed Holland, Europe and parts of the United States, always sharing what God was doing in the lives of prisoners at Bloemendaal.

It was Germany, though, that weighed on Corrie's heart. There was so much work to do there because it was the center of death and destruction. It was Germany where millions of people wandered around the country looking for food. It was

Germany where nine million citizens were dislodged because of the war. They stayed in abandoned factories, trucks, trains, or bombed out buildings; wherever people could find shelter they existed in utter poverty. Thus, it was Germany where people needed to hear of the hope of heaven, so Corrie went and preached in their churches.

One day she was at a church in Munich, speaking to a group that included former Nazis and survivors of their brutality. Corrie spoke about forgiveness, redemption and the promise of heaven. When Corrie finished speaking she positioned herself in the back of the church to shake hands with those who had come to hear her speak.

That was when she saw *him*. A former SS officer from Ravensbrück. He was a balding man in a gray overcoat, but Corrie's mind flashed pictures of a cruel guard in a blue uniform with a leather crop swinging from his belt. And he was coming toward her now.

Corrie darted her eyes away. *No it couldn't be him, could it Lord?* She glanced back at the smiling man who was next in line to shake her hand and it all came back to her in a rush of emotion. He was there, standing guard at the shower room door when Corrie and Betsie arrived at Ravensbrück. She remembered those men mocking the women as they took off their clothing and threw it on a large mound of dirty dresses. He was there, she remembered, right next to them, participating in their degradation, forcing the women to endure unspeakable humiliation.

As the man approached her, Corrie stood, frozen, recalling the horror in Betsie's face as she was forced to strip and suffer being searched by the man standing before her.

"How grateful I am for your message, Fräulein," the former concentration camp guard said to her.

He held out his hand to Corrie.

"To think that, as you say, Jesus has washed my sins away," the man said, still beaming with uplifted hand.

No movement from Corrie.

How could she?

Her mind was brewing with anger and resentment. She also thought of Bloemendaal and how she encouraged the patients to forgive those who had harmed them. This was the first time Corrie had encountered an SS guard she recognized. It was the first real test to her message of healing.

The man waited and Corrie kept silent. Even in her rage she recognized the sin in her heart at that moment. *Jesus Christ has died for this man. Am I going to ask for more?* Corrie prayed, *Forgive me Lord, and help me to forgive this man.*

Corrie tried to smile but her lips would not move. She tried to raise her hand but it remained frozen at her side. She felt nothing, no warmth, no charity; the sight of her frail sister came to mind. At that moment, the man embodied every evil that Ravensbrück meant to her, including the death of Betsie. So Corrie stood, wooden, unable to respond to the offer of friendship from the guard.

The man, not knowing that Corrie recognized him, took the initiative. "I know that God has forgiven me, Fräulein, but I would like to hear it from your lips as well, as one who has suffered under us Nazis at Ravensbrück."

Oh, he has no idea what he is asking, Corrie thought. No concept of the emotional hollowness she experienced because of that camp. Corrie was at a crossroads; her message to others either meant something or it did not. She desperately wanted to forgive the man but could not form the words. She prayed again, *Jesus, I cannot forgive him. Give him your forgiveness.*

With that prayer, Corrie felt her hand move toward his until they clasped. From the feeling of first touch, a current seemed to extend from Corrie's hand, up through her arm, and into the rest of her body. A love for the stranger standing before her filled her heart and almost overwhelmed her.

"I forgive you brother," prisoner 66730 affirmed at last with tears. "I forgive you with all my heart!"

Former prisoner and SS guard embraced.

The pain and anguish seemed to melt away, along with the final remnants of pride and pity.

Her war was over.

Corrie ten Boom was free.

CHAPTER 40

Spandau

"Go on, get up," shouted the American guard walking down Albert Speer's corridor.

"Get up, get up! Breakfast is coming. Get dressed!"

Speer opened his eyes. He was dreaming of Margarete. It was cold in his cell and he did not want to get out from his blanket just yet.

"Get dressed!"

Speer noted the same words were repeated up and down the hallways in the entire building.

It was 7 a.m.

The exact thing happened every morning at that time.

"Cups, cups!" yelled the coffee man.

Speer could procrastinate no more.

He threw back the blanket, stood, slipped on his pants and buttoned his white shirt. Soon, a metal clink on his door. He put his coffee cup through the chamber door of his prison cell and hot liquid was poured into it. The coffee was black, with nothing added to it, but it was appreciated.

A few minutes later, the main course arrived. Speer could hear his fellow prisoner delivering breakfast to the other prisoners.

"Bread. Bread. Bread." The declaration of breakfast came closer and closer to Speer's cell until there was a knock on the door.

"Bread."

Four pieces of white bread were handed to Speer.

Silence.

At 9 a.m. more commotion.

The prisoners were brought out to march in the yard. Then they were given steel wool and ordered to scrub the iron pots and pans in the galley. At 11:30 a.m. they were returned to their cells.

At noon lunch was served.

Speer received two pieces of corned beef, two pieces of bread and hot tea without sugar. In a few minutes the corridor was woefully quiet. Speer, brooding in his cell for hours, thought of the past.

5:00 p.m., a visit from the American Army chaplain.

"How are you getting along?" chaplain Henry Gerecke asked courteously in broken German.

Speer noticed they were about the same age. He had gotten to know him in chapel but had never asked how old he was.

"I'm okay, considering," Speer replied in English. "I am probably eating better than my family."

"That could be," said the chaplain. "From what I hear, things are pretty bad out there. The Allies and the Red Cross are trying to help but it is a big task."

"Out of curiosity, how old are you?" asked Speer.

"I'm 53," answered Gerecke. "How about you?"

"I'm 41. I thought we looked close in age but I was wrong."

"I actually have two grown sons in the military."

The men shared a moment of camaraderie. Speer knew Gerecke liked speaking to him more than the others. It was as if they had been friends for a long time.

The chaplain said, "I think you will be out of here and in Berlin before the New Year."

Speer did not respond.

"Do not fear going to Spandau."

Still, no response from the forlorn Speer. The prisoners were fearful of a prison where the Russians would have influence over them.

"Is there anything I can do for you?" the chaplain asked.

"Please pray for my family," Speer responded.

"I will."

"Thank you. Margarete and my six children are staying in the cow barn attached to our former gardener's house. It is a challenge…"

"I understand. I will pray for them, and for you."

With a few more words of comfort the chaplain departed.

6:00 p.m., supper is served.

More corned beef, bread and a few crackers.

After supper, Speer was ordered out into the corridor for escort to the shower.

The corridor was sixty meters long with sixteen cells on each side. The doors to each cell were heavy wooden structures surrounded by metal. A cement floor led prisoners to the end of the hall where they entered the bathing room.

Speer undressed and turned on the shower. Only a trickle. He did the best he could with the small amount of water dripping from the spigot. He dried himself off with a laundered towel laid out for him, then returned to his cell.

Speer sat on his cot for the last twenty minutes of light and wrote a letter to his wife.

A guard rapped on the door.

It was 7 p.m.

Speer handed him his glasses and pencil.

The lights were turned off.

Speer slipped off his pants and laid down on his cot. Because of the cold he decided to take two socks and put them on his hands. He closed his eyes and tried to sleep. He had been in Nuremburg for over a year now, and soon he would be transported to Spandau Prison in Berlin.

<hr>

It was October 15, 1946, and Speer could not sleep. There was construction work going on somewhere in the prison. Hammers, nails, banging. *Would it ever stop?* Speer wondered.

He thought of the men condemned to die. This would be their last night in their cells. Speer had worked closely with these men for the past several years. Soon, they would no longer be alive. He knew the prison doctor had provided a sedative to each man going to the gallows. Speer wondered if all the noise and commotion was actually the erection of the gallows where his acquaintances would hang.

Speer thought of Hermann Göring, defiant until the end. Göring refused to admit any guilt. Many of Göring's associates turned against him on the witness stand. One man even told the court about a tea his wife attended at the Göring mansion. Hermann appeared in a Roman toga and sandals, with large jewels ornamenting his entire body. He went on to say that Göring's face was painted and he had red rouge on his lips.

"The way I behave in my own house is my affair!" Göring later exclaimed. "Besides, I didn't have on lipstick."

Judge Jackson, in his closing arguments against Göring, brought up the fact that the number two man of the state declared he knew nothing of the excesses of the Gestapo which he himself created. And further, that Göring denied knowing about the extermination of the Jews though he had signed over twenty decrees which brought about the persecution of their race.

Judge Jackson concluded his thoughts on Göring: "No other half century ever witnessed slaughter on such a scale, such cruelties and inhumanities, such wholesale deportations of peoples into slavery, such annihilations of minorities. There is a strange mixture of wind and wisdom which makes up the testimony of Hermann Göring. Within the crimes of Nazi oppression and terrorism within Germany, the large and varied role of Göring was half militarist and half gangster. He stuck a pudgy finger in every pie. He was adept at massacring opponents and at framing scandals to get rid of stubborn generals. He was among the foremost in harrying the Jews out of the land.

"The defendants now ask this Tribunal to deny that they are guilty of planning, executing and conspiring to commit this long list of crimes and wrongs. They stand before the record of this trial as bloodstained Gloucester stood before the body of his slain king and begged the widow queen, *'Say I slew him not' and the queen said, 'Why then he is not dead; but dead he is, and, devilish slave, by thee.'* If you were to say of these men that they were not guilty, it would be as true to say that there has been no war, there are no slain, there has been no crime."

In Göring's final defense he declared, "I did not want war, and I did not bring it about. After the war started, I did everything to assure victory. I stand behind the things I have done. The only motive which guided me was my ardent love for my people, and my desire for their happiness and freedom. For this I call on the Almighty and the German people as witnesses."

In Speer's cell that evening, he heard commotion in the part of the prison where those condemned to death were held. A French guard walked by Speer's cell and Speer asked, "What is going on down there?"

The guard looked around to insure no one would hear him, then he quietly whispered through Speer's cell door, "It is Hermann Göring. He swallowed some poison. By the time the guards got to him it was too late. He is dead."

"Dead?" replied Speer. "But he was to be hanged tonight. How did he get the poison?"

"No one knows. No one is telling. I must keep moving."

"Thank you," said Speer, grateful the guard took the time to tell him what was happening. He was stumped how Göring might have accomplished this. The guards would all be interrogated. Speer remembered that after Göring received his death sentence, he protested the inglorious way the Allies executed high officials by hanging. Göring requested to be shot by a firing squad. He was turned down and now he is dead. This was a big change of plans for the Allies because the Reichsmarschall was supposed to be the first one hanged. *Checkmate!* In a final, desperate act, Göring usurped his opponents from enacting justice.

———————

"Ribbentrop!"

After the name was called out, Speer heard a cell door open and then footsteps reverberating down the hall. *They are going to the gallows!*

"Keitel!"

Speer noted that it took nearly a half hour for the deed to be done. He also knew he would not get any sleep that night. His fellow Germans were being executed for their crimes. It could have very easily been Speer as well.

"Kaltenbrunner!"

"Rosenberg!"

"Frank!"

"Frick!"

"Streicher!"

"Sauckel!"

At this particular name, Speer swallowed hard. Sauckel was his deputy, in charge of garnering slave laborers from the occupied territories. It was unusual for a second-in-command to get the death penalty when the supervisor received a lighter sentence. Speer had successfully convinced the court how he had tried to save Germany from destruction and turned against the man who gave him power. Sauckel tried to shift his blame to Speer and told the court that it was Speer who had greater legal and moral responsibility because Sauckel was just obeying Speer's orders. The court rejected this notion and held Sauckel responsible for the work that he did. The court held that it was one small facet of Speer's job, not his entire mission.

"Jodl!"

"Seyss-Inquart!"

Quiet filled the prison but Speer lay awake in the dark. He could not stop thinking about the limp, lifeless bodies of the men who were now being burned in a furnace, their ashes to be secretly scattered.

———————

Early the next morning, the seven inmates still in Nuremburg — Speer, Hess, Dönitz, Raeder, Funk, Neurath and Shirach — were ordered to clean out the cells of the ten hanged men. Then, Speer and the others were marched to the gymnasium where the executions took place. They were instructed to sweep and mop the floor. *This must be for effect*, thought Speer. The floor was already sparkling clean.

As Albert Speer mopped the place where the gallows recently stood, he could not help but think about what transpired there the night before. The condemned men were executed and their bodies incinerated in a furnace. They no longer existed. Speer's punishment would last for twenty years. He did not know if he could bear it.

On Good Friday, April 3, 1947, a U.S. Army chaplain walked into Speer's cell with tears in his eyes. He handed Speer a telegram stating that his father died in his sleep three days prior. Speer was speechless. He wondered about the funeral and wished he could have been there.

Located in the far western side of Berlin, Spandau Prison was built in 1876 as a military confinement facility with a capacity of six hundred inmates. A large, heavy stone structure, during the 1930s through World War II, it was used as a transit station for civilian prisoners en route to concentration camps. In 1946, the United States, Great Britain, France and the Soviet Union decided to utilize Spandau as a prison solely for the seven Nazi war criminals of the high government.

The occupying Allied powers were to share responsibility for the operation of Spandau. There were four directors — one each from France, America, Great Britain, and Russia — who would lead the prison on alternating months. All four nations contributed guards who would stay an entire year but each national director would only serve three months a year.

Albert Speer and the other six prisoners were transferred from Nuremburg to Spandau on Friday, July 18, 1947. For the first time in two years Speer returned to Berlin, by way of an American DC-3 passenger plane. As the plane circled above the large city, Speer eyed the Olympic Stadium he had designed for Hitler, the bombed out Chancellery and other buildings he helped to construct. Sadly, he noticed, the Teirgarten was destroyed; all its trees demolished by bombs or chopped down.

The seven men left the plane and traveled by a bus with barred windows and corrugated steel sides to the high, green gates of Spandau Prison. They exited the bus and walked under the large, front stone archway into the dark building that would be their new home. They were told to wait in a holding room and sit on a long wooden bench. They each received a new prison outfit for Spandau which, ironically, was former concentration camp clothing — all blue, and stiff to the touch. Then, they marched into another room where they were ordered to strip naked and be examined by a Russian physician. Next, they were all given a haircut. The order in which the seven inmates marched through the offices became their official prison number; Speer was given the number five and was identified as "five" for his entire time at Spandau.

Speer was escorted to his cell and once he entered, turned to see the door closing behind him. The large steel door with a peep hole was six feet high and nearly three feet wide. His room was painted dark green half-way up and then cream. It was nearly nine feet long by seven-and-a-half feet wide and the walls were eleven feet high. The curved ceiling was painted white and the floor black. He had a window on the back wall crisscrossed with iron bars and there was a toilet at the end of his bed with a black seat and cover. The walls were nearly two feet thick.

Speer sat on his mattress and looked around. His light consisted of two bulbs and the fixture was barred to keep inmates from putting their fingers in the socket and electrocuting themselves. There was a small steel button located next to the toilet that would buzz the guards. It was a bleak situation for Speer. He would have a long go of it and he hoped he could endure mentally.

"Ahhhhhhhhh!"

The blood-curdling scream penetrated every cell of the long corridor in Spandau. One of the prisoners was at it again, screaming in wild pain in the middle of the night.

"I can't take it anymore!" yelled Admiral Raeder from his cell. "This continual screaming is driving me mad. Guards, help us, please!"

The culprit was prisoner number seven, Rudolf Hess; it was always Hess. With his deep-socketed dark eyes perpetually in panic, and with his bushy eyebrows, Hess looked half crazy. He screamed almost every night and complained of severe stomach pain. His moaning would last for hours but the doctors could find nothing wrong with him.

Hess did not get out of bed when he was supposed to, he complained all the time of sickness, and the least little change in their schedule or routine would set off a tantrum. The other prisoners suspected him of being a calculating malingerer, which they did not mind, but they *did* want their sleep. His ghastly howls would echo down the cavernous hallways of Spandau each night and keep the others awake.

Everyone knew Hess's sicknesses were a ruse, even the guards. They would give him placebo injections of distilled water when he complained of intense stomach cramps, and Hess would always calm down. His comrades suspected Hess of insanity since his notorious trip to Britain. On May 10, 1941, Rudolf Hess, then the Third Reich Deputy, left Adolf Hitler without his sanction on a secret mission of peace. He climbed into a Messerschmitt 110 loaded with extra fuel tanks and flew to Scotland. It was a daring five hour, 900-mile flight over the North Sea. Hess hoped to speak to the British and negotiate peace, but they knew this rogue defector did not speak for Adolf Hitler so they locked him up in prison until the end of the war. It was the only reason Hess, the deputy Führer, was not executed at Nuremburg but given a life sentence; he had entirely missed the last four years of the war. And now he was at Spandau tormenting everyone, especially his fellow prisoners.

The prison director ordered Hess's mattress and blanket be removed from morning to evening. Hess sat on a chair and howled all day. This annoyed the two former admirals, Raeder and Dönitz, even more. After four days, the physician gave Hess a fake injection which made Hess calm down and quit screaming for a while.

Speer tried to help Hess when he could. Their prison cells were next to each other. When Hess was sick, Speer brought him his food and cleaned his room for him. When Hess complained of not being able to walk, Speer would do his laundry for him. The other prisoners ignored Hess but for some reason Speer felt it his duty to take care of him.

Hess was kind, but never showed any real affection toward Speer because he felt, like the others, that Speer had double-crossed them all at Nuremburg. In fact, Speer was outwardly despised by most of the others because of his position on their *collective* guilt. The old statesmen, Konstantin von Neurath, at seventy-four-years of age was the only inmate pleasant for Speer to be around, choosing to remember the pre-Hitler days of Germany as a source of energy. But the other men — Shirach, Dönitz, Funk and Raeder — constantly clashed with Speer over his disloyalty to Hitler.

For Admiral Karl Dönitz, his primary resentment of Speer rested in his assumption that in the final days of the war, Speer convinced Hitler to name Dönitz as his successor. The Admiral believed that this was the only reason he was charged to ten years imprisonment at the Nuremburg trials. *Speer must be to blame!*

For the other inmates, they somehow still held that even in the end Hitler was the rightful leader and worthy to be followed. This was something Speer could not stomach.

One day in the yard, Erich Raeder vehemently rebuked Speer for saying Hitler despised everyone, even his friends and his country. "It is easy for you to say that now, Speer, when Hitler isn't around to defend himself," said Raeder.

Baldur von Shirach quickly picked up the attack, "Yes, and you cannot say that the Führer was disloyal since he fought for Germany down to his last minute. He was true to himself to the very end, holding hope that Germany would succeed."

"How is it loyal to destroy commerce, factories and government infrastructure in German towns?" asked Speer. "A nation cannot succeed when it is destroyed by its own government. Hitler declared that himself in *Mein Kampf!*"

"There you go again stating your scorched earth ideas," said Walther Funk. "We had to shut down factories and destroy bridges so the Allies could not take advantage of them. I can't believe you do not accept that. This is one reason we lost the war, Speer. You are one of the reasons we lost the war by countermanding all of Hitler's edicts on this issue. You were the grand betrayer."

Dönitz stood by glowing. He considered Speer an arrogant young upstart who made life difficult on everyone by trying to walk on the moral high ground. "Hitler was the Chancellor, Speer, and I was in charge of the Navy," said Dönitz. "I had to obey his orders. He was my Commander-in-Chief. We were all forced to obey his orders until he died. Each of us was on trial because of our loyalty to the Reich, not because of war crimes. I never committed war crimes, I simply followed orders given to my navy during wartime."

"But the government we supported was corrupt!" barked Speer.

The conversation continued for a while, then when it was over each returned to his cell. Speer reflected on what caused the fight — a simple comment on Hitler not being a loyal man.

What does it mean to be loyal anyway? Speer wondered. *Is loyalty a good thing? Only if it supports good conduct. If not, then loyalty is a bad thing. It appears to be a lesser virtue and could be inherently evil because one definition of it could be blind acceptance. Loyalty presupposes an ethical blindness. If leaders and governments were truly ethical and upright, people could be loyal to themselves only and do okay. They could be loyal to do the right thing, and they would be fine. The only true loyalty is toward morality, and knowing what the right thing to do is.*

<hr />

When the prisoners first arrived at Spandau, the guards noticed that the seven men grew more and more depressed. Their cells were cramped and there were no books in the library yet. When the four national directors conferred on this dilemma they decided to allow the prisoners to work outside in the garden area during the day. The prison courtyard, surrounded by a fifteen-foot wall, held a garden area of nearly an acre and a half. It contained many old nut trees and massive lilac bushes. Though full of weeds in the beginning, the prisoners planted many types of vegetables and fruit trees.

Speer took a special interest in the garden and normally spent six or more hours there when the weather permitted. He built a terraced promenade and pathways throughout. One day he took an inventory and found over 100 chestnut trees. He planted an additional 50 walnut seedlings. He built a rock garden and reworked the plots for vegetables.

The prisoners were supposed to bring all produce to the kitchen but many of the prisoners smuggled vegetables for their own consumption, especially during the Russian Director months when the rations barely sustained them. Most of the guards pretended not to notice the prisoners eating raw vegetables, but not the Russians; prisoners were punished by the Soviets for committing the smallest infraction.

After several months, even the garden did not help Speer with his boredom. He decided he would walk around the entire garden path several times for exercise. If he walked around the outer path thirty times it was approximately seven kilometers. One day he decided to pretend he was on a hike from Berlin to Heidelberg. He thought about what he would see on the journey while he walked. Next he decided to hike to Italy through the Alps, which took many days. Again, his imagination made the kilometers melt away.

Speer wrote a letter to a friend of his, Rudi Wolters, who was looking after Speer's family for him. Speer told his friend of a plan he had to hike around the entire world and asked Wolters to send pictures of the places he would pass on his journey east of Berlin. Wolters complied and sent Speer as much information about the journey as possible.

After looking at travel magazines and photos of Eastern Europe and Asia, Speer hoped to use his imagination to journey through Siberia, India and even Alaska. With pictures from historical art magazines and reading about the terrain in books and clippings his friend would send, Speer could easily imagine the landscapes complete with rivers, valleys, mountains and architecture. Speer walked and walked, every day, even in the rain and snow. The only time he took a break was when his heel was in pain.

The other activity Speer used to divert his mind was to keep a diary of daily events. The guards expressly warned the prisoners not to keep any notes of their activities. The prisoners handed in all their papers and notebooks at the end of the day and they were shredded. However, Speer began writing on toilet paper and concealing the pieces in his underwear, especially if the content pertained to Hitler.

A Dutch medic, Toni Proost, alerted Speer that he would smuggle out letters for him. Speer knew this was a tremendous opportunity and a great risk for Proost. He took him up on his offer immediately. Speer gave Proost several pieces of paper containing journal entries and memories he had written about Hitler. Over time, the medic not only took his letters but provided Speer writing paper and pencils. Speer sent all his journal notes to Rudi Wolters through Proost.

There is often a certain irony in the way Providence works. Albert Speer was one of the most hated men in the world, and forced to serve twenty years in prison for crimes against humanity. But during his incarceration a unique door for help opened to him and Speer decided it was time to take a step of faith. This door came by the way of Georges Casalis, a Protestant minister who conducted Saturday services at Spandau as the prison chaplain.

All seven prisoners at Spandau were Protestant so the Allies decided to bring in Casalis to conduct services once a week. Casalis was a Frenchman who had spent years in the French resistance movement, actively working against the Nazis. He was fluent in German as a result of his love of church history and academic research on the reformers. He was already a pastor to a French congregation in Berlin so he seemed an obvious choice.

All the inmates attended Casalis' service except for Hess. However, after a few months, Hess asked the guards to leave his door open so he could hear the men singing hymns down the hall. After the very first service, Speer felt a connection with the lively French pastor. They talked and Speer decided to take some action.

"I need help," Speer told Casalis. "Will you help me become a different man?"

"Why certainly," answered Casalis. "What do you have in mind?"

"I need direction," confided Speer. "What should I read besides the Bible? How should I pray?"

"I can help you with those things." Casalis, who was a lover of John Calvin and the study of God's sovereignty, responded, "Have you heard of Karl Barth's works *Church Dogmatics*?"

Casalis spoke to the prison directors and was allowed to bring in books for the inmates to use. Speer took advantage of the opportunity more than anyone else and read volume after volume of Barth's opus *Church Dogmatics*. Through meeting with

Chaplain Casalis, Speer developed a genuine interest in spiritual matters for the first time in his life. For several years, Speer and Chaplain Casalis met and discussed theology. They also discussed Speer's relationship with Hitler and his work with the Third Reich. Speer grew to trust Casalis and the two became very close friends.

Unfortunately, the wardens swapped out prison chaplains on a routine basis so Casalis only ministered at Nuremburg for a few years. This became a frustrating interruption to Speer's spiritual journey.

The wailing continued long into the night. Hess was at it again. He seemed to be having some sort of an attack.

"Ohhhhh. Help! Ohhhhh. Help me, someone please. Ahhhhhhh."

Raeder could not take it anymore. He began to imitate the tormented Hess. "Oh someone, help, help!"

Speer did not like this, yet he understood how annoyed everyone was with Hess. They had all lived in Spandau for several years now and every few months Hess would revert back to his old ways.

"Oh, my God!" shouted Hess. "Help me, please. How can anyone endure this?"

"Oh, my God," mimicked Raeder. "Help me, help me!"

"Ahhhh!" Hess shrieked louder after hearing Raeder.

"Ahhhh!" shrieked Raeder in derision.

Speer lay still. The cavernous, dark prison was awash with sounds of a madman and an evil tormentor. These were the leaders of the Third Reich just a few years earlier. *What irony,* Speer thought.

"Someone, please help me!" shouted Hess.

A guard and a medic came down the hallway and unlocked Hess's door. He was given an injection and told to be quiet. Soon, Hess calmed down and the prison became quiet again.

The next morning Hess refused to eat. When the guards threatened to force feed him he still resisted. Then, two of the guards held him down, filled a syringe with milk and told Hess they would insert it directly into his stomach if he did not comply.

"Oh, all right then. I'll drink it," Hess said.

Later that day Hess talked to Speer in the garden.

"I can't go on Herr Speer," said Hess. "Believe me, I am losing my mind and cannot last much longer."

"Sure you can," encouraged Speer. "You go through these episodes two or three times a year and you always get better."

"Oh my God, you mean this has happened to me before?" asked a confused Hess.

That evening, Raeder suggested to the others that if Hess screamed again they should all let out bloodcurdling shrieks at the same time.

After a church service, the officiating chaplain asked to speak to Speer for a moment.

"I am sorry to tell you this," the chaplain started, then hesitated. "However, your mother died four days ago."

Soon after the chaplain delivered his news, the prisoners were sent to the garden area. Speer weeded alone.

The date was March 19th, Speer's birthday. Nothing special happened all day. Speer, or Prisoner Number Five as he was called by the guards, had no special meal or gifts sent from home. After supper, however, Neurath stopped by Speer's cell to wish him well.

"What can I wish you?" the aged Neurath asked sadly.

Speer did not respond.

Neurath took Speer's hand and quietly held it awhile.

No one spoke. Speer, paralyzed by the simple gesture of humanity, noticed Neurath held a distant gaze to the ground.

Finally, Neurath released Speer's hand, said goodnight and returned to his cell.

Speer nearly cried.

The days dragged on.

Up at 6 a.m.

Go to the washroom to bathe.

Eat breakfast.

Mop the hallway.

Go outside for a walk.

Eat lunch.

Spend time in the library.

Go outside.

Eat supper.

Write a letter.

Lights out.

Day in and day out, the routine continued.

Speer found himself periodically in fights with the others about Hitler and the war.

Hess would have episodes.

There would be a fight amongst the admirals over who used Dönitz's favorite broom.

Speer continued to reach new milestones on his "journey" around the world.

He met with the chaplain on Sundays.

He read letters from his family.

One thing that was especially painful to Speer was when his family would come for a visit. It became an opportunity for a setback, reliving the past and the mistakes he made, mistakes that now had him incarcerated and not present with those he loved. Margarete, Albert, Hilde, Arnold, Fritz, Margret and Ernst were replaced by Hess, Dönitz, Raeder and Shirach.

On one particular visit Margarete sat across from Speer and a Russian guard stood in the corner of the room. There was much more than the steel table between them and Speer was having a hard time finding words. They discussed the children, finances, and the possibility of an early release. There was no joy, no laughter. The visit was only thirty minutes, but for the rest of the day Speer thought of nothing else. He was suffering at Spandau and he could clearly see that his wife was suffering as well.

That evening, for the first time in months, Speer asked for a sedative to help him fall asleep. He could not get the picture of Margarete and her sad eyes out of his thoughts.

"Did you hear me? I said to get up!"

No answer.

"All right mate, have it your way," the guard said as he entered Hess's cell room. The British guard physically rolled the groaning Hess off his bed and onto the floor. Then he took Hess's mattress and blankets and threw them into the hallway.

"Up and at 'em, right now! Your fellows are already in the garden and here you try to sleep."

No answer.

"All right, look mate, you cannot stay here. You either go outside to the garden or you go to the punishment cell."

Hess stood, then walked down the hall to the punishment cell for the rest of the day.

The former Reich Minster of Foreign Affairs, Konstantin von Neurath, was allowed to leave Spandau on November 6, 1954. Because of his age and bad heart he was released half-way through his fifteen-year sentence. The reality that one of the seven had been swept into freedom was hard on the remaining six. Dönitz was seen visibly weeping. Speer, also, could not hold back his tears. Neurath was not even allowed to say goodbye. He was taken from his cell one evening on a false pretense and departed Spandau prison late that night in civilian clothes with his daughter.

Good old Neurath, thought Speer. He never once criticized another or was harsh on any of the other six prisoners. Once freed, Neurath was in contact with the chaplain and sent a message to their Saturday service. The chaplain relayed that it grieved Neurath not to be able to say goodbye but that he wished them all well.

Speer tried to get his mind off the freedom Neurath was enjoying and the change it caused to the little band of men there at Spandau. Nothing worked. At the end of Speer's usual walk he decided to keep going. He was trying desperately to get his mind off Neurath and freedom. He walked his thirty laps, then another thirty, and he kept going. Prior to that day he had only walked 61 laps. When he finished Speer had counted 89 laps, totaling over 21 kilometers. On his walk around the world he had left Germany and was now in Eastern Europe.

"You're perverse," Shirach said to Speer when he finished.

The next day Speer stayed in bed. His knees were swollen and his ankles hurt. He had learned a painful lesson.

⬥

Speer, now walking through Yugoslavia in the Spandau garden, set his sights on Istanbul and hoped to be there by the end of the year. Speer finished his walk early because of some commotion. It looked like Raeder was in trouble.

"What is going on with Raeder?" Speer asked Hess.

"I don't care," Hess replied, and looked away. "Besides, I'm having a heart attack."

Speer soon learned that Raeder had ever-increasing abdominal pain and was taken away by the medic to get help. Over the next few days it was discovered that he had a bad prostate. At night Raeder would toss and turn with chills and fever. Though not screaming out, the others knew he was not feeling well and feared for his health.

On one of these nights when it was deathly still and dark in the massive 600-inmate building, Hess started up again with his wailing.

"Ahhhhhhhhhh," screamed Hess. "Somebody help! Oh my God!"

Surprisingly, Admiral Raeder, once in charge of the entire Third Reich Navy as Grand Admiral, found the energy to mock Hess even though Raeder himself was suffering.

"Oh my God, oh my God," Raeder parodied.

But the others could tell that Raeder was much weaker now.

More of Hess screaming and wailing.

A little bit of mocking from a frail Raeder.

Hess.

Raeder.

Hess.

Raeder.

Hess won the contest that night.

A few days later, on September 26, 1955, Raeder was released from Spandau. Though the admiral was given a life sentence at Nuremburg, because of his ailing health all four countries agreed to let him leave.

Again, the little group had to readjust their routines. *Who would sweep the middle of the hall now?*

⬥

Two of the seven war criminals of the Third Reich High Government had been released early. This gave hope to the remaining five — Speer, Hess, Dönitz, Funk

245

and Shirach. Rumors swirled that because of world events the four nations would grow weary of manning a prison in Berlin. Besides, Germany was now free to have their own army and navy. Dönitz felt sure the officers he once worked with would demand his release. But it remained quiet outside the walls except for the news that Neurath died at his home at the age of 83.

In September, 1956, Admiral Dönitz closed in on the conclusion of his ten year term. On October 1st, he would be a free man.

Before that day arrived, Speer and Dönitz began a conversation about the old claim Dönitz perpetuated that Speer influenced Hitler's decision to make Dönitz his successor, thus resulting in his captivity in Spandau. Dönitz was ready to depart the prison but wanted to settle the score and hear it from Speer's own mouth one final time — *that Speer was to blame for his misery!*

"You're the reason I've lost ten years of my life!" an agitated Dönitz exclaimed. "Can't you admit that?"

Speer could see the look of disgust on Dönitz's face as the man railed at him.

"Because of you I've been treated like a common criminal. I could have been free, Speer, free to be with my family if you hadn't influenced Hitler. I hold you responsible. I will never command a ship again."

"You being here is not my fault," answered Speer forcefully.

"It *is* your fault! Why else would Hitler think to put me in charge? I am no politician. I should be out on the sea. All my subordinate officers are sailing again and I have been stuck in prison for ten years. I didn't even *know* Hitler that well. I am not responsible for his war crimes. Look at me, my career is ruined."

Dönitz stood up, ready to leave. He was furious. Speer would obviously never own up to his great mistake. Dönitz finished, "And you always remain aloof and say nothing about it. To me that means one thing, guilty."

Speer stood and faced Dönitz.

"May I say something please?" asked Speer.

Dönitz waved his right hand to give consent, "Go ahead."

"For ten long years you have slandered, disparaged and ostracized me. For the most part I have taken Neurath's sage advice and ignored you, but it has not been easy. Do you think I don't know how frequently you, Funk and Shirach speak evil of me behind my back? I can often hear you. But I have left it alone. We are all in misery here and I have chosen to ignore all of your abuse, chalking it up to therapy for you to survive.

"All three of you blamed me for acting dishonorably at the end of the war, but you yourselves, I guess, all behaved honorably. You sure talk enough about honor and loyalty around me with very snide comments. But I have to ask you before you depart here, do you ever think about the fact that many millions were murdered by our regime, by our government that we served? All seven of us were leaders of an institution that annihilated millions of lives in the war we fought. But it seems like your ten years here perturb you more than forty million people dead. And your last words to me are about your *career?* Go ahead and be mad at me when you leave, I don't care."

Dönitz turned around and began walking away, "Suit yourself!"

On October 1, 1956, Dönitz departed Spandau a free man.

Shirach and Funk celebrated, then wept.

Hess howled with stomach pain.

Speer turned the page.

<hr />

Speer was in India on his endeavor to walk around the world.

Funk was sick in bed with liver problems.

Shirach had taken Raeder's place to report Hess to the guards.

Hess completed five days in isolation for not cleaning up the washroom.

Speer completed architectural drawings for an American guard to build a new home. When asked how much the guard owed him, Speer told him "Twenty marks, but take the money to buy your wife some flowers."

Speer had another visit with Margarete. Though it was a short meeting, there were periods of awkward silence. Both thought the other had aged.

The prison directors met and decided to release Funk.

It was May 16, 1957, when Funk left Spandau. He had been bedridden for days before his release.

The three remaining prisoners were not allowed to say goodbye. They had not been told that Funk would be released. The news came to Speer as he was walking in the garden. He stared at the outer wall and tried to understand why the Spandau directors refused prisoners the opportunity to say farewell.

<hr />

On May 31, 1960, Walthur Funk, former Reich Minister for Economic Affairs, died at his home.

On November 6, 1960, Erich Raeder, former Grand Admiral of the Third Reich Navy, died at his home.

The three prisoners still in custody, Speer, Shirach and Hess, took the news about their former colleagues stoically. They realized that life was being sucked out of them at Spandau. The rituals, the lack of food during the Russian months, the way they were treated by some of the guards, and the way they treated each other, all were taking a toll.

Hess decided to take action. He ceased eating his meals and complained of stomach cramps every night. Usually, after an injection of distilled water Hess would shut up and go to sleep but not this time. The guards suspected that he was ingesting laundry detergent so they closely monitored the prisoners when they washed their clothes.

One day, while Speer walked in the garden, Hess remained in his cell. He broke his glasses and cut the veins in his wrists with a shard of glass. He hoped to bleed himself out. He was successful for three hours until a medical doctor on his daily rounds found Hess and stitched him up.

When Speer visited Hess the next day, he noticed a playfulness about him, like a schoolboy who had been caught in a prank.

"I was almost successful," Hess said with a smile.

"Well, here is to your unsuccess," said Speer.

Hess took to eating again.

The days drifted onward.

Each day seemed the same.

One day, Speer sat on a bench in the garden and watched the hawks and sparrows flying here and there. He realized what it might be like to be a monk, totally detached from the outside world — absolute serenity. Not counting days by events, but as segments of time to enjoy God's creation. Shirach never availed himself to the quiet and peace available at Spandau and Hess seldom noticed it. Speer was alone in his garden cathedral, loving his trees, flowers, vegetables and birds.

No ambition.

No vexation.

Time stood still.

Distant memories of the past.

Nothing to hope for in the future.

Only the present.

Speer felt prison was making him mentally deformed.

Even when released, he knew he would still be locked in Spandau.

As the years advanced, Speer walked more and more toward his goal. By 1966, Speer had walked over 30,000 kilometers. He was now in North America. He became more melancholy regarding his release. An ambivalence filled his heart. He knew he would be an eccentric on the outside, unable to deal with all the changes through which his family had journeyed. His health was being affected as well: shortness of breath, panic attacks, cardiac issues. Strangely, sometimes Speer envied how Hess would never have to face the day of his release.

On the afternoon of September 30, 1966, Hess asked the guards to lock him in his cell. He knew his two cellmates would depart that evening and he wanted to be left alone. When supper was over, he instructed the guards to turn out his lights and administer a strong sedative to him.

Speer went to the dark cell to say goodbye but Hess waved him away.

"Herr Hess, I would like to speak to you one last time," said Speer kindly.

"Make it short," replied a flustered Hess.

"Goodbye, Herr Hess. I want you to know..."

"No! No! No! Oh... let it go."

Speer returned to his cell and lay on his bunk.

At 11:30 p.m. Speer and Shirach were brought their civilian clothes to change out of their prison garb. In plain clothes the two left their cells and were escorted to the director's office. They were given their possessions they had when entering prison at Nuremburg. Speer, Shirach and the four directors awkwardly chatted while the last few minutes passed.

"Take good care of Hess," said Speer facing the directors.

"We will," said the American director, Eugene Bird. "We feel sorry for him that he will be left alone here to die."

At one minute to midnight, the directors escorted the two Reich Ministers to the outer door.

A black Mercedes waited in the courtyard.

Speer and Shirach shook hands.

The large door opened.

Blinding television spotlights flooded the entrance.

Thousands of people had gathered to watch.

The two men walked outside.

Margarete ran up the steps to greet Speer and instead of hugging, gave Speer a handshake, and then led him to the car.

Flashes of light from photographers flickered all around them.

The Mercedes slowly departed the noisy Spandau courtyard.

As the tires rolled over the crunchy gravel there was an awkward quiet within the vehicle.

Each passenger looked out their own window in stony silence.

No one knew what to say.

The significance of the event was not lost on the couple, but it erased any capacity for small talk.

His war was over.

Albert Speer was free.

POSTSCRIPT

Adolf Hitler's rise to power resulted in 18 million battle deaths, and an additional 20 million civilian deaths. Nearly every country in Europe was devastated by Hitler's ideological fanaticism. Poland itself lost twenty percent of its entire population during the war and the German Reich killed outright over three million Russian POWs. Hitler seethed in nationalistic ideals that included every form of racism, bigotry and hatred for others imaginable. Yet it would not be quite right to describe Hitler as a madman. He was a promulgater of evil, but also a coherent and meticulous schemer. Some 21st Century tutorials on Hitler merely depict him as a screaming warmonger. This book exposes the other side of Hitler, the side which might be a little uncomfortable for the reader. It was the side of Hitler that Albert Speer knew well, and loved.

Adolf Hitler was a warm, friendly and charismatic leader to his cabinet members and their families. He spent years cultivating personal relationships with his staff, and hours upon hours of casual time building his team at three primary locations: the Chancellery, the Berghof, and the Wolf's Lair. As hard as it is to imagine, Hitler knew human nature; he could play people against each other like a pro. It seemed as if he possessed a special knack for keeping the people around him happy and loyal. The perks associated with being part of Germany's national leadership team were paid for with patience; by enduring hours of Hitler's repetitive monologuing, in laughing at his jokes as if it was the first time they were ever heard, and with constant team rivalry to garner Hitler's approval. Nazi leaders desperately wanted Hitler's favor, and they were eager to emulate his idealism with ferocity.

One example of the ruthlessness that Hitler's devotees possessed was illustrated by the man sitting next to Speer at Nuremburg — Arthur Seyss-Inquart, the Reichskommisar of the Netherlands. Seyss-Inquart was proud of his 'step-by-step' achievement against Holland's Jews. First, he removed them from all professional life. Next, he confiscated their property (allowing them to keep only wedding rings and four pieces of silverware). Then, he methodically deported them to German work factories or extermination centers. As Airey Neave chronicled in *Nuremburg*, under Seyss-Inquart's governorship of Holland, a greater proportion of Dutch Jews were to die in extermination and forced labor camps than in any other West European country. Of the nearly 150,000 Dutch Jews, only 17,000 survived extermination from Nazi death camps in Poland. The few thousand who remained in country were hidden by friends and fellow Hollanders like Corrie ten Boom who took sympathy on them at great personal risk. Those who perished were the result of one man's vision to systematically annihilate another race, and his persuasion on faithful followers.

Adolf Hitler is terrifying to comprehend when you consider that one human being could possess such hatred, intellect and power all at the same time. But despite Hitler's ease with people, there was something missing in what I would call his *personhood*. Joachim von Ribbentrop, Hitler's foreign minister, worked tirelessly for Hitler for years, and attempted a personal relationship with the Führer, as he would another man. Yet Ribbentrop told the Nuremburg psychologist, G. M. Gilbert, he did not think anyone could ever have a heart-to-heart talk with Hitler as a close friend. He said that Hitler was warm and friendly but was incapable of intimacy. He never knew Hitler to really bare his soul to anyone.

Albert Speer echoes these thoughts when he described Hitler in his book *Inside the Third Reich*. Speer wrote that there was always something misbegotten about Hitler's attempts to radiate warmth in order to receive it. Also, Speer described how there was something insubstantial about Hitler; something missing. It seemed to Speer that the violent outbursts the German leader displayed were not capable of being stopped by typical human emotions. What Speer suggests is that Hitler was devoid of a normal human conscience; the Führer could not let anyone get too close to his inner self because it simply did not exist. Never in Speer's life had he met a person who so seldom revealed his true feelings. It crossed Speer's mind that Hitler might be controlled by evil. He wrote that '*one seldom recognizes the devil when he is putting his hand on your shoulder.*'

<hr />

Albert Speer and Corrie ten Boom both survived the horrors of World War II and each began a new journey in 1945. For Speer, it was the Nuremburg Trials, then twenty years in Spandau Prison.

For Corrie, she developed a home of refuge for concentration camp survivors at Bloemendaal, then traveled to Germany and began ministering to Germans. At first she lived in a factory where thousands of people without homes scraped out an existence, their lives separated only with bed sheets hung between cots. Corrie led Bible studies, counseled and spoke to the Germans of God's love and forgiveness.

One day in the factory, a director of a relief organization invited Corrie to inspect a concentration camp in Darmstadt. The camp was newly released by the government, and the relief organization felt Corrie was the perfect person to restore it and minister to hundreds of Germans still suffering. It was hard for Corrie to walk through the large gates and behind the walls still terraced with barbed wire. She nervously viewed the barracks with the hundreds of cots and reflected on some of Betsie's last words to her:

> *This concentration camp has ruined many, many lives and there are camps like Ravensbrück all over Germany. After the war they will not have use for them anymore. I have prayed that the Lord will give us one in Germany and we can use it to build up lives.*

Corrie made an agreement to lead the ministry after the relief director leased the camp in 1949. The former concentration camp at Darmstadt soon held 160 displaced German people and kept a long waiting list. Corrie made her rounds, always teaching, leading, and personally encouraging each person. The camp stayed open until 1960. Corrie then traveled the world as an evangelist visiting over 60 countries. She wrote numerous books including *The Hiding Place*, and worked with various Christian ministries. She was knighted by the Queen of the Netherlands, and honored in 1968 by the Israeli Government at Yad Vashem as a Righteous Gentile among the Nations. Together, Corrie and Jewish leaders planted a tree in her honor on the Avenue of the Righteous because of the hundreds of Jewish families she aided. Corrie died on her birthday, April 15, 1983, at 91 years of age.

Corrie's life story is admirable. She did not let her circumstances define or limit her. She used her past as a launching pad to bring greater glory to God. For her, it was about being an instrument for God to use, a paintbrush who knew full well that her life was about the Painter. Certainly she struggled at times with anger and despair, but these emotions did not defeat her. Corrie found the higher way, not the path that spiraled down in asking God *Why?* Instead, looking up she asked *What next? And what more can I do for You?* She knew her God and in faith allowed Him to control every aspect of her life. In essence, she poured out her entire existence in order to unlock people's understanding of how much God loves them — even deep into a pit of human misery.

On the day she embraced the German guard and offered him her forgiveness, she wrote the following in her journal that evening: *It is not on our forgiveness any more than on our goodness that the world's healing hinges, but on God's. When He tells us to love our enemies, He gives, along with the command, the love itself.*

Before Corrie died she recorded an audiotape to be played in the Beje museum: *Was it a mistake of God that He allowed the arrest to happen? No it was not. God never makes a mistake. My sister Betsie's death and my father's death were not mistakes. I will tell you something, when the worst happens, in the life of a child of God, the best remains.*

Albert Speer left Spandau Prison in 1966. He, like Corrie, wrote books and achieved a certain success offsetting the hard times his wife and children endured immediately following the war. Sadly, he was estranged from some of those closest to him, like Rudi Wolters who had helped his family financially for years. Also, several of his children had a difficult time relating to their father upon his release. Though Speer made some gains in seeking forgiveness with a Jew named Raphael Geis who befriended him, he was forever haunted with questions from a curious public: *What did he know? When did he know it? And why didn't he do anything about it?*

Gitta Sereny, in her book *Albert Speer: His Battle with Truth*, concluded her non-fiction tome discussing how Speer, near the end of his life, gave to a Jewish group a raw disclosure of his tacit acceptance of the persecution and murder of millions of Jews; Speer wrote to them of his guilt in the face of his knowledge.

During the trial in Nuremburg, Speer advocated for a general blame, or total responsibility, as a member of the high government. But here, at last, in correspondence with a group of Jews, he admitted personal knowledge: *I still see my main guilt in my having approved of the persecution of the Jews and of the murder of millions of them.* Sereny rightly states that if Speer had uttered those words in Nuremburg, he would have hanged.

I took on this endeavor to highlight the startling contrast between the remarkable lives of Corrie ten Boom and Albert Speer. Corrie operated solely from a position of weakness, never faltering to use and recognize publicly the supreme power of God. She credited God for her release from Ravensbrück in the nick of time. A few days after Corrie left, over 4,000 prisoners her age and older were gassed.

Corrie was never theologically trained, yet she possessed a simple faith in the gospel and shared this faith publicly in many countries. Through Albert Speer's studies of the Bible, the thirteen-volume *Church Dogmatics,* and meetings with Pastor Georges Casalis, the Spandau chaplain, I have to presume that Speer knew the gospel message intellectually. Yet it never seemed to penetrate deeply into his soul and change his identity as true believers experience. Thus, Speer did not have the mark of a *witness.*

Corrie's faith was a fountain and the message of her life. Speer's faith seldom trickled out. He spoke about Fate and Providence, but not about a personal God nor a Savior. Markus Barth (son of the famed Swiss Reformed theologian, Karl) and his wife Rosemarie, both met with Speer after his release from Spandau. They stated that in a final assessment of Speer's faith the former Nazi could only speak the language of responsibility, not repentance.

As far as history records, Corrie ten Boom and Albert Speer never met, but with their lives the reader is able to look through the two lenses of cause and effect in war. *The Lion and the Lamb* describes in detail how Corrie suffered under Speer's policies. It was Speer who negotiated the mass recruitment of workers to run his Axis factories. It was Corrie who worked at the Siemens plant. It was Speer who fought with Himmler and Goebbels to keep his stockpile of foreign workers. It was Corrie who slept in crowded, filthy conditions with foreign bunkmates and led them in Bible studies. It was Speer who cut deals with the Industrialists and located factories next to concentration camps. It was Corrie who marched to work each day, happy for the extra meal the factory workers received. It was *not* Speer who caused the fierceness of the Gestapo in prison, but it *was* Speer who helped create the perfect war machine that channeled Corrie into the horrors of Ravensbrück Concentration Camp.

This is the reason the Nuremburg judges found Speer guilty. It was not because he had crafted an extermination mechanism like Hitler, Heydrich, or Himmler; it was because he was complicit in their every decision. And, more specifically, it was because Speer brought untold suffering because of his effectiveness as a War Minister. Speer fought to acquire millions of workers, then fought harder to keep them working without harassment or conscription. The better Speer performed his job, the more people languished under the Nazi war machine. Corrie and her family were the collateral damage of Speer's wartime success.

Speer's superior achievements for Hitler during a span of four years from 1942-1945 prolonged the war and brought Corrie and millions of others into German factories. This is why the Russians wanted Speer hanged. And this damage was the work Corrie fought hard to reverse in her years of charitable service after the war.

Speer's efforts in the first few months of 1945 no doubt saved many German lives when he thwarted Adolf Hitler's scorched earth policies, but the Armaments Minister stayed quietly complicit too long. His break with Hitler was not powerful enough to combat Hitler's evil, and not early enough to impact millions of innocents like Corrie ten Boom. Speer's moral corruption was rooted in his deep, emotional attachment to Hitler, and he struggled with this linkage until confronted with the graphic images at Nuremburg. Corrie was attached to God, Speer to Hitler.

Despite the tremendous contrasts between Albert Speer and Corrie ten Boom, their lives retained a few similarities. Both spent time in prison; Speer for war crimes, Corrie for crimes during war. They were both assisted in prison by Hollanders; Corrie from a nameless Dutch nurse in Scheveningen who smuggled her scripture, Speer from a Dutch medic in Spandau named Toni Proost who smuggled his letters. Both lost loved ones while in prison and both were ridiculed, Corrie from the guards, Speer from his fellow inmates.

In Betsie and Georges Casalis, they both had spiritual mentors who helped them process life events. Also, both worked in gardens to help with post-war healing, Corrie with former prisoners in Bloemendaal, Speer with his fellow inmates, confiscating vegetables during the Russian director months. Corrie and Albert published books from their wartime experience selling millions of copies each, and both gave interviews regarding their Holocaust experiences until they died.

From G. M. Gilbert's *Nuremburg Diary* it is obvious that Speer was genuinely disgusted at the results of Nazism in Europe. He worked hard to convince his co-defendants at Nuremburg not to align with Hermann Göring, but to take responsibility for their actions, just as they would have if they had been victorious. Most of his pleas fell on deaf ears, except with Baldur von Shirach. Speer's daily influence helped Shirach break from Göring's united front, denounce Hitler, and take ownership for Nazi war crimes. Both men were spared life sentences at Nuremburg because of their sincere rejection of the Hitler cult.

Unfortunately, Albert Speer did not end his life well. He wrote a confusing and controversial book about Himmler which brought him additional wealth, but was not well-received like his first two books. Also, Speer died in a nondescript London hotel room after filming an interview with the BBC and Margarete was not the woman who accompanied him. Even out of prison Speer was an ever-distant husband and father.

To conclude the story on Spandau Prison after Speer and Shirach departed, prisoner number seven, Rudolf Hess, continued to live in the 600-inmate facility by himself for another twenty years. The guards reported loud nocturnal howls throughout the empty prison — an eerie taps to the end of Nazism. Even with his many illnesses and antics, Hess outlived all the other Nazis with whom he was imprisoned. He lived alone for the rest of the 1960s, the '70s and most of the '80s, walking in the garden, eating in his room, and cleaning the hallways and bathrooms. Hess suffered this daily monotony until one morning, at the age of 93, he found a piece of rope a guard accidentally left in the garden shed and hanged himself. The former Deputy Führer's prison time was recorded in a book written by one of the wardens called *The Loneliest Man in the World*. Spandau Prison was demolished that year so it would not become a Nazi shrine.

Shirach died in '74.

Dönitz died in '80.

Speer died in '81.
Hess died in '87.
Martin Bormann was never found.

The End

"Rescue those who are unjustly sentenced and led away to death; save them as they stagger to their slaughter. Do not excuse yourself by saying, "Look, we did not know," for the God who understands all hearts sees you, and He will repay all people as their actions deserve."
Proverbs 24:11 — 12

REFERENCES

Bird, Eugene K. *The Loneliest Man in the World*. The Bronx: Ishi Press, 1974.

Bradley, John. *Lidice: Sacrificial Village*. New York: Ballantine Books, 1972.

Buber-Neumann, Margarete. *Under Two Dictators: Prisoner of Stalin and Hitler*. London: Pimlico, 2008.

Gallagher, Hugh Gregory. *By Trust Betrayed: Patients, Physicians, and the License to Kill in the Third Reich*. New York: Henry Holt and Company, 1993.

Gerwarth, Robert. *Hitler's Hangman: The Life of Heydrich*. New Haven: Yale University Press, 2011.

Gilbert, G. M. *Nuremburg Diary*. New York: Da Capo Press, 1947.

Höss, Rudolph. *Death Dealer: The Memoirs of the SS Kommandant of Auschwitz*. Amherst, New York: Prometheus, 1992.

Kitchen, Martin. *Speer: Hitler's Architect*. New Haven: Yale University Press, 2015.

Longerich, Peter. *Goebbels: A Biography*. New York: Random House, 2015.

Longerich, Peter. *Heinrich Himmler*. New York: Oxford University Press, 2012.

Manvell, Roger and Heinrich Fraenkel. *Goering: The Rise and Fall of the Notorious Nazi Leader*. New York: Skyhorse Publishing, 2011.

Morrison, Jack G. *Ravensbrück: Everyday Life in a Women's Concentration Camp 1939-45*. Princeton: Markus Wiener Publishers, 2000.

Neave, Airey. *Nuremburg*. London: Hodder & Stoughton LTD, 1982.

Newland, Samuel J. and Clayton K.S. Chun. *The European Campaign: Its Origins and Conduct*. Carlisle, Pennsylvania: Strategic Studies Institute, 2011.

Read, Anthony and David Fisher. *The Fall of Berlin*. New York: W. W. Norton & Company, Inc., 1992.

Reitlinger, Gerald. *The Final Solution: The Attempt to Exterminate the Jews of Europe, 1939-1945*. London: Sphere Books Limited, 1961.

Roseman, Mark. *The Wannsee Conference and the Final Solution: A Reconsideration*. New York: Metropolitan Books, 2002.

Sereny, Gitta. *Albert Speer: His Battle With Truth*. New York: Alfred A. Knopf, 1995.

Sereny, Gitta. *Into That Darkness: An Examination of Conscience*. New York: Vintage, 1974.

Shirer, William L. *The Rise and Fall of the Third Reich*. New York: Crest Books, 1959.

Smith, Bradley F. *Reaching Judgment at Nuremberg*. New York: Basic Books, Inc., 1977.

Smith, Emily (Ed.). *More Than A Hiding Place-the Life Changing Experiences of Corrie ten Boom*. Haarlem, The Netherlands: The Corrie ten Boom House Foundation, 2010.

Speer, Albert. *Infiltration*. New York: MacMillan Publishing, 1981.

Speer, Albert. *Inside the Third Reich: Memoirs*. New York: Simon and Schuster, 1970.

Speer, Albert. *Spandau: The Secret Diaries*. New York: Pocket Books, 1977.

Stolfi, R. H. S. *Hitler: Beyond Evil and Tyranny*. New York: Prometheus Books, 2011.

Ten Boom, Corrie. *A Prisoner and Yet...* London: Christian Literature Crusade, 1954. Publication rights held by Baker Book House Company, Grand Rapids, Michigan.

Ten Boom, Corrie. *In My Father's House*. Grand Rapids, Michigan: Fleming H. Revell, a division of Baker Book House Company, 1976, 2000. Publication rights held by Baker Book House Company, Grand Rapids, Michigan.

Ten Boom, Corrie. *Not Good If Detached*. London: Christian Literature Crusade, 1957. Publication rights held by Baker Book House Company, Grand Rapids, Michigan.

Ten Boom, Corrie with John and Elizabeth Sherrill. *The Hiding Place*. Chappaqua, New York: Chosen Books LLC, 1971.

Ten Boom, Corrie. *Tramp for the Lord*. Grand Rapids, Michigan: Fleming H. Revell, a division of Baker Book House Company, 1974, 2000. Publication rights held by Baker Book House Company, Grand Rapids, Michigan.

Toland, John. *Adolf Hitler*. New York: Anchor Books, 1976.

Townsend, Tim. *Mission at Nuremberg: An American Army Chaplain and the Trial of the Nazis*. New York: HarperCollins, 2014.

Whitlock, Flint. *The Beasts of Buchenwald. Karl & Ilse Koch, Human-Skin Lampshades, and the War-Crimes Trial of the Century*. Brule, Wisconsin: Cable Publishing, 2011.

As the following sources are used frequently, they will be abbreviated as shown.

SPEER *Albert Speer: His Battle With Truth*
RISE *The Rise and Fall of the Third Reich*
ITTR *Inside the Third Reich*
SPAN *Spandau: The Secret Diaries*
APAY *A Prisoner and Yet*
THP *The Hiding Place*

PROLOGUE
1. Story of Cocky, **THP,** 106.
2. Story of Martin and Eike, **SPEER,** 309.

CHAPTER ONE
1. Speer in Dnepropetrovsk, ITTR, 189.
2. Speer at the Wolf's Lair, **ITTR**, 191.

CHAPTER TWO
1. Corrie at the Beje, **THP**, 97.
2. The Dutch Resistance Movement, Nieuwstraten, Jaap. 2015. *The Netherlands During the Second World War.* As printed in Smith, Emily (Ed.). *More Than A Hiding Place-the Life Changing Experiences of Corrie ten Boom.* Haarlem, The Netherlands: The Corrie ten Boom House Foundation, 2010.
3. Corrie riding her bike with Kik, **THP**, 99.

CHAPTER THREE
1. Reinhard Heydrich assassination, Gerwarth, Robert. *Hitler's Hangman: The Life of Heydrich.* New Haven: Yale University Press, 2011. 10-13. **RISE**, 1289. Longerich, Peter. *Heinrich Himmler.* New York: Oxford University Press, 2012. 568-9.
2. Story of Lidice, Gerwarth, Robert. *Hitler's Hangman: The Life of Heydrich.* New Haven: Yale University Press, 2011. 280-282. **RISE,** 1290.

CHAPTER FOUR
1. Speer's visit to Göring at Carinhall, **ITTR**, 179.
2. Göring's possessions from the Jews, Manvell, Roger and Heinrich Fraenkel. *Goering: The Rise and Fall of the Notorious Nazi Leader.* New York: Skyhorse Publishing, 2011. 284.
3. Carinhall, **ITTR**, 205.
4. Göring with Rommel, "You can pile everything on my shoulders." Manvell, Roger and Heinrich Fraenkel. *Goering: The Rise and Fall of the Notorious Nazi Leader.* New York: Skyhorse Publishing, 2011. 270.

CHAPTER FIVE
1. Corrie and Mr. Weil, **THP**, 86.
2. The secret room, Ibid. 102.
3. Corrie and the police chief, Ibid. 136.
4. The buzzer, Ibid. 119.
5. The pastor, Ibid. 114.

CHAPTER SIX
1. Zyklon B, **RISE**, 1263, 1266. **SPEER**, 344, 356. Höss, Rudolph. *Death Dealer: The Memoirs of the SS Kommandant of Auschwitz.* Amherst, NY: Prometheus, 1992. 155.
2. Gas chambers, Longerich, Peter. *Heinrich Himmler.* New York: Oxford University Press, 2012. 563.

CHAPTER SEVEN
1. Speer, Goebbels and Göring, **ITTR**, 260. **SPEER**, 372.
2. The Führer meeting, **ITTR**, 264. **SPEER**, 375.

CHAPTER EIGHT
1. Nollie with the Gestapo, **THP**, 126. Annelies is the same as *The Hiding Place's* Annaliese.
2. Practice drills in case of a raid, Ibid, 121, 130.
3. Message regarding Annelies, Ibid, 127.

CHAPTER NINE
1. Birthday party at Carinhall, **ITTR**, 322.
2. Veldenstein memory, Ibid, 279.

CHAPTER TEN
1. Corrie and the visitor, **THP**, 140.

CHAPTER ELEVEN
1. The number of Jews killed by the end of 1943, Longerich, Peter. *Heinrich Himmler*. New York: Oxford University Press, 2012. 619.
2. Speech to the Wehrmacht generals, Ibid, 539, 689. **RISE**, 1259.
3. Sobibor and Treblinka, Sereny, Gitta. *Into That Darkness: An Examination of Conscience*. New York: Vintage, 1974. 115.

CHAPTER TWELVE
1. The Ten Boom house invaded, **APAY**, 18. **THP**, 142. In *The Hiding Place* Willemsen is spelled Willemse, and Kapteyn is spelled Kapetyn.
2. At the police station, **APAY**, 22. **THP**, 149.

CHAPTER THIRTEEN
1. Speer in the hospital, **ITTR**, 330. **SPEER**, 416.
2. Speer hearing Hitler's speech, **ITTR**, 15. **SPEER**, 80.
3. Hitler's visit, **ITTR**, 335.
4. Second Göring phone call, Ibid, 338.
5. Speer with Hitler, Ibid, 341.

CHAPTER FOURTEEN
1. The interrogation, **THP**, 152-153.
2. Casper and Corrie say goodbye, **APAY**, 26. **THP**, 114.

CHAPTER FIFTEEN
1. The Max Heiliger account, **RISE**, 1267.

CHAPTER SIXTEEN
1. Corrie at Scheveningen, **APAY**, 28. **THP**, 153.
2. Corrie at the medical clinic, **THP**, 159.
3. Hitler's birthday party episode, Ibid, 166.

CHAPTER SEVENTEEN

1. Hitler giving Speer the production of Air Armaments, **ITTR**, 349.
2. Events of June 6th, **ITTR**, 354. **SPEER**, 432. **RISE**, 1347. Toland, John. *Adolf Hitler*. New York: Anchor Books, 1976. 784.

CHAPTER EIGHTEEN

1. Höss, Rudolph. *Death Dealer: The Memoirs of the SS Kommandant of Auschwitz*. Amherst, NY: Prometheus, 1992. 156-164.
2. Number of Hungarian Jews and the Sonderkommando, **SPEER**, 464-465.

CHAPTER NINETEEN

1. Corrie's memory of the train ride, **THP**, 41.
2. The letter from Nollie, **APAY**, 46. **THP**, 169.
3. The General, **APAY**, 51.
4. Interviews with the Lieutenant, **APAY**, 40. **THP**, 172.
5. The woman in the cell with Corrie, **APAY**, 50.
6. The reunion, **THP**, 178.

CHAPTER TWENTY

1. Conversation with Stauffenberg, **SPAN**, 212.
2. Details of Operation Valkyrie, **SPEER**, 443-447. **ITTR**, 380-389. **RISE**, 1361-1388. Longerich, Peter. *Goebbels: A Biography*. New York: Random House, 2015. 640-641. Toland, John. *Adolf Hitler*. New York: Anchor Books, 1976. 795-800. Longerich, Peter. *Heinrich Himmler*. New York: Oxford University Press, 2012. 696.

CHAPTER TWENTY-ONE

1. Finding Betsie, **APAY**, 54. **THP**, 183.
2. Transport and march to Vught, **APAY**, 54. **THP**, 184.
3. Memories of Karel, **THP**, 56-61. As the book *More Than A Hiding Place* points out, Karel is not his real name.
4. Life at Vught, **APAY**, 56. **THP**, 185.
5. The train ride, **APAY**, 89. **THP**, 198.

CHAPTER TWENTY-TWO

1. The days after Valkyrie, **RISE**, 1389-1405. Toland, John. *Adolf Hitler*. New York: Anchor Books, 1976. 812-822.
2. Speer at the Wolf's Lair, **ITTR**, 389.
3. Rumors about Speer, **SPEER**, 451.
4. Hitler moaning, Toland, John. *Adolf Hitler*. New York: Anchor Books, 1976. 814.
5. Speer, Goebbels and Bormann episode, **ITTR**, 398.
6. Scorched earth policy, Ibid, 403.
7. Discussion of fighters with Galland, Ibid, 407-410.
8. Speer receives warning from a friend about Upper Silesia, Ibid, 375-376. **SPEER**, 463.
9. Speer meeting with Göring, **SPAN**, 214.

CHAPTER TWENTY-THREE
1. Fate of Hofacker and Stuelpnagel, **RISE**, 1395-1398.
2. Story of Rommel, Toland, John. *Adolf Hitler*. New York: Anchor Books, 1976. 829. **RISE**, 1398-1401.

CHAPTER TWENTY-FOUR
1. Horrible train ride, **APAY**, 90-93. **THP**, 200.
2. Life at Ravensbrück, **APAY**, 93-173. **THP**, 201-236. Ten Boom, Corrie. *Not Good If Detached*. Fort Washington, PA: Christian Literature Crusade, 1957. 49-53. Ten Boom, Corrie. *Tramp for the Lord*. Grand Rapids, Michigan: Fleming H. Revell, a division of Baker Book House Company, 1974, 2000. Publication rights held by Baker Book House Company, Grand Rapids, Michigan. 14-22. Morrison, Jack G. *Ravensbrück: Everyday Life in a Women's Concentration Camp 1939-45*. Princeton: Markus Wiener Publishers, 2000.
3. Walking past the gate guards, **APAY**, 99. **THP**, 205.
4. Story of the little girl in the vest, **APAY**, 105.
5. Giving thanks for fleas, **THP**, 210.

CHAPTER TWENTY-FIVE
1. Saur is the genius, **ITTR**, 415.
2. Hitler telling Speer about offensive, Ibid, 415.
3. Speer's memory of the train ride, **SPAN**, 187.
4. The world's most inhibited man, **SPEER**, 153.
5. Speer observing the offensive, **ITTR**, 416-418.
6. New Year's Eve toasting, Ibid, 419.
7. Levee en mass discussion with Goebbels outburst, Ibid, 419.

CHAPTER TWENTY-SIX
1. Work at the Siemens plant, **APAY**, 110. **THP**, 212.
2. The Snake, **APAY**, 120, 150.
3. Story of Betsie shoveling, **APAY**, 132. **THP**, 215.
4. God can shovel without a shovel, **APAY**, 133.
5. Oh, Corrie, this is Hades, Ibid, 139. Corrie said it was Hades also, Ibid, 150. The actual word they used was the common word Jesus used in the New Testament 'Hell' but this word was edited by the publisher.
6. Story of the sick transport at night, Ibid, 114-115. **THP**, 223.
7. I am beginning to love the multitude, **APAY**, 154.
8. The punishment block and bunker, Buber-Neumann, Margarete. *Under Two Dictators: Prisoner of Stalin and Hitler*. London: Pimlico, 2008. 214.
9. The story of Mrs. De Boer and Mrs. Goede, Ten Boom, Corrie. *Not Good If Detached*. London: Christian Literature Crusade, 1957. Publication rights held by Baker Book House Company, Grand Rapids, Michigan. 49-53.

CHAPTER TWENTY-SEVEN
1. Journal entries from Rudolf Höss, Höss, Rudolph. *Death Dealer: The Memoirs of the SS Kommandant of Auschwitz*. Amherst, NY: Prometheus, 1992. 364-369.

CHAPTER TWENTY-EIGHT
1. Betsie in the hospital, **APAY**, 160. **THP**, 219.
2. Rempli de tendresse, **APAY**, 143.
3. Red-light Commandos, Ibid, 154.
4. The fleas explained, **THP**, 220.
5. The Snake and the memorial service, **APAY**, 150.
6. Corrie and Maryke, **THP**, 226.
7. Corrie and Mimi, Ibid, 229. Mimi is called Mien in *The Hiding Place*.

CHAPTER TWENTY-NINE
1. Morrison, Jack G. *Ravensbrück: Everyday Life in a Women's Concentration Camp 1939-45*. Princeton: Markus Wiener Publishers, 2000. 278-281.

CHAPTER THIRTY
1. The Russian woman, **APAY**, 162.
2. Punishment block women, Ibid, 163.
3. Corrie processing out, **THP**, 232.
4. Corrie in the hospital, **APAY**, 167. **THP**, 234.
5. Gypsie story, **THP** 235.
6. Out-processing, **APAY** 171, **THP** 236. Ten Boom, Corrie. *Not Good If Detached*. London: Christian Literature Crusade, 1957. Publication rights held by Baker Book House Company, Grand Rapids, Michigan, 52.

CHAPTER THIRTY-ONE
1. Meetings with Hitler, **ITTR**, 434-439.
2. Meeting with Göring, Ibid, 427.
3. Notes from *Mein Kampf*, Ibid, 429.
4. Meeting with Dieter Stahl, Ibid, 430.
5. Evacuation, Ibid, 438.
6. Hitler and Speer, Ibid, 439.

CHAPTER THIRTY-TWO
1. Berlin conversation with young girl, **AYAP**, 175.
2. Groningen and conversation with Truus, **AYAP**, 179.
3. Visit with Willem, **THP** 239.
4. Memory of Casper at the Beje, **THP** 44. Ten Boom, Corrie. *In My Father's House*. Grand Rapids, Michigan: Fleming H. Revell, a division of Baker Book House Company, 1976, 2000. Publication rights held by Baker Book House Company, Grand Rapids, Michigan. 31-32.

CHAPTER THIRTY-THREE
1. Speer working in defiance, **ITTR**, 446-450. **SPEER**, 482-486.
2. Speer saying goodbye to parents, **SPEER**, 487.
3. Speer stripped of power, **ITTR**, 450.
4. Speer's meetings with Hitler, Ibid, 451-456. **SPEER**, 491-498. Toland, John. *Adolf Hitler*. New York: Anchor Books, 1976. 856.
5. Speer's letter to Hitler, **ITTR**, 454.
6. Hitler's decree on Speer's behalf, Ibid, 455-456.
7. Speer working against time, **ITTR**, 457-460. **SPEER**, 498-504.
8. Dr. Brandt and Eva Braun story, **SPEER**, 505. **ITTR**, 465.

CHAPTER THIRTY-FOUR
1. Red Cross phone calls, Longerich, Peter. *Heinrich Himmler*. New York: Oxford University Press, 2012. 728.
2. Death march, Morrison, Jack G. *Ravensbrück: Everyday Life in a Women's Concentration Camp 1939-45*. Princeton: Markus Wiener Publishers, 2000. 300-304.
3. Ravensbrück freed by Russians, Ibid, 305-306.

CHAPTER THIRTY-FIVE
1. Speer's concert, **SPEER**, 506-507.
2. The bunker, Toland, John. *Adolf Hitler*. New York: Anchor Books, 1976. 857-858.
3. Roosevelt's death, **ITTR**, 463.
4. Göring departing the bunker, Ibid, 474-475.
5. Speer's last meeting with Hitler, Ibid, 478-485. **SPEER**, 518-532.
6. Göring's treachery, Manvell, Roger and Heinrich Fraenkel. *Goering: The Rise and Fall of the Notorious Nazi Leader*. New York: Skyhorse Publishing, 2011. 313-318. **RISE**, 1448-1449.
7. Final hours in the bunker, **SPEER**, 533-543. Toland, John. *Adolf Hitler*. New York: Anchor Books, 1976. 882-891. **RISE**, 1450-1475.
8. Misch and the Goebbels' children, **SPEER**, 540-541.

CHAPTER THIRTY-SIX
1. Speer's visit and conversation, **SPEER**, 525.
2. The demise of the Architect, Longerich, Peter. *Heinrich Himmler*. New York: Oxford University Press, 2012. 732-736. **RISE**, 1480.
3. The speech on dead bodies, Longerich, Peter. *Heinrich Himmler*. New York: Oxford University Press, 2012. 539, 689.

CHAPTER THIRTY-SEVEN
1. Back in the underground, **THP**, 242-243.
2. Shaved heads, **APAY**, 185-187.
3. Betsie's visions, **THP**, 223, 226, 244.

CHAPTER THIRTY-EIGHT
1. Dönitz and Speer, **ITTR**, 487-488.
2. Speer weeps, Ibid, 488.
3. Speer in transition, Ibid, 495-506.
4. Speer and his collective responsibility, G. M. *Nuremburg Diary*. New York: Da Capo Press, 1947. 25. **ITTR**, 520. **SPEER**, 560, 577.
5. Göring and Speer's argument, Gilbert, G. M. *Nuremburg Diary*. New York: Da Capo Press, 1947. 102.
6. Göring's belligerence, Manvell, Roger and Heinrich Fraenkel. *Goering: The Rise and Fall of the Notorious Nazi Leader*. New York: Skyhorse Publishing, 2011. 340.
7. Göring speaking of Speer, Gilbert, G. M. *Nuremburg Diary*. New York: Da Capo Press, 1947. 398. **SPAN**, 269.
8. Dr. Kaufman's questions of Rudolf Höss, Nuremburg Trial Transcript.
9. Judge Jackson's examination of Speer as a defendant, Nuremburg Trial Transcript.
10. Story of the death pit, Reitlinger, Gerald. *The Final Solution: The Attempt to Exterminate the Jews of Europe, 1939-1945*. London: Sphere Books Limited, 1961. 219-220. Gilbert, G. M. *Nuremburg Diary*. New York: Da Capo Press, 1947. 425. **RISE**, 1252.
11. Speer walking to hear his sentence, **SPAN**, 1.
12. Speer's conversation with Hess, Ibid, 2.
13. Speer's conversation with the psychologist, Ibid, 2.

CHAPTER THIRTY-NINE
1. Corrie's conversations with Mrs. De Haan, **APAY**, 188. **THP**, 244-245.
2. Corrie's encounter with the former SS officer, **THP**, 247.

CHAPTER FORTY
1. The kind American Army chaplain, **SPEER**, 632.
2. Göring statements and death, Manvell, Roger and Heinrich Fraenkel. *Goering: The Rise and Fall of the Notorious Nazi Leader*. New York: Skyhorse Publishing, 2011. 340. 383-393.
3. Judge Jackson's prosecution summation, Gilbert, G. M. *Nuremburg Diary*. New York: Da Capo Press, 1947. 415-417.
4. Names called out for execution, **SPAN**, 9-10.
5. Mopping the floor, Ibid, 10-11.
6. Speer's dad dies, Ibid, 58.
7. In processing at Spandau, Ibid, 71-72.
8. The description of Speer's room, Bird, Eugene K. *The Loneliest Man in the World*. The Bronx: Ishi Press, 1974. 5.
9. Hess and his bedding, **SPAN**, 217.
10. Speer rebuked for his disloyalty to Hitler, Ibid, 220.
11. Thoughts on loyalty, Ibid, 211. These thoughts were actually taken from a letter written to Speer from a woman named Mrs. Anne Fremantle.
12. Speer's meeting with Georges Casalis, **SPEER**, 22-23. 608-614.
13. Speer discussion with Hess, **SPAN**, 219.

14. Hess groaning and Raeder mocking, Bird, Eugene K. *The Loneliest Man in the World*. The Bronx: Ishi Press, 1974. 101. **SPAN**, 300, 305.
15. Speer's mom dies, Ibid, 220. Date is June 29, 1952.
16. Neurath's gesture on Speer's birthday, **SPEER**, 638. Date is March 19, 1953.
17. Neurath's departure and Speer's long walk, **SPAN**, 285-6.
18. Raeder is released from Spandau, Ibid, 307. Bird, Eugene K. *The Loneliest Man in the World*. The Bronx: Ishi Press, 1974. 115.
19. Dönitz discussion with Speer and his departure, Ibid, 327-329. Bird, Eugene K. *The Loneliest Man in the World*. The Bronx: Ishi Press, 1974. 118.
20. Funk departure from Spandau, Bird, Eugene K. *The Loneliest Man in the World*. The Bronx: Ishi Press, 1974. 121. **SPAN**, 342-3.
21. Hess suicide attempt, Ibid, 380-381.
22. The day of departure for Speer and Shirach, Bird, Eugene K. *The Loneliest Man in the World*. The Bronx: Ishi Press, 1974. 145-150. **SPAN**, 498-500.

POSTSCRIPT
1. Seyss-Inquart story, **SPEER**, 500. Neave, Airey. *Nuremburg*. London: Hodder & Stoughton LTD, 1978. 179-81.
2. Ribbentrop's view of Hitler, Gilbert, G. M. *Nuremburg Diary*. New York: Da Capo Press, 1947. 108.
3. Speer's view of Hitler, **ITTR**, 100-101, 297. **SPEER**, 233.
4. Story of Corrie and the concentration camp, **THP**, 248-9.
5. Corrie honored by Jewish leaders, **APAY**, 189. **THP**, 265.
6. Corrie's quote on forgiveness, **THP**, 248.
7. Corrie's quote on if God makes mistakes, Smith, Emily (Ed.). *More Than A Hiding Place-the Life Changing Experiences of Corrie ten Boom*. Haarlem, The Netherlands: The Corrie ten Boom House Foundation, 2010. 84.
8. Story of Speer and Jewish leaders, **SPEER**, 707-8.
9. Women gassed at Ravensbrück in February 1945. Buber-Neumann, Margarete. *Under Two Dictators: Prisoner of Stalin and Hitler*. London: Pimlico, 2008. 263. Of the over 130,000 women who came to Ravensbrück, approximately 50,000 died there.
10. Markus and Rosemarie Barth assessment of Speer, **SPEER**, 699.
11. Speer's moral corruption, Ibid, 368.
12. Speer's influence on Shirach, Gilbert, G. M. *Nuremburg Diary*. New York: Da Capo Press, 1947. 348.
13. Speer's death, Ibid, 715-717.
14. Imprisonment of Hess, Bird, Eugene K. *The Loneliest Man in the World*. The Bronx: Ishi Press, 1974.
15. Bormann's whereabouts. Martin Bormann was tried in absentia at Nuremburg for war crimes. On October 15, 1946, he was found guilty and sentenced to death by hanging. On December 7, 1972, construction workers found human remains near Lehrter Station in West Berlin. After an autopsy and much forensic examination, the West German government declared Martin Bormann dead. These results were further proved by genetic testing in 1998. Bormann's remains were cremated and his ashes scattered over the Baltic Sea in 1999.

BOOK CLUB QUESTIONS

1. In your opinion, who was the lion and who was the lamb in this story? Did your opinion change during your reading of *The Lion and the Lamb*?

2. Describe the pivotal points in the story for Speer and for Corrie? What changes did those events cause in the two? What were growth points? What were barriers?

3. Both Speer and Corrie endured a prison sentence; how were they similar and dissimilar?

4. How do events in *The Lion and the Lamb* help us learn about God? Are there any of His attributes that especially stand out in this story?

5. Why do you think a Reich Minister was called the Architect? What did he oversee for the Nazis? How did you feel about the way his story concluded?

6. What do you think was the most challenging part of Corrie's concentration camp experience? Why?

7. Speer was torn in his relationship with Hitler. Why did he continue to serve with him when the man repulsed him so much? Why do you think Speer had to have a final goodbye? Do you think Speer was a person of integrity?

8. In the chapter *Shaved Heads*, how does Corrie respond to Holland's victory activities? Was it justified for Hollanders to attack each other? What would you have done?

9. What provoked Speer to finally break with Hitler? What were his risks? Did he have a safety net? Did he ever truly acknowledge who the real Hitler was?

10. What character in *The Lion and the Lamb* are you most like? What character did you admire the most?

11. How did Hitler play his staff against each other? Do you think it served his purposes well? Is there any correlation to the upper management team in the corporation you currently serve?

12. Have you ever been in a situation like Speer in the "An Attempt to Save Germany" chapter? What was the end result?

13. What do you think about the actions of Rudolf Hess? Do you believe he was insane? What about the other people with whom Hitler surrounded himself? Were they the best and brightest?

14. Are there events happening today that remind you of Nazi Germany?

15. What did you learn from Corrie? What did you learn from Speer? Was there another character in the book from whom you learned something?

16. Are you, like Speer, currently in a relationship with someone who is leading you down the wrong path? Do you have someone like Betsie in your life?

17. What was your favorite part of the book and why? Do you have any favorite quotes?

18. In your opinion, what is the message or moral of *The Lion and the Lamb*?

ACKNOWLEDGMENTS

First off, I thank my beautiful wife Lauri for her encouragement, patience and love during the years this book was written. While researching and writing we experienced two Army moves and she worked tirelessly to ensure every last detail was planned and executed. Lauri also read through an early version of the manuscript and a late version giving me helpful advice. Her personal sacrifice and support cannot be measured, or duly praised.

Next, I thank my editor Vicki Zimmer who has been an integral part of this project since the beginning, giving me feedback and volunteering many hours to look over proposals and ideas. Vicki scrutinized every sentence of *The Lion and the Lamb* and provided valuable insights on how to write what she believed I was trying to communicate. She also researched several key points for me to validate their historical accuracy and sent me recent news stories about the Holocaust. Thankfully, Vicki was already a Corrie ten Boom enthusiast, and like me, wanted to make sure Corrie's part of the story was precise. This book is intelligible because of her. I'm thankful to Vicki for taking this project on, and being a true friend for thirty years.

This book would never have been written without the permission and support of two Netherlanders, Dr. Frits Nieuwstraten, the Director of the Corrie ten Boom House Foundation, and his son, Jaap Nieuwstraten, PhD, who read over every chapter of the book to ensure Corrie was represented well. They also provided many facts regarding Holland, World War II, and Corrie's life that I could not have found or included on my own. They were tremendous supporters and so gracious and generous to work with, they will always have my deep admiration and respect.

I am grateful to Colonel Brett Weigle, a professor at the Army War College in Carlisle Barracks, Pennsylvania, and to Dr. Loyd Melton, director of the doctoral program at Erskine Seminary in Due West, Scouth Carolina. Brett spent hours of his limited free time editing *The Lion and the Lamb* and giving me straight forward feedback. It was a tremendous shot in the arm for me to receive his support because he is an expert in the military writing style, and over the years has taught many of the Army's senior leaders. Dr. Melton, in the midst of reviewing doctoral dissertations and leading classes, invested his limited personal time to read through my book at home and provide a review for readers.

I humbly thank my friends who volunteered to read through the full manuscript and give me feedback: Cabot Ashwill, Kasia Ashwill, Virginia Emery, Mike Fleischhacker, Henry Foster, Craig Pache, Robert Payne, Ed Sonksen, Charlie Yost and Mark Zimmer. They found many of my mistakes and graciously gave me ideas on how to better write parts of the story. They are the real deal and I will always appreciate them for making this book more readable.

I am pleased that artists William S. Phillips and Kyle Carroll agreed to partner with me to enhance *The Lion and the Lamb*. I thought the William S. Phillips painting called *On Wings and A Prayer* was a great fit for the front cover and it was graciously provided by Mr. Phillips. His paintings can be viewed at www. GreenwichWorkshop.com. Kyle Carroll worked with me six years ago with *In Danger*

Every Hour and he provided the maps of Germany for this book. He is a talented historical artist whose works have appeared on magazine covers, buildings, and in galleries at Gettysburg. Kyle's website is www.KyleCarrollArt.com.

I also want to thank my agent, Dan Balow from the Steve Laube Agency, for his advice and support along with a few humble people who kindly mentored me in my early years: Chris Smith, EW, Chaz Fitzgerald, Gretchen Gee, Erik Petrik, Keith Davy, Bill Culbertson, Doug Rietema, Robert Coleman, Don Carson, Scott Manetsch, Dean Johnson, Steve Simpson, and Ken Kirk. Instead of trying to hammer God into my life they displayed authentic Christianity, spoke truth when I made mistakes, and taught me grace.

On one particularly snowy day when the Pentagon was shut down and schools were closed, my daughters invited over a couple of friends to ride out the storm with us. Little did they know I had just completed Section I and needed some guinea pigs for a plot review. Madison Causey, Hannah Causey, Elizabeth Goldwater and Helena Mulder, thank you for being *The Lion and the Lamb's* first focus group and reading over an early draft of the opening ten chapters. Your great attitudes and feedback truly helped this book. Finally, I want to thank my sons Nickolas and Isaiah Causey, who, along with the three women in my immediate family, are my constant supporters and add perspective on why I work on projects like this. Nickolas, Madison, Hannah and Isaiah, stars of my life, you are the next generation; may you see error early, have courage to stand against tyranny and, if ever in danger, possess absolute confidence in the power of God.

CPSIA information can be obtained
at www.ICGtesting.com
Printed in the USA
LVHW01s2346040718
582675LV00003B/383/P